Wiktoria Kudela-Świątek

ETERNAL MEMORY:

Monuments and Memorials of the Holodomor

Translated from the Polish
by Guy Russell Torr

Preface
by Frank E. Sysyn

KIYC CIUS
Canadian Institute of Ukrainian Studies Press
in cooperation with Księgarnia Akademicka
Edmonton, Toronto 2021 Cracow
WYDAWNICTWO KSIĘGARNIA AKADEMICKA

Canadian Institute of Ukrainian Studies Press

University of Alberta
Edmonton, Alberta
CANADA T6G 2H8
<www.ciuspress.com>

University of Toronto
Toronto, Ontario
CANADA M5S 2C3

Ksiegarnia Akademicka
ul. św. Anny 6
31-008 Kraków, Poland
<https://akademicka.com.pl>

ISBN 978-1-894865-61-6 (paperback)

Library and Archives Canada Cataloguing in Publication

Title: *Eternal Memory: Monuments and Memorials of the Holodomor* / Wiktoria Kudela-Świątek; translated from the Polish by Guy Russell Torr.

Names: Kudela-Świątek, Wiktoria, author. | Torr, Guy Russell, translator.

Description: Translated from the Polish; original manuscript title unknown. | Includes bibliographical references and index.

Identifiers: Canadiana 20210107677 | ISBN 9781894865616 (softcover)

Subjects: LCSH: Holodomor memorials. | LCSH: Holodomor memorials—Ukraine. | LCSH: Collective memory—Ukraine. | LCSH: Memorialization—Ukraine. | LCSH: Ukrainian diaspora.

Classification: LCC DK508.8372 .K83513 2021 | DDC 363.809477—dc23

Cover design: Paweł Sepielak
Cover photo: Ludmilla Temertey designs the Holodomor monument in Edmonton, Canada, 1983 (Photography by Michael Slobodian. The private archive of Ludmilla Temertey)

Publication financed under the program of the Minister of Science and Higher Education under the name "National Development Program of Humanities" in 2016–2020 (agreement no. 0243/NPRH4/H3a/83/2016)

NATIONAL PROGRAMME
FOR THE DEVELOPMENT OF HUMANITIES

ETERNAL MEMORY:

Monuments and Memorials of the Holodomor

Deacon: *In a blessed falling asleep, grant, O Lord, eternal rest unto Thy departed servants and make their memory to be eternal!*

Choir: *Memory eternal! Memory eternal! Memory eternal!*

Memory Eternal. Eastern Orthodox Memorial Hymn

Table of Contents

Acknowledgments

This work has been realized thanks to the trust and support of numerous individuals. The list of all who have been involved in my research into memory culture and the Holodomor is an extensive one.

First and foremost, I thank those closest to me: my husband, Adam, for his enormous patience with me and my academic research, and my two sons, Antoni and Ignacy, for understanding my absences from home, and especially for all of the hugs, kisses and handmade cards that greeted me on my return from every research trip.

I would like to express my deep gratitude to Professor Krzysztof Zamorski from Jagiellonian University in Cracow, my first academic supervisor, for his enthusiastic encouragement for my first steps in visual history research. He provided me with the theoretical and methodological tools that I needed to choose the right academic direction.

This book also bears witness to the many who, convinced of the importance of the subject matter, showed me such kindness and support. And here I would like to thank the Holodomor Research and Education Consortium in the persons of Marta Baziuk, Valentina Kuryliw, Professor Frank Sysyn, Dr. Bohdan Klid and Andriy Makuch (d. 2019) for their assistance in organizing my research work in Canada and support in preparing the manuscript. I would also like to thank Professor Daria Darewych of Toronto for the consultations she afforded me and her invaluable input with regard to Ukrainian iconography, which constituted a lodestar for me. I am also grateful to Ksenya Kiebuzinski, head of the Petro Jacyk Central and East European Resource Centre (University of Toronto Libraries), and Halyna Ostapchuk of St. Vladimir Institute in Toronto, whose commitment and support helped me complete my extensive literature and archival queries. Thank you also to Dr. Serge Cipko for his inspiring comments and suggestions for the manuscript. I am also most grateful to Guy Russell Torr for translation the manuscript, Agnieszka Polakowska and Iryna Mycak for editorial works and to Halyna Klid and Olha Klymenko, from whom I learned more about the numerous materials held by CIUS and HREC.

In every country, I was assisted by artists, local scholars, archivists, survivors, and colleagues, without whose time and hospitality this book would not have been possible. For sharing their profound knowledge, resources, and insights, for opening their homes to me, I thank them from the bottom of my heart. I would like to thank Ludmilla Temertey for our inspiring discussion on the role of the Holodomor monument in her artistic work and for providing the photograph for the cover. I am also indebted to Bohdan Kowal and Halyna Kowal for the hospitality shown to me as a guest in their home in Winnipeg and for the rich archival materials constituting the legacy of Roman Ivan Kowal that I have employed in this book. Larysa Kurylas gave generously of her knowledge and her insights into the Washington memorial-making process.

I am also most thankful to the Ukrainian-Canadian Research and Documentation Centre, especially Bozhena Gembatiuk-Fedyna and archivist Iroida Wynnyckyj, for the amiable environment for my research in Canada and for their help in contacting those whom I was to interview. I also thank Bohdan Ihor and Lydia Shulakewych for their immense enthusiasm and most animated discussion during my fieldwork.

I would also like to extend thanks to Oksana Rewa, the initiator of the project to construct a monument in Toronto, for supplying me with archival materials, for the discussions on changes in Holodomor memory culture as experienced abroad and for showing me the Toronto unknown to tourists. I also thank Bożena and Jerzy Głowacki for their hospitality during my stay in Winnipeg and for our discussions about life in emigration. In Hamilton, Orysia Sushko, chair of the Holodomor Museum Committee, was generous with her time and resources. And the help of Ihor Ostrovski's family was also invaluable here.

I would like to thank Dr. Marta Havryshko of I. Krypiakevych Institute of Ukrainian Studies, National Academy of Sciences of Ukraine, for the research she conducted on my behalf in Australia and Professor Tomasz Pudłocki of the Jagiellonian University for his compilation of important photographic documentation from his stay at South Bound Brook in New Jersey. I am also hugely indebted to Prof. Hubert Chudzio of the Pedagogical University of Cracow for photographing the monument in Los Angeles and Dr. Tetiana Pastushenko from Institute of History of Ukraine, National Academy of Sciences of Ukraine, for the photograph of the first Holodomor Monument in Kyiv. I thank Prof. Valentyna Kharkhun for taking the photographs of the Ukrainian section of the cemetery in Washington, DC, and the Nizhyn Holodomor Monument. I would also like to thank Mykhailo Potupchyk for taking pictures of many symbolic burial places of Holodomor victims that are found in this book. I would like to give particular thanks to Michael Andrec, Ph.D. from Ukrainian History and Education Center, Somerset, NJ, for providing me with videos of the 1973 Holodomor Memorial Day commemoration in South Bound Brook and other graphic material that added greatly to this book.

My special thanks to Professor Taras Koznarsky at the University of Toronto for his translation of Ukrainian poetry.

Finally, I would like to thank the "Księgarnia Akademicka" Publishing House and the Holodomor Research and Education Consortium of the Canadian Institute of Ukrainian Studies for their professionalism and support in the realization of this publication.

Abbreviations

CDA	– Critical Discourse Analysis
CIUS	– Canadian Institute of Ukrainian Studies
CMHR	– The Canadian Museum for Human Rights in Winnipeg
CPSU	– Communist Party of the Soviet Union
DOBRUS	– Demokratychne Ob'iednannia Buvshykh Represovanykh Ukraïntsiv Sovietamy [Democratic Union of The Ukrainians Formerly Persecuted by the Soviets]
HREC	– Holodomor Research and Education Consortium
HURI	– Harvard Ukrainian Research Institute
KGB	– Komitet Gosudarstvennoy Bezopasnosti [Committee for State Security]
MAUP	– Mizhrehional'na akademiia upravlinnia personalom [Interregional Academy of Personnel Management]
NKVD	– Narodnyi Komissariat Vnutrennikh Del [People's Commissariat for Internal Affairs]
NRU	– Narodnyi rukh Ukraïny [People's Movement of Ukraine]
ODUM	– Ob'iednannia demokratychnoï ukraïns'koï molodi [Association of Democratic Ukrainian Youth]
OSCE	– Organization for Security and Co-operation in Europe
SUM	– Spilka ukraïns'koï molodi [Ukrainian Youth Association]
TsDAHOU	– Tsentral'nyi derzhavnyi arkhiv hromads'kykh ob'iednan' Ukraïny [Central State Archive for Ukrainian Community Organizations]
UCC	– Ukrainian Canadian Congress (originally Ukrainian Canadian Committee)
UCCA	– Ukrainian Congress Committee of America
UCRDC	– Ukrainian Canadian Research and Documentation Centre
UCP	– Ukrainian Communist Party
UCPBC	– Ukrainian Canadian Professional and Business Club
UHEC	– The Ukrainian History and Education Center

UINR	–	Ukraïns'kyi instytut natsional'noï pam'iati [Ukrainian Institute of National Remembrance]
UNF	–	Ukrainian National Federation of Canada
UNR	–	Ukrainian National Republic
UNWLA	–	Ukrainian National Women's League of America
UPA	–	Ukraïns'ka povstans'ka armiia [Ukrainian Insurgent Army]
USSR	–	Union of Soviet Socialist Republics
UWC	–	Ukrainian World Congress
WCFU	–	World Congress of Free Ukrainians
WFUWO	–	World Federation of Ukrainian Women's Organizations

Preface

On July 19, 1935, Lesio Sysyn of Garfield, New Jersey, published an extensive letter in the Passaic *Herald News* condemning the Soviet Union for its persecution of Ukrainian intellectuals and suppression of Ukraine's churches.[1] As point six on his list of atrocities he asserted: "The Ukrainians accuse the Government of Russia of deliberately killing millions of the Ukrainian population by starving them to death under the pretext of Ukrainian opposition to the Soviet plan of *Pyatiletka* (Five-year plan of economic building)." He wrote that the Lviv newspaper *Dilo* had reported that as many as six million people had starved to death and that the Soviet government denied that a famine had occurred. He concluded: "The method of exterminating a 32 million-strong race by hunger is the most fiendish of all ever conceived by anybody and worthy of the Soviet rulers."

Lesio Sysyn, an immigrant from the Boiko Carpathian region in Western Ukraine, was propagating the concept of the Famine as a Soviet-organized assault on the Ukrainian nation, although his own native village of Mshanets was far from Soviet Ukraine. As recent studies have demonstrated, considerable evidence of the Holodomor was available as it was occurring, and a national and genocidal (*avant la lettre*) interpretation had emerged already in the 1930s.

Throughout his long life, Lesio Sysyn continued to disseminate information on the Ukrainian Famine, and by the early 1950s, his activities had taken on a new resonance. When in 1963 he addressed an assembly of Ukrainian Americans in Passaic as part of the thirtieth-anniversary commemorations, his audience included numerous Famine survivors who had escaped the Soviet Union or been taken to

---

[1] "Soviet Russian Crime against the Ukraine" written on July 16 was published in the July 19 issue of *The Herald News*, Passaic, New Jersey. It was reprinted in the Jersey City Ukrainian daily *Svoboda*, July 25, 1935, p. 4.

Germany as forced laborers.[2] Many had managed to avoid forcible repatriation to the Soviet Union and arrived in the US and Canada as displaced persons. His address was followed by the main speaker, an eyewitness of the Famine, Viacheslav Davydenko.[3] By the time of this gathering, the Ukrainian diaspora had engaged in recording eyewitness testimonies and translating them into English, in particular, in the two-volume work *The Black Deeds of the Kremlin*.[4] At the Passaic event, a collection was taken for the completion of St. Andrew Memorial Church in South Bound Brook, New Jersey, the site of the major community commemoration on that sad anniversary under the aegis of the Ukrainian Orthodox Church in the US. The Memorial Church and its cemetery became a primary "place of memory" for what in time came to be known as the Holodomor.

In her innovative study, Wiktoria Kudela-Świątek has harnessed Pierre Nora's concept of *lieux de mémoire* or "places of memory" to examine the memorialization and commemoration of the Ukrainian Famine, both in Ukraine itself and in the diaspora. Forming the heart of the work is her analyses of dozens of individual monuments, complemented by numerous illustrations. The number of monuments is notable given that for more than fifty years on the territory where it transpired, the Famine was virtually banned from public discourse by the perpetrating authorities. The decimation in the 1930s of the churches and religious rites through which generations of Ukraine's rural dwellers had memorialized their dead compounded the damaging impact of this silencing.

Soviet denials added urgency and significance to the memorialization efforts in Ukrainian diaspora communities. Kudela-Świątek discusses these diaspora models of remembrance, including the conceptualization of the Famine as a genocide and even the terminology "Holodomor." She describes the efforts of what she calls the Holodomor generation, the refugees who arrived in the West after World War II, some of whom were Famine survivors, and examines develop-

---

[2] Prysutnii, "Trydtsiat'littia holodu v Ukraïni vidznachyly v Passeiku, N. Dzh.," *Ukraïns'ke pravoslavne slovo,* vol. 15, no. 2 (February 1964), p. 19. Issues of the journal dealing with Ukrainian Famine commemorations are available on the website of the Holodomor Research and Education Consortium (HREC) under the rubric Resources-Memorialization. Accessed February 5, 2021, https://holodomor.ca/resources/memorialization/.

[3] For an article he wrote ten years later for the fortieth anniversary, see Viacheslav Davydenko, "Sorokrichchia Velykoho holodu 1932–33 r.," *Al'manakh Ukraïns'koho narodnoho soiuzu na rik 1973* (Jersey City–New York: Vydavnytstvo "Svoboda," 1973), pp. 95–112.

[4] On the two volumes published in the 1950s, see Bohdan Klid, "The Black Deeds of the Kremlin: Sixty Years Later," *Genocide Studies International* vol. 8, no. 2 (Fall 2014), pp. 224–35.

ments in their countries of settlement and their acclimation to cultures and forms of memorialization in the West. She also considers the role of politics for the anti-Soviet majority in these communities and various scholars' hypotheses of why the Famine became such a pervasive force in Ukrainian community life.

Dr. Kudela-Świątek traces the evolution of Holodomor commemorative practices in diaspora communities with particular attention to the fiftieth anniversary in 1983, the height of these activities. It was the planning for this anniversary year that resulted in the publication of Robert Conquest's *The Harvest of Sorrow*, which brought the Famine to the attention of the scholarly community as well as a broader public.[5] Also in connection with the fiftieth anniversary, the documentary film *Harvest of Despair* found a wide audience, including political and governmental circles.[6] Following on this momentum, the US Congress established the Commission on the Ukraine Famine, which included an ambitious project to collect survivor testimony in the US. In light of these initiatives, Soviet claims that no Famine had occurred or that the Soviet government bore no responsibility became less tenable, although as late as 1987 Soviet authorities engaged in a campaign to discredit those who drew attention to the Ukrainian Famine. It was in fact the decision to attack the efforts of "Ukrainian bourgeois nationalists" that opened the door for researchers in Ukraine to examine the Famine, led by the leading scholar of the period, Stanislav Kulchytsky.[7] As a consequence of glasnost and perestroika, the Famine soon became a public issue in Ukraine, and with the dissolution of the Soviet Union and the proclamation of Ukrainian independence, a major topic in Ukrainian memory politics. Kudela-Świątek reflects on how memorialization and research conducted in the West became intertwined with these developments in Ukraine. The decision of James Mace, a major researcher on the Famine and director of the US Congress Commission, to relocate to Ukraine is indicative of this process.

---

[5] For discussion of the impact of Robert Conquest's book, see Frank E. Sysyn, "Thirty Years of Research on the Holodomor: A Balance Sheet." *East/West: Journal of Ukrainian Studies* vol. 2, no. 1 (2015), pp. 3–15. Also available on the HREC website, accessed February 5, 2021, https://holodomor.ca/wp-content/uploads/2020/04/Sysyn_Thirty_Years_of_Research_on_the_Holodomor_A_Balance_Sheet_anhl.pdf.

[6] For discussion of these activities, see Frank E. Sysyn, "The Ukrainian Famine of 1932–3: The Role of the Ukrainian Diaspora in Research and Public Discussion," in Levon Chorbajian and George Shirnian, ed. *Studies in Comparative Genocide* (New York: St. Martin's Press, 1999), pp. 182–215. Also available on the HREC website, accessed February 5, 2021, https://holodomor.ca/wp-content/uploads/2020/05/Sysyn-Famine-Role-of-Diaspora.pdf.

[7] Stanislav Kulchytsky, *The Famine of 1932–1933 in Ukraine: An Anatomy of the Holodomor* (Edmonton–Toronto: CIUS Press, 2018).

Among the strengths of Kudela-Świątek's work is her ability to untangle the strands of tradition in the diaspora within the emerging culture of memorialization in independent Ukraine. While these topics have been discussed by other scholars, her research on monuments, museums, and other "places of memory" constitutes a fresh and illuminating approach. She draws from an extensive theoretical literature on memorialization to provide new insights into the process by which Ukrainians have sought to come to terms with the Holodomor. Her examinations of the monuments, including investigations of designs that were never realized, shed light on the intentions of the artists and the communities that engaged them. She also assesses the place of the Holodomor within the memory politics of various Ukrainian governments. Kudela-Świątek has managed through her exploration of places of memory to create a composite of the developing image of the Holodomor. Her book is both wide-ranging in its themes and personal in its aesthetic assessments and expression of her evolving understanding. The reader-viewer who contemplates the manifold forms of Holodomor commemoration explored in this book will be grateful to have Dr. Kudela-Świątek as a guide.

The Holodomor Research and Education Consortium, a research project of the Canadian Institute of Ukrainian Studies of the University of Alberta, funded by the Temerty Foundation, is pleased to make this book, originally conceived in Polish and reconceived in English, available to a wider public.

Professor Frank E. Sysyn
Head, Executive Committee
Holodomor Research and Education Consortium,
CIUS, University of Alberta

HREC
HOLODOMOR RESEARCH AND EDUCATION CONSORTIUM
Canadian Institute of Ukrainian Studies
University of Alberta

The Holodomor Research and Education Consortium
was established and funded by the Temerty Foundation in 2013.

Introduction

The notions of memory and forgetting are of interest not only to historians but to academics in a range of disciplines, including sociology, cultural studies, social psychology and the political sciences. The work of the French scholar Maurice Halbwachs in the 1920s launched an academic and public debate on the topic, but it was only in the second half of the twentieth century that historical memory and "places of memory" became the subjects of intensive and multifaceted investigations, particularly by Pierre Nora, and Jan and Aleida Assmann.[1]

Much has been written about the needs that historical memory fulfills in society. Two functions are of primary interest to historians, namely, the legitimization of authority and the existing social order, and the creation of collective identity.[2] The legitimizing force of the past means that every society has a polemical relationship with the form of memory as manifested by its national history.[3] The second involves the construction of a relevant cultural canon, with the canon understood here as a series of historical events and figures that must be remembered if one is to feel a sense of belonging to the national community that created said canon.[4] Referencing the research of American sociologists, Barbara Szacka points out the close connection between memory and identity: "Memory helps one to feel continuously oneself, even though we live in another time and in another place than we once did. Who we are at a given moment in time, in turn, defines which recollec-

---

[1] Cf. Ewa Rewers, "Interferencja pamięci. Ku transkulturowości," in *Pamięć i zapominanie w Europie przełomu wieków*, ed. Zbigniew Drozdowicz (Poznań, 2001), p. 77; Anna Wolff--Powęska, "Zwycięzcy i zwyciężeni. II wojna światowa w pamięci zbiorowej narodów," *Przegląd Zachodni*, № 2 (2005), https://iz.poznan.pl/plik,pobierz,1039,9fdc38aa0517576b9575cd2920e2ac27/pdf/naka_panfu2013.pdf.

[2] Barbara Szacka, "Pamięć zbiorowa i wojna," *Przegląd Socjologiczny*, № 2 (2000), p. 15.

[3] Ibid., p. 16.

[4] Jerzy Szacki, "O kanonie kultury europejskiej uwagi sceptyczne," *Znak* 470, № 7 (1994), pp. 18–9.

tions we unearth from our memory."[5] Awareness of a common past, of a joint existence within time, allows members of a given social group to define themselves as "we," resulting in a bonding effect. Benedict Anderson has emphasized that modern nations (and this would include Ukrainians) constitute communities within which the role of collective memory is especially important to the process of uniting and defining their identity.[6]

The collapse of the Soviet Union had far-reaching consequences for memory culture in the former communist bloc. The scale of the contradictions and tensions between individual recollections and officially sanctioned memory that served the aims of the Soviet regime was nowhere more manifest than in the Soviet republics that became independent in the 1990s. Ukraine's situation was unique for its inclusion of the memory of the Great Famine of 1932–33 that was finally open for discussion in the 1990s. The intense competition between the memory of heinous Nazi crimes and recollections of Stalinist cruelty constitutes one of Ukraine's current socio-political problems today.

Even the most democratic states impose certain cultural paradigms to homogenize society,[7] which is also why symbolism of the national past that constitutes a "place of memory" is consciously shaped through the selection of certain historical moments or motifs.[8] Independent Ukraine, reestablished in 1991, began to build its historical politics on the idea of "the Ukrainian nation's eternal struggle for independence."[9] Politicians, social activists and representatives of the intellectual elite all engaged in shaping a Ukrainian canon of national memory that could be accepted by the heterogeneous Ukrainian society.

The symbols of contemporary Ukraine are at first glance the same as those adopted in the years 1917–18 by the government of the *Ukraïns'ka Narodna Respublika* [Ukrainian National Republic (UNR)]: the *tryzub,* dating from the Rurik dynasty (trident), the blue and yellow national flag, and the national anthem *Shche ne vmerla Ukraïna* [Ukraine has not yet perished]. On closer inspection, however, it turns out that the canon of Ukrainian national culture consists of mutually exclusive symbols that divide rather than unite society. The mixing of national and Soviet symbols, along with many others, has fueled confrontation between

---

[5] Szacka, "Pamięć zbiorowa," p. 16.

[6] For more on this concept, see Benedict Anderson, *Imagined Communities: Reflections on the Origin and Spread of Nationalism* (New York, 2016).

[7] *Po co nam historia,* transl. Maria Mróz, introd. Tadeusz Łepkowski (Warsaw, 1985), p. 12.

[8] Alexander J. Motyl, *Dilemmas of Independence: Ukraine after Totalitarianism* (New York, 1993), pp. 85–7.

[9] Stefan Kozak, *Z dziejów Ukrainy. Religia, kultura, myśl społeczna. Studia i szkice* (Warsaw, 2006), pp. 339–48.

ideological positions that were already in fierce competition in Ukrainian society.[10] Moreover, the social or collective memory of Ukrainians is *in statu nascendi* as they continue to search for the roots of their identity.[11]

The Great Famine of 1932–33 known as the Holodomor is one of the pages from Ukrainian history to which successive Ukrainian presidents (and Viktor Yushchenko in an exceptionally consistent way) have turned in an effort to strengthen the sense of national identity among Ukrainians. The Verkhovna Rada (Ukraine's parliament) declared the Great Famine to be an act of genocide in February 2003. It was the state apparatus that incorporated the Great Famine within the scope of independent Ukraine's official historical symbols.[12] Both the memory of the Holodomor and the places associated with it continue to constitute a powerful force that binds the historical memory and shapes the national identity of Ukrainians.[13]

Three decades of Ukrainian independence have produced a series of symbols that embody the Great Famine in social memory, influenced by cultural exchange between the western Ukrainian diaspora and the independent Ukrainian state. Ukraine's independence brought about enormous changes in the nation's social memory. At present, monuments to the Great Famine are a noticeable element of contemporary Ukraine's cultural landscape. They impact the response to and experience of the historical space chiefly by acting on our reflective and emotional realms.

Post-communist Ukrainian society, however, faced the problem of memory's revision, something incomprehensible for representatives of the Ukrainian diaspora in the West who had honed a canon of Ukrainian collective memory before the country became a sovereign state. The Ukrainian diaspora has been the creator of both public and academic discourse on the Great Famine 1932–33. Undoubtedly, from the 1930s to the 1990s, memory around the Holodomor was shaped by achievements in scholarly research and numerous civic initiatives of communities outside Ukraine. On the Ukrainian diaspora initiative, a whole series of "places of memory" dedicated to the Great Famine exist in Western Europe, the US, Canada, and South America. The Ukrainian diaspora is also a community that still cultivates its historical memory. These efforts have prompted significant interest among researchers and

---

[10] Andrew Wilson, *The Ukrainians: Unexpected Nation* (New Haven–London, 2015), pp. 223–4.

[11] Oksana Levkova, "(U)movy samo-(za)buttia," *Nezalezhnyi kul'turolohichnyi chasopys «Ї»*, № 40 (2005), http://www.ji.lviv.ua/n40texts/levkova.htm.

[12] Oleksandra Veselova, "Uvichnennia pam'iati zhertv holodomoru-henotsydu 1932–1933 rokiv v Ukraïni," *Ukraïns'kyi istorychnyi zhurnal*, № 2 (2004), pp. 50–67.

[13] Ola Hnatiuk, *Pożegnanie z imperium. Ukraińskie dyskusje o tożsamości* (Lublin, 2003), pp. 74–6.

even controversy, including the question of the motivation of Ukrainians in the diaspora in cultivating the memory of the Holodomor.

This work in its initial conception was motivated by the question of the extent to which the Ukrainian government's actions reflect the needs of Ukrainian society as opposed to being an element of a political game. One fruitful approach is to examine the discourse of the Holodomor (understood as national "realms of memory" in Pierre Nora's conception of *lieux de mémoire*) and to explore symbolic places in which memory is anchored ("places of memory" in Nora's conception). In the case of the commemoration of the Great Famine 1932–33 in public space, it is the combination of these two concepts of *lieux de mémoire* that can offer the most effective result.

I understand "places of memory" to mean the unique depositories of collective memory of the "community of memory" that brought them into existence. I see "places of memory" as not merely topographic, but also metaphoric locations. Accordingly, the Holodomor's "places of memory" are spaces directly connected with the dead victims (for example, the cenotaphs at previously unmarked mass graves, reconstructed or discovered on the basis of witness accounts), as well as monuments, museums, or commemorative plaques – places that only symbolically frame this experience. I have considered little known "places of memory" as well as the designs for Holodomor monuments that were never realized but which are, nevertheless, present in its iconography. My attention was also captured by the eclectic, rich and heterogenic Holodomor iconography found around the world.

As a historian, I have undertaken to examine the "places of memory" of the Ukrainian Holodomor for several reasons. To begin with, I was driven by a desire to discover and understand the various meanings that are bestowed on these "places of memory," both in Ukraine and in the Ukrainian diaspora. Research curiosity, amplified by the perception of the political nature of Ukrainian collective memory of the Holodomor, demanded that its "places of memory" be viewed in the context of the varied memory cultures of the Great Famine in Ukraine and the Ukrainian diaspora. The different tones that the "places of memory" strike and means of expression they employ allow for the assessment of both political tendencies at the time of their creation (in the case of national "places of memory") and of the perceptions of the "community of memory" that funded them (in the case of the "places of memory" beyond Ukraine's borders).

It is worth noting that research into Holodomor "places of memory" has not been the subject of academic analysis.[14] Among those who

[14] Indigenous Ukrainian historiography since the 1980s, in turn, has concentrated on researching the Great Famine as a historical fact and has amassed a sizeable volume

have looked at monuments to the Great Famine 1932–33 as "places of memory" are Oleksandra Veselova,[15] Tatiana Zhurzhenko,[16] Tetiana Katargina,[17] and Vitalii Ogiienko.[18] These researchers have concentrated on a single, either metaphoric or architectural, aspect of monumental representations. While Veselova and Katargina probed the means of commemorating the Holodomor, Zurzhenko and Ogiienko focused their attention mainly on the discursive practices resulting from the specific historical policies pursued in Ukraine. As an element of social activity among the Ukrainian diaspora in North America, monuments also figure in the work of Tamara Marusyk and Olena Kovalchuk.[19]

The discussion of the Holodomor as a "realm of memory" (symbolic figure) commenced relatively recently and largely outside of Ukraine,[20] with the Holodomor culture of memory in Ukraine often cast as a phe-

---

of research in this area. For a more extensive bibliography on the subject, see Volodymyr Kalinichenko and Ielyzaveta Iatsenko, "Istoriohrafiia holodomoru 1932–1933 rokiv v Ukraïni," in *Holod – henotsyd 1933 roku v Ukraïni. Istoryko-politolohichnyi analiz sotsial'no--demohrafichnykh ta moral'no-psykholohichnykh naslidkiv. Materialy Mizhnarodnoï naukovo--teoretychnoï konferentsiï na vidznachennia 65-richchia trahediï ukraïns'koho narodu, Kyïv, 28 lystopada 1998 r.*, eds. Stanislav Kul'chyts'kyi [et al.] (Kyiv–New York, 2000), pp. 15–25; Liudmyla Grynevych, "The Present State of Ukrainian Historiography on the Holodomor and Prospects for Its Development," *The Harriman Review* 16, № 2 (November 2008), pp. 10–20.

[15] Oleksandra Veselova, "Memorial'ni znaky i pam'iatnyky zhertvam holodu-henotsydu 1932–1933 rr. v Ukraïni," *Kraieznavstvo*, № 1–2 (2009), pp. 169–79.

[16] Cf. Tatiana Zhurzhenko, "Commemorating the Famine as Genocide: The Contested Meanings of Holodomor Memorials in Ukraine," in *Memorials in Times of Transition*, eds. Susanne Buckley-Zistel and Stefanie Schäfer (Cambridge, 2014), pp. 221–41; Tatiana Zhurzhenko, "'Capital of Despair': Holodomor Memory and Political Conflicts in Kharkiv after the Orange Revolution," *East European Politics & Societies* 25 (2011), pp. 597–639.

[17] Tetiana Katarhina, "Skryzhali skorboty. Zarubizhni pam'iatky Holodomoru-henotsydu 1932–1933 rr. v Ukraïni," *Kraieznavstvo*, № 1 (2013)," pp. 65–80.

[18] Vitalii Ohiienko, "Vizual'na kul'tura pam'iatnykiv zhertvam holodomoru v Ukraïni," *Hileia. Naukovyi visnyk* 65 (2012), pp. 114–9; Vitalii Ohiienko, "Memorial'na polityka vshanuvannia pam'iati zhertv Holodomoru 1932–1933 rr. v Ukraïni," *Hileia. Naukovyi visnyk* 61 (2012), pp. 72–7.

[19] Olena Koval'chuk and Tamara Marusyk, *Holodomor 1932–1933 rr. v USRR i ukraïns'ka diaspora Pivnichnoï Ameryky* (Chernivtsi, 2010).

[20] On the Holodomor as a Ukrainian 'realm of memory' see Johan Dietsch [Öhman], *Making Sense of Suffering: Holocaust and Holodomor in Ukrainian Historical Culture* (Lund, 2006), pp. 223–53; Georgiy Kasianov, "The Open Grave: The 1932–1933 Famine in Ukrainian Historiography, Politics, and Mass Consciousness," *Ab Imperio*, № 3 (2004), p. 3; Stefan Troebst, *Postkommunistische Erinnerungskulturen im östlichen Europa. Bestandsaufnahme, Kategorisierung, Periodisierung / Postkomunistyczne kultury pamięci w Europie Wschodniej. Stan, kategoryzacja, periodyzacja* (Wrocław, 2005), pp. 33–57; Wilfried Jilge, "Holodomor und Nation. Der Hunger im ukrainischen Geschichtsbild," *Osteuropa* 54, № 12: *Vernichtung durch Hunger. Der Holodomor in der Ukraine und der UdSSR*, eds. Rudolf A. Mark and Gerhard Simon (2004), pp. 147–63; Jurij Šapoval, "Lügen und Schweigen. Die unterdrückte Erinnerung an den Holodomor," *Osteuropa* 54, № 12 (2004), pp. 131–45.

nomenon of a political nature. The role of the diaspora was mentioned very briefly. The "places of memory" were not analyzed. The first extensive study of the Holodomor culture of memory was presented in *Danse macabre...*[21] by Georgiy Kasianov. Exploring the process of the development of the Ukrainian public and academic discourses on the Great Famine of 1932–33, Kasianov distinguished between the Holodomor as a historiographic, even political, concept (and therefore proposed that it be written as "Holodomor"), and the disaster of famine: a historical event from the 1930s. In an annotation to the book, the author even noted that it was intended exclusively for academic use. Admittedly, Kasianov did not pay particular attention to the "places of memory" connected with the Great Famine or the social rituals performed around them; he was more interested in the controversies that accompanied the building of a monument in Kyiv called "The Candle of Memory," presenting it as an example of the Holodomor's politicization.

At the same time, Swedish researcher Per Anders Rudling touched on the visual culture of the Great Famine (Holodomor) indirectly by way of studying the Ukrainian Insurgent Army's "community of memory" in Canada. Of particular note here is his analysis of the monument to the victims of the Holodomor in Edmonton.[22] In 2015, Tatiana Zhurzhenko published an article in the journal *Ukraïna Moderna* about the politicization of the Holodomor in Ukraine's public sphere under the presidency of Viktor Yushchenko.[23] Italian scholar Simone A. Bellezza analyzed the monuments of the Holodomor in post-communist Ukraine against the background of the Soviet monuments coexisting in the country. He was one of the first to point out that the Holodomor monuments were built much earlier than the occurrence of the Orange Revolution.[24] However, also circulating in the literature on the Holodomor was the view that it had been used during the Cold War by the US in its fight against the Soviet Union. Work by Dmytro Vedeneyev and

---

[21] Heorhii Kasi'anov, *Danse macabre. Holod 1932–1933 rokiv u politytsi, masovii svidomosti ta istoriohrafiï (1980-ti – pochatok 2000-kh)* (Kyiv, 2010).

[22] Cf. Per A. Rudling, "Memories of 'Holodomor' and National Socialism in Ukrainian Political Culture," in *Rekonstruktion des Nationalmythos? Frankreich, Deutschland und die Ukraine im Vergleich*, ed. Yves Bizeul (Göttingen, 2013), pp. 227–58; Per A. Rudling, "Multiculturalism, Memory, and Ritualization: Ukrainian Nationalist Monuments in Edmonton, Alberta," *Nationalities Papers* 39 (2011), pp. 733–68.

[23] Tetiana Zhurzhenko, "Vshanovuiuchy holod iak henotsyd: superechlyvi znachennia memorialiv zhertvam Holodomoru," *Ukraïna Moderna*, November 28, 2015, accessed July 30, 2020, https://uamoderna.com/md/zhurzhenko-holodomor-memorials.

[24] Simone A. Bellezza, "Building Memory: National Identities and Monuments in Post-Soviet Ukraine," in *Ukraine Twenty Years After Independence: Assessments, Perspectives, Challenges*, eds. Giovanna Brogi, Marta Dyczok, Oxana Pachlovska, and Giovanna Siedina (Rome, 2015), pp. 241–64.

Dmytro Budkov on commemorations of the fiftieth anniversary of the Holodomor is a case in point.[25]

Years before, American-Canadian researcher Frank Sysyn had drawn attention to earlier forms of commemorating the Holodomor in the Ukrainian diaspora, and more recently, he has written on the construction in the 1960s of the Memorial Church in South Bound Brook, NJ.[26] In 2018, in the second edition of Kasianov's book, published under the title *Rozryta mohyla,* he referred to Sysyn's work and specified that he himself was only interested in the political discourse in Ukraine during the period 1980–2000s. Kasianov also emphasized that social initiatives and the most important social actors involved in their creation were not the object of his study.[27] Once again, he omitted the Holodomor "places of memory," stating that he understands the Holodomor in terms of "realms of memory" in Ukraine.

It so happened that this issue would not give me peace because the above-mentioned authors created mutually exclusive images of the building of memory around the theme of the Holodomor, the origins of its creation in the diaspora and in independent Ukraine, and the needs that this memory fulfills in Ukrainian society and for people of Ukrainian heritage outside of Ukraine. I soon realized that contemporary rituals of Holodomor remembrance are seen in isolation from the historical context of the emergence of a culture of memory, which took shape within the North American diaspora long before the Holodomor's fiftieth anniversary and then influenced the formation of the culture of memory in Ukraine. In the 1930s, numerous Ukrainian communities abroad staged protests and organized street demonstrations against Kremlin policies in Soviet Ukraine. Ukrainians in interwar Poland organized protests to bring attention to the Famine and sought to secure foreign aid. The diaspora press wrote about famine in the Ukrainian countryside, which was also covered in Western newspapers.[28] Research in diaspora publishing houses enabled me to establish that the

[25] Dmytro Viedienieiev and Dmytro Budkov, *Zaruchnytsia hlobal'noho protystoiannia. Trahediia Velykoho Holodu 1932–1933 rr. v Ukraïni v konteksti „kholodnoï viiny" 1945–1991 rokiv* (Kyiv, 2013).

[26] Frank E. Sysyn, "The Ukrainian Famine of 1932–3: The Role of the Ukrainian Diaspora in Research and Public Discussion," in *Studies in Comparative Genocide,* eds. Levon Chorbajian, George Shirinian (London, 1999), pp. 182–215; Frank E. Sysyn, „The Ukrainian Orthodox Church: Memory and Memorialization of the Holodomor", accessed July 30, 2020, https://holodomor.ca/wp-content/uploads/2016/05/boundbrook.pdf.

[27] Heorhii Kasi'anov, *Rozryta mohyla: Holod 1932–1933 rokiv u politytsi, pam'iati ta istoriï (1980-ti – 2000-ni)* (Kharkiv, 2019).

[28] Examples of the diaspora's responses at the time of the Holodomor can be found through the website of the Holodomor Research and Education Consortium: https://holodomor.ca/resources/diaspora-reactions/.

first monuments to the Holodomor in the emigration were created already in the mid-1950s, around the twenty-fifth and thirtieth anniversaries of the Great Famine.

In my previous works I conducted an initial analysis of monuments to the victims of the Holodomor in Ukraine. In 2008, it seemed to me that a division into three basic groups – "the Ukrainian holocaust," "spiritual revival," and "famine horror" – was sufficient to convey these monuments' main features.[29] With time, I came to view this typology as inadequate, and monuments created in subsequent years continue to elude the categorization. In addition, there are some monuments that straddle the typological boundaries of the three initially proposed groups. Indeed, Holodomor monuments are characterized by a certain eclecticism due to the frequent fusion of funereal (religious) symbolism with Ukrainian national and folk symbolism. As it turned out, a far more exciting approach was to reflect on the image of the Holodomor as a historical event as manifested in "places of memory" by the "communities of memory" that created them. Many years of interest in this subject resulted in my first book about the practice of Holodomor commemoration. My intention then was to examine the Ukrainian culture of memory of the Great Famine 1932–33 as an event that was formative for the new Ukrainian nation, born from an antagonism toward everything that had hitherto been deemed 'Soviet'. In the first place, I was curious whether this remembrance was merely a replication of the post-communist aesthetic of reparations for past wrongs and a filling in of the "blanks" of the Ukrainian past. A question that remained was whether the visual culture of the Great Famine was still intentionally limited to communicating national messages tied to understanding the Famine as genocide committed against the Ukrainian nation by the Soviet regime.[30]

The aim of this book is to present the results of my research on the "places of memory" of the Holodomor in the context of the functioning of various "communities of memory" that arose from this historical event.[31] I formulated my main hypothesis as follows: First, the memory of the Holodomor and its victims was that of Ukrainians living in the 1930s outside Soviet Ukraine during the Great Famine 1932–33 and the unsuccessful attempts to combat Stalin's genocidal policy aimed

---

[29] Wiktoria Kudela-Świątek, "Pamięć i 'miejsca pamięci' Hołodomoru. Krajobraz po bitwie," *Nowa Ukraina* 5–6, № 1–2 (2008), pp. 114–5.

[30] Wiktoria Kudela-Świątek, *Miejsca (nie)pamięci. O upamiętnianiu ukraińskiego Wielkiego Głodu z lat 1932–1933* (Cracow, 2014).

[31] This book examines a number of issues that I have addressed in previously published works. In the ten years that I have worked on this subject, many of my views have changed or evolved. Thus, in this work, I wish to present many new conclusions and reflections.

primarily at the Ukrainian peasantry. Second, the first "communities of memory" were connected mainly by people living in exile or in the southeastern voivodeships of the Second Polish Republic (today's Western Ukraine) and thus who did not experience this famine. Third, social rituals in the diaspora related to this event developed in parallel to rituals in independent Ukraine in the 1990s. These were two independent paths for cultivating the memory of the Holodomor. At the beginning of my research, I assumed that they may have similar rituals and symbols.[32] However, my in-depth study of the memorials and monuments revealed unanticipated and stimulating results.

I have sought to give these communities a say, facilitating their reflection on the commemoration of the Holodomor and on what they have achieved in terms of remembrance of this event for future generations. The subject of my reflection and analysis is thus the culture of memory of the Holodomor in Ukraine and beyond its borders in its institutional aspects, as imposed from above, as well as the artistic embodiments of these notions as created by artists at particular "places of memory." I analyze the process of bestowing specific political significance to the experience of the Great Famine 1932–33 for the national identity of Ukrainians. Monuments are known to be catalysts for such social processes,[33] and thus the scope of my analysis includes memorials and monuments (including real and symbolic places of burial) that commemorate the Holodomor as "places of memory."

Establishing the actual number of such monuments irrespective of their form (mass graves, symbolic cemeteries, cenotaphs, etc.) is a complicated task. For various reasons, local governments in smaller towns and communities have erected monuments to the victims of *both* the Great Famine and Stalinist crimes generally, suggesting the validity of Viktor Yushchenko's historical policy, which stressed that the Great Famine was part of a broader attack directed against the Ukrainian nation. Thus, estimating the number of Ukrainian "places of memory" of the Great Famine of the 1930s is difficult. In 2003, an estimated 437 monuments and mass graves in Ukraine commemorated the Holodomor, with the largest number found in the Poltava, Kyiv, and Vinnytsia oblasts. Ukraine's eastern regions have been less active; between 1991 when Ukraine gained independence and 2003, only seven monuments to Holodomor victims had been unveiled in the Dnipropetrovsk Oblast, and none in the Donetsk and Zaporizhzhia oblasts.

---

[32] Wiktoria Kudela-Świątek, *W labiryncie znaczeń. Pomniki ukraińskiego Wielkiego Głodu 1932–1933* (Cracow, 2020).

[33] Yuliya Yurchuk, *Reordering of Meaningful Worlds: Memory of the Organization of Ukrainian Nationalists and the Ukrainian Insurgent Army in Post-Soviet Ukraine* (Stockholm, 2014), pp. 8–10.

Over the past decade, the number of monuments has noticeably risen, chiefly as a result of the seventy-fifth anniversary of the Holodomor. In 2010, a map was published marking places where monuments to the Great Famine had been erected, with illustrations of exemplary "places of memory" from across the country. Establishing the precise number of Holodomor "places of memory" is not paramount here. Indeed, there are works on this topic that are statistical to some extent, based on detailed research into Ukrainian and foreign journals that published information on unveiling ceremonies or mentioned the creators of monuments.[34]

In the earlier stages (from 2006 to 2008), my analysis was based on the registry of monuments I had received from the Ukrainian Ministry of Culture. In later years (from 2012 to 2014), I used a catalogue compiled by Vitalii Ogiienko, an employee of the Ukrainian Institute of National Remembrance.[35] Additionally, I drew on the inventorizing works of Oleksandra Veselova[36] and analyzed a catalogue compiled by German researchers under the direction of Anna Kaminsky that contains descriptions of monuments and burial sites in Ukraine up until 2008.[37] I also became acquainted with the first draft of Tetiana Katargina's compilation of diaspora sites of remembrance.[38] The works of these researchers cannot easily be compared because of the differences in the methodologies employed, their definitions of "places of memory," and the geographic scopes of their analyses. Some of these studies contain contradictory information as to the dates, founders, and creators of certain "places of memory." In the final stages of preparing this monograph for publication, I also made use of an on-line catalogue of Holodomor burial sites in Ukraine,[39] although it covers only the places of symbolic and real burial of the famine's victims. In short, to date, we do not have an exhaustive catalogue of Holodomor monuments at our disposal.

I conducted my archival and library research in Ukraine in 2015, and in Canada in 2017. In 2018, Dr. Marta Havryshko conducted research in

---

[34] Veselova, "Uvichnennia pam'iati," pp. 50–67; Oleksandra Veselova, "Pam'iatni znaky i pam'iatnyky zhertvam Holodu-henotsydu 1932–1933 rr. v Ukraïni," *Problemy istoriï Ukraïny. Fakty, sudzhennia, poshuky* 13 (2005), pp. 434–41; Katarhina, "Skryzhali skorboty," pp. 65–80.

[35] "Holodomor monuments in Ukraine," The Ukrainian Canadian Research & Documentation Centre, accessed February 25, 2020, http://www.holodomor-monuments.org/.

[36] Veselova, "Memorial'ni znaky," pp. 169–79; Veselova, "Pam'iatni znaky," pp. 434–41.

[37] Anna Kaminsky, ed., *Erinnerungsorte an den Holodomor 1932/33 in der Ukraine*, revised by Ruth Gleinig, and Ronny Heidenreich (Berlin, 2008).

[38] Katarhina, "Skryzhali skorboty," pp. 65–80.

[39] "Mistsia masovoho pokhovannia zhertv Holodomoru-henotsydu," Holodomor Museum, accessed February 25, 2020, https://map.memorialholodomor.org.ua/.

Australian libraries for the purposes of the present volume. Thanks to Prof. Tomasz Pudłocki's kindness, I obtained valuable visual materials from South Bound Brook, NJ, US. Moreover, throughout the last ten years I have visited the majority of the monuments analyzed here, in Poland, Canada, and larger cities in Ukraine, while also keeping up to date on unveilings.

The present study confirms the imprecise nature of information contained in an array of inventory works. My deliberations have a qualitative character and prioritize iconological and discourse analysis of Holodomor "places of memory" over their enumeration and individual description. The uniqueness of this study stems from it being the only work on this subject that diverts from the schematic of viewing the Holodomor exclusively in the context of Ukraine's politics of memory and reconstructs the process of the shaping of the "communities of memory" of the Holodomor, both in the diaspora and in independent Ukraine, processes that began as two separate currents but that grew mutually dependent over the last two decades. As a work dealing with the history of Holodomor monuments, this study can further our understanding of Ukrainian diaspora identity (responsible for the remembrance model) on the one hand, and trends in the politics of memory in Ukraine on the other. In the latter case, both the objective and the functional aspects of these "places of memory" are of interest; that is, both the content they convey and the means of conveyance.

This study consists of six chronologically related chapters. In the first, I discuss the theoretical basis of my reflections and my research methodology. It serves as a theoretical introduction to the subject of "places of memory" and addresses the applicability of the notion of "places of memory" in Pierre Nora's understanding to the analysis of the symbolic spheres in commemorating the Great Famine in Ukraine. In searching for appropriate theoretical models, I also reference Aleida Assmann, Krzysztof Pomian, Lech Nijakowski, and Roma Sendyka. This chapter also explains my methodological approach, which is based in reception theory (Stuart Hall) and critical discourse analysis (Gunther Kress, Teo van Leeuwen, Norman Fairclough, and Ruth Wodak), as well as iconology (Erwin Panofsky and Peter Burke).

The second chapter draws on the concept of a "community of memory" to shed light on the process that shaped the rituals of remembrance of the Great Famine and the creation of its first monuments in the diaspora and independent Ukraine. It is here that I reflect on whether, in the context of the Great Famine, we are dealing with multiple "communities of memory" or a single, heterogenic one.

In the third chapter, I discuss the Holodomor memorialization process outside Ukraine. I am interested in publications of the Ukrainian diaspora press in which the proposals to build Holodomor monuments first appear. And I also present the history of the creation of the most essential Holodomor "places of memory" in the diaspora. A separate subsection is devoted to the history of building the Memorial Church in South Bound Brook, NJ.

The fourth chapter looks at initiatives undertaken in Ukraine immediately after it gained independence as well as those of the Ukrainian diaspora and émigré communities in the West. Of particular interest to me are joint initiatives and those in Ukraine that were funded by the diaspora. This chapter looks at successive monuments to the Holodomor to outline how its culture of memory was shaped. It also references the present state of the Holodomor discourse, and to this end analyzes Ukraine's historical policy from 1991 to 2016.

In the fifth chapter I undertake an iconological analysis of select places of Holodomor remembrance – Edmonton, AB (1983) and Winnipeg, MB (1984) in Canada; Lubny (1993) and Kyiv (1993, 2002, 2008) in Ukraine; and Washington, DC (2015) in the US – providing an extensive justification for this selection in the course of analysis. Here I present the results of my iconological analysis of selected "places of memory" that played a very important role in shaping the visual culture of the Holodomor in Ukraine and abroad.

Finally, chapter six is devoted to the specifics and uniqueness of Holodomor commemoration in the context of other twentieth-century historical traumas. To this end, I consider various aspects of monumental architecture, starting with the Ukrainian architectonic symbolic tradition and continuing on to examine sources of inspiration, means of creating architectonic constructs in a symbolic dimension, and finally, the shared characteristic traits of monuments commemorating the Great Famine's victims, regardless of the time and place of their creation.

The structure of this book is intended to explore the titular subject in a multidimensional way while also supplying the reader with examples of how narration through monuments may enhance or counterbalance written narratives. I would argue that in the public sphere, the places of Holodomor remembrance are far more persuasive in their recounting of the event than even the best works of scholarship or reportage. It is for this reason that we must think about the stories told by these "places of memory," to whom they are addressed, and what the future of Holodomor monuments and memorials may hold.

Chapter I

Holodomor "Places of Memory": Between Theories and Methods

According to Maria Lewicka, "place" as a subject of research in the humanities and social sciences was first defined by so-called humanistic geographers (Yi-Fu Tuan, Edward Relph, Anna Buttimer, and David Seamon) as well as by architects (for instance, Christian Norberg-Schulz). Their conceptualizations of "place" bestow the space in question with a particular significance that is in turn understood as the content of the mental (or cognitive) representations that can shape personal recollections, family accounts, national or religious symbols, and the memory of historical events.[1] In this context, "place" becomes a skeleton key for opening the door to an unlimited number of processes that build new cultural experiences, both existential and aesthetic.[2]

If we are able to speak of "place" as a research category – a point in the universe, together with the material assembled in it, containing a story or a utopia, a sense of threat or security, an identity or memory[3] then we can also acknowledge that a place serves as a point of reference for how we perceive our social reality. Places thus play a crucial role in the creation and cultivation of individual and collective memories. Yi-Fu Tuan believed that memory is best served by tangible evidence of the past: old furniture, buildings, monuments, museum collections. Such places "anchor" time since the power of the past is still present within them;[4] they are memory's natural environment.

---

[1] Maria Lewicka, "Aurea mediocrita, czyli o tym, czy jakość może przejść w ilość," *Roczniki Psychologiczne* 13, № 1 (2010), p. 53.

[2] Ewa Rewers, *Post polis. Wstęp do filozofii ponowoczesnego miasta* (Cracow, 2005), p. 161.

[3] Lewicka, "Aurea mediocrita," p. 53.

[4] Yi-Fu Tuan, *Space and Place: The Perspective of Experience* (Minneapolis, MN–London, 2001), p. 193.

After the appearance of Frances Yates' *The Art of Memory* in 1966, the connection between memory and place became the subject of a broader study. Yates posited that memory as an uncontrolled subject – mobile, uncertain and changeable – not only arouses fears of losing control over memory but also prompts societies to seek various means for its preservation. For centuries, the art of memory has been tightly bound with "places of memory": *loci memoriae*. In Cicero's time, orators were advised to stipulate a construction of associations-symbols-places to reference during a speech.[5] When we actively refer to a given place to aid memory in the process of memorializing, we turn it into a "place of memory."

Nevertheless, research into *loci memoriae* is most strongly associated with the multi-volume publication *Les lieux de mémoire*,[6] edited by Pierre Nora and published between 1980–93. The central ideas of this work found adherents in various European countries relatively quickly,[7] and the concepts advanced by Nora have become prevalent in the field of historical research into monuments (and not only). Among historians, however, monuments are extremely rare as objects of reflection.[8] This is due, at least in part, to the absence of a theoretical concept that responds to the needs of contemporary historiography and would allow a place or moment to become the independent object of research.

Thus, this chapter aims to present the theoretical framework and methodological assumptions applied to the fundamental questions I raise in the work – namely, does a Holodomor monument brings us closer to the event it commemorates, i.e., allow for it to be remembered, or does it equally distance us, creating a "substitute for memory," an image of social construction designated by the name *Holodomor* (as suggested by Kasianov)? Or if the aim is to recount the event, does the

---

[5] Frances A. Yates, *The Art of Memory* (London, 1966), pp. 3–4.

[6] Pierre Nora, dir., *Les lieux de mémoire*, vol. 1–7 (Paris, 1984–93).

[7] See i.a. David Lowenthal, *The Past Is a Foreign Country* (Cambridge, 1985); John Bodnar, *Remaking America: Public Memory, Commemoration, and Patriotism in the Twentieth Century* (Princeton–New York, 1992); John R. Gillis, ed., *Commemorations: The Politics of National Identity* (Princeton, 1994); Raphael Samuel, *Theatres of Memory* (London, 1994); Simon Schama, *Landscape and Memory* (New York, 1995); Jan Assmann and Tonio Hölscher, eds., *Kultur und Gedächtnis* (Frankfurt a. M., 1988); Jan Assmann, "Die Entdeckung der Vergangenheit. Innovation und Restauration in der ägyptischen Literaturgeschichte," in Jan Assmann, *Stein und Zeit, Mensch und Gesellschaft im Alten Ägypten* (München, 1991), pp. 303–13; Jan Assmann, *Das kulturelle Gedächtnis. Schrift, Erinnerung und Politische Identität in frühen Hochkulturen* (München, 1992); Maurice Halbwachs, *Das Gedächtnis und seine sozialen Bedingungen* (Frankfurt a. M., 1985); Maurice Halbwachs, *Das kollektive Gedächtnis* (Frankfurt a. M., 1991); Reinhart Koselleck, *Vergangene Zukunft. Zur Semantik geschichtlicher Zeiten* (Frankfurt a. M., 1995); Edgar Wolfrum, *Geschichte als Waffe. Vom Kaiserreich bis zur Wiedervereinigung* (Göttingen, 2001).

[8] Robert Traba and Hans Henning Hahn, eds., *Polsko-niemieckie miejsca pamięci*, vol. 1–4 (Warsaw, 2012–3).

monument enable history to survive the prospect of oblivion, influencing the context of a Ukrainian national canon that has only recently taken shape?

I began my quest for a theoretical model from a discussion of the concepts of "realms of memory" and memorialization advanced by Pierre Nora, Aleida Assmann, James Young, Lech Nijakowski, Roma Sendyka, and Krzysztof Pomian, deliberating over their applicability to research into monuments as "places of memory" for the Holodomor.

1.1 The *Lieux de mémoire* according to Pierre Nora: A redefinition

Nora's ambitious attempt at describing the topography of the collective memory of the French consists of an extensive anthology of more than one hundred articles by various authors, each devoted to a "place of memory." In these volumes one can find articles about the French national flag, La Marseillaise, Joan of Arc, French wine, the French National Library, to mention only a few entries. They all anchor time, play the role of symbols, and serve as the nation's "places of refuge, sanctuaries of spontaneous devotion and silent pilgrimage, where one finds the living heart of memory."[9]

By way of introduction, it must be stressed that the premises formulated in Nora's work were not fully developed at the time of its publication. Many aspects required more precise specification, especially given their internally incongruent character. Nora did not define the notion of a "place of memory" directly, leaving readers the possibility of arriving at their own elaborations and understanding of the phenomenon conveyed as *lieux de mémoire.*[10] Moreover, the French scholar was in large measure inconsistent, not fully differentiating between the places, the carriers, and the mediums of memory.[11] Paradoxically, the ambiguity of the *lieux de mémoire* allows it to function as a skeleton key, allowing for any number of interpretations of Nora's premises[12] and proving most

---

[9] Nora, Pierre. "Between Memory and History: Les Lieux de Mémoire," *Representations*, № 26, Special Issue: Memory and Counter-Memory (Spring, 1989), p. 23.

[10] Cf. Andrzej Szpociński, "Miejsca pamięci (lieux de mémoire)," *Teksty Drugie*, № 4 (2008), p. 12; Kaja Kaźmierska, *Biography and Memory: The Generational Experience of the Shoah Survivors*, transl. Katarzyna Maciejczyk (Boston, 2012), pp. 87–9; Kornelia Kończal, "Miejsca pamięci. O niebywałej karierze pewnej koncepcji badawczej," in *Polsko-niemieckie miejsca pamięci*, vol. 4, *Refleksje metodologiczne*, eds. Robert Traba, Hans Henning Hahn, cooperation Maciej Górny, Kornelia Kończal (Warsaw, 2013), pp. 80–4.

[11] Kończal, "Miejsca pamięci," p. 80.

[12] Ibid., pp. 83–4.

attractive to his potential followers. Indeed, their expectations have been given full expression in numerous works that either relate to, or directly reference this concept.

Nora's *lieux de mémoire* are not places in the strictly geographical meaning of the term and are to be understood metaphorically and symbolically:

> These *lieux de mémoire* are fundamentally remains, the ultimate embodiments of a memorial consciousness that has barely survived in a historical age that calls out for memory because it has abandoned it. They make their appearance by virtue of the deritualization of our world — producing, manifesting, establishing, constructing, decreeing, and maintaining by artifice and by will a society deeply absorbed in its own transformation and renewal, one that inherently values the new over the ancient, the young over the old, the future over the past.[13]

For Nora, the term *lieux de mémoire* signifies locations "in which memory is rooted" for a given society.[14] The basic function of these places is to secure the memory of a group of people, and for this reason "realms of memory" can include people, events, objects, buildings, books, songs, or geographical locations that are "enveloped in a symbolic aura."[15] Practically every preserved object and phenomenon reflects the past; even dates themselves maintain memory of past events through the custom of anniversary commemorations.[16] Thus the main role of "places of memory" is thus to function as symbols that are called on to develop a society's perception of itself and its history. A key characteristic of these places is that they can convey various meanings that are themselves subject to change. According to Nora, "places of memory" are not shared by all cultures, and he repeatedly emphasized that his methodology was exclusive to the boundaries of French culture. Applying this concept to analyze phenomena outside of French culture without adequate reflection could result in a less than effective methodological copy.

Researchers of "realms of memory" focus on how they are reflected in our consciousness as opposed to their physical or historical cores. They describe how society remembers its past rather than the past as it was. At the centre of the majority of discussions published therein lies the question of when a given "realm of memory" gained one or another symbolic meaning and how this meaning changed over time. Nora's conceptualization suggests that "realms of memory" should be viewed

---

[13] Nora, "Between Memory," p. 12.

[14] Ibid., p. 22.

[15] Ibid., p. 19.

[16] Marcin Kula, *Nośniki pamięci historycznej* (Warsaw, 2002), pp. 7–8.

as symbols made permanent by cultural and collective memory, the ties that bind a given society. As Nora writes:

> (...) the notion of "places of memory" suggests a sense of belonging, the experience of membership within a community, an inscription in time, as well as a period of manufacture, fermentation. It suggests frameworks, tradition, the creation of collective imagination and a set of collective representations. In short, it indicates the existence of a history that is naturally perceived as shared.[17]

Sources for researching "realms of memory" include texts, images, and objects that provide information about an event, person or idea. They can extend to relics of historical thought, articles in the press on the unveiling of monuments, speeches given to mark historical jubilees, historical paintings, and everyday objects. However, the researcher who looks for concrete pointers in Nora's work will be disappointed given the intuitive nature of Nora's deliberations. In describing phenomena connected with the culture and history of France, he accidently discovered something that could explain and classify places and phenomena hitherto lacking a common denominator, but which comprise the essence of "Frenchness."

In Nora's initial conceptualization, "realms of memory" replace the "genuine" and "authentic" living memory that had been with us for decades, even hundreds of years, but which had ceased to exist.[18] In addition, *lieux,* in Nora's understanding, by functioning as the embodiment of memory, take on the role of guarantors of a memory that lives in them, accessible to anyone who is interested. In other words, "realms of memory" exist where cultural memory is present.[19] Pierre Nora emphasizes that the places are artificial and deliberately created in order to help us recall the past, which is necessary to give meaning to life in the modern world. The fundamental aim of such places is "to stop time, to block the process of forgetting, to establish a state of things, to immortalize death, to materialize the immaterial."[20] The place remains active as long as someone notices and interprets it in the way intended by its creator. The creation or activation of a place is decided also by the intellectual horizons of a given epoch and views on many matters. Some potential "realms of memory" are not activated, while the active role of others, in turn, can expire. After all, not all old build-

---

[17] Pierre Nora, "W poszukiwaniu europejskich miejsc pamięci," *Borussia. Kultura, Historia, Literatura,* № 41 (2007), p. 7.

[18] Charles Maier, "A Surfeit of Memory? Reflections on History, Melancholy and Denial," *History and Memory* 5, № 2 (1993), pp. 136–51.

[19] Nora, "Between Memory," p. 19.

[20] Ibid., p. 12.

ings and ruins, town squares and archives, cemeteries and libraries become "realms of memory." Only those chosen for us by our forefathers and those selected by us for our heirs are elevated to remembrance, interrupt the process of forgetting, and suggest common values that unite people as nations.[21] From this perspective, "realms of memory" are places whose symbolic significance is understood by contemporaries who label them as such.

Since the 1980s, research into nation-building processes has increasingly involved the symbolic aspect of the process that shapes national identity. An attraction to mementoes from the past grows out of the need to possess tangible objects that 'can support a sense of identity'.[22] As Tim Edensor writes: "nations provide individuals with sacred centres, objects of spiritual and historic pilgrimage, that reveal the uniqueness of their nation's "moral geography."[23] As a rule, these spatial symbols evoke historical events and serve as evidence of a given nation's past existence;[24] they point to its glorious past and commemorate significant episodes of a usually retrospectively reconstructed national history. In other words, the most important events in a nation's life are recalled through monuments, ceremonies, texts, documentary broadcasts, and institutions, and they constitute the most important symbolic figures in the memory of a society. According to Jan Assmann, these symbolic messages of the past are emotionally linked with our collective identity.[25] "Realms of memory" in this sense are conceived as spaces symbolizing time, and thus as spatial transpositions. There are also examples of "places of memory" that attempt to "embody" time in space.

The collective memory of any society is not a constant phenomenon but subject to changes in the course of historical processes. Over time, the traditional associations that support the meaning of these places cease to be read in the way originally intended by their creators. The illegibility of the message that can follow socio-political transformations is obvious in the large-scale processes of removing communist monuments across Ukraine and all of Eastern Europe following the system's collapse and, in many cases, their replacement with monuments

---

[21] Elena Trubina, "Mesta pamiati, monumenty i 'novaia demokratiia'," *Topos*, № 3 (2000), accessed July 30, 2020, http://journals.ehu.lt/index.php/topos/article/view/485.

[22] Tuan, *Space and Place*, p. 197.

[23] Tim Edensor, *National Identity, Popular Culture and Everyday Life* (Oxford, 2002), p. 45.

[24] See more: Barbara Szacka, *Wprowadzenie do socjologii* (Warsaw, 2003), pp. 241–4; Barbara Szacka, "Pamięć zbiorowa i wojna," *Przegląd Socjologiczny*, № 2 (2000), pp. 11–28; Barbara Szacka, "Historia i pamięć zbiorowa," *Kultura i Społeczeństwo*, № 4 (2003), pp. 3–15; Barbara Szacka, "Transformacja społeczna a świadomość historyczna," in *Ofiary czy współwinni. Nazizm i sowietyzm w świadomości historycznej* (Warsaw, 1997), pp. 43–64.

[25] Anna Wolff-Powęska, "Zwycięzcy i zwyciężeni. II wojna światowa w pamięci zbiorowej narodów," *Przegląd Zachodni*, № 2 (2005), http://www.iz.poznan. pl/pz/pz/22_2005_2_wybrany_art.pdf.

to national heroes from other epochs.[26] The aims of "places of memory" can also be thwarted by the changing basis of aesthetic knowledge and convention.[27] Varied interpretations point to the ways such places are bestowed with different identities and affiliations, thereby signaling the link between a given place and the person narrating its tradition.[28]

1.2 The Holodomor and "realms of memory" and "places of memory"

In these deliberations, I am satisfied with the position positing that *lieux de mémoire* can be both material and imaginary in nature. For the sake of clarity, it must be added here that the Great Famine of 1932–33 itself – an event seen as decisive in the history of Ukraine and the subject, on the one hand, of an intense cult among some Ukrainian communities abroad and, on the other, of bitter debate for other communities (primarily in Ukraine) – is a *lieu de mémoire,* understood as an imagined "realm of memory." Recollections of this event, in turn, cultivated in places bestowed with symbolic significance to maintain intergenerational bonds and fortify the spirit of unity, constitute the "places of memory" of the Great Famine, namely, places understood as actual spaces of memory about the given event.

Applying the concept of "realms of memory" in the context of the Great Famine of 1932–33 leads to the observation that the Holodomor has become "a symbolic element of the legacy of memory" for the Ukrainian nation in Ukraine and that its analysis will benefit from the classic understanding that Nora brought to memory studies.[29] In order to employ Nora's concept to study the formation of Ukrainian memory about the Great Famine, a certain fundamental difference between the French and Ukrainian contexts must be stressed at the onset. Namely, the work of Nora was aimed at counteracting a process that he saw as "the rapid loss of French national memory." Thus, the "realms of memory" analyzed by Nora and the historians with whom he worked were understood as already entirely formed and complete national phenomena.[30]

---

[26] Aleksandra Leinwand, "Z cokołów," *Karta,* № 19 (1996), pp. 62–6.

[27] Edensor, *National Identity,* p. 66.

[28] Ibid., p. 67.

[29] Agnieszka Niewiedział-Bédu, "Sprawiedliwi wśród Narodów Świata w Polsce 1989–2003. Gry znaczeń w konstrukcji miejsca pamięci," in *Historia, pamięć, tożsamość. Postaci upamiętniane przez współczesnych mieszkańców różnych części Europy,* eds. Maria Kujawska and Bogumił Jewsiewicki (Poznań, 2006), p. 139.

[30] Ibid., p. 140.

In the case of the Great Famine in Ukraine, we do not observe a transition from *milieux de mémoire* (the real environments of memory) into *lieux de mémoire* (places that remind us of the past) that would save the Great Famine from oblivion, following on Nora's conceptualization. Memory of the Great Famine had not faded with the passage of years. There are a few source references describing how, in 1943 in the Reichskommissariat Ukraine during the German occupation, the Great Famine was commemorated by marking mass graves, but this was a brief moment breaking the silence that after the re-establishment of Soviet power would again hang over the subject in Ukraine.[31] However, the memory of the Great Famine (the Holodomor) had not faded with the passage of years. Although this memory was not part of social consciousness, even among those that with time would be known as the generation of Holodomor survivors (this would change later, given the politics of memory in the Soviet Union), in the 1990s the Great Famine was rescued from amnesia and bestowed with major social significance. Indeed, it was to become a key element in the construction of the new Ukrainian memory canon. It must be noted that under communism, the Holodomor's *milieux de mémoire,* which Nora understood as spaces of memory in which a "living memory" of an event was present, simply did not exist. The fact that the Holodomor had taken place was ignored by the historical narratives created about Soviet Ukraine's past, which destined it to being forgotten.

It appears that in describing Holodomor monuments, there is a notion that may be more appropriate and that is, in a sense, encompassed in *lieux de mémoire,* namely, that of a *site,* meaning a place established to commemorate an event deemed worthy of being remembered in the present by a given "community of memory." The shaping of an awareness of "places of memory" is a common phenomenon in processes of social development.[32] The idea of a shared heroic past, for example, is fundamentally important to the sense of identity of ethnic minorities, towns and regions. It also plays an important role in shaping national

---

[31] In 1943, a cross was placed on the grave of Ukrainians who died of famine in the village of Marchenky (near Myrhorod). *Uriadovi dunaievets'ki visti,* № 82 (October 10, 1943), p. 3; *Sums'kyi visnyk,* July 23, 1943, p. 2; *Holos Okhtyrshchyny,* July 30, 1943, p. 4; *Myrhorods'ki visti,* № 53 (July 15, 1943), p. 4. On July 4, 1943, a funeral service was held in the village of Pishchane (Reshetylivka Raion) in the presence of 1,500 local people. *Holos Poltavshchyny,* № 94 (274) (29 July, 1943), p. 2. In July 1943 a wooden cross was established in the center of the village of Riasne (Nekhvoroshcha Raion). *Tarashchans'ki visti,* № 60 (218) (August 8, 1943), p. 4.

[32] Bertrand Taithe, "Monuments aux morts? Reading Nora's Realms of Memory and Samuel's Theatres of Memory," *History of the Human Sciences* 12, № 2 (1999), pp. 123–39; Hue-Tam Ho Tai, "Remembered Realms: Pierre Nora and French National Memory," *The American Historical Review* 106, № 3 (2001), pp. 906–22.

ideology. National symbolism, which most often derives from history, plays this role. Mementoes of important events from the lives of nations, cities, or other types of communities also serve this function. The "places of memory" or "sites of memory" connected to the Great Famine are thus aimed at making it (or rather its present image) manifest within the cultural landscape, which is not consistent with a desire "to block the process of forgetting" but rather with the need to promote awareness of facts from the nation's history that had been buried in times of communist totalitarianism. For obvious reasons, they constitute a sign of the presence of a Ukrainian symbolic domain on these lands.

The impact of the Great Famine 1932–33 on individuals has become only more noticeable with time. Despite the many years of silence on the subject, the consequences have not disappeared – to the contrary, they manifest in the public sphere out of a necessity for closure in social mourning. There are even those who argue that the phase of actual awareness and understanding of the Great Famine is still to dawn because, although it happened eight decades ago, the perpetrators obscured the truth.[33] Against the backdrop of such declarations, it does not seem rash to assert that the Great Famine represents an extraordinary historical experience, the influence of which on one or several generations cannot yet be evaluated. Given the difficulties of establishing the boundaries of the "community of memory" of the Great Famine, as well as this event's mythologization, it is difficult to determine the number of generations enveloped by the experience. Consequently, the past has not yet passed; it continues on at the levels of emotion, self-awareness and political orientation, and as an effect of interpretations that endow it with meaning that necessitates a revision of one's own identity.

As already mentioned, during the first decade of Ukraine's independence, "places of memory" of the Great Famine were consciously established, both to habituate the symbolic realm and to populate the new state's cultural landscape. Over time, and particularly during the period of "passive (non)remembrance" under Leonid Kuchma's presidency, these places became an element of the counter-memory sphere and only occasionally drew public attention. Under Viktor Yushchenko's government, both existing places and those that were being established (including museums) gained in significance, only to be ignored in the public sphere during the years of Viktor Yanukovych's presidency. The complete lack of a historical policy under Yanukovych meant that these places became part of his "Ukrainophile" predecessor's legacy. It isn't easy to pin down the meanings and significance that Ukrainians will impart to these places (or whether they will

---

[33] Oksana Levkova, "(U)movy samo-(za)buttia," *Nezalezhnyi kulturolohichnyi chasopys «Ї»*, № 40 (2005), accessed July 30, 2020, http://www.ji.lviv.ua/n40texts/levkova.htm.

establish new places). In light of the current difficult internal situation in Ukraine, these "places of memory" could either play a consolidating role in society or be relegated to the back burner, giving way to new heroes and symbols emerging from the culture of memory that is presently developing around the "Revolution of Dignity." In my opinion, the process of giving social meaning to Holodomor "places of memory" is ongoing and is thus a historical phase of commemoration in the public space.

1.3 Monuments and memorials to the Holodomor as "places of memory"

In discussing actual "places of memory" of the Holodomor, my analysis addresses monuments and memorials as well as real and symbolic places of burial. It is worth noting at the onset that we are dealing with "places of memory" that came into being at different times. As a result, as symbolic "places of memory," they represent vastly different images of the Great Famine and embody this event's varied memory cultures. For this reason, I am interested in real "places of memory" (*site de mémoire*) as part of "realms of memory" *(lieux de mémoire)*, which the Great Famine constitutes for Ukrainians, regardless of where they now live.

1.3.1 Monuments and memorials

Site de mémoire can refer to a monument, among other things, and according to Witold Szolginia, can mean, for example, a sculpted and/or architectonic work, statue, memorial stone, obelisk, or memorial plaque raised to commemorate a historical person or event.[34] I also favour the definition advanced by Sigfried Giedion, Jose Luis Sert, and Fernand Lager in their 1943 manifesto *Nine Points on Monumentality*:

> Monuments are human landmarks which men have created as symbols for their ideals, for their aims, and for their actions. They are intended to outlive the period which originated them and constitute a heritage for future generations. As such, they form a link between the past and the future.[35]

---

[34] Witold Szolginia, *Architektura* (Warsaw, 1992), p. 126.

[35] Sigfried Giedion, Jose Luis Sert, and Fernand Lager, "Nine Points on Monumentality," in *Architecture Culture 1943–1968: A Documentary Anthology*, eds. Joan Eigen and Edward Ockman (New York, 1993), pp. 29–30.

In an urban setting, monuments arise from the desire of a local society to commemorate in an abstract form (assumed by a permanent, material object) the values and ideas of significance to the collective, as well as out of an aesthetic need to distinguish particular points of the urban space.[36]

Agnieszka Gębczyńska-Janowicz considers a monument to be a significant element of an urban landscape that changes its hitherto neutral surroundings into an element of its own context, even as it becomes incorporated in the cityscape itself and part of a greater area. In this way, a monument becomes a reference point amid other elements of the landscape, one of many topographic hubs in a network that orients a person's recollections and carries a symbolic meaning both within the physical sphere as well as our memory.[37]

In this context, a "place of memory" is a physical and visual carrier of collective memory. It comes into existence as a result of the transformations of a space that flow from the meanings and attributes bestowed upon it over time. The place itself does not possess such power but becomes a "place of memory" through the projections of its visitors' recollections. A place as such is unable to convey information about an event, so some visualization of memory is necessary to present basic facts. Straightforward information plaques and tablets as well as a monument's design can serve this aim.[38]

A monument is one of the simplest signs of identity – an artistic synthesis of national memory. Erected with the aim of remembrance, it usually constitutes a dominant element of the cultural landscape. It memorializes the people who made history and who are the reason why our world today looks as it does, and not otherwise. It also answers the needs of the memory collective that gave it life, including the artists who designed it, exemplifying their interpretation of a given event. The manner in which a monument's symbolic meaning and its expressiveness as a work of art are interpreted depends on its viewer's cultural, intellectual, and aesthetic background. Likewise, the sense bestowed on a work by its creators will be variously interpreted.[39] For those who witnessed the commemorated events directly, a monument stands as important evidence of that time; for others, including those not particularly interested in history, it provides an opportunity to reflect, to visit an "alternative" reality and

[36] Agnieszka Gębczyńska-Janowicz, *Polskie założenia pomnikowe. Rola architektury w tworzeniu miejsc pamięci od połowy XX w.* (Warsaw, 2010), p. 81.

[37] Ibid., p. 83.

[38] Ibid., p. 105.

[39] Kurt Forster, "Monument: Memory and the Mortality of Architecture," *Oppositions*, № 25 (1982), p. 8.

be carried away by passions and emotions converted into form by an artist-creator.[40]

As images that illustrate and evoke specific ideas, monuments have an important function outside of the historical sphere. Popularized through photographs, they sometimes become icons of memory – an element of our imaginings and recollections about space. They are also the "places of memory" of specific experiences. As part of wedding rituals in Ukrainian cities and towns today, couples often go to Holodomor monuments to take photos. Monuments can be part of a narrative matrix that shapes the collective vision of history, or what the American researcher James Young calls the "texture of memory."[41]

As is the case with many "places of memory" that commemorate tragedies of twentieth-century history, Holodomor monuments possess a force that is difficult to grasp, an aura that allows for the simultaneous perception of the distance and the proximity of history in both its factual and psycho-social dimensions.[42] The global array of Holodomor monuments is far from uniform with respect to intent, aesthetics, or politics. Nevertheless, these monuments contribute to a collective function; on the one hand, they bring together a "community of memory" in mourning the deceased victims, and on the other, they play a role in recounting and educating about an event that is crucial to the Ukrainian experience and to twentieth-century history more generally.

Given the problems in applying Nora's classical category of *lieux de mémoire* to Holodomor "places of memory" and reflecting on the version of the Great Famine's history that is told in the monumental representations of this event, I turn now to Aleida Assmann's conceptualization of "places of memory." In contemplating such places and their presence in urban spaces, she differentiates between two types, namely, places of commemoration and traumatic places. The former are places that function without a local connection in the present. They commemorate historical events of significance to local society, but ones that are separated by a chasm from contemporary reality. What links such places to passersby is the conviction that they belong to the history of a given society. Communing in and with such a place facilitates sensory contact with the reality conveyed, thereby evoking specific emotions and aesthetic experiences. These places are called into being to allow people to contemplate the spirit of their forefathers and events

---

[40] Maciej Lewandowski, "Rzecz o pomnikach," *Przeszłość i Pamięć*, № 4 (1998), p. 5.

[41] James E. Young, *The Texture of Memory: Holocaust Memorials and Meaning* (London–New Haven, 1993).

[42] Tomasz Kranz, "Miejsca pamięci czy pamięć miejsc? Rozważania o roli upamiętniania w przekazie społeczno-historycznym," *Przeszłość i Pamięć*, № 1 (2000), pp. 58–9.

both lofty and terrifying in their essence. Their purpose is to make the present more luminous by means of the past.

Places of trauma, unlike places of commemoration, do not allow for an affirmative interpretation of the commemorated past. In such places, the sensual, concrete, and emotional tone all work to deepen an otherwise intellectual grasp of past events through personal reflection and intellectual assimilation of history.[43]

In considering monuments to the Great Famine as "places of memory," we encounter those that possess both commemorative and traumatic traits as identified by Assmann. Holodomor monuments are closer to places of recollection despite the fact that they recall exceptional suffering since their places of commemoration are intended to convey a positive message to future generations. According to Assmann, "both religious and national memory is full of blood and victims, yet it is not traumatic since it carries positive connotations and can participate in the shaping of a collective identity."[44] In this context, history brings permanence to a place of commemoration that recounts it, and vice versa – such places make real the historical narrative. Thus, Holodomor monuments have an identity function in presenting the victims of the Great Famine in a noble and praiseworthy manner that speaks to the sacrifices made by the Ukrainian nation on its road to independence.

Holodomor monuments share with places of trauma the fact that they prompt us to recall something that can still cause pain and from which the "community of memory" cannot and does not want to distance itself. Holodomor monuments do not aspire to give meaning to or positively interpret this event but to symbolize a still open wound and the suffering that is passed from generation to generation. For some memory communities, as a matter of ethics the crime of the Holodomor must always remain present in social memory and cannot be allowed to expire, which makes historical distance from the event that much more undesirable.

As a result, it is not possible to divide Holodomor monuments into traumatic places and places of commemoration because these same "places of memory" have, at different moments in history, fulfilled one or both of these social functions. However, it is certain that Holodomor monuments are not erected to forget about the Holodomor, its perpetrators, or their victims. That said, the monuments analyzed and presented within the empirical part of this book can be divided into those memorializing the victims and those honouring the heroism of the

---

[43] Aleida Assmann, "Das Gedächtnis der Orte – Authentizität und Gedenken," in *Firma Topf & Söhne – Hersteller der Öfen für Auschwitz: Ein Fabrikgelände als Erinnerungsort?*, eds. Aleida Assmann, Frank Hiddemann and Eckhard Schwarzenberger (Frankfurt–New York, 2002), p. 197–212.

[44] Ibid.

survivors. Assmann's concept was formulated with a broad understanding of social processes within the circle of cultures of memory. It is important to note that in the case of the Holodomor, these sites cannot always be differentiated. In many cases, the monuments were erected in small localities on lands that, as discovered years later, were actual mass burial sites for victims of the Famine.

I initially termed these places "cemetery sites."[45] In fact, these sites are typically found in the vicinity of local cemeteries, although some exist in suburbs and even urban centres, where their role is akin to that of monuments. The diversity of this group of memory sites makes it difficult to define them and to propose a suitable typology. In many cases they are marked with simple crosses, although markings of a non-Christian character are also encountered. Some recall the mass Holodomor casualties at a given location as a fact, while others fulfill an added interpretative function of narrating the experience of those buried there.

1.3.2 Cemetery sites

A cemetery is not merely a place for the burial of human remains and for remembrance of the deceased; it is also a cultural text that evidences human fates while simultaneously illustrating attitudes toward death characteristic for each age. Our perception of death, in turn, is a clear measure of our attitude towards life; hence cemeteries often tell us more about the living who attend to burials and conduct rituals of mourning than those who are buried there. While the actual substance of a cemetery consists of the remains under the earth, the real signifiers of all that a cemetery evokes are part of its above-ground repository. It is primarily these visible elements that transform a cemetery into an important cultural phenomenon – a "cultural text." According to Jacek Kolbuszewski, a Polish philologist and specialist in thanatological literature, the cemetery is a place where the present tangibly rubs shoulders with the past. A cemetery develops not only in space but also across time, adopting a certain temporal expression. The dates on the gravestones of the deceased, along with the other personal information, become metatexts integral not only to the cemetery's history but also the history of the local community that frequents it. The cemetery is, to some degree, "a chronicle of the history of the countryside," at times revealing its links with the history of the state and the nation.[46]

---

[45] Wiktoria Kudela-Świątek, *Miejsca (nie)pamięci. O upamiętnianiu ukraińskiego Wielkiego Głodu z lat 1932–1933* (Cracow, 2014), pp. 161–9.

[46] For more on the cultural significance of cemeteries see Jacek Kolbuszewski, *Cmentarze* (Wrocław, 1996), pp. 30–7.

A monument at a cemetery, well-maintained and remembered, can express both a sense of community and private, familial ancestral worship. Graves and cemeteries are created not only to satisfy laws that require the removal of corpses from living spaces for reasons of hygiene; they are also spaces of remembrance of all that makes human life meaningful, including the belonging of the deceased to a clearly defined community.[47] The traditions and customs of many religions call for reverence of the memory of the deceased and a spiritual connection with them at the place of their burial through prayer, displays of mourning, and individual and collective reflection.[48] Philippe Aries, writing on the role of symbolic monuments in cemeteries in France, noted that they were erected after 1870 for French soldiers who had died far from home (veterans of the Franco-Prussian War and/or colonial wars). World War I then gave the civic cult of the dead a popularity and prestige that it had not experienced previously, after which the burying or burning of the dead on the field of honor was no longer tolerated. Entire cemeteries, conceived as architectural landscapes, were devoted to endless rows of identical crosses. The cross was chosen as the common symbol of death and hope. According to Aries,

> It is very significant that the church and the cemetery were the two places that welcomed the first two monuments to the dead: the church, because the Catholics and the clergy regarded those who had died in such a just war as comparable to martyrs and because the Church considered its vocation to honor the dead and maintain their cult; the cemetery, because it was the place where the living went to remember and had actually been a kind of competitor of the church since the time the two had been legally separated. (...) And each commune of France, in each *arrondissement* of Paris, a tomb was erected to the slain soldiers. An empty tomb, "the monument to the dead," was generally located opposite the town hall. (...) It really was the symbol of unanimous national feeling, almost until our own time.[49]

In other words, the grave, headstone, and inscription as "counter balance" now symbolize the person, replacing the emotional and social space once materialized around the deceased. The deceased receives these as the final gift from his or her loved ones. In cases where an entire local community funds the grave, it serves – as Kolbuszewski wrote – as a trace of the deceased on earth, testifying to a person's existence and significance to others. The mere act of identifying the deceased on

---

[47] Ibid., p. 33.

[48] Kranz, "Miejsca pamięci," p. 59.

[49] Philippe Ariès, *The Hour of Our Death: The Classic History of Western Attitudes toward Death over the Last One Thousand Years*, transl. Helen Weaver (New York, 2008), pp. 591–2.

the headstone and thus individualizing the grave speaks to the essence of the unrepeatable singularity of one human fate.[50] Mourad Djebabla, a Canadian researcher of the memory of the Great War, emphasizes that in representing a "community of memory," a monument to the memory of the deceased also relates to a very personal, individual mourning, which invites both understanding and consensus. The monument thus becomes the departure point of collective memory that focuses a given community on the same recollection.[51] It becomes a place of pilgrimage ("practices of commitment") for memory that provides a symbolic sense of belonging to a community.

Cemetery monuments in places that represent the Holodomor experience as an act of genocide, as suffering and extermination, arouse feelings of fear, mourning, and emotional overload, which are linked to a history of negative models. As material proof of a historical phenomenon, these places play a crucial role in shaping an appropriate "community of memory" of the Holodomor by virtue of their joint reinterpretation and attainment of "place of memory" status. Real places retain their full transmission power even when the viewer has, in actual fact, little to see. As Anna Ziębińska-Witek notes, the sense of place is the most emotional part of the experience of such spaces.[52] At stake is the so-called affective remembrance transmitted via *lieux de mémoire* in "cemetery places," arousing certain emotions, including empathy, communitarianism, and hope.[53]

The Polish sociologist Barbara Szacka wrote: "certain points in public space play the role of 'commemorative places.' In testifying to what happened, they counter forgetting and become memory's stable footholds. (...) Commemorative places make the past tangible and allow us to overcome time. Spending time where something happened, discovering the traces of those who died and events long since passed, makes them more real and creates a sense of direct involvement with them."[54] Retaining contact with the past is of highest importance here, with the past's materiality becoming the subject of an affective and sensual

---

[50] Kolbuszewski, *Cmentarze*, p. 31–2.

[51] Mourad Djebabla, "Pamięć zaklęta w kamieniu. Czytanie pomników ofiar Wielkiej Wojny w Québecu (1919–1939) jako miejsc pamięci," transl. Kamilla Kuźmicka, in *Inscenizacje pamięci*, eds. Izabela Skórzyńska, Christine Lavrence, and Carl Pépin (Poznań, 2007), p. 261.

[52] Anna Ziębińska-Witek, "Estetyki reprezentacji śmierci w ekspozycjach historycznych," in *Obóz-muzeum. Trauma we współczesnym wystawiennictwie*, eds. Małgorzata Fabiszak and Marcin Owsiński (Cracow, 2013), p. 32.

[53] Luiza Nader, "Afektywne pamiętanie. Moim przyjaciołom Żydom Władysława Strzemińskiego," *Zagłada Żydów. Studia i materiały*, № 8 (2012), pp. 188–213.

[54] Barbara Szacka, "Pamięć społeczna a identyfikacja narodowa," in *Trudne sąsiedztwa. Z socjologii konfliktów narodowościowych*, ed. Aleksandra Jasińska-Kania (Warsaw, 2001), pp. 43–4.

experience. At the heart is the process of communing with the relics, or remains, of a reality now passed that is based in being at a place connected with this past and experiencing it directly, physically.[55]

As sacral places, cemeteries constitute a principal element of collective memory. The Holodomor monuments located there gain in symbolic strength because of the surrounding landscape. They are usually dedicated to victims of totalitarianism and are intended to symbolically serve as a grave for those lacking a place of burial for an array of reasons.[56] The creators of these monuments remain anonymous as a rule, with the sponsors more often receiving mention. The weight of this symbolic recompense is underscored by the fact that these symbolic tomb monuments were often funded by survivors of the Great Famine. The location becomes part of their symbolic background rather than their historical context; the aesthetics of mourning are viewed across Ukraine as the most appropriate form of remembering Holodomor victims.

In considering theoretical categories appropriate to the task of studying real and symbolic burial sites, I have been drawn to a concept developed by Roma Sendyka, who has made reference in her works to forms of commemorating/remembering traumatic historical events involving local society. In my view, such places belong to the category of "counter or non-places of memory". These sites do not belong to the category of anthropological spaces, which allow individuals to embody their identities. "Non-places" can be understood as inauthentic and ahistorical. The notion of a non-place was first defined by Marc Augé, who emphasized that these places encompass space in general (airports, motorways, supermarkets, etc.), and as products of the era of modernization, they do not provide answers to questions about our identity or history.[57] In turn, Claude Lanzmann, proposed the term "non-places of memory" to define so-called deformed places such as sites of the mass execution of Jews. In his understanding, the notion is the complete opposite of Nora's "places of memory."[58] A non-place can be the result of what evolves when a local community does not see the need to commemorate a place and more broadly speaking, the memory of the event connected to it.

Roma Sendyka expanded the definition of "non-place" to cover sites where acts of mass violence had taken place.[59] These are scattered and

---

[55] Marc Ferro, *The Use and Abuse of History: Or How the Past is Taught* (London, 1984), p. 11.

[56] Lech Nijakowski, *Domeny symboliczne* (Warsaw, 2006), pp. 69–70.

[57] Marc Augé, *Non-Places: An Introduction to Anthropology of Supermodernity*, transl. John Howe (London–New York, 1992), p. 79.

[58] Claude Lanzmann, "Les Non-lieux de la mémoire," in *Au sujet de Shoah. Le film de Claude Lanzmann*, ed. Michel Deguy (Paris, 1990), pp. 280–93.

[59] Roma Sendyka, "Pryzma – zrozumieć nie-miejsce pamięci (non-lieux de mémoire)," *Teksty Drugie*, № 1–2 (2013), pp. 323–44.

connected to forms of institutionalized violence that lack, at present, any form of signposting or remembrance, or where an event has been inappropriately documented. Their shared characteristic, according to the author, is the presence of human remains at the site. "Non-places" do not necessarily possess common topographic features or physical properties and include urban and rural areas.

Sendyka's conceptualization, inspired by scholarship on Holocaust remembrance, is primarily concerned with "places of memory" in which the community topographically tied to a given location does not see the need or reason for connecting its memory to a given site. In the case of the Holodomor, at stake are places where, due to various circumstances, the local community begins to see the need for remembering previously unmarked mass graves. During the Holodomor, as deaths mounted and the living weakened, funeral customs were degraded and burials had a mass, dehumanizing character, with bodies taken to a nearby cemetery or simply away from residential areas, deposited in ditches prepared for the purpose, buried rolled up in a blanket or without any covering. Witnesses have described cases of the ground moving after burials because victims still barely alive were thrown into the shallow graves along with the dead, thereby saving those tasked with transporting corpses a second trip.[60] The oral histories often recall the spontaneous creation of such mass graves. The locations of these mass graves were most often unmarked. Interestingly, crosses that symbolically commemorate the events have started to appear at some cemeteries independent of the process of locating actual burial sites.[61]

Although useful in operationalizing the empirical part of my research, the concept as presented within the subject literature does not provide a theoretical framework sufficient for explaining the specifics and uniqueness of Holodomor memory culture. The specificity of this type of "place of memory" follows from the fact that, on the one hand, these sites can be interpreted as places of living memory (*milieux de mémoire* as understood by Nora) while, on the other, they constitute "(counter)places of memory," given that their discovery serves as a reminder of a forgotten past. In this way, they become places worthy of remembrance. Communing at such a place in a cemetery leads to awareness of the Holodomor's proximity, making it real in juxtaposition to the multitude of "inauthentic" monumental and museum pres-

---

[60] Oleksandra Veselova, "Uvichnennia pam'iati zhertv holodomoru-henotsydu 1932–1933 rokiv v Ukraïni," *Ukraïns'kyi istorychnyi zhurnal*, № 2 (2004), p. 50.

[61] Oleksandra Veselova, "Uvikopomnennia zahyblykh vid holodnoho moru," in *Holod – henotsyd 1933 roku v Ukraïni. Istoryko-politolohichnyi analiz sotsial'no-demohrafichnykh ta moral'no-psykholohichnykh naslidkiv. Materialy Mizhnarodnoï naukovo-teoretychnoï konferentsiï na vidznachennia 65-richchia trahediï ukraïns'koho narodu, Kyïv, 28 lystopada 1998 r.*, eds. Stanislav Kul'chyts'kyi [et al.] (Kyiv–New York, 2000), p. 232.

entations. An abstract realm linked to a distant, extraordinary, and often incomprehensible event in a nation's history is, in turn, transformed into something familiar, allowing for contact with the experience of the Famine victims buried at the site. This type of "place of memory" also powerfully articulates the extent of death during the famine years.

A concept within the notion of "places of memory" as proposed by Krzysztof Pomian is appropriate for this discussion. Following his division of "places of memory" into "dominating" and "dominated,"[62] cemetery monuments in the context of the Holodomor's memorial culture undoubtedly belong to the latter group, largely because they are erected by local community representatives, and often the initiative is part of a broader plan to commemorate victims of the Great Famine.[63] This said, it should be added that cemetery monuments stemmed from the desire to provide a symbolic grave for those who were not buried respectfully during the famine years. It is a way for the local community to symbolically restore the dignity of its dead fellow-countrymen. For this reason, the planners of these monuments seek the opinions of the oldest local residents who are requested to identify places where the dead were buried. The unveiling ceremonies of such monuments and memorials are usually connected to religious services in memory of those who tragically perished.

In fact, dominant in Ukraine are monuments constructed in the twentieth and twenty-first centuries by Ukrainian state authorities (the initiatives of presidents on anniversaries of the event). Holodomor cemetery monuments would constitute the second group, mainly because they have been erected by local communities despite the initiatives' connections to the fulfillment of a broader plan to memorialize victims of the Great Famine. One may underscore that these came into being, first and foremost, out of the needs of the heart and the desire to create a symbolic grave for those who were not buried with proper respect and solemnity.

In the case of the Ukrainian diaspora, it is only in the last decade that "dominating" monuments have started to appear, that is, monuments advocated by Ukrainian diplomatic missions in various countries as part of efforts to build good-neighbourly relations with European Union countries and counteract Russian influence. Earlier monuments to the Holodomor were built on the initiative of Ukrainians in emigration as residents of their new countries, reflecting the local memory of the national and denominational community constituting an ethnic

---

[62] Krzysztof Pomian, "Miejsca pamięci w Europie Środkowo-Wschodniej. Doświadczenia przeszłości. Przesłanie na przyszłość," *Przegląd Polityczny*, № 89 (2008), pp. 4–11.

[63] Veselova, "Uvichnennia pam'iati," pp. 50–67; Veselova, "Uvikopomnennia zahyblykh," pp. 218–42; Oleksandra Veselova, "Pam'iatni znaky i pam'iatnyky zhertvam Holodu-henotsydu 1932–1933 rr. v Ukraïni," *Problemy istoriï Ukraïny. Fakty, sudzhennia, poshuky* 13 (2005), pp. 434–41

minority in the given country. Hence, for our purposes, Pomian's concept can be applied only partially because of its European nature and lack of attention to the specifics of post-Soviet states.

1.3.3 The choice of a theoretical concept

In the search for a theoretical concept, I have also examined "sociology of a monument," a metaphor of a sociological basis suggested by Polish sociologist Lech Nijakowski. He proposes monuments as "varied forms of commemoration and places symbolizing important events from the past such as the designation of the sites of battles, houses inhabited by great compatriots, concentration camps."[64] Nijakowski treats the subject of sociological research so defined to be a common denominator for all places that are "expanses of memory" and "non-places of memory." To a certain extent, this theoretical concept bonds all of the theories mentioned above.

It is Nijakowski's conviction that, in terms of sociology, a monument may be researched in four different ways:

1. As a material object, a work possessing a creator, a symbolic dimension, potential viewers, and aesthetic value. The fundamental significance of the sociology of a monument on an aesthetic level is the analysis of the work-recipient relationship (within the social context).[65]
2. As a composite part of a communicative subsystem. A monument in the modern national state has become a valuable instrument of official propaganda, engaged in the shaping of a homogeneous cultural environment.[66]
3. From a micro-sociological and anthropological perspective (first and foremost that of the anthropology of everyday life), as an object adapted to the daily practices of ordinary people. Many additional subjective and inter-subjective meanings are attributed to a monument, such as its significance to individual biographies as well as collective ones.[67]
4. From a macro-sociological and political science perspective. Legal norms regulate commemorations, and state institutions regulate this sphere of civil activity and the shaping of state policy in relation to social memory. Additionally, monuments can be viewed from the perspective of their social functions: the maintaining and shaping

[64] Nijakowski, *Domeny symboliczne*, p. 66.
[65] Ibid., p. 81.
[66] Ibid., p. 86.
[67] Ibid., p. 89.

> of social memory, the mobilization of groups, the legitimization of authority, and also the unintentional consequences of the "action" flowing from a monument: social conflict, questioning of state authority, etc.[68]

In this work, I am equally interested in the monument as an aesthetic model and as a communicative subsystem or element acting within the public discourse. The empirical research that served as the basis for my analysis to a large degree skews towards this understanding of what constitutes a monument, including the sociological typology of monuments proposed by Lech Nijakowski. In fact, Holodomor monuments erected at cemeteries and near houses of worship, as Nijakowski noted based on entirely different examples taken from Polish courtyards, derive their symbolic power from the aura of the places where they are erected. And yet, the very first Holodomor monuments were built by the Ukrainian diaspora on the grounds of Ukrainian Orthodox and Greek Catholic parishes in North America and Australia, likely the result of practical (and not symbolic) considerations; these plots were the property of the local Ukrainian communities residing in emigration. It was in the mid-1980s that the first monuments were erected on property belonging to Canadian municipalities – Edmonton in 1983 and Winnipeg in 1984.

Moreover, the symbolism of the Great Famine (Holodomor) has changed over the years and will undoubtedly undergo further transformation. Clearly, this is not a rigid phenomenon as it has a range of regional variations (particularly noticeable in the numerous examples of how the commemoration of the Holodomor is observed in the diaspora) and is representative of both political memory and grassroots initiative. Ukrainians, in the absence of their own non-religious model of commemoration, have adopted some known examples of the commemoration of traumatic events from the history of humanity, transferring and adapting social rituals of their countries of residence to their own cultural and social contexts (the lighting of graveside candles, wreaths from ears of corn hung on house doors, etc.).

It seems impossible to find and employ a single theoretical model to analyze places of real and symbolic burial as well as Holodomor monuments. Nora's conceptualization will be pertinent in cases where real places of burial have been transformed into symbolic ones. Assmann's ideas, in turn, are significant for the analysis of the social function played by monuments to the Holodomor's victims, while Sendyka's theories allow us to grasp the social aspect in the functioning of "places of memory" at the local level or how society ignores them. Finally, Pomian's

[68] Ibid., p. 90.

approach only strengthens my belief that the burial places at cemeteries cannot be categorized as "places of memory" in urban environments.

Most important to note from the perspective of historical research is that none of the concepts outlined here supposes that a design for a monument that was never erected could be the subject of research. However, during the course of my research conducted in Canada and Ukraine, I uncovered archival materials documenting the processes that resulted in the creation of certain monument designs and viewed submissions for design competitions that were never realized (for example, the Marian Kots competition for a monument in Kyiv and the 2003 Kyiv competition) as well as materials bearing witness to the change in political (national) context affecting the choice of design (the monument in Kyiv in 2008). Therefore, it became imperative for me to understand the substantive reasons for the rejection of specific proposed designs. Consequently, it was also helpful to consider theoretical concepts that examine three-dimensional images in broad contexts.

I was tempted to limit my research scope to theoretical concepts and avoid the specifics and uniqueness of the monuments, including the reflections of the changes, the transformations within Ukrainian politics of memory, and the coming of age of Ukrainian society in its fight for its own dignity. Yet as a historian, the opportunity to examine how discourse about the Great Famine of 1932–33 was shaped and how it evolved into a discourse of the Holodomor itself was for me an opportunity to explore in-depth the evolution of a culture of memory for a specific event. My approach has allowed me to elucidate a symbolic world constructed around and encompassing a definite historical subject and to explore how symbolic content evolves and changes in a context within which historical events have been incorporated into the public expanse (the relation between the politics of memory and everyday memory itself, i.e., the "communities of memory").

Aleida Assmann is ultimately convinced that awareness (consciousness) of the variety of perspectives is critical to analysis of the "places of memory":

> (...) the memory of places is heterogenous and inevitably complicated. Its complexity results from the fact that an array of emotions is tied to a single place. (...) A place is what is sought there, what is known about it and what is connected to it. Despite being objectively concrete, it changes depending on the viewer's perspective.[69]

By adopting different theoretical assumptions, therefore, the viewers' perspective of one and the same "place of memory" can change. My work is eclectic in terms of theory, referencing the conceptualizations

---

[69] Assmann, "Das Gedächtnis der Orte," p. 205.

presented above on an "as needed" basis, stemming from an effort to provide the most exhaustive answers to my research questions as is currently possible. Theories and methodologies are not ends in themselves nor are they ever the last word, and a significant part of any research within the humanities is the creation of one's own research methods, one's own theory and methodology.[70] As Kathy Charmaz writes, acts involved in theorizing foster revelations of possibilities, establishment of connections, and the asking of new questions.

> Theorizing means stopping, pondering, and rethinking anew. We stop the flow of studied experience and take it apart. To gain theoretical sensitivity, we look at studied life from multiple vantage points, make comparisons, follow leads, and build on ideas. Because you chart your direction through acts of theorizing, you may not be able to foresee endpoints or stops along the way.[71]

Therefore, in my research and analysis into "places of memory," I take advantage of all of the important concepts discussed above, and in many instances, I have examined the same phenomena employing research tools of varied disciplines. Finally, I always sought methods that expanded theoretical possibilities, avoiding the imposition of set images and predetermined answers.

1.4 Reading images of the Holodomor

As a historian studying the visual culture of the Holodomor, I do not use visual data in an auxiliary or supplementary manner. I place the work of art – the monument or museum exposition, along with its creators and sponsors – at the centre of my analysis. Consequently, my research falls within the scope of various academic disciplines, among them history, cultural anthropology, and art. From the many methods available, I also selected a few that support my analysis of visual and textual sources.

1.4.1 Eyewitnessing the Holodomor

This study is indebted to Erwin Panofsky's theory relating to iconography and iconology. Iconology is fundamental to the interpretation

---

[70] Ewa Domańska, "Jakiej metodologii potrzebuje współczesna humanistyka," *Teksty Drugie*, № 1–2 (2010), p. 52–4.

[71] Kathy Charmaz, *Constructing Grounded Theory: A Practical Guide through Qualitative Analyses* (London–Thousand Oaks–New Dehli, 2006), p. 135.

of the commemorative Holodomor memorials and monuments under analysis as it helps to unlock the meanings in the symbols found in the sculptures and to explain how visual images can communicate ideas far beyond the space of a given "place of memory" in the public domain in Ukraine and abroad.

Panofsky, the founder of iconology as the study of the symbolism and content of visual imagery, discussed it as interpretive iconography. A scholar working in the framework of iconology aims to expose a visual work's successive semantic layers through a series of analytical activities:

1. Pre-iconographical description (identification of all that can be perceived with the naked eye in a given work, including objects and events);
2. Iconographical analysis (establishment of the theme and study of the work's conventional significance based on cultural knowledge);
3. Iconological interpretation (surmounting an artwork's conventional perception).[72]

Peter Burke, referencing Panofsky and writing about the use of iconological and iconographic analysis in historical research, emphasizes that

> (...) historians need iconography but also need to go beyond it. They need to practice iconology in a more systematic way, which may involve making use of psychoanalysis, structuralism and especially reception theory (...).[73]

Conducting an iconological analysis reveals the iconographic motifs that are significant from a symbolic perspective and facilitates their interpretation in the context of the meanings bestowed by the collective memory and the artist, whose work anticipates and attempts to meet this community's expectations and notions about how best to remember the Holodomor. I see iconological analysis as an opportunity to consider forms of narration about the past other than the historiographic and yet to be fully valued by historians.

In terms of the methodology employed in my analyses, I start from a conviction akin to that of Alon Confino, namely, that research into collective memory is first and foremost a reflection on the shape and essence of a group identity shared by members of a given community, an identity that binds this group despite its members' varied interests and

---

[72] Erwin Panofsky, "Iconography and Iconology: An Introduction to the Study of Renaissance art," *Meaning in the Visual Arts* (1970), pp. 53–7.

[73] Peter Burke, *Eyewitnessing: The Uses of Images as Historical Evidence* (London, 2001), p. 42.

motivations.[74] I focus less on the ways that the past manifests itself in the present than I do on the reasons why some images of the past have gained recognition while others have been rejected. Therefore, in my investigations I attempt to combine reflection on memory as such with reflection on memory politics along with possible counter-memories. It is only in grasping the whole of the phenomenon, without isolating its individual aspects or arranging them in a particular order (for example, chronological), that the essence of a memory's complexity can be conveyed – both in the form of memory representations and in their adoption or rejection.[75]

Stuart Hall, who came up with the encoding/decoding model of communication, notes a difference between information as it is encrypted and as it is decoded. The content ascribed to a work by its recipients will depend on their experiences and the environment in which they live. This explains why one recipient fully accepts the symbolism intended by the author while another rejects it or simply does not understand it.[76] Gunther Kress and Teo van Leeuwen stress the need to consider the variety of ways in which any particular visual representation can be understood and analyzed through cultural experience:

> Visual communication is always coded. It seems transparent only because we already know the code, at least implicitly – but without knowing what it is we know, without having the means for talking about what it is we do when we read an image. A glance at the "stylized" arts of other cultures should teach us that the myth of transparency is indeed a myth. We may experience these arts as "decorative," "exotic," "mysterious," or "beautiful," but we cannot understand them as communication, as forms of "writing," unless we are, or become members of these cultures.[77]

Sometimes, however, we see in a monument what is not there. Specifically, the fate of children during the Holodomor is dramatically represented on the monument in Los Angeles, which presents a tragic scene of a mother wailing over the loss of her children. The viewer comes to a Holodomor monument with certain expectations, and our empathy with the victims may be reflected in it as in a mirror. For

[74] Alon Confino, "Collective Memory and Cultural History: Problems of Method," *The American Historical Review* 102, № 5 (1997), p. 1390.
[75] Ibid., p. 1399.
[76] Stuart Hall, *Encoding and Decoding in the Television Discourse* (Birmingham, 1973), pp. 166–7.
[77] Gunther Kress and Teo van Leeuwen, eds., *Reading Images: The Grammar of Visual Design* (London–New York, 2006), pp. 32–4.

example, Oleksandra Veselova has suggested that the image represents a mother killing her child to lessen its suffering.[78]

According to the analysis of Holodomor monuments and memorials examined in this monograph, it is important here to reiterate this highly relevant aspect of the social semiotic approach adopted. My position is that a monument's meaning lies somewhere between its creator's assumptions and its viewer's interpretation. The recipient cannot decipher all of the meanings encoded by the artist; each party decodes the monument's symbolic meaning in an individual, unique way. In other words, in this work I am interested in "places of memory" of the Holodomor as an element of a cultural landscape.

As a rule, the "places of memory" of the Great Famine are viewed outside of their socio-cultural context, within a sphere set by given state borders (Ukrainian and/or diaspora). Meanwhile, the juxtaposition of the two memories of the Holodomor (the traditional diaspora perspective and the new Ukrainian one) allows us to grasp both the degrees of kinship and the differences in commemoration as practised in Ukraine and abroad. This is an important point in relation to the data examined in this study; the Holodomor monuments and memorials under analysis are not all of Ukrainian origin, created for a Ukrainian audience, or placed in the Ukrainian public space. I analyze both monuments created by Ukrainian artists or artists of Ukrainian origin and monuments built by foreign artists; monuments created for a Ukrainian audience and monuments built as a warning to other nations; and monuments created in Ukraine and those created abroad. If the full potential of their meaning is to be established, it is important to employ theoretical approaches that can address the relevance of culture. Consequently, I do not write about "ours" and "others" and have not divided these places into "national" and "diaspora" ones because, regardless of geographic location, these places are linked by shared symbolic content that is re-created and transformed in "places of memory" the world over. We can speak then of the existence of a single, albeit differentiated, visual culture that understands the Holodomor as an act of genocide committed against the Ukrainian nation.

In my considerations, I have tried to avoid imposing my reading of the images and ideas I gleaned from the symbolic layers of the Holodomor monuments and memorials. For this reason, I worked on visual images as texts in their specific contexts. In each of the analyzed cases, I looked for the context and often reconstructed it from diverse and fragmentary information.

---

[78] Veselova, "Uvichnennia pam'iati," pp. 50–67.

1.4.2 Critical Discourse Analysis (CDA)

The meanings conveyed by the Holodomor monuments and memorials are bestowed on them by the "community of memory" that ensured their creation (in diaspora settings) or which has formed around them (in Ukraine). In order to comprehend the meaning, it is necessary to interact with the "community of memory" that not so much funded the monument as "gave it life," bestowing it with a specific meaning and purpose. Given that Holodomor monuments interest me as part of a broad social and historical backdrop, I found it necessary in my analysis of the Ukrainian émigré and diaspora Holodomor culture of memory to analyze the discourse itself.

The significance of contextual factors to an understanding of visual culture is reflected within the discipline of Critical Discourse Analysis (CDA). CDA is evident in this study on two levels. On the one hand, it helps us get to know the broader context in which a monument is created. Because for an understanding of monuments as "places of memory," it is essential that our analysis goes beyond an interpretation of images and that it extends to an exploration of the context in which they were produced. On the other hand, a conveyor of a message employs an image and words in composing a statement, so it was necessary to employ textual and semiotic instruments to understand the relationship between the visual image and the inscription on a monument.

In this study I point to an important aspect of monumental sculpture: whereas a painting is best displayed against a neutral background of walls, floor, and ceiling, which is conducive to reflection and immersion in the world created by the painter, works of monumental sculpture commune with individuals in their environment and should be understood from the perspective of the various angles from which they can be viewed. It is only in tandem with surrounding architecture that monuments find their artistic expression. This means that for me the location of the monument and the inscription on it should be analyzed equally with the rituals of social cultivation of the memory of the Holodomor in public space.

Subsequently, the source materials that inform my research include the Ukrainian diaspora press published after 1940, government documents defining the principles of Holodomor remembrance in the public space (such as the decrees of the Verkhovna Rada (Parliament) of Ukraine and Ukraine's successive presidents), the anniversary speeches of Ukraine's presidents, articles in national and regional media covering the unveiling of Holodomor monuments, and the commentary on these monumental projects provided by their creators.

Important sources included the recollections of those involved in the construction of the monuments as published in the Ukrainian diaspora press, recorded during in-person interviews, or available on the internet. My attention was riveted by the journal and newspapers sources that published information about Holodomor commemorations over successive anniversaries (with the event initially being referred to as the Great Famine, or the Famine-Genocide) as well as the appeals and proclamations of social activists and hierarchs of the Ukrainian Orthodox and Catholic (Uniate) Churches abroad. I looked at publications from the 1940s, 1950s, 1960s and 1970s, and thus long before the so-called "explosion of memory" in the 1980s. In my analysis of these materials, I trace the process of the creation of a "community of memory" and its characteristic rituals of commemoration and unique symbolism by considering both individual initiatives and mass-scale commemorations.

The use of CDA in social research can be attributed to Norman Fairclough. For him, discourse is a kind of social practice and the embodiment of social structure. Fairclough created his model as a three-dimensional framework comprising text, discourse practice, and social practice. This three-dimensional model has implications for the way we treat a text. An analyst may identify several different representations within a given text that, as Fairclough states, can be viewed as a separate discourse, and in turn a discourse is accomplished by generating many specific representations. The relationships between different discourses are an element of the relationships between different people – they may complement one another, compete with one another, one can dominate others, and so forth.[79]

How do we go about identifying different discourses within a text? Fairclough suggests thinking of a discourse as representing some distinct part of the world from a particular perspective.[80] The distinguishing features of a discourse are the vocabulary used. But rather than focus minutely on different ways of wording the same aspects of the world, I focus on how different discourses affect the world differently, and therefore, on the semantic relationships between words. I seek the global meaning of the piece to be deciphered and interpreted, subjecting the text to a laborious process involving its segmentation (the separation of all structural components) followed by a reconstruction of the discursive strategies by means of which the speaker shapes the recipient's opinion about the informative content conveyed in the analyzed text (for example, news items about plans to build monuments). The results of each analysis were compared with the results of the iconological analysis. The final combined product served as the basis for the considerations and reflections presented in this study.

---

[79] Norman Fairclough, *Analysing Discourse, Textual Analysis for Social Research* (London, 2003), p. 124.

[80] Ibid., p. 129.

As Ruth Wodak and Norman Fairclough have explained, CDA considers how language works within institutional and political discourses as well as specific discourses in order to uncover overt, or more often, covert inequalities in social relationships. At the basis of CDA lies the assertion that discourse is a prerequisite element of the social world, that it is the prime mover within social constructs.[81] Language use in writing is seen as a social practice, which implies a dialectical relationship between a particular discursive event and the situations, institutions, and social structures that frame it.[82] For Małgorzata Lisowska-Magdziarz, the aim of analyzing media discourse is "to show the formulated, social and unnatural specifics of cultural texts; an analysis of the possible effects that the action of various discourses have."[83] In this context, I am interested in the analysis of the conceptual structures expressed in written language. Reading a text in context involves looking at its socio-cultural and intertextual features in relation to other discourses produced at other times or other topics at the same time in the same society ("communities of memory").

The textual analysis employed here involves detailed description of the ceremonies and events associated with the construction or unveiling of a given monument; the elaboration of the design concepts that were to be realized; the opinions and letters of readers on the subject of these initiatives; announcements about collections to fund the building of such a monument. In other words, in CDA, discourse is essential to explain the social world, and through CDA, it is possible to discover the forces that exploit a specific image of the Holodomor, what this image is and why it has become the imposed canonical representation of this event within the public space.

1.5 Conclusions

Within this theoretical framework, the consumer of a work of art (in this case, a monument to the victims of the Holodomor in Ukraine) is not passive in encountering it, each time negotiating its significance anew. My semiotic analysis of the symbolic layers of Holodomor monuments is based in each case on knowledge of specific symbols and their

---

[81] Norman Fairclough and Anna Duszak, "Wstęp. Krytyczna analiza dyskursu – nowy obszar badawczy," in *Krytyczna analiza dyskursu. Interdyscyplinarne podejście do komunikacji społecznej*, eds. Anna Duszak and Norman Fairclough (Cracow, 2008), p. 16.

[82] Ruth Wodak and Norman Fairclough, "Critical Discourse Analysis," in *Discourse as Social Interaction*, ed. Teun A. van Dijk (London, 1997), pp. 258–84.

[83] Małgorzata Lisowska-Magdziarz, *Analiza tekstów w dyskursie medialnym* (Cracow, 2006), p. 23.

significance in Ukrainian culture (including folk and funerary art), as supported by relevant literature. Where possible, I also reference the broad European context of symbols that constitute the canon of Holodomor visual memory culture, as well as the views of both artists and sponsors regarding the ideas expressed with particular monuments. The process of creating and realizing these projects is an important element of my analysis. I am particularly interested in the artist's choice of symbols and the reasons behind the rejection of other symbols or designs. For me, the artist is also a historian whose account of the Holodomor is based on historical knowledge, biographical experience and artistic reflection.

My analysis is limited to real monuments, excluding virtual monuments, art installations and performative forms of representing the Holodomor experience. In thinking through a monument's symbolic layer and its message to its viewers, I pay attention to the creative process that precedes construction. I do not view a monument simply as a finished project with a concrete meaning but rather as the effect of a process involving multiple compromises and concessions on the part of both the artist and the community of memory behind the project. My analysis extends to the inscriptions etched into these monuments, which often supplement the work's symbolic layer and convey specific meanings bestowed by its creator or funders.

By approaching the visual analysis from a social perspective and incorporating historical, cultural, ethnic, and political contextual information, I try to demonstrate the significance of taking a holistic view of the "places of memory": their historical contexts; the modes of communication that make up the whole; and the role of the viewer as a reader of the monuments. I will discuss both aesthetic questions and issues around Holodomor commemoration in Ukrainian "places of memory" and those outside its borders. With emphasis placed firmly on the symbolic and aesthetic component of the message, political whirlwinds occupy a noticeably less prominent role in my discussion. However, I fully understand that politics and poetics are sometimes inseparable in the context of Holodomor commemorations.

Chapter II

The Communities of Memory of the Great Famine (1932–33)

This chapter is intended to provide the context for my discussion and interpretations of visual culture of the Holodomor. Monuments to the Great Famine have been erected by various "communities of memory" around the world, invested with a multitude of meanings, in an array of historical circumstances. They do not constitute a homogeneous group and become indecipherable and incomprehensible without social, historical, and cultural background. Moreover, in the absence of context, only the aesthetic and artistic qualities of these works of art would lend themselves to analysis in the framework of Holodomor studies in and outside of Ukraine. My position, however, is that the symbolic layer is closely connected to the way that this event was commemorated by various "communities of memory" at different moments in history and reflects their level of knowledge and interpretation of it.

This chapter begins with an attempt to define the complex notion of "community of memory." My use of the term "communities of memory" denotes those communities that were instrumental in the process of Holodomor symbolization. Therefore, later in this chapter, I attempt to answer the question of why the diaspora made a tremendous effort to honour the victims of the Holodomor and what the course of that process was over the years. I also present the most significant symbols that emerged in the social symbolization process and were later reflected in the symbols of Holodomor "places of memory." To that end, I employ critical analysis of media discourse. Moreover, I consider the role that the Holodomor generation, which consists of the survivors, played in cultivating that memory and subsequently, in the emergence of "communities of memory." Finally, I will focus on the key institutions established for the purpose of uniting individuals engaged in Holodomor-related research, education, and social projects.

2.1 Who creates a "community of memory" and why?

The notion of a "community of memory" is usually defined intuitively, mainly with reference to the subordinate concept of "community."[1] "Community" is understood here as a type of collective based on the strong internal bonds of a group, generally informal in structure. In this light, a "community of memory" is a social group that is defined by its past and the memory of this past.[2] The decisive factor behind the creation of a "community of memory" is the conviction of its members regarding the exclusivity and exceptionality of their experience in relation to other groups.[3] Thus understood, it is a kind of enclave for a specific lifestyle. Its members participate in so-called "practices of commitment," meaning rituals of memory devised and accepted by the given group as proof of its stability. Hence, ritual becomes a way of professing the group's values.[4] Creating narratives about a shared past and notable individuals is a significant part of the tradition, which is key to "communities of memory." For such a community, recollecting, cultivating, and ritualizing a shared past is the main goal rather than a means of defining group characteristics.

The most commonly cited definition of "communities of memory" is the one advanced by Maurice Halbwachs. In his understanding, a "community of memory" (*la communauté de souvenir*) is a real living social group that has come together as a result of a common experience of the past and which possesses and cultivates its own images of this past (called figures of memory) that are valued in a way specific to the group.[5] Halbwachs believes that exceptional collective memories develop within every society which cultivates the memory of events considered significant exclusively to the given collective. The fewer first-hand witnesses of a given event remain, the more vested with significance the memory of it becomes. Everyone belongs to several "communities of memory," either at the same time or successively, and every "community of memory" contracts and expands over time and space.

In the works of Jan Assmann, we encounter the notion of *Erinnerungsgemeinschaft*, meaning a "community of remembrance" (or of

---

[1] Lech Nijakowski, *Polska polityka pamięci. Esej socjologiczny* (Warsaw, 2008), p. 145.

[2] Robert N. Bellah [et al.], *Habits of the Heart: Individualism and Commitment in American Life* (New York, 1985), p. 152.

[3] Jan Assmann, *Cultural Memory and Early Civilization: Writing, Remembrance, and Political Imagination* (New York, 2011). In this translation the term 'memory community' was used. However, I use the term 'community of memory', because I recall works that were originally written in English, e.g., Iwona Irwin-Zarecka and Robert N. Bellah.

[4] Bellah [et al.], *Habits of the Heart*, p. 154.

[5] Maurice Halbwachs, *On collective memory*, ed., transl., introd. Lewis A. Coser (Chicago–London, 1992), pp. 59–60, 224.

commemoration). According to Assmann, a social group defined as such focuses on two aspects of functioning: specificity of character and longevity. In constructing its external image, the group underlines its exceptionality, while internally it attempts to eradicate existing differences. Internal transformation or diversification, if noticed, would be difficult to accept and lead to the group's cessation. In its focus on longevity, "communities of memory" try to eliminate internal differences with a selection of facts to remember that will specifically ensure a sense of continuity.[6]

Iwona Irwin-Zarecka looks at the concept of "community of memory" as the common denominator for groups united by a shared experience of the past. In her view, shared suffering or being part of the same generation helps individuals with distinct biographies to define themselves as "we" and has a bonding effect. The group in question coheres around the experience of an exceptional event that is usually traumatic in character.[7] Flowing from this definition, individuals who come together in "communities of memory" share an experience of suffering and have a sense of social exclusion, stigmatization, and marginalization in public discourse.

Similar views on the subject of "communities of memory" can be found in the works of Charles S. Maier. In Maier's conceptualizations, trauma constitutes a foundation for both individual and collective identity, which makes empathy in relation to other "communities of memory" that emerge from a similar experience of suffering more difficult. Both Irwin-Zarecka and Maier believe that it is impossible to empathetically comprehend the suffering of another even when it is similar to one's own (for example, for a victim of communist repression to empathize with victims of Nazism and *vice versa*). Understanding is instead intellectual in form, a grasping of facts rather than genuine persuasion. "Communities of memory" built around trauma, therefore, constitute a closed and narrow group of individuals who witnessed an almost identical traumatic experience. For example, the "community of memory" of former extermination camp inmates comprises significantly smaller "communities of memory" of survivors from specific concentration camps at Treblinka, Majdanek, or Auschwitz.[8]

When a "generation" is conceptualized as a "community of memory," scholars make recourse to Karl Mannheim's definition of a gen-

---

[6] Assmann, *Cultural Memory*, p. 26.

[7] Iwona Irwin-Zarecka, *Frames of Remembrance: The Dynamics of Collective Memory* (New Brunswick–New Jersey, 2009), p. 47.

[8] Charles S. Maier, "Hot Memory… Cold Memory. On the Political Half-Life of Fascist and Communist Memory," IWM, accessed November 26, 2013, http://www.iwm.at/read-listen-watch/transit-online/hot-memory-cold-memory-on-the-political-half-life-of-fascist-and-communist-memory/; Irwin-Zarecka, *Frames of Remembrance*, pp. 47–52.

eration and emphasize that it does not refer to an "age cohort" but rather a group of people who experienced a formative event at a similar stage in life.[9]

In his conceptualization, Polish scholar Lech Nijakowski defined a "community of memory" as an aggregate – a group of people bound by a specific biographical experience, not always of a traumatic nature, that includes descendants who have adopted the familial memory. A "community of memory" rejects not only the disparate "objective" story of some of its representatives but also the individual perspective of its members.[10] Nijakowski develops the original understanding of "communities of memory" as proposed by his predecessors. For him, such communities comprise both first-hand witnesses and participants of the formative event as well as all those who identify with it. A "community of memory" is thus constructed as a result of a social process of symbolization that takes place among the participants and witnesses of the formative event. It is limited to a specific area and identifies itself with a local or regional group, although it can also include individuals of vastly different ethnicities dispersed across a country.[11] In this sense, in speaking of a "community of memory" we signal that it is based on categories and models characteristic of its cultural realm.[12] A sense of unity of the biographical experiences of group members underpins the creation of "communities of memory" (understood as collectives of individuals with similar biographical experiences who, moreover, produce the same images of these experiences). "Communities of memory" exist, therefore, beyond generational, social, ethnic, or racial divides. Varied social identities can come together in one and the same "community of memory." What is key is that they identify with the formative experience, and the forms of its remembrance developed and cultivated by the given community.

In the case of the Great Famine of 1932–33, logic dictates that the core of a "community of memory" ought to be comprised of representatives of the victim generation and their descendants, only later gaining impetus from the initiatives of those consciously remembering the event. However, in Soviet Ukraine, that event was not experienced in a social context. How is it possible then, that "communities of memory" emerged outside of Ukraine, shaping rituals connected with commemorating that event and creating "places of memory" in which the Holodomor was embodied?

---

[9] Irwin-Zarecka, *Frames of Remembrance*, pp. 53–4.

[10] Nijakowski, *Polska polityka pamięci*, p. 145.

[11] Ibid., pp. 145–7.

[12] Kaja Kaźmierska, *Biography and Memory: The Generational Experience of the Shoah Survivors*, transl. Katarzyna Maciejczyk (Boston, 2012), pp. 96–7.

2.2 The first Holodomor "communities of memory" in the Ukrainian diaspora and Ukrainian émigré communities

The term "diaspora" is of Greek origin and denotes dispersal. Initially used to refer to the Jews who, as a result of Babylonian captivity, were exiled from and lived dispersed beyond their homeland's borders, the term has subsequently been applied to other ethnic groups forced to emigrate from their homelands, whatever the reason. The term "Ukrainian diaspora" was initially used by the sociologist Volodymyr Starosolskyj.[13] It took on a broader meaning after Ukraine attained independence in 1991. Currently, the notion of the Ukrainian diaspora refers to the entire Ukrainian ethnic group residing outside of Ukraine. Its representatives are all those who, regardless of where they were born or their knowledge of the Ukrainian language, preserve an awareness of their Ukrainian roots, display an interest in Ukrainian culture and Ukraine's national interests, and cultivate a sense of Ukrainianness.[14] A subdivision into western and eastern diaspora has also been noted, the latter arising in the wake of the collapse of the Soviet Union and the establishment of fifteen independent nation states that now include Ukrainian populations.

The western and eastern diasporas differ in many ways. Ukrainians residing in Western Europe, the Americas, and Australia, who have experienced wide-ranging democratic freedoms, have preserved their ethnic distinctiveness and developed a range of social organizations.[15] The Soviet communist authorities, however, promoted a negative image of the diaspora, presenting it as hostile to the Ukrainian nation. As a result, Ukrainians abroad were forced to function in complete isolation from their home culture but nevertheless managed to cultivate their traditions and mother tongue.[16] At the same time, Ukrainian diaspora circles raised awareness of issues that tarnished the Soviet Union's image in the world. The eastern diaspora, in turn, has had to contend for years with the problem of internal self-determination. For

---

[13] Tetiana Bilenko, "Funktsional'nist' khrystyians'koï symvoliky u tvorakh ukraïns'koï diaspory XX viku," in *Literatura emigracyjna Rosjan, Ukraińców i Białorusinów*, eds. Anna Woźniak and Lubomir Puszak (Lublin, 2001), p. 143.

[14] Włodzimierz Wilczyński, *Leksykon kultury ukraińskiej* (Cracow, 2004), p. 50.

[15] Cf. Symon Narizhnyi, *Ukraïns'ka emihratsiia. Kul'turna pratsia ukraïns'koï emihratsiï 1919–1939. Materialy, zibrani S. Narizhnym do chastyny druhoï*, eds. Oleksandr Fedoruk [et al.], compilation Larysa Iakovleva [et al.] (Kyiv, 1999); Fedir Zastavnyi, *Ukraïns'ka diaspora. Rozselennia ukraïntsiv u zarubizhnykh kraïnakh* (Lviv, 1991).

[16] Michael Marunchak, *The Ukrainian Canadians: A History* (Winnipeg–Ottawa, 1982), p. 826.

many Ukrainians living in former Soviet republics, the creation of an independent homeland was confusing, and frustrations were heightened by deepening economic crises in their countries of residence.[17]

During the period in question, specifically from 1933 to 2016, Ukrainians outside of the Russian sphere of influence were engaged in the cultivation of the Holodomor's memory. Prior to World War II, the groups engaged in commemoration of the Holodomor included Ukrainian communities in the United States, Canada, Brazil, Argentina, and Europe, including the territories of Eastern Galicia and Volhynia (part of the Second Polish Republic), Bukovyna (in Romania), and Transcarpathia (in Czechoslovakia). In the post-war period, until the end of the 1980s these groups included Ukrainian communities in Germany, the United Kingdom, France, Australia, Brazil, Argentina, the United States, and Canada. From the 1990s to the present, memory of the Holodomor has been actively cultivated in the United States, Canada, Brazil, Argentina, Australia, France, Great Britain, Germany, and Poland. In other European countries, the cultivation is driven by Ukrainian diplomatic missions, often in isolation from the intergenerational messages and traditions of the "communities of memory" formerly active there.

When referring to the Ukrainian diaspora, I include ethnic Ukrainians permanently residing outside Ukrainian borders who declare Ukrainian nationality. Certainly, I am aware that this is a greatly simplified definition and that this broad notion has always included communities that are diverse in denominational, political, and social scope. In this study I will analyze various initiatives, the aims of which were to publicize the Famine in Ukraine in the late 1930s, and later, pay tribute to its victims. For this reason, I draw upon the concept of a "community of memory," thanks to which, against the background of the heterogeneous community of Ukrainians living abroad, I have been able to discern those communities that share a conviction about the need to raise awareness of the Great Famine 1932–33 as an overlooked crime against humanity.

The western diaspora broached the subject of Holodomor commemoration from the beginning, in the 1930s. In one of his works, Mykhailo Marunchak listed numerous initiatives undertaken by Ukrainians outside of Soviet Ukraine in 1932–33.[18] The aim of these was to draw the attention of not only the authorities but also the general public in Europe and both Americas to the situation in Soviet Ukraine. To this end,

[17] Bohdan Lanovyk [et al.], *Istoriia ukraïns'koï emihratsiï. Navch. posibnyk dlia stud. vyshch. navch. zakladiv osvity* (Kyiv, 1997), pp. 9–12.

[18] Mykhailo Marunchak, *Natsiia v borot'bi za svoie isnuvannia: 1932 i 1933 roky v Ukraïni i diiaspori* (Winnipeg, 1985), pp. 44–64.

demonstrations were organized,[19] numerous articles were written in the press,[20] and fundraisers were organized.[21] And numerous works illuminating the genesis, course, and consequences of the Great Famine appeared (and are still being published) in the United States, Canada, Great Britain, and Australia.[22] I stress here, however, that the events in question failed to contribute to the establishment of "communities of memory" due to the fact that, at that time, these diaspora communities were not bringing together those who had themselves experienced the Great Famine of 1932–33. It was solidarity with the Famine victims that united the communities.

In the post-war period, as subsequent waves of Ukrainian emigrants from various European countries continued to arrive, conflicts started to develop between the newly arrived and the existing diaspora structures and organizations in countries that accepted displaced persons. The waves of emigration discovered that a mutual declaration of Ukrainian nationality was the main unifier. Victor (Vic) Satzewich described the situation:

> In fact, during the postwar years, the diaspora was divided between socialists and communists, and between longer-settled nationalists and their descendants who, in turn, were made up of a combination of labor migrants and political refugees who had begun to accommodate themselves to life in the diaspora. It was also fractured by the new political refugees, for whom the struggle for an independent Ukraine, and eventual return, were the most important priorities of organized diaspora life. In other words, a common ethnicity was not enough in itself to bring Ukrainians in the diaspora together into a coherent and united front.[23]

A connecting factor for the varied émigré groups at that time turned out to be their need to display their Ukrainianness in its exceptionality.

---

[19] Olena Koval'chuk and Tamara Marusyk, *Holodomor 1932–1933 rr. v USRR i ukraïns'ka diaspora Pivnichnoï Ameryky* (Chernivtsi, 2010), pp. 59–101.

[20] See: Stanislav V. Kul'chyts'kyi, Olha F. Botushans'ka, and Volodymyr Motyka, eds., *Holodomor v Ukraïni 1932–1933 rr. Bibliohrafichnyi pokazhchyk*, compilation Larysa M. Bur'ian, and Inna E. Rikun (Odesa–Lviv, 2001). However, there were also interesting initiatives not included in this bibliography, including articles written for the local press, i.e., newspapers aimed at a readership wider than the diaspora. A very interesting example is an article by Lesio Sysyn, "Soviet Russia's Crime against the Ukraine," *Svoboda*, № 171 (July 25, 1935), p. 4.

[21] Koval'chuk and Marusyk, *Holodomor 1932–1933 rr. v USRR*, pp. 59–101.

[22] Oleh Bazhan, "Initsiatyvy ukraïns'koï diaspory, pov'iazani z vshanuvanniam zhertv holodu 1932–1933 rr. u 80-ti roky," in *Holod – henotsyd 1933 roku v Ukraïni. Istoryko-politolohichnyi analiz sotsial'no-demohrafichnykh ta moral'no-psykholohichnykh naslidkiv. Materialy Mizhnarodnoï naukovo-teoretychnoï konferentsiï na vidznachennia 65-richchia trahediï ukraïns'koho narodu, Kyïv, 28 lystopada 1998 r.*, eds. Stanislav Kul'chyts'kyi [et al.] (Kyiv–New York, 2000), pp. 48–52.

[23] Vic Satzewich, *The Ukrainian Diaspora* (Routledge, 2002), p. 106.

Regardless of how they felt about each other or about the communist authorities in Ukraine, they all sought to show the uniqueness of Ukrainian culture and traditions in a public manner, organizing folk embroidery and Easter egg exhibitions, dance performances and art displays, and showcasing Ukrainian traditions during religious holidays and festivities.[24] Yet the subject of the Great Famine is perhaps even more significant as a common link for both communities. The diaspora circles that formed in North America at the turn of the nineteenth and twentieth centuries played a role in publicizing the situation in Ukraine during the Famine, and they were both aware of and engaged in Ukraine's political situation and social issues. It was only the post-war generations, however, that arrived with or were brought up in conscious opposition to the communist system and who considered informing the world about the Ukrainian tragedy of the Great Famine as their basic duty. This was especially true of circles linked to Ukrainian military units from World War II. As early as the 1940s, the Great Famine was presented in the press as a historical fact that could be repeated if the Ukrainian military formations active in the anti-communist underground were to lay down their arms.

Among the émigrés who left for the West after World War II, there were, in fact, many witnesses of the Great Famine,[25] but they did not form a united front on the subject, particularly on the question of its genocidal character. Some individuals and diaspora organizations remained silent on the issue of Holodomor commemoration in the public sphere of the so-called "free world." On the other hand, there were émigré circles that placed publicizing the Great Famine at the very heart of their activities, seeing it as a moral obligation.[26] Of note in this context are *Soiuz ukraïntsiv zhertv rosiis'koho komunistychnoho teroru* [Association of Ukrainians Victims of Russian Communist Terror], *Svitova federatsiia ukraïntsiv kolyshnikh politychnykh v'iazniv* i *represovanykh sovietamy* [World Federation of Ukrainian Former Political Prisoners and Victims of the Soviet Regime], and *Demokratychne Ob'iednannia Buvshykh Represovanykh Ukraïntsiv Sovietamy* [Democratic Union of The Ukrainians

[24] Oleksandr Shevchuk, *Natsional'no-kul'turni initsiatyvy ukraïns'koï diaspory (kinets' 50-kh – pochatok 90-kh rr. XX st.)* (Kyiv, 1997).

[25] Stanislav Kul'chyts'kyi, "Problema holodu 1932–1933 rr. ta yïi mistse v suspil'no-politychnomu zhytti Ukraïny kintsia 80-kh – pochatku 90-kh rr.," in *Holod – henotsyd 1933*, pp. 27–45.

[26] Cf. *The Black Deeds of the Kremlin: A White Book*, vol. 1: *Book of Testimonies*, ed. Semen O. Pidhainy, transl. Alexander Oreletsky and Olga Prychodko, introd. George W. Simpson (Toronto, 1953); vol. 2: *The Great Famine in Ukraine in 1932–1933*, eds. Semen O. Pidhainy, Petro P. Pavlovych, and Vasyl I. Hryshko, transl. M. Coach, J. Hladun, and Olga Prychodko, introd. Charles J. Kersten (Toronto, 1955); Iurii Semenko, compilation, *Holod 1933 roku v Ukraïni. Svidchennia pro vynyshchuvannia Moskvoiu ukraïns'koho selianstva* (Munich, 1963).

Formerly Persecuted by the Soviets] which included among its publications a work that contained some of the first published Holodomor eyewitness testimonies, *The Black Deeds of the Kremlin: The White Book*.

According to John Paul Himka, given the lack of contact between Ukrainian emigrants and their homeland, their image of Ukraine was gradually idealized, and in terms of history, it was viewed exclusively from the position of Ukraine as victim.[27] The diaspora press reported on events in Soviet Ukraine as they happened.[28] Ukrainian emigrants sought to demonstrate Ukraine's distinctiveness from other Soviet republics and to promote awareness of the Soviet political system that was repressing its citizens. Meetings and lectures were organized with individuals who, starting in the mid-1950s, visited the Soviet Union, including Ukraine, as tourists.

Holodomor literature includes other conceptions of the significance of memory for successive generations of Ukrainian emigrants. On the one hand, we come across the opinion that the Ukrainian diaspora in North America, faced with the threat of assimilation and the blending of subsequent generations of Canadian and American Ukrainians with English-speaking communities, had placed great faith in its consolidation through the cultivation of the memory of the Holodomor. On the wave of an emerging culture of memory, the Great Famine grew in status to an event that symbolically bonded the Ukrainian diaspora in North America, despite differences in the provenance of its members.[29] Diaspora circles could combine forces by engaging in restoring the memory of the Holodomor.[30] Olena Kovalchuk, a Ukrainian scholar of the diaspora in North America, asserts that Canadians of Ukrainian origin faced unavoidable assimilation of their second and third generations beginning in the 1940s.[31] During the 1950s and 1960s in Canada, more than fifty different titles by Ukrainian-language publishers came out in print. This number fell to just twenty-four in the Ukrainian language and two in English in 1984. With the onset of the 1990s, a significant decrease of interest in Ukrainian-language publications can be observed among this ethnic group in Canada, especially among its youth. A survey of Ukrainian-Canadians at this time reveals that

[27] John Paul Himka, "War Criminality: A Blank Spot in the Collective Memory of the Ukrainian Diaspora," *Space of Identity* 5, № 1 (2005), pp. 9–24.

[28] Kul'chyts'kyi, "Problema holodu," *passim*.

[29] Dmytro Viedienieiev and Dmytro Budkov, *Zaruchnytsia hlobal'noho protystoiannia. Trahediia Velykoho Holodu 1932–1933 rr. v Ukraïni v kontekstі „kholodnoï viiny" 1945–1991 rokiv* (Kyiv, 2013), pp. 45–6.

[30] Satzewich, *The Ukrainian Diaspora*, pp. 177–87.

[31] Volodymyr B. Ievtukh and Olena O. Koval'chuk, "Etnokul'turna diial'nist' ukraïns'kykh kanadtsiv. Zdobutky i problemy," *Ukraïns'kyi istorychnyi zhurnal*, № 9 (1991), pp. 42–50.

20.2 percent read the Canadian Ukrainian-language press regularly; 9.5 percent, occasionally; 4.9 percent, rarely; and 65.2 percent, never.[32] Despite great pressure placed on learning the national/mother tongue,[33] it no longer seemed possible to build community bonds solely on the grounds of a language community; an identity constructed on the basis of shared symbolic values was needed. Indeed, the process of victimization is an important part of social consciousness that can contribute to the tightening of social bonds and coalescence in defense of collectively held values. Narratives about the Holodomor's victims, in addition to aiding the Ukrainian diaspora leadership in cultivating empathy within their adopted societies, could help bring people together and support their sense of ethnic identity. As Victor (Vic) Satzewich writes:

> The famine also provides Ukrainians with a common object of concern and symbolizes the historical suffering of the Ukrainian people. It is important because it says to the wider diaspora community that millions of "our" ancestors died because they were Ukrainian, that the Ukrainian people survived in the face of terrible atrocities and ordeals, and that therefore the spirit of Ukrainian ethnicity and identity must not die a natural death through assimilation. The famine and war crimes issues bridge most political and ideological divisions in the community, and so mobilization around them is part of the process of ethnic community-building. Mobilization around these events also builds a bridge between members of the diaspora who are dispersed through a number of countries of settlement. These dynamics are particularly important to understand considering the less-than-hoped for benefits that Ukrainian independence was to bring to the organized Ukrainian diaspora.[34]

On the other hand, there is an array of opinions about the level of politicization (for various reasons) of initiatives undertaken to commemorate the Holodomor. Some are convinced that such initiatives enjoyed support from the American authorities, particularly in the 1970s–80s. According to Maksym Masl'onko, the Ukrainian diaspora's efforts would have had no chance of success if not for the support, including financial, of the American authorities. Masl'onko argues that during the Cold War, the "bloody stains" in the Soviet Union's history and their investigation were key in the rivalry between the two superpowers and in entrenching the image in the West of the USSR as an "evil empire." During Ronald Reagan's presidency particularly, a series of academic, popular, and literary works were published with the aim of stigmatizing the Kremlin's crimes. Demonstrations and marches

[32] Iurii O. Zhluktenko, *Ukraïns'ka mova na linhvistychnii karti Kanady* (Kyiv, 1990), p. 43.
[33] Ievtukh and Koval'chuk, "Etnokul'turna diialnst' ukraïns'kykh kanadtsiv," pp. 42–50.
[34] Satzewich, *The Ukrainian Diaspora*, p. 194.

were organized, including in front of Soviet diplomatic missions, that placed the blame for the genocide against the Ukrainian nation during the 1930s on Soviet authorities.[35]

Dmytro Viedienieiev and Dmytro Budkov see the actions of the diaspora as undertaken more or less consciously to combat the representation of Ukrainians as anti-Semites and Nazi collaborators, which had some traction in American social memory at that time.[36] Himka argues that victimizing one's own historical experience was a means of redirecting attention away from crimes committed by Ukrainians during World War II by individuals who had emigrated.[37] The Commission of Inquiry on War Criminals in Canada, also known as the Deschênes Commission, was established with the aim of tracking down war criminals who had settled in Canada after World War II. Per Anders Rudling contends that public debate around the question of the participation of nationalist Ukrainian military forces in the Holocaust was the impulse behind the diaspora's determination to take up the subject of the Great Famine in the 1980s. Rudling points to members of an association of SS Galizien veterans, the Brotherhood of Former Soldiers of the First Ukrainian Division of the Ukrainian National Army, as being among initiators of the first monument in Canada to the victims of the Great Famine, erected in 1983 in Edmonton.[38]

In his point of the view the campaigns of the diaspora to commemorate the Great Famine starting in the 1980s can be interpreted as attempts to produce a new Ukrainian national mythology by constructing an image of Ukraine as a nation-victim of the communist system and thus mitigate the perception of Ukrainians as collaborators.[39] His erudite works and conclusions about the cultivation of Holodomor memory and the intergenerational transmission of its image by Ukrainian diaspora circles are based on varied sources (including archival documents and works of Sovietology) but tend to omit those produced by the diaspora, such as the documents of various Ukrainian organizations, the daily and the religious press publications, as well as memoirs.

---

[35] Maksym Masl'onko, "Holodomor iak chynnyk zovnishn'oï polityky Ukraïny. Istoriia chy isteriia?," in *Problemy mizhnarodnykh vidnosyn*, vol. 1 (Kyiv, 2010), pp. 232–47, accessed February 1, 2021, http://dspace.nbuv.gov.ua/handle/123456789/58858.

[36] Viedienieiev and Budkov, *Zaruchnytsia hlobal'noho protystoiannia*, pp. 52–3.

[37] Himka, "War Criminality," pp. 9–24.

[38] Per A. Rudling, "Multiculturalism, Memory, and Ritualization: Ukrainian Nationalist Monuments in Edmonton, Alberta," *Nationalities Papers* 39 (2011), pp. 733–68.

[39] Peter A. Rudling, "Memories of 'Holodomor' and National Socialism in Ukrainian political culture," in *Rekonstruktion des Nationalmythos? Frankreich, Deutschland und die Ukraine im Vergleich, ed. Yves Bizeul* (Göttingen, 2013), pp. 234–5; Per A. Rudling, "Long-Distance Nationalism: Ukrainian Monuments and Historical Memory in Multicultural Canada," in *Public Memory in the Context of Transnational Migration and Displacement*, ed. Sabine Marschall (Cham, 2020), pp. 95–126.

Canadian researcher Frances Swyripa, writing about the settling of the Canadian prairies by various immigrant groups, has written about monuments as a kind of "domestication" or "taming" of the landscape, referencing heroes and victims associated with the departed country. She does not see any political intentions in these initiatives.

> Ukrainians as other religious groups in Canada also identified strongly with their overseas dead. (…) The Ukrainian diaspora consciousness, constructed around old-world dead, and fed by the post-1945 displaced persons, produced memorials like that to Ukraine's freedom fighters in Edmonton's St. Michael Ukrainian cemetery, or those to the artificial famine in Soviet Ukraine in 1932–33 outside Edmonton and Winnipeg city halls. The Ukrainian Centennial Memorial Park at Selo Ukraina also remembered both the famine and victims of Soviet tyranny more generally, bringing to the Canadian countryside an event in the homeland that never personally touched the families of pioneers with origins in Western Ukraine. In the late twentieth century, the churchyards and cemeteries of the old rural settlement area modestly echoed this politicized and old-world Ukrainianness. (…) In other instances, the Ukrainianness articulated was purely secular – a trident added to the entrance gate, Ukraine's flag alongside Canadian and provincial flags, or, less aesthetically, the stones of the cairn erected for the golden jubilee of Ukrainian settlement in 1941 painted patriotic blue and yellow.[40]

Rostyslav Chomiak has written about the need of Ukrainians to erect symbolic graves in places of temporary residence in the post-war period in Germany:

> True, creating a burial mound was not at stake here. Burial mounds – admittedly brotherly and symbolic – have had their day. Symbolic graves still stand on only some of our resort estates. Such a mound stood in our displaced persons camp in Mittenwald. It was raised by the camp's inhabitants without reservations or objections, next to the Orthodox church. When I went to Mittenwald several years later, the camp was being used by a German Highlanders' regiment, who had razed our mound and moved the Orthodox church to a barrack garage, as was the case under the Third Reich. Everything was just as it had been once, only the metal eagle no longer held a swastika in its talons.[41]

The establishment of a "place of memory" when one is no longer a citizen of one's homeland underlines the impermanent nature of a "place of memory." It shows that the meaning of a "place of memory"

---

[40] Frances Swyripa, *Storied Landscapes: Ethno-Religious Identity and the Canadian Prairies* (Winnipeg, 2010), pp. 212–3.

[41] Rostyslav L. Khomiak, "Iaka efektyvnist' nashykh pam'iatnykiv u Vashingtoni?" *Svoboda*, № 1 (January 1, 2009), p. 5.

is attributed by the "community of memory," which has certain hopes attached to it. Studying the issue of Holodomor commemoration in various aspects, I have come to the conclusion that none of the above-mentioned opinions on the genesis of the Holodomor discourse is adequate. It is not about research methods or the range of source material but about assessing the attitudes of the participants of this discourse, including the authors of various texts on the Holodomor and the intentions of the creators of the monuments. Some of the scholars mentioned above assume that the issue was politicized or had a colonial character (in the sense of marking a new territory) and based on this starting point, they invoke arguments in favour of their theses.

I do not intend to evaluate whether the subject of the Holodomor was used by the American intelligence or security services, or whether it was intentionally showcased in the days of the Deschênes Commission in Canada, or whether it was used to counter assimilation processes within the Ukrainian diaspora. Why? I believe that the ardent commemoration by Ukrainian communities abroad following World War II developed as individuals from the so-called "Holodomor generation" came to live in the West and were able to share accounts of their experiences in the public space of countries in which they settled. Within the diaspora they contributed to the core of the numerous "communities of memory" that emerged after World War II as demonstrated by the early "practices of commitment" that appeared in the public space during this time. Of course, private, not entirely patriotic, needs could also be satisfied, which happens inside other "communities of memory" as well.

2.3 The Holodomor generation

The generation of Holodomor survivors constituted neither a uniform milieu nor a "community of memory." In contrast to Holocaust survivors, those who survived the Holodomor typically have not presented this experience as a foundation of their identity. It is also worth noting here that I use the terms "victim generation" or "Holodomor survivors" to indicate those who experienced the Great Famine and its psycho-physical effects during the course of their lives. The historical landscape following World War II, however, which shifted borders and led to the emigration of many Ukrainians to Western Europe as well as North and South America, meant that this survivor generation lived in many countries. Among the displaced persons who found themselves in the US, Canada, Australia, and Great Britain, the witnesses of the Holodomor played a significant role in cultivating the diaspora's memory of the Great Famine. The opportunity to speak about their trauma had a soothing effect, allowing them to mourn the death of loved ones and instilling hope in the future. Worth remembering is that the majority of new immigrants came from Eastern Galicia and had not experienced the Famine personally but saw it as a shared Ukrainian national tragedy.

Those who remained in Ukraine had the fewest opportunities to begin the process of mourning and work through the experience of the Famine and, consequently, of investing it with meaning on the level of biographical experience or participating in its memorialization in the public sphere. Many died before this instrument of Stalinist terror was openly spoken about in an independent Ukraine. Those who did live to see the return of independence had a chance to share their memories, although in the public sphere in post-communist Ukraine, testimonies of the Holodomor were most often used as an element of accusatory rhetoric directed at the Russian Federation, the symbolic inheritor of the Soviet Union's ideological legacy.

In my opinion, the recording of the Holodomor generation's memories constituted a crucial stage in creating "communities of memory," both in Ukraine and abroad. The emotional interaction with surviving witnesses had a tremendous impact, as evidenced by the attendance of Holodomor survivors at many events connected with creating "places of memory" (conventions, manifestations, or monument unveiling ceremonies). Their testimonies were used in museum exhibitions and documentaries as voices of authenticity.

Holodomor testimonies were utilized in emigration beginning in the 1950s.[42] These were the fruits of initiatives of local Ukrainian communities aimed at preserving the memories of those individuals who were important to them.

Research into the Great Famine and dissemination of information gained ground in the West throughout the 1980s. The Ukrainian Canadian Research and Documentation Centre (UCRDC) was founded in 1982. In 1984, a young American scholar, Leonid Heretz, began collecting famine survivor accounts. The U.S. Commission on the Ukraine Famine 1932–1933 was established December 13, 1985, under the direction of James Mace.[43] The most significant event, however, was the publication (in 1988 and 1990) of three volumes of research gathered under Mace's direction. Edited by Mace and Heretz, the volumes included the accounts of 179 survivors of the Great Famine.[44] Testimonies from

---

[42] For more on the subject: Oleksandra Veselova, "Svidchennia ochevydtsiv Holodomoru 1932–1933 rr. v Ukraïni iak dzherelo doslidzhennia ioho prychyn ta naslidkiv," *Problemy istoriï Ukraïny. Fakty, sudzhennia, poshuky* 19 (2010), pp. 82–98.

[43] James Mace and Leonid Heretz, eds., *Oral History Project of the Commission on the Ukraine Famine*, 3 vols. (Washington, 1990).

[44] Ibid.

the UCRDC collection are found in volume three of the publication. They comprise twenty-one interviews tape-recorded and transcribed in the years 1981–86.[45] Stanislav Kulchytsky, citing fragments of the victim testimonies collected by the U.S. Commission on the Ukraine Famine 1932–1933, wrote:

> (…) the accounts cited here were selected in a way that displays the most important thing: under the guise of collecting grain reserves, all food was either taken away or destroyed with the sole intention of causing death by hunger. Although official documents confirming this intent do not and cannot exist, this action of annihilation (…) enveloped the whole of Ukraine.[46]

Active in documenting the testimonies of Holodomor survivors since the eighties, UCRDC, in cooperation with the Ukrainian Canadian Congress, undertook in 2008 an extensive documentation project to record the stories of Holodomor survivors. Hundreds of individuals were filmed across Canada and in some other diaspora communities, and eighty of the interviews were featured with the *Share the Story* project marking the eightieth anniversary of the Holodomor in 2013. Most of the interviewees, men and women from 78 to 99 years of age, had been children during the Famine.[47] In 2008, a massive four-volume work based on James Mace's multi-year project of collecting Holodomor survivor testimonies appeared in Ukraine.[48]

Thus, the memories of the Holodomor generation have been recorded as video material, which entirely alters the perception of such testimony. Recorded (as opposed to written) testimonies are more compelling for those for whom the events of the 1930s are in the distant past as the viewer has the experience of hearing directly from a witness of the events. Indeed, oral history archives are the most likely means for preserving the intergenerational message inside the Holodomor "communities of memory."

In Ukraine, the first attempts to reference the memories of Holodomor survivors were made with the onset of *perestroika*. The first such initiative involved drawing up lists of those who had perished from

---

[45] Mace and Heretz, eds., *Oral History Project*, vol. 3, pp. 1464–659.

[46] Stanislav Kul'chyts'kyi, *Holodomor 1932–1933 rr. iak henotsyd: trudnoshchi usvidomlennia* (Kyiv, 2008), p. 306.

[47] The homepage of the project highlights eighty survivors of the Holodomor – eighty stories for the eightieth anniversary. These stories, as told by survivors living around the world, are representative of the millions who experienced the wrath of a genocidal policy aimed at destroying a nation. See: http://www.sharethestory.ca/index.html.

[48] *Velykyi holod v Ukraïni 1932–1933 rokiv. Svidchennia ochevydtsiv dlia Komisiï Konhresu SShA*, 4 vols., compilation Dzheims Meis (Kyiv, 2008).

starvation, in particular towns and villages.[49] In 1989, the newspaper *Sil's'ki visti* [Rural News] was the first to publish the recollections of famine victims, with more than one hundred such accounts featured on its pages.[50] The appeal, signed by Stanislav Kulchytsky and titled *"33-ii: Holod". Zaproshuemo do stvorennia knyhy-memorialu* [Famine of 33: An invitation to create a memorial book], was first published on December 9, 1988. An editorial board was established to oversee the investigation of the causes of the 1933 famine with Volodymyr Maniak as editor-in-chief. The appeal for eyewitness accounts included a number of questions. Letters were to be sent to *Sil's'ki visti* or Maniak's home address.[51] On January 3, 1989, the newspaper published a report on the progress of the memorial book along with excerpts from some of the letters.[52]

In the spring of 1990, on the initiative of Volodymyr Maniak, a National Week of Memory for the Victims of the Great Famine 1932–33 and of Stalinist Repression took place, while in September of 1991, the memorial book *1933-ii Holod* [Famine of 1933] was published. This work deserves particular attention for combining recollections with archival documents, historical scholarship, documentary photographs, and artistic works.[53]

Edited by Maniak and his wife Lidiia Kovalenko, the memorial book is a collection of witness accounts with a structure reminiscent of books known from Soviet historiography documenting World War II events. The book contains fragments extracted from individual accounts that dramatically illustrate starvation in the Ukrainian countryside in the 1930s. The published recollections underwent substantive literary editing aimed at easing the engagement of readers from diverse backgrounds. This editing diminishes the scholarly value of the book, but it was never intended as an academic work. From the start, the aim of the project was to mobilize society and draw attention to this "blank spot" in Ukrainian history. The Holodomor Research and Education Consortium (HREC) is publishing full transcripts online of hundreds of the letters from the Maniak Collection, some accompanied by English translations.[54]

---

[49] For example, towards the end of 1988 in the village of Tarhan, Kyiv Oblast, a list was compiled by those who themselves had survived the Holodomor. In this village, 360 died in the period 1932–33, while during World War II – 52. See Oleksandra Veselova, "Uvikopomnennia zahyblykh vid holodnoho moru," in *Holod – henotsyd 1933*, p. 230.

[50] Liudmyla Stakhors'ka, "Holodomor ochyma suchasnykiv," in *Holodomor 1932–1933 rokiv iak velychezna trahediia ukraïns'koho narodu. Materialy Vseukraïns'koï naukovoï konferentsiï. Kyïv, 15 lystopada 2002 r.* (Kyiv, 2003), p. 209.

[51] *Sil's'ki visti*, № 282 (December 9, 1988).

[52] *Sil's'ki visti*, № 2 (January 3, 1989).

[53] Volodymyr Maniak and Lidiia Kovalenko-Maniak, *1933-ii: Holod. Narodna Knyha-Memorial* (Kyiv, 1991).

[54] The Maniak Collection thus consists of the letters that were sent to *Literaturna Ukraïna*, *Sil's'ki visti*, and the Maniak-Kovalenko residence in late 1988 to mid-1989. It ap-

These letters from survivors and witnesses that were sent to the newspaper editorial office and to Volodymyr Maniak's private address constitute "raw material" detailing a variety of experiences. There are many memories from survivors who write in a spontaneous and direct fashion about starvation. There are also letters from people who ask

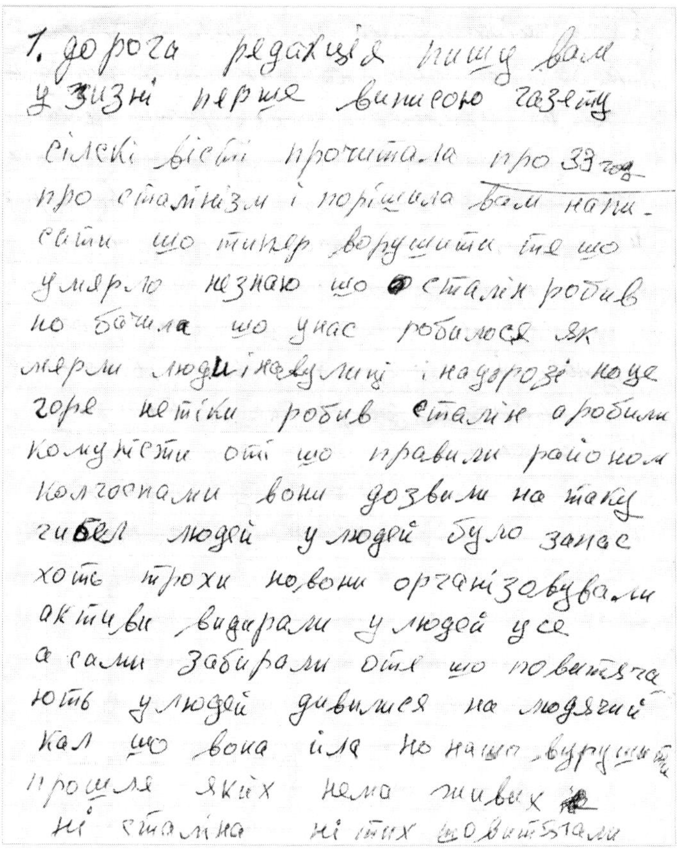
1. Дорога редакція пишу вам
у жизні перше виписою газету
Сілскі вісті прочитала про 33 год
про сталінізм і порішила вам напи-
сати що тепер ворушити те що
умерло незнаю що Сталін робив
но бачила що унас робилося як
мерли люди і на вулиці і на дорозі но це
горе не тіки робив Сталін а робили
комунести оті що правили районом
колгоспами вони дозволи на таку
гибел людей у людей було запас
хоть трохи но вони орґанізовували
активи видирали у людей усе
а сами забирали оте що повитяга-
ють у людей дивилися на людячий
кал що вона іла но наша вирушити
прошлая яких нема живих
ні Сталіна ні тих шо витягали

Fig. 1. A page from a letter by K. N. Lymar to the editorial board of Sil's'ki visti *(February 27, 1989, Lishchynivka)*

pears that close to six thousand letters were received, some published in *Sil's'ki visti,* and some, apparently, in *Literaturna Ukraïna*. More than five hundred abridged letters were included in *Holod: 33*, edited by Maniak and Kovalenko, and the rest were to be published in a planned volume. Maniak was killed in a bizarre road accident in 1992, and Kovalenko passed away not long after, in 1993. As a result, the fate of many of the original letters remains unclear. Roughly seven hundred letters were passed on by the Maniaks to Father Wolodymyr Bojczuk, their French-Ukrainian acquaintance, who later shared them with HREC. HREC website: https://holodomor.ca/resource/maniak-collection/.

the editors to give up their idea for a Memorial Book and leave the past in the past.[55]

Following the unfinished initiative of Maniak, other smaller-scale social campaigns aimed at preserving local memory also multiplied. The testimonies of Holodomor survivors and witnesses opened up new avenues for historians and social activists, and journalists. There was an explosion of "reclaimed memory" among the generation of victims, who could now remember and discuss things as they actually were. Conducting interviews and writing down and publishing recollections enabled the restoration of memory as well as lost historical consciousness. The practice of gathering accounts of the Great Famine had two fundamental aims at that time: first, to prove the criminal character of the communist authorities, who were understood to be the external driving force that led to genocide on Ukrainian lands; and second, to present Ukraine as a victim of the Soviet system.

Many of the projects to collect Holodomor testimonies were undertaken outside of academia, and thus the quality is highly inconsistent. Those engaged in collecting witness accounts of the Holodomor had a unique opportunity at the onset of the 1990s, and the fact that the opportunity was not taken advantage of fully is a reflection of the state of Ukrainian society at the time. Civic organizations engaged in the subject of the Holodomor constituted communities whose identities were based in the cultivation of memory about the experience of loss and suffering. As such, these initiatives were only in small part an expression of individual or social drive to come to terms with the experience of loss and to publicly honour the victims and survivors. In essence, these efforts were aimed at the creation of a symbolic realm that would enable sustained contact with a bygone world (an idealized notion of a world before the Holodomor).[56]

The documentation of Famine recollections considerably declined under Leonid Kuchma's presidency, although ethnographers and members of the academic community were still engaged in gathering and publishing such accounts. They initiated such efforts during this period despite the lack of support from the authorities. Lacking the necessary funds, these efforts were not undertaken methodically.

At the same time, a team of Ukrainian researchers led by ethnographer William Noll performed field studies in Ukraine that resulted in

---

[55] K.N. Lymar to editor of *Sil's'ki visti*, February 27, 1989, Maniak Collection, HREC, accessed February 1, 2021, https://holodomor.ca/letters/lymar-k-n/.

[56] In contemplating the importance of testimonies for research into the Holodomor, I have come to understand that in striving to comprehend traumatic biographical experience in the realm of social memory, I am always doomed to chase the shadow of the past. See: Wiktoria Kudela-Świątek, "From Private Memory to the Collective Image of the Ukrainian Holodomor," *Wrocławski Rocznik Historii Mówionej*, № 6 (2016), pp. 33–65.

a unique collection of "Holodomor generation" memories, which Noll uses as the basis for his work *Transformation of Civil Society: Oral History of Ukrainian Village Culture of the 1920–30s*. In the years 1993–95, interviews were carried out in 126 Ukrainian villages. The main goal was to collect first-hand accounts of village life and community organization prior to, during, and after the forced collectivization of the Ukrainian farmers. Using an elaborate and carefully crafted questionnaire, the researchers recorded 429 interviews with elderly villagers across Ukraine. The interviews served as primary data for the analysis of dramatic sociocultural changes experienced by the Ukrainian rural communities in the 1920–30s. The villagers' testimonies offer accounts of life before, during, and after collectivization and personal insights into one of the most dramatic and devastating periods of Ukrainian history. In partnership with the Humanities and Fine Arts Digital Research Centre at the University of Saskatchewan, project data was digitized and made available in open access format.[57]

The victims' generation found itself at the centre of attention again thanks to the project "Ukraine 3000" initiated by Kateryna Yushchenko, the wife of Ukraine's third president.[58] However, this project was undertaken too late and thus resulted in the documentation of the Holodomor's oral tradition (as was the case with the testimonies collected by Valentina Borysenko).[59] Unquestionably, such recordings are of great value as documentation of the role of the Holodomor in the consciousness of Ukrainian rural communities. However, they cannot be viewed as oral history or the testimony of the Holodomor generation.

According to Georgiy Kasianov, the published recollections that were the fruit of these oral history and ethnographic projects were, for the most part, compilations of materials carefully selected and edited to promote a specific image of the past.[60] Of course, the selection process for these editions necessarily reflects some overriding goal.

Eric Santner's concept of "narrative fetishism," which has played a significant role in the development of trauma studies in English-language scholarship, may be relevant here. In "History Beyond the Pleasure Principle: Some Thoughts about the Representation of Trauma,"

---

[57] https://drc.usask.ca/projects/pcuh/transformation/eng/search.php?all=TRUE.

[58] "Ukraïna 3000" – an undertaking by Kateryna and Viktor Yushchenko, the aim of which is to promote Ukrainian cultural models, preserve and cultivate memory about the history of Ukraine as well as charity work. For more: Mizhnarodnyi blahodiinyi fond "Ukraïna 3000," accessed May 13, 2005, http://www.ukraine3000.org.ua. The site is in Ukrainian, Russian, and English.

[59] Valentyna Borysenko, *A Candle in Remembrance: An Oral History of the Ukrainian Genocide of 1932–1933* (New York, 2010).

[60] Heorhii Kasi'anov, *Danse macabre. Holod 1932–1933 rokiv u politytsi, masovii svidomosti ta istoriohrafiï (1980-ti – pochatok 2000-kh)* (Kyiv, 2010), p. 252.

published in 1992 in a book dealing with issues of representation in the context of the Holocaust, Santner explains "narrative fetishism" as a tendency within post-traumatic societies to use past trauma narratives without accounting for changes in individual and social identities in the present. This adaptive strategy reduces the process of working through trauma to documenting the stories about a traumatic historical event. The end result is a situation where experiences of trauma and its consequences are superseded by narration about losses and suffering. In this way, the past is reconstructed in a form that makes room only for victims' and survivors' voices.[61]

These efforts marked the beginning of a working through of the trauma of the Holodomor. At the same time, this effort to fill the public space with these testimonies, which guided the first activists who recorded the memories of the survivors, served the additional purpose of establishing without a doubt that the Great Famine had indeed taken place. Ten years earlier, denial of the Holodomor was still quite common in post-communist Ukraine.

The general positivist belief in the superiority of written sources, not uncommon among scholars, has led some historians to dismiss the value of witness and survivor recollections. An additional factor in the case of the Holodomor, in my opinion, is that we are often dealing with testimonies of poorly educated people. Their straightforward and blunt descriptions of events that took place in the Ukrainian countryside in the 1930s are sometimes off-putting or shocking, Liudmyla Hrynevych has emphasized that at the beginning of the 1990s, Ukrainian society was not ready to accept the dramatic and sometimes horrific stories flooding the public discourse.[62] Unfortunately, while society had perhaps matured over the years and became better able to deal with these accounts (for instance, of cannibalism), fewer and fewer people were left who could share such recollections.

As an oral historian, I understand that those who testify are those who survived and not those who experienced the suffering in its most extreme form. Witnesses are almost exclusively those who miraculously managed to stay alive, whether through luck or the ability to adapt to a new reality. Despite this limitation, however, the historical value of testimony is rooted in its difference from propaganda texts and its emotional authenticity. Allowing the witnesses of history to speak within

---

[61] Eric Santner, "History Beyond the Pleasure Principle: Some Thoughts About the Representation of Trauma," in *Probing the Limits of Representation. Nazism and the "Final Solution,"* ed. Saul Friedländer (Cambridge, 1992), pp. 143–54.

[62] Liudmyla Hrynevych, "Vid zaperechuvannia do vymushenoho vyznannia: pro mekhanizm vkhodzhennia temy holodu 1932–1933 rr. v ofitsiinyi publichnyi prostir u SRSR ta URSR naprykintsi 1980-kh rr.," *Problemy istoriï Ukraïny. Fakty, sudzhennia, poshuky* 18 (2008), p. 241.

the public sphere is key to working through the traumatic experiences of the past.[63] The numerous published recollections were meant to become an element in the healing process of Ukrainians and in the discovery (or in large measure construction) of their Ukrainian national identity.

Nevertheless, it was only after the collapse of the communist system that a generation of victims had the chance to speak. Private recollections carried enormous political and propagandistic value at this time. Reprinted in magazines and newspapers, they reflected twentieth-century history through the eyes of ordinary human beings. In light of these accounts, the collapse of the Soviet regime took on a completely different aspect and inclined many to reflect on a future without the Soviet Union.

Despite the drawbacks mentioned above, the existing body of memoirs more than refutes any claims challenging the artificial or planned nature of the Holodomor.

For generations that inherited the memory of the tragedy from their surviving forbearers, recording their grandparents' recollections became a kind of social ritual that shored up identity and guaranteed affiliation with a "community of memory." These initiatives promise the continued existence of the "communities of memory." The use of these testimonies in public spaces (particularly in museums and education) guarantees the survival of many "communities of memory" of the Holodomor even after the passing of the representatives of the formational generation.

2.4 "Practices of commitment"

The tone of discourse about the Holodomor has been shaped by the diaspora and Ukrainian emigration. I believe that the early stages of social rituals connected with the remembrance of the victims can be traced to the initial demonstrations in the 1930s in defence of the starving people in Ukraine. In some cases, these were not single protest actions but initiatives with a broader resonance. It is important to note that some were meant to herald forms of honouring the victims. In a sense, they provided an example of how to respect the memory of the victims and condemn the communist regime. At that time, however, the international community largely ignored their efforts.

On October 28, 1933, a demonstration was organized in Lviv by the *Hromads'kyi Komitet Poriatunku Ukraïny* [Civic Committee to Save

[63] Barbara A. Misztal, *Theories of Social Remembering* (Maidenhead, 2003), pp. 160–1.

Ukraine], as reported in the Lviv weekly *Meta* [Goal].[64] The initiative was semi-secular and semi-religious. Two important components of the social experience of the memory of the Holodomor emerged that would be repeated in social rituals on subsequent anniversaries. The demonstrators walked through the streets of the city and ended the meeting in a church where a memorial service (*panakhyda*) was held. Participants in events in North American cities such as New York and Chicago also marched through the streets and held public meetings.[65]

It is worth noting that later demonstrations were of a very similar nature. I see them as certain "practices of commitment" that safeguard the survival of "communities of memory." Due to their engaging and emotional nature, they are bond-forming.

At this point, I will turn to how Ukrainian newspapers abroad influenced the formation of a "community of memory" of the Great Famine in the diaspora from the 1940s onward. From the succession of articles that dealt with the subject of the Great Famine in the context of its anniversaries (fifteenth and subsequent ones), I was drawn to those that incorporated the subject of the Great Famine with the cultivation of memory and establishment of social rituals tied to honouring both famine victims and survivors.

2.4.1 The early stages of Holodomor discourse in the diaspora

The first mentions in the Ukrainian press abroad about the need to honour the victims of the Holodomor came fifteen years after the Famine, in 1948. An article entitled *Richnytsia pro iaku ne zhaduiut' Soviety* [The anniversary not mentioned by the Soviets], which appeared in the *Svoboda* newspaper in 1948, serves as one example.[66] That same year, a proclamation by the editorial board of *Vyzvol'nyi shliakh* appeared appealing to Ukrainians in emigration to mark the fifteenth anniversary of the Great Famine:

> The whole Ukrainian emigration is in mourning over this tragic event. (...) Let us pay our respects to the memory of those Ukrainians who died at the hand of the Muscovite executioner. Let us organize evenings

---

[64] *Meta*, (October 22, 1933) and *Meta*, (October 29, 1933). Quoted after Marunchak, *Natsiia v borot'bi za svoie isnuvannia*, pp. 100–4.

[65] "Nasha tserkva na linii protestu proty holodu," *Dnipro*, № 20 (October 15, 1933), p. 1; *The Ukrainian Weekly*, № 2 (October 13, 1933), p. 1; № 6 (November 10, 1933), p. 1; № 7 (November 17, 1933), p. 1; № 8 (November 24, 1933), p. 1; № 9 (December 1, 1933), p. 1.

[66] V. Iar, "Richnytsia pro iaku ne zhaduiut' Soviety (sposterezhennia ochevidtsia)," *Svoboda*, № 95 (April 24, 1948), p. 3; № 97 (April 27, 1948), p. 3; № 98 (April 28, 1948), p. 3.

> of grief, sorrow, and homage for our brothers. Let us pray at memorial services to Him in whom we believe, that He, along with the whole free world, hears us, Ukrainians, and comes to our aid.[67]

In 1948, demonstrations on the occasion of the fifteenth anniversary were organized by Ukrainians living in Displaced Persons (DP) camps in Germany. The magazines *Na storozhi* and *Avangard* wrote about the events in Munich.[68] The event was initiated and organized by the Ukrainian Youth Association (*Spilka ukraïns'koï molodi* – SUM). SUM chose Munich because it was the largest city in the American zone of occupation. The Munich action was held on March 14, 1948, with six thousand people participating. The authorities permitted the demonstration on the condition that there would be no political speeches. Leaflets about the Holodomor were prepared in German and hung throughout the entire city. The central point of the event was the Church of Saint Luke, where the parish of the Ukrainian Autocephalous Orthodox Church gathered. Only hierarchs of the UAOC made speeches during the ceremony. At the end, 158 wreaths brought by the participants (individuals and organizations) were laid in the centre of the church in the shape of a symbolic grave.

It is worth mentioning that writer Ivan Bahrianyi was at the memorial ceremony in Munich. His reflections (*Nasha Pravda*) were published in the newspaper *Ukraïns'ki visti* [Ukrainian news]:

> This symbol – it becomes reality, pushing out the heavy walls of this structure, St. Luke Church in the centre of Europe, it doesn't fit inside, just as our great Ukrainian tragedy does not fit within any walls nor the minds of the civilized world. ...Hecatombs for millions. A communal grave, made of an infinite number of wreaths, that flow together in the tear-filled grieving eyes into an endless sea of our national mourning. And in the centre, on top of the woven ribbons and common words, a loaf of bread and a few apples were placed... This is what "they" were lacking! So, in this grave, under that piece of bread, lay six, maybe seven, or even eight million of them! Seven million victims – our mothers, brothers, and sisters, and small children, and grey grandfathers, tortured with a horrific hungry death in God's year of 1933 in the "most prosperous country of the world" – in "the sunlight of Stalin's constitution." ... There it is – our truth! That Truth, that we, like a heavy cross, carried from the banks of the Dnipro, Kuban and the Don, and laid down in the centre of Europe. Laid it down, finally, in the open on the fifteenth anniversary of the great tragedy of our nation. Look, world![69]

---

[67] "15-richchia zhakhlyvoho holodu 1933–1948," *Vyzvol'nyi shliakh*, pt 5 (1948), p. 22.

[68] *Avangard*, № 3 (1948), pp. 1–3; *Na storozhi*, № 3–4 (1948), p. 30.

[69] *Ukraïns'ki visti*, № 24 (March 20, 1948).

The newspapers *Svoboda* and *Ukraïns'ki visti* wrote about events in April of that year in Hanover,[70] at which participants wore a paper badge with the dates 1933–48 on it and a trident and a black ribbon as a sign of mourning.[71] Floral wreaths brought by the participants were arranged at a symbolic grave in front of the church.

In articles about these events, the Great Famine is described as a "Ukrainian Golgotha." At the same time, the purpose of these demonstrations was to draw attention to the efforts of the Soviet Union to conceal or cover up the fact of the Famine. Two years earlier, Bahrianyi had written his well-known agitational pamphlet *Chomu ia ne khochu vertatys' do SSSR?* [Why do I not want to return to the Soviet Union?] in which he writes of the Great Famine of 1932–33 among other tragic consequences of Soviet policy. Bahrianyi's position, expressed with literary clarity and simplicity, is a forceful summary of the contemporary understanding of the essence of the Holodomor for the Ukrainian nation. The overriding aim of these commemorations seems to have been to "tell the truth" about events being ignored by international opinion.[72] I find the reference to Christian values in these rituals spontaneous and intuitive, and do not see any evidence that they were purposefully introduced into social rituals at the time.

But in five years it would change. On the occasion of the next major anniversary, articles began to appear in the diaspora press containing specific suggestions on how to respect the memory of the Holodomor victims. In 1953, The Ukrainian National Women's League of America (UNWLA), in its bilingual magazine *Nashe zhyttia* [Our Life], published an appeal to readers on the occasion of the twentieth anniversary of the Holodomor. The appeal offered suggestions on how to mark the sorrowful anniversary and underlined the significance of such commemorations for the identity of Ukrainians in emigration:

> Here is an anniversary that we will remember this Pentecost. It has been twenty years since the great, artificially induced famine in Ukraine that lay to waste hundreds of Ukrainian villages and small towns. Ukrainian inhabitants of these places are preparing to commemorate this anniversary to remind those who were there of the catastrophe and make it known to those who did not experience it; and on this example of the occupant's massive and brutal willfulness reveal its essence and danger to

[70] *Svoboda*, № 118 (May 22, 1948), p. 3; *Ukraïns'ki visti*, № 35 (1948), p. 5.

[71] Badge worn by participants at a demonstration in Hanover, Germany, on the occasion of the fifteenth anniversary of the Famine of 1932–33 in Ukraine. No later than April 11, 1948. Original, colour image. The symbol is glued to the page; it appears that the typed description accompanying the badge was made by D. Solovei, https://holodomor.ca/wp-content/uploads/2020/04/Oseredok-znachok_g15i9.pdf.

[72] Ivan Bahrianyi, *Chomu ia ne khochu vertatys' do SSSR?* (Winnipeg, 1946).

> the whole world. Ukrainian women join in honouring this anniversary. They, too, carried the immense weight of this catastrophe on their shoulders and lived through all of its horrific consequences. When women's organizations contribute to marking this anniversary, it is thus not to separate from, nor duplicate such commemorations. We desire only to highlight the distinct role played by women in this national catastrophe. It is simply an attempt to expand the remembrance of this anniversary into areas not reached by Ukrainian national appeals and academia (...). There are still other ways to honour the anniversary: modest commemorative gatherings where a paper is read or participants share their recollections, newspaper articles on the subject, or even an explanation of this anniversary's significance to other women's organizations. Each step will bring us and others to understanding the truth about the Bolshevik regime. One more internal goal remains: for women from all across the Ukrainian lands, now united by shared work toward a single task, to become better acquainted. It is not simply today's meetings and cooperation that will bring us closer; through the shocks from the past we learn mutual understanding and forgiveness and try to correct past shortcomings in our relations.[73]

In the publication's next issue, a short overview appeared in English that cited witness recollections and provided encyclopaedic information on the course and effects of the Famine:

> Today, 20 years after this government instigated and perpetrated "experiment," we who witnessed this horrible predicament cannot keep silent. Because who can assure the world today that the same plight might not arise in other countries which may decline into the communist sphere? As far as the Kremlin is concerned – oh, these masters of deceptive propaganda and perversion can "explain" any phenomenon according to their patterns, as they always did.[74]

Articles about the Holodomor, including its genesis and consequences, were in fact fairly common in the diaspora press of the 1950s and 1960s. For example, in 1958, the newspaper *Vpered* [Forward] published an article devoted to the twenty-fifth anniversary of the Great Famine.[75] Its editor-in-chief, Ivan Maistrenko (1899–1984), who was born in Opishnia near Poltava and had been imprisoned by the NKVD, wrote an article from the vantage point of an external observer rather than of a Holodomor victim or survivor. With its tone, the article about the Holodomor's twenty-fifth anniversary was intended as evidence that the 1933 famine in Ukraine was planned and man-made. He

[73] "Na aktual'ni temy: Chomu vidznachuiemo rokovyny velykoho holodu?," *Nashe zhyttia / Our Life*, vol. 5 (1953), p. 2.

[74] M.S., "The year 1933," *Nashe zhyttia / Our Life*, № 6 (1953), p. 21.

[75] *Vpered* 92, № 7 (1958).

included a fragment of a poem he had written earlier, using the history of his hometown as a backdrop:

Блукають в льохах неоплакані тіні,
Минулого жертви і жертви нові,
А хмари несуться і блискавки сяють
І кличі над степом гудуть бойові[76]

Unmourned shadows roam the vaults,
Victims from the past and new victims,
While clouds sweep and lightning bursts
And over the steppe militant calls resound.[77]

In the four cited lines, writing about the lost souls, the author underlines that those who perished were not victims of a natural disaster but of intentional actions stemming from policies that targeted the Ukrainian countryside.

The Great Famine of 1932–33 was described in a similar fashion ten years later. In 1964, the American periodical *Samostiina Ukraïna* [Independent Ukraine] featured a series of articles devoted to events of the 1930s in Soviet Ukraine.[78] The fundamental goal for the generation of Ukrainian displaced persons was to focus the attention of local inhabitants in their countries of settlement. It is worth noting that these articles were written in the Ukrainian language and appeared in publications financed by local diaspora communities. It was as if the new generation of Ukrainian arrivals wanted, first and foremost, to re-introduce the subject of its biographical and generational experience into the Ukrainian discourse in the North American diaspora.

In 1962, the newspaper *Svoboda* announced the thirtieth-anniversary commemorations of the Great Famine as follows:

> Commemorations of this tragic anniversary are to take place not only in the name of recollection but also as an open and deserved accusation against Khrushchev and his *oprichniki* for Stalinist policies of denationalizing and decimating the Ukrainian nation that are continuing today. Through this action, Ukrainians abroad should bring Moscow to account, in front of the whole world, for its crimes while under the leadership of Stalin and Khrushchev, and particularly during the 1932–33 Famine in Ukraine. Commemoration of this anniversary is to provide an impulse to publish new books about the criminal Muscovite policy against Ukraine in all languages and to distribute those already pub-

---

[76] Ibid.; Ivan Maistrenko, *Istoriia moho pokolinnia. Spohady uchasnyka revoliutsiinykh podii v Ukraïni* (Edmonton, 1985), pp. 4–5.
[77] Translated by Taras Koznarsky.
[78] *Samostiina Ukraïna* 179, № 1 (1964); 180, № 2 (1964).

> lished; directed against Moscow's murderers, it ought to be a subject of interest to the press, radio and television across all countries of the free world.
>
> Let us all work with dedication in the defence of our nation, for the policies of 1933 are still being pursued by Moscow in Ukraine, only now in a different form. (...)
>
> Let no Ukrainian remain indifferent, let no one remain a mere spectator, but work honestly, actively, and with dedication and sacrifice toward realizing these plans.[79]

In 1973, *Nashe Zhyttia* [Our Life] printed an article referencing an appeal made by the World Congress of Free Ukrainians (WCFU):

> The main challenge for Ukrainian people in all countries of the world is the dignified, meaningful and comprehensive commemoration of the tragic fortieth anniversary of the famine in Ukraine. (...) In connection with this tragic anniversary, the Secretariat of the World Congress of Free Ukrainians has issued an appeal to all Ukrainians in the free world. Addressed to all organizations and to every Ukrainian individually, it calls for the dignified presentation of this unprecedented act of genocide to the world. The day of action has been set for March 25, 1973. The executive committee of WFUWO [The World Federation of Ukrainian Women's Organizations] fully supports the appeal of the WCFU Secretariat and ardently calls on all its members to actively engage in commemorating this tragic event with the rest of Ukrainian society. Let us recall all those nameless mothers who laid down their lives to save the smallest from famine and pray for their souls to find peace.[80]

As early as the 1940s, articles were published in various Ukrainian communities abroad calling for participation in demonstrations and manifestations, and emphasizing the need to cultivate the memory of the innocent victims of the Holodomor. The issue of commemorating the Holodomor in the new countries of residence was addressed both in daily press for wider audiences and in print publications of organizations representing extremely varied political views. Nevertheless, the articles quoted in this study share one factor – a conviction about the necessity of preserving the memory of Holodomor victims and spreading knowledge about the Holodomor in the new countries of residence. The preservation of the memory of Holodomor victims was part of recalling the criminal communist system ("Moscow murderers," "the occupants"), and the "national catastrophe" was presented as the guarantor of Ukrainian identity shaped around the aspirations for independence. And independence was presented as liberation from the colonial rule of the Soviet Union.

---

79 "V 30-ti Rokovyny velykoho holodu," *Svoboda*, № 217 (November 14, 1962), p. 3.

80 *Nashe zhyttia / Our Life*, № 3 (1973), p. 23.

2.4.2 Commemoration of Holodomor anniversaries in the diaspora and Ukraine

From the 1950s onwards, the Ukrainian diaspora engaged in a range of actions aimed at drawing attention to the events of 1932–33 in Ukraine, which had an impact on the initiation of academic research and the shaping of social opinion about the form and function of Soviet totalitarianism. On the twentieth and thirtieth anniversaries, the major community commemoration in North America was held on the grounds of the Ukrainian Orthodox Church in South Bound Brook, NJ [81]. From May to July 1953, demonstrations (*zhalibna khoda*) took place in many US cities, including the largest ones in Washington, DC, New York, Syracuse, and Buffalo, NY, and Philadelphia, PA.[82]

Their essential elements were prayers for the deceased victims of the Great Famine and the joint performance of the funeral hymn *Memory Eternal*. On June 21, 1953, banners were also prepared by Holodomor survivors, indicating the culprits of the Holodomor and a symbolic cemetery was set up on the Bound Brook Orthodox parish grounds (twenty white crosses).[83]

In the 1960s, within the Ukrainian community, opinions differed in evaluating the role of the Ukrainian communists and the Ukrainian cultural elite of the 1920s and '30s.[84] In 1963, far fewer people were involved in commemorating the anniversary of the Great Famine than in previous years. Important religious ceremonies traditionally took place during the designated Sunday in South Bound Brook, NJ.[85] In December, commemoration ceremonies took place in Jersey City, NJ, and Passaic, NJ. An essential element was the celebration of Orthodox religious mourning traditions. During this anniversary, not only the funeral hymn *Memory Eternal* and patriotic songs, but also the Ukrainian National Republic anthem were sung by all participants.[86]

[81] *Svoboda*, № 135 (June 23, 1953), p. 1; *Ukraïns'ke pravoslavne slovo / Ukrainian Orthodox Word*, № 7 (July 1953), p. 15–6; № 8 (August 1963), pp. 14–5; *Svoboda*, № 108 (June 8, 1963), p. 2; № 109 (June 11, 1963), p. 1.

[82] *Svoboda*, № 135 (June 23, 1953), p. 1; № 135 (June 24, 1953), p. 1; *The Ukrainian Weekly*, № 93 (May 19, 1953), p. 1; *Ukraïns'ke pravoslavne slovo / Ukrainian Orthodox Word*, № 6 (June 1953), p. 28; № 7 (July 1953), p. 15.

[83] *Ukraïns'ke pravoslavne slovo / Ukrainian Orthodox Word*, № 7 (July 1953), pp. 15–6.

[84] V. Koval', ed., *Stalins'ko-khrushchovs'ke okhvistia* (New York–Chicago, 1964), pp. 5–15.

[85] *Ukraïns'ke pravoslavne slovo / Ukrainian Orthodox Word*, № 8 (August 1963), pp. 14–5; Prysutnii, "Trydtsiat'littia holodu v Ukraïni vidznachyly v Passeiku, N. Dzh.," *Ukraïns'ke pravoslavne slovo*, vol. 15, no. 2 (February 1964), p. 19. Issues of the journal dealing with Ukrainian Famine commemorations are available on the website of the Holodomor Research and Education Consortium (HREC) under the rubric Resources-Memorialization, accessed February 5, 2021, https://holodomor.ca/resources/memorialization/.

[86] *Svoboda*, № 228 (December 4, 1963), p. 1; *Ukraïns'ke pravoslavne slovo / Ukrainian Orthodox Word*, № 1 (January 1964), p. 19.

Fig. 2. Members of DOBRUS at a demonstration in South Bound Brook, NJ, US (June 21, 1953)

Fig. 3. Orthodox and Uniate clergy at a memorial service in South Bound Brook, NJ, US (June 21, 1953)

Whereas the earlier social and commemorative initiatives were of a local nature and limited to the various social and religious organizations, in the case of the fortieth anniversary of the Holodomor they had a broader scope. This particular engagement of the Ukrainian circles in the West in the years 1972–73 was obviously affected by a number of factors: political (international affairs), local (the communities that organized the commemorative events continued to stage them), and intracommunal (the generation that lived through the Holodomor was getting older, resulting in an increased urgency of the intergenerational message). In my opinion, most important was the troubling situation in Soviet Ukraine, including mass repressions of those in the opposition referred to as *shestydesiatnyky* [people of the sixties]. A number of protests outside the Soviet embassy in Washington were triggered by the planned visit of Soviet leader Leonid Brezhnev to the United States (June 18–26, 1973). These events were covered in the Ukrainian press published abroad as fundamental reminders of the need for unification of hostile Ukrainian factions in the West and other citizens on the essence of Soviet policy and its consequences.

The Ukrainian-language press published in the US and Canada printed articles intended to unite the divided Ukrainian circles abroad and encourage joint fortieth-anniversary commemorations. The newspaper *Svoboda* [Freedom] published many such articles throughout 1973. In one of these, Anatoliy Hudovskyi, President of the civic organization *Demokratychne Ob'iednannia Buvshykh Represovanykh Ukraïntsiv Sovietamy* [Democratic Union of The Ukrainians Formerly Persecuted by the Soviets – DOBRUS], called for commemorating the fortieth anniversary on an all-national level, in an atmosphere of national unity and loyalty with respect to the assessment of national history and the authorities of the last Ukrainian state, the Ukrainian National Republic.[87] An article by Stephanie Bukshovana reflects in a most emphatic manner the link between the Holodomor and the events of 1960s–70s in Ukraine:

> We, who have found ourselves in the free world, have partially experienced this and we know from our own experience. Thanks to a handful of determined people beyond the Iron Curtain, we know what's going on there today and what will happen tomorrow. We must not remain silent about what happened forty years ago and what is happening today. We have in mind each and every one of us (no more, no less). All of us, regardless of age, education, position, have the same duty: to oppose the inhumane crimes of the communist regime, to inform those persecuted behind the Iron Curtain that we are with them and to shake the conscience of our environment and the conscience of the world.[88]

May of 1973 saw numerous demonstrations on the occasion of the fortieth anniversary that were organized by the Ukrainian Congress Committee of America (UCCA). The largest, comparable only with the religious commemorative events staged in South Bound Brook, took

---

[87] Anatoliy Hudovs'kyi, "Do vidznachennia richnytsi holodu," *Svoboda*, № 90, (May 16, 1973), pp. 2, 5.

[88] Stefa Bukshovana, "Vystupaiemo – ale vsi!," *Svoboda*, № 49, (March 16, 1973), p. 5.

place on May 26 in Washington, DC.[89] One of the participants, Senator Pavlo Yuzyk from Canada, addressed the gathered crowd:

> Let this commemoration of the anniversary of the terrible famine in Ukraine be a sad, but at the same time a serious reminder that communism denies and destroys human values, democracy, and freedom, establishing a brutal dictatorship and a totalitarian regime with the ultimate goal of seizing power over the world. American citizens should also be reminded that Moscow's current rulers continue their policies of genocide and colonialism in Ukraine through violent Russification, persecution, arrests, deportations, and institutionalization of intellectuals who defend human rights, destroy Ukrainian churches, and persecute their religions.[90]

Once again, the emphasis is on the need to publicly address the subject of the communist crimes against Ukraine. It is worth stressing here that the program of the demonstration included two practices crucial for the emerging Holodomor culture of memory: commemorative events included references to the works of Ukrainian national poet Taras Shevchenko (*Zapovit* [Testament] was sung), and the march through the streets of Washington towards the Soviet embassy, led by a member of the community in shackles, personifying occupied Ukraine.[91] These two crucial symbolic elements of Holodomor culture of memory were present, therefore, from the very beginning, and were important for the "communities of memory," regardless of divisions among Ukrainians living abroad, such as geographic location, denomination, or political views.

Demonstrations also took place in Canada (Winnipeg and Edmonton)[92] and in several European countries, including the United Kingdom (Bury, Nottingham, London[93]), Germany (Munich)[94], France (Châlette-Vésines) and Switzerland (Zürich)[95]. On September 23, 1973, the New York chapter of the Ukrainian Congress Committee of America organized a major demonstration in memory of the Holodomor victims and as a sign of solidarity with the Ukrainian elite repressed in the Soviet Union.[96]

---

89 "Tysiachi vzialy uchast' u ukraïns'kii proty soviets'kii manifestatsiï u Vashynhtoni," *Svoboda*, № 99 (May 30, 1973), pp. 2–4.

90 Ibid., p. 2.

91 Ibid., p. 4.

92 *Homin Ukraïny*, № 17, (April 21, 1973), p. 3; № 19, (May 5, 1973), p. 12; *Svoboda*, № 44, (March 9, 1973), p. 1.

93 *Svoboda*, № 55, (March 24, 1973), p. 1.

94 *Svoboda*, № 61, (April 3, 1973), pp. 1, 6.

95 *Svoboda*, № 55, (March 24, 1973), p. 1.

96 *Svoboda*, № 169, (September 14, 1973), p. 1; № 177, (September 25, 1973), pp. 1, 8.

However, the years that followed saw a scant number of commemorative initiatives inside individual "communities of memory." It took the fiftieth anniversary for the Holodomor to become a peak moment in Holodomor discourse. The social campaign greatly transcended local initiatives and was of a more secular rather than religious nature. The social symbolization of the Holodomor in individual "communities of memory" was also reflected in the mushrooming "places of memory."

The fiftieth anniversary of the Great Famine in 1982–83 stirred the Ukrainian diaspora in North America to conduct an information campaign starting in 1982. The largest American and Canadian newspapers published articles about the Holodomor,[97] with Ukrainian academic and social organizations in the US and Canada playing an especially significant role. The Canadian Institute of Ukrainian Studies already existed at the University of Alberta in Edmonton, Canada, and the Ukrainian Research Institute, established under the leadership of Professor Omelian Pritsak, was active at Harvard University. In 1983, the University of Quebec in Montreal held an international academic conference on the subject of the Great Famine that resulted in the publication of an essay collection based on its proceedings.[98]

In Washington, DC, and a number of other American cities, demonstrations, meetings, and academic colloquia were organized to mark the Great Famine's fiftieth anniversary. The largest demonstration took place on October 2, 1983, in front of the Soviet embassy in Washington.[99] According to police sources, some eighteen thousand people participated in the demonstration alone. It was a very well-organized civic action. The demonstrators were addressed in an official letter from then President of the United States, Ronald Reagan.[100] All major news services covered the event.[101] The Ukrainian press, not unlike ten years earlier, printed articles emphasizing the importance of joint community preparations and mass participation in the commemorative initiatives organized by various Ukrainian organizations. They also offered

---

[97] Adrian Karatnycky, "Forced Famine in the Ukraine: Holocaust the West Forgot," *Wall Street Journal,* July 7, 1983, p. 22; Bohdan Nahaylo, "Famine Reports Exaggerated," *Spectator,* April 2, 1983, pp. 17–8; Alexander J. Motyl, "The Great Ukrainian Famine," *American Spectator,* August 1983, pp. 24–6.

[98] Roman Serbyn and Bohdan Krawchenko, eds., *Famine in Ukraine: 1932–1933* (Edmonton, 1986).

[99] Tsentral'nyi derzhavnyi arkhiv hromads'kykh ob'iednan' Ukraïny (later as: TsDAHOU), f. 1, op. 25, spr. 2219, ark. 61.

[100] "Ponad 18,000 Ukraïntsiv z usikh hromad v ZSA vshanuvaly pam'iat' zhertv velykoho holodu v Ukraïni v 1932–33 rokakh, vziavshy uchast' u memoriial'nii manifestatsiï u Vashynhtoni 2-ho zhovtnia; velychavym kontsertom zakincheno memoriial'nyi tyzhden' v stolytsi ZSA," *Svoboda,* № 189 (October 5, 1983), pp. 1, 3–4.

[101] Koval'chuk and Marusyk, *Holodomor 1932–1933 rr. v USRR,* p. 120.

Fig 4. Demonstrators in Washington, DC (October 2, 1983)

information about group transport and accommodation opportunities so that as many people as possible could participate in the demonstration in Washington, DC.[102]

In the newspaper *Svoboda* [Freedom], Roman Danylevych (1903–85) called for collaboration of all the greatly divided Ukrainian communities in the United States:

> Sunday, October 2, is a Memorial Day that should gather thousands of people in the US capital, especially Ukrainians, to express their deep sorrow over the deaths of millions of Ukrainians in 1932–33 during Communist Moscow's Great Famine in Ukraine. And this profound mourning must at the same time be a public act of indictment against the mass murderers who, having written on their flags the false cries of brotherhood, equality, and universal freedom, have drowned millions of people in a sea of blood for decades and carried captivity and death instead of freedom. (...) And if so, should the question be asked: to go or not to go to Washington? But unfortunately, such a request is satisfied, if we look at our reality! Many of our compatriots look at the case of the demonstration in Washington not from an all-Ukrainian perspective, but from the perspective of a narrow group or party. And that's our whole disaster! (...) It hurts to the core that many of us are still hesitant about taking part in the memorial service for the millions of our brothers and sisters who died during the Great Famine on their land of milk and honey, or were torn from it and died in the Siberian tundra.[103]

The numerous press articles analyzed here expressed the belief that the world needed to learn about the Great Famine of 1932–33 as a "Ukrainian Holocaust."[104] Participation in the demonstration was a moral imperative, reflecting the national duty of Ukrainians living in the "Free World" towards the victims of the famine.[105]

Worth remembering is that not all groups participated in the organization of the commemorations, demonstrations, and meetings. The commemorative events were in fact boycotted by UCCA,[106] which had been the lifeblood of the commemorative events on the fortieth anniversary in 1973. Moreover, no representatives of SUM[107] attended the events.

---

[102] Stepan Kuropas', "Ïdemo do Vashynhtonu na 30-te veresnia," *Svoboda*, № 173 (September 13, 1983), p. 3.

[103] Roman Danylevych, "Ïkhaty chy ne ïkhaty do Vashynhtonu?," *Svoboda*, № 180 (September 22, 1983), p. 2.

[104] Andrii Bilyk, "Memoriial'na manifestaciia zblyzhaiet'sia – chas diiaty!," *Svoboda*, № 173 (September 13, 1983), pp. 2, 4; O-ka, "Pro nahodu, iaku ne mozhna znekhtuvaty," *Svoboda*, № 182 (September 24, 1983), p. 2.

[105] O-ka, "Pro te, shcho ne mozhna robyty," *Svoboda*, № 186 (September 30, 1983), p. 2.

[106] Danylevych, "Ïkhaty chy ne ïkhaty do Vashynhtonu?," p. 2.

[107] O-ka, "Pro tykh koho ne bulo," *Svoboda*, № 192 (October 8, 1983), p. 2.

Fig. 5. Members of ODUM at a demonstration in Washington, DC (October 2, 1983)

Two important issues regarding the demonstration need to be mentioned here. First, as there was no Holodomor monument in Washington, DC, the wreaths were laid at a monument to Taras Shevchenko. Second, mothers dressed in traditional costumes marched in the demonstration carrying their small children. Thus, the image of a woman (a mother with a child in this case), and the reference to the national poet ("Bard of Ukraine," as inscribed on the monument), become indispensable elements of the Holodomor culture of memory.

To mark the semicentennial anniversary, at the beginning of 1983 representatives of Ukrainian-Canadian social organizations regularly featured the subject on the pages of local newspapers and major magazines. Similar commemorative events to mark subsequent anniversaries of the Great Famine began to be organized in countries with the largest Ukrainian diaspora and towns. Communities also organized sessions and meetings that were often accompanied by a Requiem Mass for the souls of the communist regime's victims in the Ukrainian SSR. In addition, as part of the commemorations, Ukrainian schools in Toronto and Winnipeg added material on the Great Famine to their curricula. Wasyl Hryshko's book, *The Ukrainian Holocaust of 1933*, which was published in 1983 due to the efforts and donations of the Ukrainian diaspora in the United States and Canada, became a recommended textbook for students.[108] The World Congress of Free Ukrainians chose to convene in Toronto from November 30–December 4, 1984, despite strong opposition from the Soviet Embassy in Canada. The Soviet diplomatic corps sent a letter to the Canadian Ministry of Foreign Affairs, which emphasized that:

> (...) The Soviet side does not support either the backing extended by the Canadian government to the remnants of Ukrainian nationalists, nor the lectures given by known politicians, including Brian Mulroney, who mentioned the deliberate destruction of millions of Ukrainians during the famine of 1933 in his appearance.[109]

The Ukrainian Autocephalous Church abroad and the Ukrainian Orthodox Churches in the US and Canada also played a significant role in these fiftieth-anniversary commemorations. Metropolitan Mstyslav, in an apostolic letter marking the anniversary, appealed to the clergy and the faithful to erect crosses beside Orthodox churches in memory of the victims of the Famine or to incorporate commemorative plaques on the walls of their houses of worship.[110] The Ukrainian Catholic

[108] Wasyl Hryshko, *The Ukrainian Holocaust of 1933* (Toronto, 1983).

[109] TsDAHOU, f. 1, op. 25, spr. 2716, ark. 25.

[110] *Vyzvol'nyi shliakh*, № 5 (1983), p. 536.

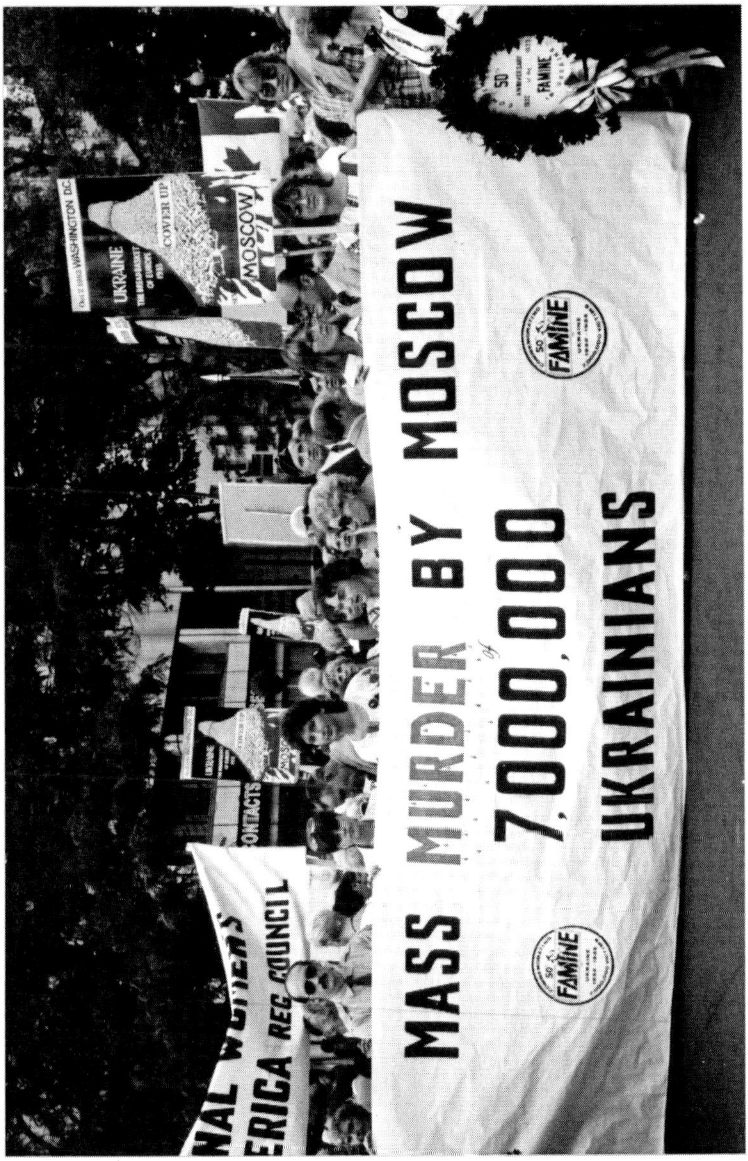

Fig. 6. Demonstrators with a banner reading "Mass Murder by Moscow – 7,000,000 Ukrainians" at a demonstration in Washington, DC (October 2, 1983)

Church organized religious events (memorial services in cemeteries and parish churches and symbolic wakes). For example, the clergy and the congregation of the Ukrainian Catholic Eparchy of Saint Vladimir the Great of Paris gathered on Sunday, October 2, in Strasbourg for a memorial service celebrated by Metropolitan Maxim Hermaniuk, CSsR, from Winnipeg,[111] and a memorial service was celebrated on Sunday, June 12, 1983, at Holy Spirit Ukrainian Catholic Cemetery in Hamptonburgh, NY, along with lectures about the Holodomor.[112]

It should be noted here that all Ukrainians regardless of religious rite were invited to participate in a fast on September 25, 1983. They were asked to skip one meal that day as a symbol of their compassion for the famine victims.[113] However, this commemorative initiative failed to take root in the "communities of memory," and it was not proposed again. In fact, it was replaced by the less demanding tradition of lighting candles, which is maintained in independent Ukraine.

Therefore, it is worth noting that the commemoration of the fiftieth anniversary, although hardly an expression of unanimity, was of a tremendous bond-forming importance to the communities cultivating the memory of the Great Famine outside of Ukraine. Numerous "places of memory" emerged in the 1980s connected with the symbolization of the Holodomor for Ukrainians living abroad.

The commemorative events marking the sixtieth anniversary had the potential to combine the initiatives of the broader diaspora with those of the communities emerging from political opposition circles that constituted the core of the Holodomor "community of memory" in Ukraine in the late 1980s. It should be remembered, however, that the commemorative events in Ukraine were primarily of a community nature. The political, social, and economic situation in Ukraine at the time did not allow for broader remembrance initiatives. The modest sixtieth-anniversary commemorations held in 1993 were the predictable outcome of this situation, and their shape, scale, and meaning were determined by local governments and local activists.[114]

The assessment of the Great Famine as a historical event at this point, however, still depended on the speaker's political views. For example, forces on the left of the political spectrum in Ukraine maintained that

---

[111] "Pomynky zhertvam holodu v Ukraïni 1933," *Shliakh peremohy*, № 40 (October 2, 1983), p. 4.

[112] Roman S. Holiad, "Na tsvyntari Sviatoho Dukha vshanuvaly pam'iat' zhertv holodu v Ukraïni," *Svoboda*, № 123 (July 1, 1983), p. 3.

[113] *Svoboda*, № 182 (September 24, 1983), p. 1.

[114] Oleksandr Hrytsenko, *Prezydenty i pam'iat'. Polityka pam'iati prezydentiv Ukraïny* (Kyiv, 2012), pp. 215–6.

Fig. 7. Metropolitan Mstyslav giving a speech at a demonstration in Washington, DC (October 2, 1983)

the Great Famine was largely an invention of Ukrainian nationalists.[115] Those interested in publicizing the Great Famine had to, so to speak, impose this knowledge on a Sovietized society. Stanislav Kulchytsky, one the first scholars of the Great Famine, conveys the crux of this problem well:

> A society that has lived through a genocide is not always aware of the violence perpetrated against it. The fact that an already dead generation

[115] Svitlana Kostylieva, "Vysvitlennia vitchyznianoiu presoiu 70-oï richnytsi holodu 1932–1933 rr.," *Problemy istoriï Ukraïny. Fakty, sudzhennia, poshuky* 11 (2004), pp. 343–53.

> was its victim complicates the matter even further. Those who survived the times of Stalinist repressions did not pass an aversion to the regime, or a hatred of it, onto their children out of fear for their safety and their own. These children, educated in Soviet schools, did not have a chance to confront the Soviet ethical values implanted in them with universal human values. The regime changed its approach to its pupils (without changing in its essence) to an extent that made it difficult for the new generation of citizens to identify the Soviet authorities with the crimes of the Stalinist era.
>
> Ukrainian scholars and ethnologists were able to graft onto the consciousness of their people the external manifestations of the Great Famine. This was carried out with shocking detail. These scholars were apparently not as convincing in explaining the logic of the successive events that followed the onset of the mass collectivization of agriculture.[116]

The Great Famine may have been known in Soviet Ukraine, but the subject was simply not discussed, like many other controversial issues. In reality, this collective memory was expressed – already in Soviet times – through varied social activities undertaken with the support of the Ukrainian diaspora that involved the creation of symbolic graves by both independence-focused groups and private individuals. This cultivation of illegal memory could be met with constant surveillance, discrimination, intimidation, and imprisonment[117] since even public conversations about the subject were perceived as anti-communist propaganda. The period of de-Stalinization did not bring any changes in this regard. Among the Ukrainian intelligentsia, internal censorship was requisite since the penal code of the Ukrainian SSR still contained Article 62 on anti-Soviet agitation and propaganda.[118] Kulchytsky recalls the 1960s and 1970s in the following way: "As a historian, I connected the inability to commemorate the Great Famine with its causes, then unknown to history studies. I saw, however, how deeply rooted it was in everyone's consciousness."[119] The events that were carefully expelled from the historical discourse in its generalized form constituted the core of a different, Soviet history, which every citizen of the Soviet Union learned from the stories of parents and grandparents.[120] Based on private experiences, these stories often did not describe the achievements and victories of the Soviet Union but rather, told of human suffering as a result of famine and violence inflicted on citizens

---

[116] Kul'chyts'kyi, *Holodomor 1932–1933 rr.*, p. 9.

[117] Andrea Gratsiozi, "Usvidomliuvannia Holodomoru," *Krytyka* 7, № 12 (2003), *passim*.

[118] Kul'chyt'skyi, "Problema holodu," *passim*.

[119] Ibid.

[120] Iurii Mytsyk, "Z dosvidu zboru svidchen' pro holodomor 1933 r.," in *Holod – henotsyd 1933*, p. 390.

of the Soviet state. It was because of this unofficially circulated history that the Great Famine could survive in the memory of Ukrainians.

The Ukrainian communities abroad commemorated the sixtieth anniversary in a modest manner. A committee was established in the United States comprising representatives of various Ukrainian organizations and led by Taras Hunczak. The Ukrainian press published calls for financial support and attendance of the event:

> This year [1993], Ukraine will commemorate the anniversary of this unforgettable national sorrow for the first time, while the Western diaspora has been accumulating knowledge about those events since the 1930s. Valuable documentary materials were collected, including eyewitness testimonies, and dozens of newspaper and magazine articles, books, including by non-Ukrainian authors, were written on this ageless topic. (…) In our opinion, the commemoration (…) should not be limited to certain days – it is important to remember as much as possible and (…) bring to mind this fact: the communist tyranny in the twentieth century made the Ukrainian people its main victim.[121]

It should be emphasized that, as often noted in the publications, the organizing committee believed that the commemoration of the sixtieth anniversary of the Holodomor through mass public actions was important not only in symbolic terms but also as an opportunity to present a political position. At a time when relations between Ukraine and the United States were normalizing, the main task before the committee was to inform the American public about Ukraine, the tragic pages in its history that resulted from its history within the USSR, and the reasons for their deep distrust of Moscow. Therefore, according to the authors of the press items, many events were aimed primarily at non-Ukrainians. Non-Ukrainian clergy were invited to the memorial service, and a conference was held in English.[122]

In Ukraine, a range of civic initiatives was held on a nationwide basis. It was initially assumed that demonstrations and manifestations would be of a more performative nature. However, it was not possible to realize all of the events that were planned for the Days of Mourning in 1993, and the agenda was executed only partially and in a conventional manner.[123] Memorial services were organized spontaneously

---

[121] Taras Hunchak, "Vidznachyty velykyi holod – obov'iazok kozhnoho ukraïntsia," *Svoboda*, № 62 (April 1, 1993), p. 3; Taras Hunchak, "Vidznachyty velykyi holod – obov'iazok kozhnoho ukraïntsia," *Nashe zhyttia / Our life*, № 5 (1993), p. 7.

[122] Lesia Bilovus, "Tematyka Holodomoru v ukraïnomovnii periodytsi diaspory SShA iak chynnyk zberezhennia natsional'noï identychnosti," *Eminak: naukovyi shchokvartal'nyk*, № 1 (21) (2018), vol. 2, pp. 135–40.

[123] Heorhii Kasi'anov, *Rozryta mohyla: Holod 1932–1933 rokiv u politytsi, pam'iati ta istoriï (1980-ti – 2000-ni)* (Kharkiv, 2019), pp. 47–8.

by social associations and local governments. The first Holodomor "places of memory" emerged at this time in Ukraine (Lubny, Kyiv), attracting individuals who were in fact creating the first "communities of memory." Many years later, Borys Oliynyk described the atmosphere of those gatherings, emphasizing their unifying, community-building nature:

> Remembering those days, that time of revival of bright memory and historical justice, I am once again convinced of the power of noble human thoughts. The initiative to honour the victims of the Holodomor really came from the people; representatives of the intelligentsia helped to implement it. People sincerely remembered, sincerely prayed for the repose of the souls of the dead.[124]

The "practices of commitment" have changed over the years. After Ukraine regained independence, rituals transformed, uniting Ukrainians around the world. In 2003, James Mace, who then lived in Ukraine, proposed the civic initiative *Zapaly svichku* [Light a Candle], which has continued in conjunction with each consecutive Holodomor commemoration. Since then, on Holodomor Remembrance Day (the fourth Saturday in November), at 16:00, candles are lit in windows of private homes and institutions, in front of monuments, and on city squares.[125]

In 2008, the International Holodomor Remembrance Flame action under the slogan *Let's Light a Candle of Remembrance* was particularly unifying for Ukrainians, both at home and abroad. It started on April 6, 2008, in Australia and travelled through thirty-three countries, ending in Ukraine in November 2008. One of its participants was President Viktor Yushchenko who, during his visit to Canada (April-May 2008), expressed in a speech his gratitude to Canadian Ukrainians for their perseverance in preserving the memory of the Great Famine of 1932–33 for future generations.[126] From the perspective of the culture of memory, it was tremendously important that during that event, Stepan Horlach [Horlatsch], a Holodomor survivor, passed a candle to Luda Monchak, a representative of present-day Canadian youth of Ukrainian descent.[127]

Organized anniversary commemorations have evolved in recent decades. Since the eightieth anniversary of the Holodomor, according to accounts published in Ukrainian-American newspapers and journals, the events follow a pattern: young people carry American, Can-

---

[124] Viedienieiev and Budkov, *Zaruchnytsia hlobal'noho protystoiannia*, p. 8.
[125] Kasi'anov, *Rozryta mohyla*, pp. 66, 233.
[126] Olena Koval'chuk, "Holodomor 1932–1933 rr. v USRR i ukraïns'ka diaspora Pivnichnoï Ameryky: informatyvni aspekty," *Ukraïna XX st.: kul'tura, ideolohiia, polityka*, № 15 (2009), pp. 193–4, accessed July 30, 2020, http://resource.history.org.ua/publ/xxx_2009_15_2_172.
[127] Ibid., p. 194.

adian, and Ukrainian flags and the flags of their youth organizations, hand out brochures about the Holodomor, lay wreaths at a monument, and conduct a march of remembrance to the religious or cultural centre of the community, where they attend an ecumenical and interfaith memorial service for the souls of the innocent victims. In the evening, events are organized featuring speeches by community as well as public and political leaders, interspersed with performances by cultural figures and short testimonies of Holodomor victims (and if there are no living eyewitnesses, by descendants and young people reading memoirs). At traditionally decorated tables, organizers serve what is known as a hungry dinner: a slice of rye bread with some honey and hot tea.[128] More recently, demonstrations have lessened in significance, and research and educational activities have come to the foreground. The newly established "places of memory" have become the centrepieces of events commemorating the anniversaries.

It should be noted that demonstrations were of a mass nature on the fortieth and fiftieth anniversaries of the Holodomor in the United States and Canada. However, from the mid-1980s, we observe a return to intracommunal initiatives and a decrease in their number. After Ukraine regained independence, these demonstrations lost some of their relevance among the diaspora in the West. The commemorative events in Ukraine, however, are of a different character in comparison with the earliest commemorative initiatives organized outside of its borders.

It is essential to consider the relationship of these rituals to other cultures of memory. The discourse about the Holodomor in the diaspora and independent Ukraine as a "silent genocide," "forgotten holocaust," and "genocide famine" did not arise in a social vacuum or without sources of inspiration. The Ukrainian tradition of remembering the dead and the Christian tradition of commemorating the martyrs for the faith were the first such contexts to which the Ukrainians in North America (especially the Orthodox) were drawn. Holodomor victims are mentioned as "innocent victims," "innocent murdered" and "innocent martyrs." Ukrainian diaspora communities have been also influenced by ways that the Holocaust has been remembered over the last thirty years. The social cultivation of the memory of the Holocaust had a much more significant impact on the Holodomor culture of memory among the Ukrainian diaspora (particularly in North America). During the 1960s–80s, adopting narrative models unequivocally associated with cultivating the memory of the genocide of the Jewish people during World War II became a characteristic feature of the Ukrain-

[128] Bilovus, "Tematyka Holodomoru v ukraïnomovnii periodytsi," pp. 135–40.

ian diaspora's rhetoric.[129] In speeches and publications, terms such as "Ukrainian ghetto," "Ukrainian Holocaust," or "Holocaust by hunger" appeared. As the Jews had suffered during World War II, the justification went, Ukrainians had suffered under Soviet rule during the 1930s. The Great Famine was a specific example of the fate that had befallen Ukrainians under foreign, Soviet rule, a horrific reminder of the enormous price paid by their forefathers on the road to independence. This narrative was the beginning of a practice of writing about the Great Famine in a spirit analogous to traditions of writing about the Jewish experience of genocide, a tendency reflected in both historiographies and art. It was natural in a situation where Ukrainian rituals of genocide remembrance did not yet exist in social memory, whereas general and socially accepted practices of commemorating a genocide, in this case, the Holocaust, could serve as a reference point.

Interestingly, the culture of memory of the Irish Great Famine had no impact on the commemoration of the Holodomor, despite the development of both memory cultures in twentieth-century North America in similar manners. Both the Irish and Ukrainian communities in the United States and Canada comprised immigrants who saw in the values of their new homelands protection from the suffering they endured. In both cases, the commemoration of the famine as the ultimate form of persecution by an imperial government was meant to emphasize the consequences of subjection to perpetrator-rulers and the need to remain independent from the oppressor (the British Empire and Soviet Russia, respectively). The Irish in the United States and Canada also used ethnic and religious symbols but to a lesser extent than Ukrainians living in the diaspora. The Irish diaspora initially located monuments on the grounds of parishes belonging to their religious communities (constituting the first "communities of memory"), but that is the extent of the similarities.[130]

In post-Soviet Ukraine, remembrance of the Great Famine was long modelled on Soviet commemorative practices. However, a core group consciously accepted and promoted the model of memory proposed by the Ukrainian diaspora, which relied on the memories of the Holodomor victim generation to constitute a "community of memory." This has changed over time as a result of educational and social activities.

[129] Glenn Sharfman, "The Quest for Justice: The Reaction of the Ukrainian-American Community to the John Demjanjuk Trials," *Journal of Genocide Research* 2, № 1 (2000), pp. 68, 70, 78; George V. Mylton, "Books Expose Famine-Genocide," *The Ukrainian Weekly* (October 8, 2000); Ihor Sawon, "Famine Memorial United Our Community," *The Ukrainian Weekly*, № 49 (December 3, 2000), p. 7; Johan Dietsch [Öhman], *Making Sense of Suffering: Holocaust and Holodomor in Ukrainian Historical Culture* (Lund, 2006), p. 242.

[130] Emily Mark-Fitzgerald, *Commemorating the Irish Famine: Memory and the Monument* (Liverpool, 2013), pp. 151–216.

2.4.3 Community and research organizations

In the shaping of the Holodomor culture of memory, an important role has been played by numerous research institutions and projects. On the one hand, we speak about scientific research and on the other, about local initiatives aimed at preserving the memories of the surviving witnesses or marking the victims' mass graves. Even though the nature and impact of such initiatives have changed throughout the years, since the mid-1980s, actions have fueled the "practices of commitment" followed by the "communities of memory."

The Ukrainian diaspora's community organizations had tried for some time to persuade the governments of their countries of residence to put pressure on the government of the Soviet Union, which, while officially admitting to the great purge, refused to consider the Famine in Ukraine as a Stalinist crime. The interest expressed in the subject of the Great Famine by the Reagan administration, which sent its representatives to some of the Ukrainian diaspora's events, was a mark of community success. The US Congress also paid particular attention to the fiftieth anniversary commemorations, as evidenced by the declaration it circulated widely (including to diplomatic posts, the United Nations, and mass media). Rumors circulated at this time that the US Congress would undertake an investigation into the events of 1932–33,[131] and on September 27 and 28, 1983, a series of special meetings with witnesses of the Great Famine were held. A number of well-known American activists participated in the debate aimed at establishing the truth about the Holodomor.[132] In the US House of Representatives, Congressman James Florio put forth a draft motion to create a commission of inquiry to investigate the Great Famine of 1932–33 in Ukraine, with the aim of disseminating information about the functioning of the Soviet system and thereby revealing the role that the Soviet authorities played in inducing the Famine. Senators Ernest Frederick "Fritz" Hollings and Pietro Vichi "Pete" Domenici approached President Reagan with a request to proclaim May 28 as the day the US Congress condemned the atrocity of the Great Famine in Ukraine. Support from Hamilton Fish Jr., the son of Senator Hamilton Fish Sr., had symbolic significance as the latter had appealed to Congress back in 1934 to condemn the situation in Ukraine and had proposed aid for the Famine victims. While Hamilton Fish Sr.'s

[131] Koval'chuk, *Holodomor 1932–1933 rr. v USRR*, pp. 172–80; Viedienieiev and Budkov, *Zaruchnytsia hlobal'noho protystoiannia*, pp. 80–8.

[132] TsDAHOU, f. 1, op. 25, spr. 2719, ark. 5–6; "Senate Foreign Relations Committee passes resolution on 1932–33 famine," *The Ukrainian Weekly*, № 46 (November 13, 1983), pp. 1–2.

proposal did not gain approval, his son's resolution passed with the support of sixty-two senators.[133]

On October 12, 1984, President Reagan approved with his signature the establishment of an investigative commission into the Great Famine in Ukraine in 1932–33; its members were to include congressmen, civil servants, and representatives of the Ukrainian diaspora.[134] On October 30, 1984, the president designated Sunday, November 4, 1984, as a Day of Commemoration of the Great Famine in the Ukraine in 1933.[135] The US Commission on the Ukraine Famine established by the US Congress comprised six scholars tasked with examining the issue on the basis of eyewitness accounts and accessible archive materials (including documents that had been captured by the Nazis and that subsequently found their way to the US from the archives of the Smolensk Oblast Committee of the Communist Party of the Soviet Union (CPSU), the State Archives of the Dnipropetrovsk Oblast in Krynychky, and the NKVD Archives in the town of Chornukhy in the Poltava Oblast).[136] The US earmarked $400,000 USD toward the research, and the commission was given two years to conduct the project, with work beginning in 1985.[137] In February 1986, James Mace, who was affiliated with the Harvard Ukrainian Research Institute, became the project's director.

The deadline for the commission's work would have most likely come at the end of the summer of 1987, but members of the Central Committee of the Communist Party of Ukraine (CPU) concluded that the American commission wished to time the announcement of its findings so as to interfere with the commemorations of the seventieth anniversary of the October Revolution in 1987. Fearing this outcome, the Central Committee of the CPU established an alternative famine commission in the autumn of 1986. Its members were expected to expose the deceptions of the "bourgeois" Ukrainian emigrants with regard to events in Ukraine. The work of the Soviet research team, however, progressed slowly.[138]

---

[133] Koval'chuk and Marusyk, *Holodomor 1932–1933 rr. v USRR*, pp. 132–4.

[134] Ibid., p. 134.

[135] TsDAHOU, f. 1, op. 25, spr. 2818, ark. 55–6; "Proclamation 5273: Commemoration of the Great Famine in the Ukraine," https://www.presidency.ucsb.edu/documents/proclamation-5273-commemoration-the-great-famine-the-ukraine.

[136] *Ukrainian Famine of 1932 and 1933: Hearing before the Committee on Foreign Relations United States Senate, Ninety-eighth Congress, Second Session on S. 2456. A Bill to Establish a Commission to Study the 1932–33 Famine Caused by the Soviet Government in Ukraine, August 1, 1984* (Washington, 1984), pp. 91–2.

[137] Koval'chuk and Marusyk, *Holodomor 1932–1933 rr. v USRR*, p. 133; "S. 2456 – 98th Congress: Commission on the Ukraine Famine Act," https://www.govtrack.us/congress/bills/98/s2456.

[138] Bazhan, *Initsiatyvy ukraïns'koï diaspory, passim.*

Meanwhile, once its government funding was exhausted, the work of the US commission continued with the material support of private sponsors from the Ukrainian diaspora. In 1988, the final findings of the research, edited by James Mace, appeared in print.[139] The in-depth analysis of the problem, which considered the mechanism of eliminating the Great Famine from the memory of Ukrainians, made a lasting impression on those who commissioned the report. As a result, the work of the commission mandate was extended until September 1990. In June 1989, during a meeting with the Soviet ambassador to the US, James Mace emphasized that the Great Famine could cease to be a "white spot" in Ukraine's historiography with the involvement and genuine cooperation of Soviet scholars. The Soviet side, however, remained silent on the matter.

In 1983, the UCRDC produced the documentary film *Harvest of Despair*. In 1986, at Harvard University's Widener Library, an exhibition entitled *Famine in the Soviet Ukraine 1932–33* was mounted with Leonid Heretz's involvement. A catalogue by Leonid Heretz, Oksana Procyk, and James Mace was published to accompany the exhibition.[140] As Frank Sysyn has noted, the Harvard Ukrainian Research Institute (HURI) in the early 1980s had concentrated on medieval and early modern studies. When the Ukrainian Studies Fund proposed that HURI mark the anniversary of the Ukrainian Famine in 1982–83 with appropriate scholarly projects, the request met with the support of HURI's academic advisory committee, the Harvard Committee on Ukrainian Studies, which included prominent specialists in the modern history and politics of the USSR, Richard Pipes and Adam Ulam. The Ukrainian Famine Project was initiated in 1980, and in 1981, Dr. James Mace from the University of Michigan joined the Institute staff to carry out research on the Famine. By mid-1981, the Institute, on the recommendation of Adam Ulam, had come to an agreement with Dr. Robert Conquest to write a monograph about the Famine. Conquest, known for his work *The Great Terror*,[141] undertook the writing of a monograph about the Great Famine, and the first edition of *The Harvest of Sorrow: Soviet Collectivization and the Terror-Famine* came out in London at the end of 1986.[142] Dr. Mace provided significant research assistance.[143]

---

139 Kul'chyts'kyi, "Problema holodu," *passim*.

140 Oksana Procyk, Leonid Heretz, and James E. Mace, *Famine in the Soviet Ukraine, 1932–33: A Memorial Exhibition, Widener Library, Harvard University* (Cambridge, MA, 1986).

141 Robert Conquest, *The Great Terror: Stalin's Purge of the Thirties* (London, 1968).

142 Robert Conquest, *The Harvest of Sorrow: Soviet Collectivization and the Terror-Famine* (London, 1986).

143 Frank Sysyn, "Thirty Years of Research on the Holodomor: A Balance Sheet," *East/West: Journal of Ukrainian Studies* 2, № 1 (2015), pp. 4–16.

Over time, research into the Great Famine inspired a growing number of Ukrainian scholars, who became the first members of the *Asotsiatsiia doslidnykiv Holodomoru-henotsydu v 1932–1933 v Ukraïni* [Association of Researchers into the Holodomor-Genocide of 1932–1933 in Ukraine], founded by Volodomyr Maniak in June of 1992.[144] Those affiliated with the Association (later *Asotsiatsia doslidnykiv holodomoriv v Ukraïni* [Association of Researchers of Famines in Ukraine]) can thus be viewed as the first "memory community" of the Holodomor in Ukraine. It was a wholly ideological community that already possessed its own place in both the topographic and metaphorical senses, to which certain rituals started to attach. Its core consisted of intellectual and artistic elites with patriotic leanings. The witnesses of the tragedy were yet to join this community, but were essential as proof of the validity of the community's very existence. This was certainly the beginning of the struggle over memory in post-Soviet Ukrainian society. As already mentioned, the Association undertook the first Holodomor monuments, conferences, projects to collect testimonies from witnesses of the Holodomor, and marking of mass graves in Ukrainian villages. In the following parts of the study, I will analyze in more detail the Association's initiatives related to the creation of "places of memory."

In August 1992, the Association proposed the establishment of an International Centre for the Study of the History of Ukraine that would engage in "the study of the demographic, medical, spiritual, cultural, economic, and political consequences of genocide policy."[145] This proposal was made again in 1998, 2000, and 2003.[146] As a result, the Centre for the Study of Genocide in Ukraine was established. Formally, it consisted of three people who are the backbone of the Association for Holodomor Studies in Ukraine (V. Marochko, O. Movchan, and O. Veselova). The Centre, which was formally a division of the Institute of History of Ukraine, for three years researched the topic "Genocide of national, ethnic, and religious groups of Ukraine in the twentieth century: historical and political and legal analysis." In the winter of 2009, the Centre was liquidated by decision of the Directorate of the Institute of History of Ukraine of the National Academy of Sciences of Ukraine.[147]

[144] At present this association is headed by Oleksandr Ushyns'kyi. Members carry out research and publishing activities and organize events commemorating each Holodomor anniversary. Of special note is the input of Marian Kots – a New York-based researcher into the Great Famine, who has enabled the publication of Ukrainian academic works abroad as well as charity work.

[145] Oleksandra Veselova, *Z istoriï stvorennia i diial'nosti Asotsiatsiï doslidnykiv holodomoru v Ukraïni (ADHU) 1933: monohrafiia* (Kyiv, 2007), p. 40.

[146] Ibid., pp. 82, 90.

[147] Kasi'anov, *Rozryta mohyla*, p. 255.

Under President Yushchenko, an Institute of National Remembrance was established, which began to function as a government institution in 2006. It included a unit with the eloquent name Department of Historical Tragedies of the Peoples of Ukraine.[148] Nevertheless, it was not strictly a research institute.

However, a research consortium was successfully established outside of Ukraine, in Canada. The Holodomor Research and Education Consortium (HREC) was established in 2013, the eightieth anniversary year of the Great Famine, as a project of the Canadian Institute of Ukrainian Studies (CIUS) at the University of Alberta. Its stated mandate is "(...) to research, study, publish, and disseminate information about the Holodomor, ensuring that the Ukrainian experience receives greater recognition in society at large and that it is represented in the teaching of history (...)."[149] Its dual mandate to promote research and education is reflected in its structure. The establishment of HREC was made possible by the financial support of the Temerty Foundation, whose founder, James Temerty, had funded the Holodomor monument in Edmonton thirty years earlier. As he emphasized in an interview featured in the *Svoboda* newspaper, "I am extremely pleased to support the Consortium, and I hope for its success and for a deeper understanding and awareness of the Holodomor tragedy."[150]

The main office of HREC is located at the Ukrainian Canadian Research and Documentation Centre in Toronto. It is overseen by an Executive Council comprised of CIUS unit directors together with an Advisory Committee and managed by Executive Director Marta Baziuk.[151]

The consortium's research division, headed by Dr. Bohdan Klid, is tasked with promoting academic research that relates to the subject of the Holodomor and supporting Holodomor studies in conjunction with scholars, universities, working groups, as well as institutions and libraries in Ukraine and abroad. The website of HREC features numerous academic articles, English translations of relevant documents, and a range of resources, including oral histories in English translation. HREC also holds an annual research grants competition to support research into lesser known aspects of the Holodomor.

---

148 Ibid.

149 "Stvoreno Konsortsiium z vyvchennia Holodomoru," *Svoboda*, № 10 (March 8, 2013), p. 1.

150 Ibid., p. 5.

151 At the time of HREC's establishment, the Advisory Committee included Frank Sysyn of the University of Alberta; Paul Robert Magocsi of the University of Toronto; Alexander Motyl of Rutgers University; Norman Naimark of Stanford University; Serhii Plokhy of Harvard University; Mark von Hagen of Arizona State University; Denis Hlynka and Orest Cap of the University of Manitoba; Mark Melnyk of the York Region District School Board; and Boris Radyo of Edmonton Catholic School District.

The educational arm of HREC develops and disseminates materials intended for teachers, students, educational institutions, libraries, and the general public and works to gain inclusion of the topic of the Holodomor in school curricula. HREC's Director of Education, Valentina Kuryliw, is a history teacher by training and the author of numerous educational and pedagogical publications, among them, an English-language Holodomor teaching resource that provides educators with teaching materials, lesson plans, and assignments that can be applied to various grade levels.[152] Like James Temerty, Kuryliw is the child of Holodomor survivors. She has taught qualification enhancement courses for history teachers in Ukraine since 1993[153] and considers spreading awareness of the Holodomor a priority in her life.[154]

In April 2015, HREC in Ukraine (Holodomor Research and Education Centre for the Study of the Holodomor) was launched as a non-governmental organization with the financial support of the Temerty Foundation. Its mission is to preserve the memory and support academic study of the Holodomor and other genocides.[155]

The creation of these entities that combine research, educational, and commemorative components is a significant shift in the way the subject of the Great Famine is promoted academically and in the public domain. It constitutes a step onto a completely different level of promoting the study of and knowledge about this genocide.

2.5 Conclusions

In analyzing the Holodomor as a formative event, the societies that can be potentially regarded as its "communities of memory" should be considered. A fundamental question that arises is the number of such communities. The memory of the Great Famine 1932–33 is a shared legacy of the Ukrainian emigration, and particularly of the post-war emigra-

---

[152] Valentyna Kuryliv, *Metodyka vykladannia istorii̇. Kurs pidvyshchennia kvalifikatsii̇ vchyteliv istorii̇* (Lviv–Toronto, 2003); 2nd ed. (Kharkiv–Toronto, 2008); Valentina Kuryliw, *The Unknown Genocide: Holodomor in Ukraine 1932–1933* (Toronto, 2008); Valentina Kuryliw, *Holodomor in Ukraine, the Genocidal Famine 1932–1933: Teaching Materials for Teachers and Students* (Toronto, 2015).

[153] Orest Subtelnyi, "Valentyna Kuryliv: Metodyka vykladannia istorii̇," *Pedahohichna dumka*, № 3 (2003); V. Fedorak, "Iak vchyty istorii̇ v suchasnii shkoli," *Istoriia v shkolakh Ukraïny*, № 6 (2003), p. 46; Oksana Zakydalsky, "Canadian Educators Change the Teaching of History in Ukraine," *The Ukrainian Weekly*, № 16 (April 18, 2004), p. 13.

[154] Interview with Valentina Kuryliw, Toronto, November 20, 2017 (the author's private collection).

[155] Interview with Liudmyla Hrynevych, Toronto, November 20, 2017 (the author's private collection).

tion wave of the so-called "DPs" ("displaced persons"), as well as members of the oldest generation living in Ukraine. These communities can be seen both as a variant of one and the same community, differing only in relation to the country in which they function, and also as completely different communities shaped by the process of restoration of memory. There could also exist a single, dynamic and diverse community whose members, regardless of where they reside, are linked by the idea of the need to cultivate the memory of the Great Famine and the conviction of its uniqueness in human history. In this case, state boundaries would have no bearing on the range and scope of the "community of memory," with the sense of belonging to this group tied to the conviction about the Holodomor's genocidal character and acceptance of the rituals of memory connected with its cultivation in national discourse.

A primary "community of memory" of the Holodomor is a group descending from the generation of the event's victims together with Western Ukrainians who accept and share the Holodomor as a common national tragedy. Within diaspora circles, it is indeed members of this generation and their descendants who identify themselves with the event and who have been a propelling force behind a range of initiatives aimed at the propagation of awareness of the Great Famine. For the "community of memory" that arose at the beginning of the 1990s in Ukraine, in turn, eyewitness accounts of the tragedy were a primary source, evidence of the barbarities of Stalinist terror. At that time, the core of the community arising in Ukraine was made up of individuals who consciously accepted the Great Famine as historical fact and postulated it as an act of genocide against the Ukrainian nation.

However, the examples in this chapter show that there are various small "communities of memory," each with its own history and tradition of commemoration. Sometimes, on the occasion of anniversaries important to all Ukrainians in a given country, the communities will unite to commemorate the memory of the victims of the Holodomor in the public space. Importantly, they are united by the borderless idea of the necessity to remember the victims, expressed every year in the "Light a Candle" civic action. "We remember and we are strong," the slogan of this initiative proclaims. Currently, this activity is the main "practice of commitment" for Ukrainians around the world.

I consider the events and initiatives discussed in this chapter as formative and decisive in creating "communities of memory," indicative of the process of the Holodomor's social symbolization. The symbolic image of the Holodomor in the examples of "communities of memory" discussed here emerged over several decades and underwent a series of transformations. In subsequent years, there were an increasing number of such initiatives, although their character changed: other elements of Stalinist policies were emphasized in the speeches on the occasion of the anniversaries, and while some rituals were religious (memorial services, the presence of religious leaders at ceremonial protests), secular means of commemorating (demonstrations, lectures) also took place.

Chapter III

Memorialization of the Holodomor Abroad

This chapter applies current literature to examine the process of symbolizing the Great Famine by the Ukrainian diaspora in the US, Canada, Brazil, Great Britain, and Australia. My analysis of numerous diaspora publications suggests that the Holodomor (then frequently referred to as the Famine of 1933 or the Great Famine 1932–33) from the mid-twentieth century on was in the process of being elevated to the rank of a symbol that supported a sense of Ukrainianness and marking a distinctiveness from other diaspora groups from the territories of the Soviet Union who left for the West after World War II.

As in subsequent subchapters I will concentrate on those events and initiatives that turned out to be exceptionally significant in creating Holodomor "places of memory" throughout the diaspora. It is the activities of the western diaspora that are most relevant in my research because the issue of the Great Famine of 1932–33 was central to its social and organizational life.

3.1 Secular *vs* sacral: The first Holodomor memorialization initiatives in North America

From the outset, both secular and religious components have been intertwined in the remembrance of the Holodomor as communities considered how to best honour the memory of the victims. In the previous chapter, I discussed demonstrations held on consecutive anniversaries as examples of "practices of commitment." They also reflect a combination of religious and secular practices in honouring the millions of people of different ages and genders whose deaths could have been avoided, a circumstance that heightens the sense of tragedy and loss. As stressed by Alexander Etkind, mass murders can be interpreted by contemporary generations in religious categories – as a sacrifice of one's own life – and in lay (political) terms – as a sacrifice for the sake of (re)gaining independence. Etkind asked a very important question: How can sacrifice be translated into secular terms?

> One could define sacrifice – e.g., a loss of soldiers at war or firemen on duty – as based on the voluntary participation of the potential victims and the retroactive acknowledgment from the public sphere. In other words, sacrifice is voluntary, public, and meaningful to the public. In contrast, a mass murder in a gas chamber or in a Soviet camp does not comply with this definition because it is not voluntary and not public.[1]

This distinction applies to the victims of mass, man-made starvation. A victim's life and death were not in the public domain of the law and court; they were at the mercy of a tyrant. Therefore, the choice of religious symbols indicates the necessity to sanctify the Ukrainian people as victims on their long road to independence, in their struggle with the oppressor ("red Moscow," or "the red hangman" – terms found in the press of the 1940s through 1980s). For many, religious rhetoric seemed most appropriate. The early forms of commemorating the Holodomor at "places of memory" were of a deeply religious nature. The earliest "communities of memory" commemorating the Holodomor originated with parish congregations, which determined the location of monuments, their form (shape, symbolic message), and their role in the "practices of commitment."

Paradoxically, in the literature on the subject, while the role of Ukrainian diaspora organizations in the cultivation of memory about the Holodomor, the building of monuments, and the organization of protests as well as educational programs, has been stressed, most studies do not consider the initiatives of the Ukrainian Orthodox Church in their analyses of the diasporic discourse on the Great Famine. As Frank Sysyn rightly notes, in the 1960s the Ukrainian Orthodox Church in the US included groups of inter-war émigrés, arrivals from pre-1939 Soviet Ukraine, including Archbishop, and later Metropolitan, Mstyslav, who built on the conceptualization of the Great Famine developed in the European centres of the Ukrainian emigration in the 1930s as they observed events in their homeland with horror.[2] After World War II, a large number of émigré Holodomor survivors and their children joined the Church.

---

[1] Alexander Etkind, *Warped Mourning: Stories of the Undead in the Land of the Unburied* (Stanford, 2013), pp. 29, 184.

[2] Frank Sysyn, "The Ukrainian Orthodox Church: Memory and Memorialization of the Holodomor," accessed July 30, 2020, https://holodomor.ca/wp-content/uploads/2016/05/boundbrook.pdf.

It is worth noting that the hierarchs and parish leaders in communities belonging to that Church were engaged in creating "places of memory" not only in the United States.[3] The Ukrainian Greek Orthodox Church in Canada fulfilled a similar mission. The Ukrainian Autocephalous Orthodox Church served Brazil, New Zealand, Australia, and Western Europe. While not recognized as canonical at the time by the greater Orthodox world, these Ukrainian Orthodox churches played a major role in the diaspora's religious, cultural, and political life. In the 1950s, the Ukrainian Orthodox Church in the US located its seat in South Bound Brook, NJ, which is why it has been referred to as the "Ukrainian Jerusalem" in the Ukrainian diaspora in North America.[4]

The Ukrainian Orthodox Church of the USA (UOC of USA) was established as an ethnically Ukrainian Church in North America at a 1950 council (Sobor) in New York City. At the head of the Church was Metropolitan Ioan (Teodorovych). Archbishop Mstyslav (Skrypnyk) became his deputy and the head of the Consistory.[5] He initiated the Ukrainian Orthodox Center in South Bound Brook, NJ, for which twenty-three hectares of land were purchased in 1951. A cemetery was established there in 1954, which became the resting place of many well-known

[3] The Ukrainian Orthodox community in the United States formed during the nineteenth century with the influx of Orthodox Ukrainian immigrants and the conversion to Orthodoxy of some Ukrainian emigrants of the Greek-Catholic faith. Ukrainians created their own ethnic parishes within the framework of the American archeparchy of the Russian Orthodox Church. After 1915 a part of these decided to break away from the Russian Church and to create a separate structure, one Ukrainian in character. In 1921, this group approached the Ukrainian Autocephalous Orthodox Church with the request to appoint a head. The head of the Church became Archbishop Ioan (Teodorovych). Although the Ukrainian Autocephalous Orthodox Church was not recognized as canonical by other Orthodox Churches, Archbishop Ioan immediately began organizing his eparchy in the United States with his arrival in 1924. But in 1929 some of the Orthodox Ukrainians living in the United States created an alternative Church (the Ukrainian Orthodox Church in America), which in 1936 was taken under the jurisdiction of the Constantinople patriarchy. Over the course of the next dozen years or so both structures were in open rivalry for influence amongst the faithful. In 1950 most of their parishes united during a joint council, creating out of the two Churches the largest Ukrainian Orthodox Church structure in the United States. At the time the Head of the Church was the earlier mentioned Metropolitan Ioan (Teodorovych). In 1971, following the death of Metropolitan Ioan, the Church was headed by Metropolitan Mstyslav (Skrypnyk). In 1990 he was declared patriarch of the restored Ukrainian Autocephalous Orthodox Church in Ukraine. He passed away in 1993. On the Church, see Nicholas Denysenko, *The Orthodox Church in Ukraine: A Century of Separation* (DeKalb, IL, 2018), and Frank E. Sysyn, "The Third Rebirth of the Ukrainian Autocephalous Church and the Religious Situation in Ukraine, 1989–1991," in Serhii Plokhy and Frank E. Sysyn, *Religion and Nation in Modern Ukraine* (Edmonton–Toronto, 2003), pp. 88–119.

[4] David Marples and Ostap Skrypnyk, "Patriarch Mstyslav and revival of the Ukrainian Autocephalous Orthodox Church," *The Ukrainian Weekly*, № 1 (1991), p. 7.

[5] Sysyn, "The Ukrainian Orthodox Church."

figures of the Ukrainian emigration. St. Andrew Memorial Church, designed by Ukrainian-Canadian architect Yuriy Kodak, opened for worship in 1965. At present, besides the church, the location is home to the St. Sophia Seminary, a museum, an archive, a printing house, and The Ukrainian History and Education Centre, which houses a 1,500-seat concert hall and a library.[6]

From the beginning, the church-monument was developed as a Holodomor "place of memory." Even during its lengthy construction (1955–65), it was the site of Holodomor anniversary events, in 1958 and 1963, and it has continued to play an important role in consecutive Holodomor anniversaries.

Similar commemorative initiatives to mark subsequent anniversaries of the Great Famine were being organized in countries with large Ukrainian communities, along with – significantly – initiatives to erect the first monuments in memory of its victims. The first such monument, which was built next to an Orthodox church, was most likely the cross unveiled in Adelaide, Australia, in 1972. The *Entsyklopediia Ukraïns'koï Diiaspory* [The Encyclopedia of the Ukrainian Diaspora] states:

> A monument in the shape of a cross was erected in 1972 in Adelaide near a Ukrainian Autocephalous Orthodox Church (on the Hindmarsh estate). As a result of the closure of the Church of the Holy Pokrova in 1993, it was transferred to St. Michael's Orthodox Church in Adelaide.[7]

In writing about the Great Famine memorial initiatives spearheaded by the Orthodox and the Eastern Rite Churches abroad, it is important to note that the overwhelming majority of monuments were built on land owned by the particular parishes. They were funded with the donations of parishioners, on whom rests the burden of care for these "places of memory." In fact, globally (with the exception of Ukraine), the Holodomor monuments that are not the property of parishes can be counted on the fingers of one hand.

Towards the end of the 1970s, at Saint George Ukrainian Orthodox Cemetery in Lachine (today part of Montreal), a place of symbolic burial marked with a cross and a memorial plaque was unveiled to mark the forty-fifth anniversary of the Great Famine. In 1983, the newspaper *Oko* [Eye] wrote that it was "the only known monument to date in Canada commemorating the Ukrainian Holocaust."[8] This example is interesting

---

[6] "Some Aspects in the Life of the Ukrainian Orthodox Church of the USA," Ukrainian Orthodox Church of the USA, accessed March 23, 2019, https://www.uocofusa.org/history.html.

[7] Roman Mykytovych and o. Ivan Shevtsiv, "Pam'iatnyky," in *Entsyklopediia ukraïns'koï diiaspory v 7 tomakh*, ed. Vasyl' Markus', vol. 4, *Avstraliia, Aziia, Afryka* (Kyiv, 1995), p. 147.

[8] *Oko*, № 6 (1983), p. 2.

in that it reveals the next stage of interpretation of the Great Famine by the Ukrainian emigration; although the memorial site in Lachine is part of a religious setting and uses religious symbols, it relies on secular narrative models with its reference to the Holocaust.

The religious initiatives have their own tradition; while to a large extent linked to secular, socio-political, and socio-cultural initiatives, they nonetheless initially created their own symbolic thesaurus derived from the Christian tradition of remembering the dead. However, the

Fig. 8. Holodomor monument at Lachine cemetery in Montreal, Canada (1972)

religious rituals and Holodomor "places of memory" do not fully present the complexity of the Soviet terror, which brought about the senseless deaths of millions of Ukrainians. It seems that references to religious rhetoric grew out of a desire to bestow meaning onto that tragedy in the public space. However, the calls to erect monuments beyond the grounds of parishes or cemeteries are evidence that a part of the "communities of memory" desired to create secular monuments that would transcend the Ukrainian communities and position the discussion of the Holodomor on an entirely different level in the societies to which they belonged.

The first initiatives connected with erecting a secular monument in memory of Holodomor victims were mentioned in the 1960s and 1970s in the Ukrainian-language press in the United States and Canada. In 1963, the newspaper *Kanadiis'kyi farmer* published an open letter signed "P. Speka" that called for the erection of a monument honouring the victims of the Great Famine.[9] Speka was the pseudonym of Pamfil Ses (1897–1992), a Ukrainian engineer who had resided in Great Britain since 1948. He dabbled in sculpture and poetry in his free time and wrote to Ukrainian-language periodicals in the US and Canada.[10] Having lived in the 1930s in what is today the city Dnipro, the author had experienced the Great Famine, although he does not reference his personal experience in the letter. Nevertheless, his personal experiences contributed to his understanding of the Great Famine and his conviction – which emerged, in turn, through his artistic interests – in the need to commemorate the event in the "free world" in the form of a monument. It is worth noting that Ses mentions the figure of fifteen million victims, which includes the victims of famines from the years 1921–22, 1932–33, as well as 1946–47.

> Let us pay homage to those who died on masse under Bolshevik rule. These victims do not rest in cemeteries as they would anywhere in the world among the cultured nations beyond the Iron Curtain. Under the communist barbarian, victims are scattered over the entire territory controlled by the executioner, walled off by an iron curtain so that no one from the outside can discover the crimes he committed. If it had not been for the war, the world would have never learned of the "cemetery" in Vinnytsia, on the site of which a park was established to hide the graves of twelve thousand Ukrainian victims. And when fifteen million such

[9] P[amfil] Speka [Ses], "Zbuduimo pam'iatnyka zhertvam Holodu v Ukraïni," *Kanadiis'kyi farmer* (September 2, 1963), pp. 3–4.

[10] Nina Ses'-Marchenko, "V'iazanka spomyniv...," in *Regensburg. Statti, spohady, dokumenty*, ed. Omelian Kushnir (New York–Paris–Sydney–Toronto, 1985), pp. 612–6; Nina Ses'-Marchenko, "U pam'iat' moho bat'ka," *Vidomosti ieparkhiial'noho upravlinnia UAPTs u Velykii Brytanii* (London), ch. 1 (1993), pp. 51–3.

> victims do not have their own cemetery, **then we, even though abroad, must build this monument-cemetery to focus our attention and to educate other nations. (...) And so will be raised the monuments of these fifteen million brothers who perished in their homeland for the sole reason that they loved it so. We shall erect a monument to these victims in a foreign country, for we cannot on our home soil.** Let us use this chance to instill fear in those who had a hand in this hideous crime against the defenseless. **Let us erect a monument and call it "The Golgotha of the Ukrainian Nation" [bold – W. K.Ś.].**[11]

In his letter, Ses postulated that the future monument should have the characteristic of a cemetery, that it be a place of reflection for future generations of Ukrainians. Interestingly, Ses employs religious references ("Golgotha") and proposes a monument-cemetery that can serve as a warning for other nations.

Ten years later, in 1973, on the pages of the Ukrainian diaspora press in the US, another proposal for the construction of a monument appeared. In the section "Readers' Voices" found in issue 49 of the newspaper *Svoboda,* devoted to the commemorations of an anniversary of the Shevchenko Scientific Society, we find a letter signed by Mykhailo Mlakovyi proposing the construction of a monument to the Holodomor's victims. Mlakovyi (1895–1976) was a Ukrainian journalist who was persecuted by the Bolsheviks in the 1930s and fought in the ranks of the Ukrainian Insurgent Army during World War II, later emigrating to the US. According to Mlakovyi, the construction of a monument to the victims of the Holodomor was essential given the fact that the event had been erased from public discourse in Soviet Ukraine and throughout the Soviet Union. The author underscored that such a monument would be far more effective than demonstrations in front of Soviet diplomatic missions or on city streets. In his view, a memorial would prevent such a momentous event in the history of the Ukrainian nation from being forgotten:

> Let us build monuments – we've already erected a few – to T. Shevchenko, L. Ukrainka... And why should we not create a monument to the deserving victims of the Great Famine, which was man-made by the Red Muscovite occupiers of Ukraine forty years ago? But such a monument will not be erected in our homeland, neither by the occupant – Red Moscow – nor its gauleiters in Kyiv.
>
> The best of our organized meetings and demonstrations planned to mark the fortieth anniversary this year, however numerous and influential they may be, will soon pass. We, and the Ukrainian friends who demonstrated alongside us, will go back to our everyday concerns the

[11] Speka [Ses], "Zbuduimo pam'iatnyka," pp. 3–4.

> very next day, while the 7 million victims of the 1932–33 famine will probably be remembered again in another ten years. **A monument located in a suitable center of the free world would be long-lasting: it would not only be a daily testament to our respect for these multitudes of innocent victims of the Red Muscovite tyranny but, since it is not possible to justly strike at the blood-stained and pillaging hands of the Red Muscovite Empire, would also serve as a powerful reminder of the threat posed to other countries of the free world by the tragedy which befell Ukrainian peasants during 1932–33**. Therefore, it is difficult to overestimate the significance of such a monument in exposing before the eyes of the world the murderous crime that Red Moscow inflicted on our people. It is not yet too late to undertake the task of erecting such a monument, which can first be announced during commemorations and demonstrations, with its actual construction beginning next year. Let us appropriately honor the seven million victims among our peasants; they albeit unarmed, fell while resisting the Red Muscovite pillager.[12]

Clearly, Mlakovyi's initiative reflects the impulse to construct a secular monument and one that would belong symbolically not only to the diaspora but to something more significant. As he writes, the Holodomor monument was to be a kind of memento, a symbolic sign present in the public sphere of the free world that would not belong exclusively to the Ukrainian diaspora "community of memory." His rhetoric is entirely different from that of Ses. He writes about "innocent victims" and the unpunished "Red Muscovite Empire," but, above all, he claims that a monument should be located in the city centre.

Both texts are exciting examples of private – and, notably, secular – initiatives to create a Holodomor monument. It was not a new idea, however, since Orthodox Ukrainians belonging to the North American diaspora had been engaged in building an Orthodox Memorial Church in South Bound Brook, NJ, for twenty years. Although many religious communities erected crosses in memory of Holodomor victims, the authors stress the need to establish a non-religious "place of memory," perhaps reflecting the need of non-religious people to commemorate the Holodomor as well. The divisions between the churches to which Ukrainians living abroad belonged may have played a role in this respect as well. Nevertheless, this secular and supra-communal idea for a monument would finally come to fruition during the fiftieth anniversary commemorations of the Great Famine 1932–33 in Canada.

The boundaries between secular and religious elements in the Great Famine memory sphere started to blur with the passage of time, giv-

[12] M[ykhailo] Mlakovyi, "Nekhai pam'iatnyk promovliaie," *Svoboda*, № 49 (March 16, 1973), p. 3.

ing rise to a common symbolic language characteristic for recalling this event in the social memory of Ukrainians the world over. At the same time, the significance of religious initiatives to the cultivation of memory about the Great Famine cannot be overestimated.

3.2 The Ukrainian Orthodox St. Andrew Memorial Church in South Bound Brook

The Ukrainian religious communities in both the Americas and Australia pursued a number of small initiatives, including building symbolic graves in parishes from the early 1950s and organizing small anniversary commemorations and meetings with Holodomor witnesses as well as local thematic exhibitions (Hamilton, Canada). But there is no doubt that the construction of the Ukrainian Orthodox St. Andrew Memorial Church in South Bound Brook is the Ukrainian diaspora's grandest initiative commemorating the Great Famine in North America in the 1950s and 1960s.

I would like to highlight several milestones in the ten-year construction history of the Holodomor memorial in South Bound Brook. I am interested in the architectural style proposed by the main architect of the project, Yuriy Kodak. It is vital to note this sanctuary's symbolic meaning as stipulated by the church hierarchs and the faithful. Attention should be paid to how this church functioned in the local community and the reaction of the Soviet authorities to this initiative. After all, a Ukrainian national pantheon was being built in South Bound Brook.

Art historians have suggested that Kodak's design was influenced by the sacral architecture along the Dnipro in Ukraine, as were most diasporic sacral buildings. Strictly speaking, Kodak's design is considered a formally expressive example of Cossack Baroque. For Vadym Kutsevych, it is a well-conceived interpretation that on the one hand, references traditional sacral buildings in Ukraine, and on the other, evokes the traditions of the new country of residence for Ukrainians who emigrated after World War II.[13] Kodak (whose real name was Yuriy Panasenko) obtained his art education in Kyiv before the war, which had a definitive impact on his artistic output in emigration. Since the Orthodox church in its conception was to be a pantheon to Ukraine's heroes and martyrs, a stylistic choice that referenced the Cossack aesthetics of sacral architecture seemed appropriate.

[13] Vadym Kutsevych, "Evoliutsiia khramobuduvannia v poselenniakh ukraïns'koï diaspory," *Ukraïns'ka akademiia mystetstva* 21 (2013), pp. 87–96.

Fig. 9. A photo of Surmach from one of her talks

Over the many years of the construction of the memorial, an event that was both significant and symbolic in nature took place, bringing the intentions of the builders of the church into sharper focus. Namely, in 1956, brick fragments that were brought from Ukraine by an American artist of Ukrainian descent, Yaroslava "Gloria" Surmach-Mills, were incorporated into the church's cornerstone. Known as Slavka Surmach in the diaspora, the artist was born in the US at the beginning of the twentieth century. Her father was the founder and for many years the owner of a Ukrainian bookshop in New York.[14] In her work, Surmach-Mills utilized elements of folk culture, including traditional Ukrainian embroidery. The young artist was among the first in the non-communist Ukrainian diaspora community to obtain a visa to visit the Soviet Union, and her first journey taking her to selected USSR republics was reported on by the diaspora press:

> Slavka Surmach, the American-born daughter of a known Ukrainian bookstore owner, M. Surmach, travelled to the most important cities of the Soviet Union between August 12 and September 2. The purpose of her journey was to view the Ukrainian folk painting collections held in Soviet museums, particularly painted Easter eggs. Ms. Surmach spent time in Leningrad, Moscow, at the Kyivan Cave Monastery, in museums of contemporary and folk art. During her stay in Ukraine, she had the opportunity to take many colour photographs. She returned via Vinnytsia, Ternopil, Lviv, and Uzhhorod, but without the chance to stop in any of them. Her train journey ended in Prague. On Sunday, October 14 Ms. Surmach organized an exhibition of photographs taken during her trip at the Ukrainian National Home in New York, accompanied by a relevant commentary.[15]

[14] "New Exhibition at The Ukrainian Museum. Yaroslava Surmach Mills: Retrospective," March 7–September 23, 2018, The Ukrainian Museum, accessed February 1, 2021, http://www.ukrainianmuseum.org/ex_180307_yaroslava.html.

[15] "Slavka Surmach vidbula poïzdku po Soviets'komu Soiuzi," *Svoboda*, № 194 (1956), p. 1.

Surmach documented her travels extensively in photographs and on her return home, shared her impressions during numerous meetings, lectures, and photography exhibits organized in Ukrainian community circles. Numerous announcements about such meetings can be found on the pages of the newspaper *Svoboda*:

> Slavka Surmach is coming to Chicago from New York to speak at the invitation of a branch of the League of Ukrainian Youth of North America on October 12. Her meetings enjoy high turnouts. She knows Ukraine well and, having been behind the Iron Curtain twice, has gathered fascinating materials for her talk, entitled "Ukraine Today" which is documented with photographs.[16]

The many meetings focusing on Surmach's trips to the historic homeland and the enthusiasm connected with them illustrate how the Ukrainian diaspora experienced its "Ukrainianness" in North America

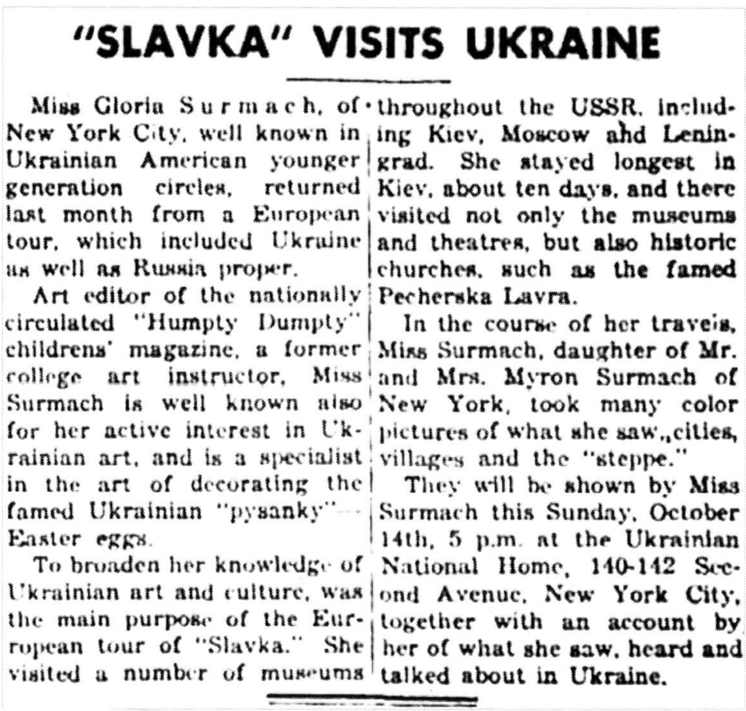

"SLAVKA" VISITS UKRAINE

Miss Gloria Surmach, of New York City, well known in Ukrainian American younger generation circles, returned last month from a European tour, which included Ukraine as well as Russia proper.

Art editor of the nationally circulated "Humpty Dumpty" childrens' magazine, a former college art instructor, Miss Surmach is well known also for her active interest in Ukrainian art, and is a specialist in the art of decorating the famed Ukrainian "pysanky" Easter eggs.

To broaden her knowledge of Ukrainian art and culture, was the main purpose of the European tour of "Slavka." She visited a number of museums throughout the USSR, including Kiev, Moscow and Leningrad. She stayed longest in Kiev, about ten days, and there visited not only the museums and theatres, but also historic churches, such as the famed Pecherska Lavra.

In the course of her travels, Miss Surmach, daughter of Mr. and Mrs. Myron Surmach of New York, took many color pictures of what she saw, cities, villages and the "steppe."

They will be shown by Miss Surmach this Sunday, October 14th, 5 p.m. at the Ukrainian National Home, 140-142 Second Avenue, New York City, together with an account by her of what she saw, heard and talked about in Ukraine.

Fig. 10. Invitation to a meeting with Gloria Surmach published in The Ukrainian Weekly

[16] Stepan Kuropas', "Shykahovska khronika," *Svoboda*, № 183 (1958), p. 3.

at that time. Continuity of generations is relevant in this context since Surmach belonged to the second generation of immigrants.

While visiting Kyiv, Gloria Surmach managed to visit the largest among its Orthodox churches. She took advantage of the opportunity to take with her fragments of bricks from two of the most important Orthodox churches for Ukrainian culture and identity, one of which was in ruins at the time (the Dormition Cathedral at Kyivan Cave Monastery). The brick fragments Surmach brought back to the US were treated as treasured relics, demonstrating that national and religious values were inseparable for the Ukrainian diaspora. The idea to

Fig. 11. Announcement of one of Surmach's talks

incorporate them in the building block of the planned church, in turn, speaks to the community's need for a symbolic connection to the lost historical homeland. The fragments also served as a symbol of the Orthodox places of worship that could not be rebuilt in Soviet Ukraine but only symbolically reconstructed abroad, such as in the form of the Memorial Church.

The fragments were incorporated into the building block on May 4, 1961, during a celebration at South Bound Brook that spoke to their symbolic significance and sanctified the event. The following description of these celebrations appeared in the newspaper *Svoboda*:

> The ceremonial act of incorporating bricks from the Sophia Cathedral and the Dormition Cathedral at Kyivan Cave Monastery into the walls of the Ukrainian Orthodox Memorial Church, in the picturesque setting of the state of New Jersey, which took place last Sunday, on the fourth of May, turned into a genuine widespread manifestation with several thousand people in attendance, including representatives of many central and local organizations. The entire Bound Brook area was taken with the celebration, with speakers broadcasting Ukrainian religious songs throughout the town. The day's ideal sunny weather lent itself to the occasion, which started at 9 a.m. with a procession of priests, parishioners, members of the women's sisterhood, and acolytes. The bricks were transferred, and a Holy Liturgy was celebrated in the already half-built memorial church. (...) All of the ceremonies were profoundly religious and patriotic in nature.[17]

The report on the event in the magazine *Ukraïns'ke pravoslavne slovo / Ukrainian Orthodox Word* stated:

> The act of incorporating bricks from the Sophia Cathedral and the Kyivan Cave Monastery shows us the deep significance of the idea to erect a Ukrainian Memorial-Church in the "Free World." First and foremost, it reveals the meaning behind the idea to incorporate in the walls of this temple bricks that come from the Dormition Cathedral, which was decimated by our nation's enemies in the process of Moscow's destruction of the oldest and greatest of Ukrainian temples, of which it is one. The walls of this temple have been the object of pious admiration for millions of Ukrainians over hundreds of years; within its walls, Ukrainian women have shed a river of tears while praying to the Mother of God to protect and safeguard their dearest ones and for a better fate for the whole nation. Why does this temple lay in ruins... Some of these ruins were brought to the USA in 1956 by a Ukrainian girl who was

[17] "Tysiachi narodu vzialy uchast' u vrochystostiakh bilia Tserkvy-Pam'iatnyka v Bavnd Bruku [vmurovannia tsehlyn z kyïvs'kykh tserkov u stiny tserkvy-pam'iatnyka peretvorylos' u vsenarodnu manifestatsiiu]," *Svoboda*, № 104 (1961), p. 1.

born here (Slavka Surmach), for her pure heart sensed the holiness of the Ukrainian Jerusalem.[18]

In its conception, the goal of building a Memorial Church was to remind future generations of Ukrainians raised in the emigration of their national roots. The burial there of many eminent Ukrainians who had settled in the US and Canada also served this purpose. The site consequently became a pantheon of Ukrainian emigration – a "place of memory." *Ukraïns'ke pravoslavne slovo / Ukrainian Orthodox Word* was writing at the time:

> Therefore, it is the sacred duty of Ukrainians in the free world to restore their glory and erect this church in the free world as well as to raise it as testimony of the gratitude of the Ukrainian spirit.
>
> All of these priceless treasures will be displayed in a museum beside the memorial church to, first of all, inspire our children and grandchildren to love all that was dear to their forefathers, grandparents and parents, and, secondly, to reveal the Ukrainian nation's past to the free world.[19]

This was an important undertaking at a time when the cultivation of Ukrainian history was unthinkable in the homeland. The fact that the church's construction was entirely financed by the faithful was also proof that diverse diaspora circles could unite in the realization of a common endeavour, doggedly striving over the course of decades toward their noble goal. The significance of this initiative for the Ukrainian diaspora could be fully appreciated only years later. On the pages of *Ukraïns'ke pravoslavne slovo / Ukrainian Orthodox Word*, the precise goals of the Memorial Church's construction were published in point form on multiple occasions:

The Memorial Church – is the joint monument on the graves of our forefathers, and family members and those dearest to us.	Церква-Пам'ятник – це спільний монумент над могилами наших попередників та рідних і найдорожчих нам.
The Memorial Church – is the expression of our deep respect for the heroes and martyrs of our Ukrainian nation.	Церква-Пам'ятник – це вияв глибокої пошани до героїв і мучеників українського народу.

[18] *Ukraïns'ke pravoslavne slovo / Ukrainian Orthodox Word*, № 5 (June 1961), p. 10.
[19] *Ukraïns'ke pravoslavne slovo / Ukrainian Orthodox Word*, № 9 (September 1965), p. 10.

The Memorial Church – is a very humble cross on the graves of millions of victims of the Great Famine ploughed over by the enemy.

Церква-Пам'ятник – це дуже скромний хрест над зораними ворогом могилами мільйонів-жертв Великого Голоду.

The Memorial Church – is merely a humble attempt to recreate the grandeur of the Ukrainian churches destroyed by Moscow in the twentieth century alone.

Церква-Пам'ятник – це лише скромна спроба відтворити велич українських святинь, що їх зруйнувала Москва тільки в XX столітті.

The Memorial Church – is the creation of the free Ukrainian spirit, inseparably connected to ancient Ukrainian Church construction.

Церква-Пам'ятник – це твір вільного українського духа, нерозривно пов'язаний з давнім українським церковним будівництвом.

The Memorial Church – is our humble contribution to the treasury of spiritual and cultural assets of the US.

Церква-Пам'ятник – це наш скромний вклад в скарбницю духовних і культурних вартостей США.

The Memorial Church – is evidence that its builders and sponsors lived not only for themselves, but also for the future generations of our nation.

Церква-Пам'ятник – це свідоцтво, що її будівничі й фундатори жили не тільки для себе, але й для прийдешніх поколінь нашого народу.

The process of building the church, which took place between 1955 and 1965, was covered in detail on the pages of *Ukraïns'ke pravoslavne slovo / Ukrainian Orthodox Word*, the press organ of the consistory. In one issue, an appeal was featured underlining the importance of creating a "place of memory" that would serve as a sanctuary and a pilgrimage destination for Ukrainians living in the "free world":

> We have written more than once about the significance for every emigrant community of a spiritual connection with the homeland and its people. We have written at length about one form of such connection in particular – the necessity of a strong bond with previous generations of the Ukrainian nation, especially with the outstanding individuals whose life's work, and on more than one occasion personal sacrifice, shaped the distinct phases and periods of our national history. As an organ of the Orthodox Church, our monthly has called for especially honoring

[20] *Ukraïns'ke pravoslavne slovo / Ukrainian Orthodox Word,* № 10 (October 1965), p. 3.

> the memory of the deceased who had served our nation. (…) In sharing our reverence for the dead, the idea to build a Memorial Church as an external manifestation of our bond with our deceased kith and kin as well as the heroes and martyrs of the Ukrainian nation, whose numbers run in the millions, was born on the pages of the *Ukrainian Orthodox Word*. Many saw the idea behind erecting a monument on their mostly unknown graves as their testament, and set an example through their actions and, first and foremost, generous donations for the construction of the Memorial Church, donations that could often be referred to as a princely sum. With gratitude to these people of good will, the work on our Memorial Church began ten years ago, but unfortunately its construction still awaits completion. It remains unfinished because many of our people have insufficiently felt the testament of our deceased kith and kin, especially those who laid down their lives for us all (…). For it is extremely hard to utter the whole truth about there being no small number of people amongst us who have been generously blessed by God with earthly goods but have a deaf conscience and a cold heart toward that which is homegrown, akin, and Ukrainian.[21]

The publication also printed letters of readers who, having donated to the construction effort, called on others to support the initiative. I was particularly drawn to those that pointed to the necessity of commemorating the Holodomor by supporting the building of the Memorial Church:

> I am astonished by how our forefathers built temples as grand as the Pochaiv Monastery, the Kyivan Cave Monastery, St. Sophia Cathedral and St. Volodymyr Cathedral as well as many, many other wonderful buildings; where did our impoverished people manage to find the money for their construction. You wonder and become embarrassed that we, political émigrés who live in prosperity never imagined, cannot share a few dollars to build a monument to the seven million of our starved compatriots.[22]

This letter's author is Makar Sydorenko (1891–1960), who was born near Poltava and experienced the Great Famine directly, losing one of his children, his daughter Nadia.[23] In his letter, the author mentions that he had, within his means, financially supported the Memorial Church's construction. He does not mention, however, his personal experience of the Holodomor, although this is the only letter to the editors printed in *Ukraïns'ke pravoslavne slovo / Ukrainian Orthodox Word* that presents the

---

[21] *Ukraïns'ke pravoslavne slovo / Ukrainian Orthodox Word*, № 7 (July 1965), p. 4.

[22] *Ukraïns'ke pravoslavne slovo / Ukrainian Orthodox Word*, № 9 (July 1960), p. 15.

[23] "In Memory of Helen Dobusz 1928–2017," Hagan-Chamberlain Funeral Home, March 23, 2019, accessed February 1, 2021, https://hagan-chamberlain.com/tribute/details/477/Helen-Dobusz/obituary.html#content-start.

Memorial Church as a monument exclusively to the famine's victims, rather than the numerous victims among Ukrainians in the course of their nation's history. The author writes with a heavy heart that he will probably not live to hear the sound of the newly built temple's bells as he is gravely ill, but he expresses the hope that his appeal will not leave Ukrainians indifferent and encourages them to make donations in support of the church's construction.

In some issues of the periodical, passionate appeals about the financial difficulties that slowed down the building's completion were also printed, as well as additional letters from donors.

Чи ви, дорогий читачу, вже зложили свою пожертву на будову Церкви-Пам'ятника, що її УПЦерква в ЗДА будує на молитовний спомин про наших найближчих та героїв і мучеників українського народу? Наколи ні — зробіть це негайно!

Fig. 12. An appeal for financial support for the construction of a Memorial Church in South Bound Brook, NJ, US

One such note is of special interest in the context of my reflections. First, it provides evidence of intergenerational transfer among the Ukrainian diaspora and the inheritance of a Ukrainian identity based on attachment to specific values and their forefathers' historical experience. Second, it establishes the role that the Memorial Church played in informed and patriotically oriented families. The note in question, published in *Ukraïns'ke pravoslavne slovo / Ukrainian Orthodox Word* in 1960, provided information about a fundraiser organized by the brothers George (Yurko) and Peter (Petrus') Feshchenko-Chopivsky, who raised $58 USD through a familial collection. Peter Chopivsky (1952–2010), who became a well-known American physician and academic,[24] was eight years old at the time and donated three dollars from his piggy bank to the cause; his brother George Chopivsky (b. 1947), now a respected lawyer and businessman and thirteen at the time, gave six dollars and fifty cents of his savings. They were the sons of Dr. Yuriy Chopivsky (1923–88)[25] and Sophia Chopivsky (née Klepachivsky),[26] who, along with other family members (e.g., their grandparents Maria and Konstatyn Klepachivsky (1887–1979), who in 1917 was President of the National Bank of Ukraine), also participated in their children's Easter fundraiser.[27] Both Yuriy Chopivsky and his wife were interred at the cemetery in South Bound Brook, and their son Peter was laid to rest beside them in 2010.[28]

---

[24] "Dr. Peter Chopivsky. Notice," *The Washington Post*, April 22, 2010, https://www.legacy.com/obituaries/washingtonpost/obituary.aspx?fhid=2177&n=peter-chopivsky&pid=142082591.

[25] His father was prof. Ivan Feshchenko-Chopivsky (1884–1952). At the end of February 1918, he was appointed Minister of Trade and Industry in Vsevolod Holubovych's government and in 1919 Vice-Premier and Minister of the Economy in Serhii Ostapenko's government. In 1922 he was appointed professor of metallurgy and metallography at the Academy of Mining and Metallurgy in Cracow. After the end of World War II, he was arrested by the NKVD and deported to a labor camp in Abez in the Komi Republic, where he died of exhaustion.

[26] Oleksandr Panchenko, "Slovo pro rodyny Klepachivs'kykh ta Chopivs'kykh," *Svoboda*, № 31 (July 30, 2010), pp. 19, 22.

[27] *Ukraïns'ke pravoslavne slovo / Ukrainian Orthodox Word* (1960), № 5, pp. 17–8.

[28] The Chopivsky-Klepachivsky family was the pride of Ukrainian society in the USA. In numerous articles published about them in the *Svoboda* newspaper, one may learn more about, among other things, the organizers of the mentioned collection at Easter 1960. A write-up appeared in *Svoboda* in 1978 to mark Petro Chopivsky's PhD defence. See: "D-r Petro Feshchenko-Chopivskyi zakinchyv medychni studiï," *Svoboda*, № 169 (August 11, 1978), p. 4. About subsequent academic successes in 1981 the following was written: "Dr Petro Chopivsky was raised in a Christian family, which is why in adopting the religious principles of his parents he leads a religious-spiritual life and belongs to the Ukrainian Orthodox Church, upholding the principles of our Orthodox-religious life.' See H.S., "Kaliforniia zbahatylas' ukraïns'koiu profesional'noiu syloiu," *Svoboda*, № 227 (December 2, 1981), p. 4.

The same note also mentions George (Yurko) Wyhinny from Chicago, who donated three dollars for the building of the Memorial Church. George Wyhinny, M.D. is the son of Dr. Peter Wyhinny (1916–2009) and the father of George William Wyhinny, an American film actor and producer.[29] George William Wyhinny graduated from St. Volodymyr School of Ukrainian Studies,[30] and today addresses the subject of the Holodomor in his creative work[31] and also shares information about the historical event.[32] These examples illustrate how the issue of the Memorial Church's construction connected different generations and how the theme of the Holodomor linked with this "place of memory" became an important issue for subsequent generations of Ukrainians that were not directly involved in the initiative.

Families such as the ones mentioned here were not numerous, however. For many years, the monument's construction was supported largely by the same set of families that donated resources to the extent of their means and sometimes – beyond. Fundraisers and collections were organized to support construction. In 1960, a thirty-minute film entitled *Living Water* was produced about the Ukrainian Orthodox Church in the US, and collections for the Memorial Church's construction were organized at its screenings. The film was screened in English and passed from parish to parish, with individual tickets priced at $15 US dollars. One issue of the *Ukraïns'ke pravoslavne slovo / Ukrainian Orthodox Word* includes a letter from a parishioner who writes that he does not regret donating money from his pension for the completion of the Memorial Church built to honour the victims of the Great Famine in Ukraine.[33]

The Orthodox Church was finally consecrated on October 10, 1965.[34] The editors of *Ukraïns'ke pravoslavne slovo / Ukrainian Orthodox Word* published an article recalling the ceremony, with its first two paragraphs of particular interest here:

---

[29] "Peter Wyhinny Ph.D.," *Chicago Tribune*, August 6, 2009, accessed February 1, 2021, https://www.legacy.com/obituaries/chicagotribune/obituary.aspx?n=peter-wyhinny&pid=131004416.

[30] "Congratulations, Graduates!" *The Ukrainian Weekly*, № 29 (July 18, 2004), p. 9.

[31] "Holodomor Remembrance Flame presented at Toronto's City Hall," *The Ukrainian Weekly*, № 19 (May 11, 2008), p. 11.

[32] "Hunger for Truth: Illuminating the Hidden History of the Holodomor: Symposium Commemorating the Ukrainian Genocide of 1932–1933: California State University, Fresno, Henry Madden Library," Fresno State, October 5–6, 2017, p. 9, accessed February 1, 2021, http://www.fresnostate.edu/socialsciences/historydept/documents/Holodomor-Symposium-web.pdf.

[33] *Ukraïns'ke pravoslavne slovo / Ukrainian Orthodox Word*, № 9 (1960), p. 15.

[34] "Speech by Archbishop Mstyslav at the dedication of St. Andrew Memorial Church (Ukrainian)," October 10, 1965, audio, 13:15, UHEC, accessed February 1, 2021, https://www.ukrhec.org/collections/archives/recorded-sound/speech-archbishop-mstyslav-dedication-st-andrew-memorial-church.

Fig. 13. Memorial Church in South Bound Brook, NJ, US (1965)

> The pathway to October 10, 1965, the day that the Memorial Church was consecrated, has been long and arduous. Initially, the very idea of building a Memorial Church in memory of the millions of bodies concealed by our nation's enemies in graves and out of sight of the human eye was generally not understood by Ukrainians living abroad. The number of people who believed in and realized this initiative grew slowly. This was due to many reasons, beginning with denominational differences and ending with organizational and political views. Our monthly has been the most active in disseminating the idea, with the remainder of the Ukrainian (including Orthodox) press limiting itself to sporadically chronicling the progress of construction. Some journals openly attacked the idea of building a memorial church, seeing it as the product of an ailing imagination or a matter of personal interest for a few individuals. These media outlets – consciously or not – invariably assumed the role of mouthpieces for the Soviet press, which understood the hostile message behind the memorial church from the start and fought it with all means at its disposal. **To recall, half a year ago someone in Canada and the US was widely disseminating an issue of the Kyivan satirical magazine *Perets'* [Pepper], which addressed the construction of the memorial church and claimed that it would "never get off the ground." The issue was bought, sought out, and borrowed by many people...**
>
> Nonetheless, Sunday, October 10, 1965, showed that the hissing of contemporary *Peppers, Octobers,* and *Soviet Ukraines* and other *Homelands*[35] had accelerated the idea's realization and galvanized people of good will, those dignified and unafraid, people of humble heart and pure mind, and, most important, people wholly devoted to serving Ukraine in all places and circumstances. As a result, October 10 became a day of triumph and victory for the free and untethered Ukrainian spirit, a quintessentially Ukrainian day that erased many existing differences between us, a day that will certainly shorten the path to a Universal Ukrainian Easter, meaning the day of Ukraine's liberation from captivity. It is only in this way that the day of the consecration of the Memorial Church will be remembered by those fortunate enough to participate directly in this immense celebration.
>
> This day shall also remain deeply significant for future generations, becoming their signpost of an enlightened goal – a free and sovereign Ukraine dependent only on the will of our people.[36]

My attention was drawn to the author's remark about a special issue of the Ukrainian satirical magazine *Perets'*, which was passed from hand to hand since it was entirely devoted to the construction of the Orthodox Church in South Bound Brook. Verifying this information may seem irrelevant, but it is in fact of utmost value. *Perets'* was one

[35] All words in italics are the names of some of the largest newspapers and magazines published in Soviet Ukraine at that time, namely: *Perets', Radians'ka Ukraïna, Batkivshchyna, Zhovten'*.

[36] *Ukraïns'ke pravoslavne slovo / Ukrainian Orthodox Word,* № 11–12 (1965), p. 11.

of the best-known satirical magazines published in the Soviet Union, in circulation since the 1920s. According to Kateryna Yeremieieva, it served as a propaganda arm of the Communist Party from the 1950s to 1970s when Fedir Makivchuk was its editor-in-chief.[37] The fact that *Perets'* covered, albeit in a manner intended to be humorous, Archbishop Mstyslav's initiative to build an Orthodox church in South Bound Brook meant that this information reached millions of homes in Ukraine. To verify the authenticity of information printed in *Ukraïns'ke pravoslavne slovo / Ukrainian Orthodox Word,* I performed an archival search of issues of *Perets'* published from 1955 to 1965. The subject of Ukrainians abroad appeared on its pages frequently in those years, with the newspaper mocking the nationalism, backwardness, and religiosity of the Ukrainian diaspora in the US and Canada. There was no special issue devoted exclusively to the topic of the Memorial Church's construction during this period, although texts about Ukrainian émigrés, including Mstyslav and his initiative, did appear.

During this time, Steve Macievich (1909–71) contributed his lampoons to *Perets'* under the pseudonym "Mykyta Vishta." He came from Volhynia and emigrated to Canada as a teenager in 1928. He was an active member of the pro-communist (at that time) Association of United Ukrainian Canadians (AUUC) and for *Perets'* wrote mainly satirically about a rival diaspora organization, the Ukrainian Canadian Committee (UCC). His articles were supplemented by caricatures of the Ukrainian diaspora in Canada, and especially of UCC members, resembling the figures from the paintings of Russian artist Ilya Repin. Significantly, his caricatures were deliberately drawn using two colors, yellow and blue, referencing the national colors of Ukraine that had been supplanted by red and sky blue during communist times. In the 1960s, Macievich reported primarily on political events in the US and Canada without paying particular attention to religious or social initiatives realized by the diaspora, including the construction of the Memorial Church in South Bound Brook.

Yurii Melnychuk (1921–63), a Soviet publicist living in Lviv, was another key figure at *Perets'* during this period. His biographical entry in *Entsyklopediia Ukraïnoznavstva* [Encyclopedia of Ukraine] states that "his work was distinguished especially by his indiscriminate lampoons of the Catholic Church and 'bourgeois nationalists.'[38] In an anniversary edition of *Perets'* dedicated to the newspaper's writers, his caricature was accompanied by a four-line poem characterizing his work for this

---

[37] Kateryna Ieremieieva, *Byty satyroiu. Zhurnal "Perets'" v sotsiokul'turnomu seredovyshchi Radians'koï Ukraïny* (Kharkiv, 2018), p. 51.

[38] "Melnychuk Iurii (1921–63)," in *Entsyklopediia ukraïnoznavstva. Perevydannia v Ukraïni,* vol. 4 (Lviv, 1994), p. 1516.

publication. Yurii Melnychuk is depicted as a knight in shining armor fighting against Ukrainian nationalism abroad. On the tip of his lance, which is red and sharpened into the nib of a fountain pen, hangs an atrocious figure clad in Cossack attire. It was this very Yurii Melnychuk who authored two of the articles about the construction of an Orthodox church initiated by Ukrainian emigrants in the US and Canada.

The author of the letter published in the newspaper *Ukraïns'ke pravoslavne slovo / Ukrainian Orthodox Word* was likely thinking about Melnychuk's first article to appear in *Perets'*, which was published in 1960.[39] It is an extensive piece that "satirically and indiscriminately" describes the figure of Archbishop Mstyslav (Skrypnyk) and his initiative to build an Orthodox church. The satire, announced on the issue's cover, is printed on the centrefold and the subsequent page and supplemented with a cartoon of a clergyman rolling around over bags full of money.

Fig. 14. Caricature of Yurii Melnychuk, the author of texts about the Ukrainian diaspora in Canada

[39] A review of the content of the *Perets'* magazine in 1955–66 indicates that there was no other article on the subject.

A year later, in 1961, the editors published another text by the same author on the subject of the building of an Orthodox church in Windsor, ON, in Canada, which referenced his previous article about South Bound Brook:

> Archbishop Mstyslav, for instance, ten years ago or so, conducted a fundraiser in Canada to build St. Nicholas' Monastery and, once the money was raised, built himself a villa. The so-called high-priest and high-impostor moved to the US and started to build himself a memorial church in Bound Brook. Having assured the faithful that the church's construction would cost $100,000, this penny-pincher extracted well over half a million dollars from them, while the building barely reaches above its foundations.[40]

From 1965 to 1966, after the Memorial Church had been completed, the subject disappeared from the newspapers. Without further research, it is impossible to say whether the temple in South Bound Brook ceased to matter to the editorial board or whether the silence was merely the result of the death in 1963 of Yurii Melnychuk, the author of the cited articles.

Fig. 15. Caricature of Archbishop Mstyslav published in the magazine Perets'

Regardless, the church in South Bound Brook played an essential role in shaping the Holodomor culture of memory in the diaspora. The story of this creation would be incomplete without attention to other commemorations related to the construction of the church and the anniversary of this historical event. The Memorial Church in South Bound Brook in the early 1960s became a central "place of memory" of the Holodomor and the commemoration of the thirtieth anniversary,

Fig. 16. Caricature of Archbishop Mstyslav published in the magazine Perets'

[40] *Perets'*, № 16 (1961), p. 4.

За гроші наївних православних українських емігрантів у США архієпископ Мстислав купив у 1956 році один, а в 1958 році другий шикарний автомобіль і зареєстрував у Тремтоні, Н. Дж., теж, як свою приватну власність.

Православні українці в Америці щораз дошкульніше відчувають широку натуру і хижу вдачу свого архієпископа. Збирав він гроші на будівництво приюту для старців і сиріт і не збудував нічого, збрехав. Проголосивши в 1953 році проект будови церкви, в підземеллі якої повинен бути обладнаний мавзолей для 62 «видатних» небіжчиків (кажуть, що це він задумав для себе бомбосховище на випадок війни), архієпископ Мстислав оголосив кошторис будівництва на 100 тисяч доларів. Щороку він безконтрольно підвищував кошти будови приблизно на 100 тисяч доларів і так дійшов до півмільйона доларів. А кінця будівництву ще не видно. Навіть у церковній пресі лунають голоси, що будівництво церкви в Савд-Бавнд-Брук Мстислав веде «споловини», що на тому будівництві він добре гріє свої загребущі руки. І на це, виходить, нема ніякого ліку. Бо що, справді, має робити сердешний архієпископ, як він не може не красти. Це вже, мабуть, від бога такий хист у нього.

Ще архієпископ Мстислав мріє про те, щоб записати всі церкви і весь маєток УАПЦ в Америці, як свою приватну власність. І що думаєте, він наполегливий, він може досягти свого. Вже й нині він має в Америці таку славу, що з ним перший-ліпший гангстер під злочинницький ростомір не стане.

Бо в усіх діяннях архієпископа Мстислава— дихання злодійського генія.

Ю. МЕЛЬНИЧУК.

Fig. 17. Lampoon of Archbishop Mstyslav by Yurii Melnychuk, published in the magazine Perets'

which took place June 9, 1963, in the still unfinished church building. The church collected names of victims and donations for services at the Memorial Church.[41] The description of the commemorative event describes the hierarchs leading thirty-seven priests (the main celebrant was Metropolitan Ioan) and four thousand faithful in the commemoration, including hundreds of youth from Plast, SUM and ODUM, followed by a banquet with the President of the UNR in exile and the heads of all Ukrainian organizations as well as many Ukrainian Catholics.[42] It appears to be a perfect example of a "place of memory" created for the entire diaspora. The commemorations firmly rooted the image of the Memorial Church in connection with the Famine.

---

41 *Ukraïns'ke pravoslavne slovo / Ukrainian Orthodox Word,* № 7 (1963), pp. 14–6.

42 *Ukraïns'ke pravoslavne slovo / Ukrainian Orthodox Word,* № 8 (1963), pp. 14–5.

The ceremony combined secular and religious elements, as we have seen in earlier ceremonies. In his speech, Archbishop Mstyslav referred to the Ten Commandments and also encouraged all present to sing the secular song *Cranes* [also *You see, my brother*].[43] The sublime atmosphere, in which the hymn *Memory Eternal* (a funeral hymn in the Orthodox Church) had been sung a moment earlier, shifted as Mstyslav turned to a song with historical significance. The song of the Sich Riflemen, written by Bohdan Lepky in Cracow in 1910, ends with the phrase "in a foreign country I will die" (*v chuzhyni umru*). Lepky had been impressed by the Polish national uprisings in the nineteenth century and moved by the fact that the Polish emigration would die in a foreign land. During World War II, Lepky's song became an anthem of the Ukrainian Insurgent Army. It also became a symbol connecting Ukrainian emigrants to their spiritual homeland and was sung at burials. The combination of these symbols, equally important for the identity of the Ukrainian diaspora, is further indication that from its very beginning, South Bound Brook was a national temple and a national pantheon.

Fig. 18. Holodomor commemoration and blessing of graves at St. Andrew Church and Cemetery, South Bound Brook, NJ, US (May 6, 1973)

[43] Ibid., p. 14.

Ten years later, the church and the cemetery in South Bound Brook were the venue for the Great Famine's fortieth-anniversary commemorations for many Orthodox Ukrainians in the US. In 1973, Metropolitan Mstyslav, who lived in South Bound Brook, prepared a pastoral letter to mark this anniversary and announced the establishment of a Remembrance Day for the Victims of the Great Famine:

> I decree this year's Antipascha (Sunday of St. Thomas), when our Holy Orthodox Church has prayed through the ages for the souls of our laudable forefathers and the just, the martyrs, and the heroes of Ukraine, as a day of national remembrance of those who suffered and were martyred by the Great Famine. Also on this Antipascha, rising in highest and fervent prayer in all Ukrainian churches of the Free World, everywhere we are joined as one with Christ, and foremost in that strongest bastion of our people – the Ukrainian Autocephalous Orthodox Church! The main memorial commemorations of the Great Famine's fortieth anniversary are to take place at the centre of Ukrainian Orthodoxy outside our country's borders, St. Andrew parish in South Bound Brook, New Jersey, US, where on Antipascha Sunday, the sixth of May, a commemorative national Prayer Service will be celebrated at the cemetery beside the Memorial Church.[44]

While *Svoboda* published the pastoral letter, the Australian publication *Vil'na dumka* [Free Thought] also included a short notice about the Great Famine commemorations in South Bound Brook.[45] The notice states that the solemn Requiem Mass, celebrated on Antipascha Sunday, namely, the Sunday after the Resurrection (Easter) in the Orthodox Church dedicated to remembering the dearly departed, had attracted some five thousand faithful wishing to participate in the scheduled memorial commemorations. Among those gathered were representatives of youth organizations as well as Ukrainian military veterans. In the presence of numerous clergy and laymen, Metropolitan Mstyslav recalled the events of the Great Famine and emphasized that Ukrainians should not lose heart and faith since the moment of historical justice would arrive and the Holodomor's perpetrators would be punished.[46]

---

[44] "Arkhypastyrs'ke poslannia z nahody 40-oï richnytsi velykoho holodu," *Svoboda*, № 51 (March 20, 1973), p. 2.

[45] "Zhalobni urochystosti. Piat' tysiach ukraïntsiv z'ïkhalosia do Bovnd Bruk," *Vil'na dumka*, № 22 (May 27, 1973), p. 1.

[46] Holodomor commemoration and blessing of graves at St. Andrew Church and Cemetery, South Bound Brook, NJ, May 6, 1973, private video from Mykola Holovs'ko, 13:08, UHEC_2012-6-20_MP01.

Fig. 19. Holodomor commemoration and blessing of graves at St. Andrew Church and Cemetery, South Bound Brook, NJ, US (May 6, 1973)

Undoubtedly, as a "place of memory" South Bound Brook combines both religious (or even ecumenical) and secular aspects. During the opening ceremony, the placing of Holodomor victims on par with those who lost their lives fighting for Ukrainian independence bestowed upon their demise the quality of national loss, experienced in a deeply religious manner. The manifestations accompanying successive anniversaries in that "place of memory" were of a secular and patriotic nature. The "communities of memory" centred around this church-monument erected it at their own expense as an embodiment of their own vision of what the Holodomor meant for Ukrainians as a nation. In other words, the religious symbols and iconography were used to create a profoundly spiritual representation of the Holodomor. And this is the essence of the uniqueness of that "place of memory."

3.3 The wave of Holodomor monuments in the 1980s

Around the world, the commemorative initiatives on the Holodomor's fiftieth anniversary included the erection of monuments, both religious and secular. The "places of memory" established at that time were diverse in terms of iconography. Many "communities of memory" expressed a desire to erect monuments, and although not all such initiatives were realized, the sheer extent of expression speaks to the process of Holodomor symbolization in public spaces. The fact that such initiatives continued to be funded for the most part with donations of private citizens demonstrates the importance of having a "place of memory" for Ukrainians living abroad.

In the wake of success in attracting the attention of the highest levels of the American government to the subject of the Great Famine, diaspora communities in the US created new "places of memory" during the 1980s, which included monuments and symbolic burial places. There were also cases in which the emotions connected to the Holodomor's sorrowful anniversary resulted in alterations to planned Ukrainian monuments.

One of the more interesting initiatives was the project to build a Ukrainian National Monument Mausoleum in the US. Information about this project was provided in *The Ukrainian Weekly* newspaper in 1982.[47]

Artist's conception of monument-mausoleum.

Fig. 20. Design of the Ukrainian National Monument-Mausoleum

Nicolas Andreadis, an engineer, came up with the idea for a mausoleum-monument that was Byzantine in style and modeled on a Greek cross. The planned entrance gate was shaped like the Ukrainian trident (*tryzub*), while the interior was to be decorated with mosaics featuring a national and patriotic theme. An eternal flame was to burn in the mausoleum, with the exterior finished in the yellow and blue colours of Ukraine.[48] Initially, it was not the intent of the project to memor-

[47] "DC mausoleum project okayed," *The Ukrainian Weekly*, № 46 (November 14, 1982), p. 11.

[48] *Homin Ukraïny*, August 24, 1983, p. 16; "Vladyka S. Sulyk poblahoslovyt' zemliu pid budovu Pam'iatnyka-Mavzoleiu," *Svoboda*, № 144 (August 2, 1983), p. 1.

ialize the Holodomor's victims. As a result of the events marking the Famine's fiftieth anniversary, however, modifications were made to the initial design to include a commemorative plaque on one of the main walls, marking a symbolic burial place for those who perished during the Great Famine. On September 10, 1983, Metropolitan of the Ukrainian Greek-Catholic Church Stephen Sulyk consecrated the ground where the Ukrainian National Monument Mausoleum was to stand.[49] In contrast to the Orthodox church in South Bound Brook, NJ, this mausoleum-monument was to be dedicated to those martyred for Ukraine's freedom and was to be built on land at Cedar Hill Cemetery in Suitland, MD (section F, 4111 Pennsylvania Avenue).[50] Ultimately, however, the project was never realized.

Meanwhile, in November 1983, a memorial stone was ceremoniously unveiled at Eisenhower Park in Westbury on Long Island, NY, in remembrance of the victims of the Holodomor. *Svoboda* newspaper reported on this event as follows:

> On Sunday, November 27, a monument to the victims of the Great Famine will be unveiled and consecrated at Eisenhower Park. (...) The monument was designed by the artist Ihor Kuchmak, the son of the deceased master Ivan Kuchmak. Eisenhower Park is the largest park on Long Island, where various events, political gatherings, and ethnic festivals take place, including the annual "Ukrainian Evening" that usually attracts between ten thousand and twenty thousand people.[51]

A year later, the Ukrainian community in Wilmington, DE, impressed by the fiftieth-anniversary commemorations of the Great Famine, decided to commemorate the historical event in their parish.[52] On July 15, 1984, a monument in the form of a black stele was raised beside Sts. Peter & Paul Ukrainian Orthodox Church. Around the same time (on July 7), an oak tree was ceremoniously planted on the grounds of a Roman Catholic university in the Bridgeport diocese – Sacred Heart University in Fairfield, CT – and a memorial stone of black granite was placed beside it to commemorate the seven million victims of the Ukrainian Famine.[53]

---

[49] *Homin Ukraïny*, October 19, 1983, p. 13.

[50] "Sulyk officiates at DC mausoleum groundbreaking service," *The Ukrainian Weekly*, № 40 (October 2, 1983), p. 3.

[51] Kateryna Myts'o, "Bude postavleno pam'iatnyk zhertvam Velykoho holodu v Ukraïni na Long Ailendi," *Svoboda*, № 205 (November 23, 1983), p. 3.

[52] Vasyl' Sheremeta, "Parafiia U.P. Tserkvy m. Vilminhton, Del. zhertvam zamuchenym holodovoiu smertiu v 1932–1933 rr.," *Ukraïns'ke pravoslavne slovo / Ukrainian Orthodox Word*, № 9 (September 1984), p. 28.

[53] "Monument to famine victims dedicated in Bridgeport," *The Ukrainian Weekly*, № 31 (July 29, 1984), p. 3.

Fig. 21. A memorial stone for the victims of the Holodomor in Eisenhower Park, Westbury, NY, US (1983)

There was also a plan to unveil a monument to the Great Famine in Los Angeles in 1983, but bureaucratic formalities delayed its construction in the centre of the city by three years. The monument, designed and created by Taras Kozbur, was unveiled ceremoniously in May of 1986. *Svoboda* described the event as follows:

> The commemorative plaque inscribed "In memory of the seven million people who fell victim to Russian communists. To the memory of those deprived of freedom, property and life on the order of the Soviet author-

ities during 1932–33." With the commemorative plaque, the sculpture depicts an emaciated human figure extending its arms to the sky and a grief-stricken woman bent over her three children.[54]

Fig. 22. The Holodomor monument by Taras Kozbur in Los Angeles, US (1986)

It is worth noting that the diaspora press, in commenting on the fiftieth-anniversary commemorations, recalled that the Memorial Church in South Bound Brook was hitherto the only monument to the victims of the Ukrainian tragedy. *The Ukrainian Weekly* published an extensive interview with Metropolitan Mstyslav about the initiative he realized

[54] "V Los Andzhelesi vidsloneno pam'iatnyk zhertvam shtuchnoho holodu," *Svoboda*, № 97 (May 23, 1986), p. 1.

in the 1950s and 1960s. These articles preceded the building of monuments in Edmonton and Winnipeg in Canada.

The Ukrainian diaspora in Canada actively joined in the commemorations of the fiftieth anniversary of the Holodomor. Two monuments of great iconographic interest were erected. On October 23, 1983, on the initiative of Canadian Ukrainians, a monument to the Great Famine's victims designed by Ludmilla Temertey was unveiled in Edmonton, the provincial capital of Alberta. A year later, another monument, designed by Roman Kowal, was erected in Winnipeg, Manitoba's provincial capital.[55] These two projects were unique for two reasons: it was the first time that a design was chosen through a competition, and both monuments were secular in character and located in their respective city centres rather than on the grounds of a Ukrainian parish.

On the wave of these events, the Ukrainian community in Toronto considered the building of a monument along with a research centre and museum, with which it would have earned a first-class ranking among the already existing sites of Holodomor remembrance. Members of the Ukrainian Canadian Congress, Toronto Branch, considered several potential locations, in consultation with the city government. The idea in Toronto was to build more than just a monument (the Edmonton initiative, aimed at immortalizing the event in an urban space, did not foresee the creation of a museum); the proposal was for a "place of memory" that would serve as a model for commemorating the Great Famine, including the messages that needed to be conveyed.

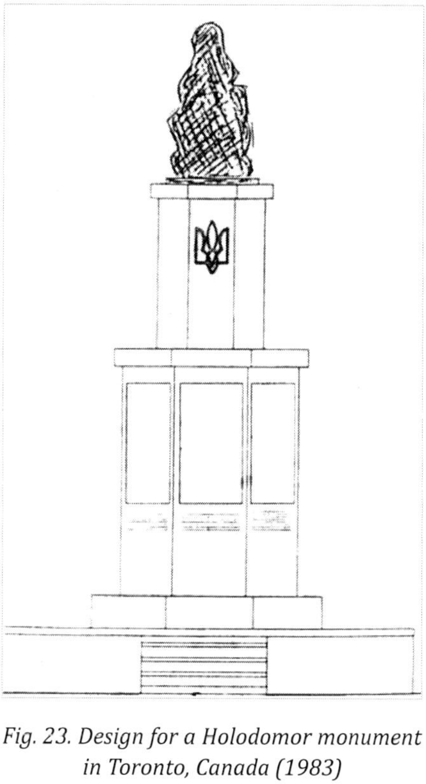

Fig. 23. Design for a Holodomor monument in Toronto, Canada (1983)

The monument was to stand over nine metres high (thirty-one feet) with a sculpture topping an octagonal base. The statue was to depict a family dying of hunger, while the

[55] Oleksandr Shevchuk, *Natsional'no-kul'turni initsiatyvy ukraïns'koï diaspory (kinets' 50-kh – pochatok 90-kh rr. XX st.)* (Kyiv, 1997), p. 50.

plinth was to show eight bas-reliefs representing events in Ukraine during 1932–33. The project's authors were of the opinion that it was essential to incorporate religious, national, and folk symbols to convey the Holodomor's complex nature. Religious symbolism was to point to the atheistic and destructive nature of the Soviet central government's social policies and politics toward particular nations of the Soviet Union. Folk symbolism, chiefly embroidery and ornaments alluding to the Cucuteni–Trypillia culture, was a reference to the continuity of Ukraine's existence through the centuries. In turn, national symbolism was meant to show that the Famine was directed against Ukrainians as a national group. Next to the monument, a Holodomor memorial centre was planned that was to include a research institute, a museum, an archive, and a library. Ultimately, however, a monument based on this design was not raised, nor was the research centre, possibly because the entire project was estimated to cost $2,655,600 CAD (the monument in Edmonton had cost the local Ukrainian community $35,000 CAD.)[56]

The Holodomor's semicentennial anniversary also resulted in the creation of some "places of memory" in Great Britain, although not on the scale seen in the US or Canada. During the 1980s, two monuments marking the tragedy were raised in Great Britain: in the Acton district of London and in Cheltenham, Gloucestershire.[57] Due to its proximity to Gloucester, the latter is often erroneously identified as being located there. Both monuments are in the form of a cross. The monument in London is located on the grounds of the Acton Ukrainian Autocephalous Orthodox Church, while the one in Cheltenham is found at a summer residence owned by the Orthodox parish in Gloucester. The solemn unveiling of the monument in Cheltenham included both scholarly and survivor accounts of the Famine and was widely covered by the diaspora press.[58]

Holodomor monuments were also built in Australia during the 1980s. In 1981, Ivan Alexandrov organized a committee to build a monument in Essendon (a suburb of Melbourne), which was unveiled on October 9, 1983, near the Protection of the Holy Virgin Memorial Church.[59] Alexandrov, who donated $5,000 AUD to the project, did not live to see its unveiling. The monument's design was drawn up free of charge by George (Yurko) Himmelreich, an Australian artist and the son of Kost Himmelreich.[60] The motto "Lest we forget," located underneath the monument's inscription, speaks to the idea behind its creation. The un-

---

[56] *Ukraïns'ki visti,* October 5, 1983, pp. 1–2.

[57] "Shche odyn khrest-pam'iatnyk v Anhliï [Cheltenham]," *Vil'na dumka,* № 5–6 (January 29, 1984), p. 4.

[58] *Vil'na dumka,* № 5–6 (January 29, 1984), p. 4; *Novyi shliakh,* № 1–2 (1984), pp. 2, 15.

[59] *Vil'na dumka,* № 41 (October 7, 1984), p. 7.

[60] *Vil'na dumka,* № 45–6 (November 6–13, 1983), p. 1.

Fig. 24. The Holodomor monument in Acton – London, England (1983)

Fig. 25. The Holodomor monument in Cheltenham near Gloucester, England (1983)

veiling event included a memorial service and readings on the subject of the Holodomor. The commemoration was intimate and community oriented, and another $500 AUD was collected at the time for the purpose of building another Holodomor monument in Australia.

With the groundswell of events commemorating the Holodomor's fiftieth anniversary, a committee dedicated to commemorating the Ukrainian Famine was established in the Australian capital of Canberra in October 1983. On October 19, 1983, its members issued an appeal to Ukrainians living in Australia:

> The Ukrainian people are not able to properly honor and build a monument to the victims of the Holodomor in their own country. Therefore, all Ukrainians living in the free land of Australia must build a monument to those who have been buried without memory or monuments. In this way we shall fulfill our national and Christian duty toward the seven million fathers, mothers and children, by telling the world what happened fifty years ago.[61]

[61] "Komitet budovy pam'iatnyka, pam'iatnyk zhertvam Holodomoru v Kanberri," in *Ukraïntsi v Avstraliï*, vol. 2 (Melbourne, 1998), pp. 172–3.

Fig. 26. The Holodomor monument in Essendon – a suburb of Melbourne, Australia (1983)

The committee published a communiqué about the future monument's design and the cost of its realization on the pages of the newspaper *Vil'na dumka*.[62] The monument was to be made of stainless steel and incorporate a silver birch cross. Artist Mykhailo Sadovsky used

[62] *Vil'na dumka*, № 35 (August 26, 1984), p. 8.

Fig. 27. The Holodomor monument in Canberra, Australia (1985)

an illustration from the book *The Black Deeds of the Kremlin*[63] to paint a larger and modified version of Mykhailo Dmytrenko's work *1933*. The painting shows a woman with a child in her arms standing amidst

[63] *The Black Deeds of the Kremlin: A White Book*, vol. 1, *Book of Testimonies*, ed. Semen O. Pidhainy, transl. Alexander Oreletsky and Olga Prychodko, introd. George W. Simpson (Toronto, 1953), p. 223.

corpses. Artist Leonid Denysenko, in turn, painted a trident framed by a thorny wreath. Based on these designs, bronze plaques were cast. Two other plaques with inscriptions in both Ukrainian and English for the sides of the monument's granite base were also commissioned.[64]

Members of the Ukrainian community in Australia were asked for their opinions of the design, and the editorial board of *Vil'na dumka* published three letters received in response. The letters suggest a lack of consensus. In Antin Daneliuk's opinion, monuments on foreign soil should not be built at the expense of the Ukrainian community at all. Such monuments, he argued, should be built in an independent Ukraine.[65] In a polemic response, I. Yushchuk wrote:

> The Jewish nation builds monuments and speaks of its "holocaust" the world over. The Poles have built a huge monument to the Katyn victims in London. And we are to be silent? (...) Are we unable to raise $30-$40,000 dollars to honor at least partially those martyred by hunger? The land on which the monument is to stand belongs to us, Ukrainians, and its location – almost in the centre of the capital – will be a valuable warning to others, reminding them of the holocaust* of our nation.[66]

In his letter, Leonid Tryzna expressed doubts about both the monument's cost and artistic design. For him, the planned monument was insufficiently dignified to honour the memory of the Holodomor victims; his preference was for a granite monument that would feature a family emaciated by hunger in the centre.[67]

The next issue of *Vil'na dumka* included an announcement from the committee stressing that the opinions of the Ukrainian community were both valued and always welcome, and should be sent directly to the committee henceforth.[68] Despite this declaration, however, none of the suggestions were taken into consideration, and the monument was built as initially conceived. $49,000 AUD was raised in individual donations (with contributions ranging from one to one thousand dollars). In fact, it was built at the lower cost of $40,539 AUD, with the remaining funds set aside for the monument's future maintenance.

In May 1985, the Sunset building company was commissioned to create the monument in black marble, with the work due within three months. The city, however, did not assign a suitable site for the monument. Consequently, the committee members approached the Ukrainian Autocephalous Orthodox Church in Canberra, which designated

---

[64] "Komitet budovy pam'iatnyka," pp. 172–3.
[65] *Vil'na dumka*, № 38 (1984), p. 7.
[66] *Vil'na dumka*, № 42 (1984), p. 6.
[67] *Vil'na dumka*, № 45 (1984), pp. 7–8.
[68] *Vil'na dumka*, № 46 (1984), p. 2.

a square located at 6 McKay Gardens, Turner, for the purpose. In its final form, one of the side plaques was etched with the names of donors who contributed more than one hundred dollars (171 individuals and 37 organizations in total). The unveiling of the monument took place in October 1985 and was attended by James Mace, who took the opportunity to give several lectures about the Great Famine.[69]

Fig. 28. The Holodomor monument in Curitiba, Brazil (1983)

A monument to Holodomor victims was unveiled on November 2, 1983, on the fiftieth anniversary of the Great Famine 1932–33, in Curi-

[69] "V Avstralii̇ vshanuvaly pam'iat' zhertv holodu," *Svoboda*, № 224 (November 22, 1985), pp. 1, 8; "Komitet budovy pam'iatnyka," p. 173; Michael Lawriwsky, "The Great Famine of 1932–33. A Symposium 22 October, 2003, 'Australia and the Holodomor: 50 Years of Remembrance'," p. 6, accessed February 1, 2021, http://archive.cym.org/au/archives/Holodomor.pdf.

tiba, Brazil. A memorial service was celebrated in the parish of Nossa Senhora Auxiliadora at Rue Martim Afonso. Attended by Ukrainians of both the Greek Catholic and Orthodox Churches, the mass was celebrated by Bishop Yefrem (Kryvyi) of the Order of Saint Basil the Great, Bishop of the Curitiba Eparchy of St. John the Baptist. The second part of the event took place on Ukraine Square (Praça da Ucrânia), where a stone marker in memory of the victims of the Holodomor was unveiled.[70]

Diverse diaspora communities created the "places of memory" that appeared worldwide as part of the fiftieth-anniversary commemorations and immediately following, and the monuments reflect that diversity. They include symbolic burial places at cemeteries, crosses and monuments on the grounds of Orthodox and Greek Catholic parishes, and a few monuments centrally located in Canadian and American cities.

The fiftieth anniversary of the Great Famine, which was commemorated by Ukrainians all over the world with the exception of the Soviet Union, was groundbreaking for several reasons. First, the events of 1932–33 in Ukraine began arousing the interest of historians, politicians, and journalists. For many, the fact that the Soviet Union categorically denied that the Great Famine had taken place only heightened the desire to find answers to the many questions raised by the tragedy. With the support of American politicians and community activists, the Ukrainian diaspora's efforts to immortalize the victims of the Great Famine elevated discussion of the event to the level of state affairs, which subsequently and naturally generated discussion around the world, including in Soviet Ukraine.

The fifty-fifth anniversary of the Holodomor did not receive as much publicity as the fiftieth. Although a number of monuments were erected outside of Ukraine towards the end of the 1980s (for instance at the Ukrainian National Federation's (UNF) Camp Sokil in Hawkestone, ON, on the shores of Lake Simcoe), the scale of these initiatives was much smaller. The idea to erect a monument in Hawkestone first arose in 1987 in connection with the upcoming millennial celebrations of the Christianization of Kyivan Rus' (988). Several affiliated organizations initiated the undertaking: UNF Ridna Shkola and Ukrainian Studies Courses, and the Toronto-West Branch of the UNF. The monument's foundations and future location were prepared at this time.[71] The design featuring a cross on a stone slab along with an etched inscription

---

[70] Kornelii Shmulyk, "Brazyliia v pokloni zhertvam holodu," *Shliakh peremohy*, December 11, 1983, p. 5.

[71] "Filiia ukraïns'koho natsional'noho ob'iednannia – Toronto-Zakhid," in *Narys istoriï konhresu ukraïntsiv Kanady v Toronti* (Toronto, 1991), pp. 536–47.

Fig. 29. The Holodomor monument in Hawkestone, Canada (1989)

was produced and delivered two years later by Smith Monuments. The inscription read: "To the eternal memory of the 7,000,000 freedom-loving Ukrainians who were martyred by the hostile Muscovite-Soviet regime through death by starvation in Ukraine from 1932 to 1933."[72]

The monument built in 1988 was unveiled on July 23 1989, with the unveiling ceremonies described in the newspaper *Novyi shliakh* [New Pathways] as follows:

[72] "Pam'iatnyky zhertvam Holodomoru, vstanovleni v Kanadi," accessed March 23, 2019, http://canada.mfa.gov.ua/ua/ukraine-ca/holodomor-remembrance/holodomor-remembrance-canada/holodomor-remembrance-canada-monuments.

> The choice of location in the beautiful surroundings of the UNF Camp Sokil was apt. As the President of the WCFU Yuri Shymko rightly noted, the monument will remind thousands of visitors to this beautiful district in spring, summer, and fall, and especially the Ukrainian youth, of the tragic sacrifice of victims of the Great Famine in Ukraine. We must ennoble in our hearts and minds the memory of the innocent victims of the Great Famine in Ukraine. In remembering their terrible, shocking death at the hands of Muscovite-Kremlin assassins, we have to raise the level of consciousness and awareness in the Western world and portray the Ukrainian Holocaust of 1923–33 as a holocaust of holocausts* – the most terrible of human crimes. This holocaust must always remind us that the Ukrainian people are still engaged in a fierce battle with the same Kremlin assassin, the famine's instigator in Ukraine. And this we must never forget.[73]

The main goal of monuments erected during the 1980s, regardless of their founders' political beliefs, was to disseminate information about the Great Famine around the world.

The varied political and religious communities of Holodomor memory established in the Ukrainian diaspora as early as the 1940s were a response to the silencing of this event in the Soviet Union. I would argue that these memorial efforts highlight the Holodomor's tremendous significance in the cultural memory of North American Ukrainian diasporic communities. At the same time, the public commemorative initiatives demonstrate how members of the North American diaspora have drawn on their collective memory of the Holodomor in order to participate actively in the civic life and democratic objectives of their communities. To be clear, these events and others like them offer scholars of cultural memory rich opportunities to consider how diasporic communities negotiate their memories of the past and their new-found citizenship within "host" nations. By making the topic of the Holodomor visible within the public sphere of their countries of residence, Ukrainian communities aroused the interest, and at times even the understanding and empathy, of their adoptive societies, along with support and good will toward their commemorative initiatives.

3.4 Monuments abroad commemorating Holodomor anniversaries (1991–2016)

At the beginning of the 1990s, after Ukraine regained independence, one could observe changes in the commemoration of the Great Famine

---

[73] *Novyi shliakh*, № 31 (August 5, 1989), p. 7.

1932–33 also outside its borders. Monuments were still erected on the occasion of subsequent anniversaries of this event, but the commemorations were modest and local.

A monument to Holodomor victims on the occasion of the sixtieth anniversary was built in Chicago in December 1993. It was the work of Anatoliy Kushch, the Ukrainian sculptor who designed the famous Independence Monument in Kyiv. The close proximity of the Chicago Orthodox Church of St. Andrew was likely a decisive influence on the monument's religious nature. The monument depicts the figure of a mother sitting under a cross and crying over the body of her starving child. An inscription etched into the monument's side reads: "Stop and pay homage to the innocent victims. This monument was erected in 1993 by the Ukrainian Community of the Chicago metropolitan area on the sixtieth anniversary of the Great Famine in Ukraine."

Fig. 30. The Holodomor monument in Chicago, US (1993)

Plans for the ceremonious unveiling of the monument were announced on the pages of *Svoboda*:

> The community committee of Chicago and surrounding areas, established to build a monument to the victims of the Famine in Ukraine, has concluded its fundraising efforts as well as work on the monument, which was made by the Ukrainian sculptor Anatoliy Kushch and will be unveiled on Saturday, December 4, at 2 p.m. with the participation of the local Ukrainian communities. The monument stands in proxim-

> ity to the Orthodox Church of St. Andrew in Bloomingdale, near Chicago. It was consecrated by Constantine, Metropolitan of the Ukrainian Orthodox Church in the US, together with all Ukrainian Orthodox hierarchs and clergy. The monument will be unveiled by members of the ODUM, Plast and SUM youth organizations. After the consecration of the monument, a modest memorial lunch will be held in the parish hall with the local Ukrainian community, American state dignitaries, and the Ukrainian consul. The artistic program will include performances by the Surma Choir, St. Andrew's Choir and Oksana Rodak-Lutsenko, member of the ODUM band. The cost of attending the lunch is $10/person. All attendees will receive as an entry ticket a commemorative program with articles on the Famine, greetings and a list of all donors who funded the monument.[74]

The Chicago monument was often visited by Ukrainian politicians and became a meeting place on the occasion of subsequent Holodomor anniversaries.[75]

At this time, a monument to the Holodomor was also unveiled in Parma, OH. Standing in the vicinity of St. Vladimir Ukrainian Orthodox Cathedral, it is a work of great interest as it highlights the national dimension of the tragedy through its form, the *tryzub* (trident), a symbol featured on Ukraine's coat of arms.[76] The newspaper *Svoboda* reported on this unveiling as well:

> Parma, Ohio. On October 30 and 31 of this year, parishioners of St. Vladimir Ukrainian Orthodox Cathedral in Parma, Ohio, are honouring the famine victims from 1921–1933 in connection with the sixtieth anniversary of these sad events. Archbishop Antony will lead a prayer service and perform the consecration (...). Delegations of priests and parishes from among local Orthodox communities in Cleveland, youth organizations, veterans and American dignitaries, are kindly invited. The monument stands ten feet tall in the square next to the Cathedral on one of Parma's main streets and has the shape of the Ukrainian *tryzub* with a cross. It was designed and made out of dark red granite by Andrii Zeleniak of the Cleveland Memorial Company.[77]

---

[74] "V Chykaho vidkryiut' pam'iatnyk zhertvam holodu," *Svoboda*, № 219 (November 17, 1993), p. 1.

[75] [Myron B. Kuropas], "Standing Resolute in the Face of Evil: Reflection on the Great Famine," *The Ukrainian Weekly*, № 41 (October 14, 2001), p. 6; "Ukraïns'ka vystavka u Chykaho [Zokrema pro pokladannia vitse-prem'ier-ministrom D. Tabachnykom kvitiv do pam'iatnyka zhertvam Holodomoru, Bluminhdeil, SShA]," *Uriadovyi kur'ier*, December 16, 2006, p. 3; Taras Konowal, "Patriarch Filaret visits Parish in Bloomingdale," *The Ukrainian Weekly*, № 47 (November 19, 2006), p. 11.

[76] V. Ivanchuk, "Zhertvam holodomoru 1932–1933 rr. [Pam'iatnyk u Parmi, Ohaio, SShA]," *Ukraïns'ki visti*, December 5, 1993, p. 5 (photo); "Pam'iatnyk zhertvam holodu [Parma, Ohaio, SILA]," *Ukraïns'ki visti*, October 10, 1993, p. 3.

[77] "Volodymyrs'kyi sobor v Parmi vidsloniuie pam'iatnyk zhertvam Velykoho holodu," *Svoboda*, № 192 (October 8, 1993), p. 1.

Importantly, toward the end of the 1990s, such monuments started appearing in Ukrainian communities outside of North America. The Ukrainian diaspora in Australia marked the sixtieth anniversary of the Holodomor by moving a monument from one parish in Adelaide to another. In 1999, in turn, a monument designed by the artist Ihor Novosilets was unveiled in Calgary. Its inscription reads: "Let us all stand on guard against tyranny, violence and inhumanity."[78]

On the 16th of October, 1993, at the initiative of Mykhailo Vasylyk, the Ukrainian Central Representation of Argentina erected a symbolic grave in memory of the victims of the Holodomor in Ukraine. Thanks to the help of the Taras Shevchenko Foundation in Argentina, this monument was located in the Ukrainian Esteban Echeverría Cemetery in Monte Grande (suburb of Buenos Aires). The monument is in the shape of a cross on a hill. In this way, it resembles traditional Ukrainian military graves (burial mounds).[79]

In 1997, a monument was also unveiled at the Oakridge Cemetery in the town of Goshen, IN. In the Ukrainian diaspora context, it is an atypical initiative because the monument is located in a cemetery (which is also the case in the Lachine borough of Montreal).[80] As noted in *Svoboda*:

> On September 20 at the Oakridge Cemetery in Goshen, Indiana, the unveiling and consecration of a monument to the victims of the Great Famine 1932–33 in Ukraine were effectively organized. Archbishop Vsevolod celebrated the memorial service at the Holy Trinity Orthodox Church together with Orthodox and Greek-Catholic priests from Chicago and northern regions of the State of Indiana. The procession to the cemetery included more than 150 people and took place under a police escort to avoid traffic problems.[81]

The seventieth anniversary of the Holodomor in 2003 brought increased recognition of this event as an act of genocide, including by the US House of Representatives and the Canadian Senate, which intensified commemorative efforts of the Ukrainian diaspora. One of the more publicized initiatives, spearheaded by the Ukrainian Canadian Civil Liberties Association, focused on attempts to have Walter Duranty's Pulitzer Prize in journalism revoked. It had been awarded in 1932 for a series of articles on the progress of communism in the USSR.

---

[78] For a report on the building and unveiling ceremony of the monument see: "Holodomor Monument Unveiling," produced by *Echoes of Ukraine TV*, February 4, 2015, YouTube video, 23:20, https://www.youtube.com/watch?v=t2N24tf28u8&feature=youtu.be.

[79] Mykhailo Vasylyk, *Ukraïntsi Argentyny: istoriia ta suchasnist'* (L'viv, 2009), p. 236.

[80] "Vidkryttia pam'iatnyka zhertvam holodu v SShA [Hoshen, Indiana]," *Vil'na dumka*, November 26–December 3, 1997, p. 32.

[81] "Vidkryttia pam'iatnyka zhertvam Holodu 1932–33 rokiv v Ukraïni," *Svoboda*, № 199 (October 18, 1997), p. 4.

While the initiative did not achieve revocation, the matter was widely reported throughout the world.

The seventieth anniversary was also marked with installation of a commemorative plaque in Vienna, Austria, and a stele-shaped monument on the grounds of St. Michael's Ukrainian Orthodox Church in Genk, Belgium. The latter, made from white sandstone, is the work of Ukrainian artist Mykola Telizhenko[82] and depicts a mother and two children, with the woman's image following typical Marian Orthodox iconography.

Fig. 31. The Holodomor monument in Genk, Belgium (2003)

The Holodomor monument built in 2005 in Windsor, ON, is another important act of commemoration. The monument, unveiled in a ceremony that took place on Sunday, November 13, had the support of the Windsor branch of the Ukrainian Canadian Congress. It was the third monument to be built in Canada. Located in the Queen Elizabeth II Gardens, also known as Jackson Park, it was funded with private donations, and approximately two hundred people participated in the unveiling ceremony. This stele-shaped monument is made of black granite and was designed by Halyna Mordowanec-Regenbogen

[82] "Z namy bula vsia planeta," *Uriadovyi kur'ier*, April 17, 2004, p. 7.

and Tom Regenbogen. A map of Ukraine was carved into one of its sides, marking famine-stricken areas as verified in consultation with Dr. Ihor Stebelsky of the University of Windsor. Among the guests at the unveiling were representatives of the Ukrainian Canadian Congress and municipal authorities, as well as Stefania Korostil, a survivor of the Holodomor who shared her childhood recollections.[83] The monument in Windsor serves as a place where the Ukrainian diaspora gathers on anniversaries and memorial days. During a meeting of the Ukrainian community of Windsor and Essex County on November 25, 2012, Ihor Stebelsky urged the community to participate in commemorating and promoting awareness of the Holodomor:

> The Windsor community is doing what it can. To promote public awareness, and in keeping with the resolution of the Senate of Canada, the Ukrainian Community of Windsor and Essex County, headed by the Ukrainian Canadian Congress, Windsor Branch, on November 2005, unveiled the monument in Jackson Park dedicated to all the victims of the Famine genocide of 1932–33 in Ukraine.[84]

Over the years, the number of monuments commemorating the Great Famine has continued to grow. In 2005, in the French town of Holtzheim, a modest stele commemorating the victims of the Holodomor was placed at 1 Place de la Fontaine, acting also as a symbol of friendship between Ukraine and France.[85]

In 2006, two monuments appeared in Central Europe. In the Slovak town of Prešov, a cross was consecrated to honour victims, bearing an inscription in both Ukrainian and Slovak: "To the victims of the Holodomor in Ukraine in 1932–33. This holy cross was consecrated on November 2, 2006."[86] That same year, a memorial called *Gloria Victis* in memory of 100 million victims of communism, which included a small stele dedicated to the Holodomor's victims, was unveiled at a cemetery near Budapest.

Many commemorative initiatives marked the seventy-fifth anniversary of the Holodomor during Viktor Yushchenko's presidency. At this time, the Ukrainian president emphasized the importance of the

---

[83] [Pawlo Berezniak], "Pam'iatnyk zhertvam Holodomoru 1932–1933 u Vindzori," *Novyi shliakh*, February 9, 2006.

[84] *Homin Ukraïny*, № 10 (March 15, 2013), p. 12.

[85] "Histoire ukrainienne, entre génocide, makhnovtchina et pyramides," accessed August 30, 2020, https://www.paperblog.fr/7060673/histoire-ukrainienne-entre-genocide-makhnovtchina-et-pyramides/.

[86] "Ukraïntsi v Priashevi takozh vshanuvaly pam'iat' zhertv Holodomoru v Ukraïni (FOTO)," *Zakarpattia online*, accessed April 3, 2019, https://zakarpattya.net.ua/Special/187571-Ukraintsi-v-Priashevi-takozh-vshanuvaly-pam%E2%80%99iat-zhertv-Holodomoru-v-Ukraini-FOTO.

Ukrainian diaspora's commemorative undertakings. All initiatives marking the event in Ukraine involved state authorities and often included representatives of other nations that had officially recognized the genocidal nature of the Famine. The most widely publicized commemorations tied to this relay took place in the US, Canada, Australia, and Great Britain.

Fig. 32. The Holodomor monument in Holtzheim, France (2005)

Coinciding with the seventy-fifth anniversary, a memorial plaque dedicated to Great Famine victims was unveiled inside the Metropolitan Cathedral in Buenos Aires, Argentina. Also at this time, a monument was unveiled at the centrally located Plaza de Armas in Encarnación, Paraguay. A monument was also unveiled at the Ukrainian Catholic Cathedral of the Intercession of the Mother of God and St. Andrew in Munich, Germany. On November 20, 2009, in turn, a memorial stele to the victims of the Holodomor was unveiled in the English town of Rochdale. The same year, a monument was unveiled in a Ukrainian memorial park in Curitiba, PR (Brazil).[87] All of these monuments, regardless of location, are quite similar.

[87] "Ministro ucraniano inaugura monumento no Parque Tingui," Fundação Cultural de Curitiba, accessed July 28, 2020, http://www.fundacaoculturaldecuritiba.com.br/noticias/ministro-ucraniano-inaugura-monumento-no-parque-tingui/.

In Poland, monuments were erected on the occasion of the seventy-fifth anniversary in Cracow and Warsaw. In Cracow, a relief sculpture was added to a side wall of the Greek-Catholic Church of the Exaltation of the Holy Cross (on Wiślna Street) in 2008. Entitled "The Great Famine in Ukraine," it was designed by Stefan Dousa, a Cracow sculp-

Fig. 33. Relief sculpture dedicated to victims of the Holodomor, in Cracow, Poland (2008)

tor and professor at the Tadeusz Kościuszko University of Technology, whose artistic oeuvre includes monumental sculptures, smaller spatial forms, and medals. His bas-relief on the Greek-Catholic church's wall, following a tendency in the diaspora to locate these monuments on the grounds of a Uniate or an Orthodox church, does not reference the it history in any way. Instead, it reflects ideas about identity shaped over the course of recent decades and held by a new community of believers, mainly parishioners from a "new wave" of Ukrainian immigrants. The construction of the Holodomor memorial on the site of this particular church appears to have stemmed from the desire of its parishioners to create a "refuge," a safe harbor for people united not only by faith and rite but also by a similar perception of their Ukrainianness. The bas-relief is an independent work of art, although it was designed to complement the church's façade. While discreet in form (reminiscent of an enlarged medal), it is worth considering why it is not located inside the house of worship, or on the church façade, but instead on a side wall overlooking the Planty Park, a popular destination for tourists and locals. This memorial in Cracow is thus, on the one hand, an expression of the church's parishioners and their Ukrainian identity, while on the other, it is a Polish sculptor's artistic representation of the horrors of the Holodomor to be shared with Cracow's residents and visitors.

In the context of the author's body of work, the monument's symbolic dimension instinctively evokes a comparison to Dousa's monument to the *Victims of Communism*, which stands at the Rakowicki Cemetery in Cracow. In both cases, the creators use the motif of hands that are trying to find support, something to grab onto (a cross, in the case of the Rakowicki Cemetery monument), in order to escape and liberate themselves from suffering. On the Holodomor memorial, these hands are intertwined with faces whose features are blurred, creating the impression of deformed bodies cast into a boiling cauldron. This association with infernal fire did not emerge immediately but formed slowly as I contemplated both this monument and Dousa's other martyrological works. For this artist, the essence of the Great Famine appears to be enslavement, the impossibility of escaping Stalin's "burning infernal fire." At the centre of the bas-relief is a circle that can be interpreted in many ways. The location of this memorial at a church may evoke Eucharistic symbolism, the Christian ritual of breaking the host and Holy Communion. Inside the circle's rim are two interlinked female figures (a mother and daughter) with, significantly, indistinct facial features, which in my interpretation signals the mass nature of the Holodomor. The blurred faces prevent conceptual identification with a single individual, portraying instead the scope of the annihilation. In terms of Dousa's symbolic framework, this monument, to a large degree, incorporates elements found in the Holodomor monument in

Fig. 34. The monument to the Victims of Communism at the Rakowicki Cemetery in Cracow, Poland (1995)

Edmonton as well as the Holodomor memorial in Kyiv near the city's St. Michael's Monastery. Its similarity to other Holodomor monuments in Poland is much less pronounced.

A year later, a Holodomor memorial was unveiled at the Orthodox Cemetery in the Wola District of Warsaw. It is the work of Giennadij Jerszow, a Ukrainian immigrant and an artist working in Gdańsk. Having come to Poland in 2001, his artistic ideas are rooted in Ukrainian traditions. Jerszow's monument embraces Christian traditions, although it does not resemble the artist's other religious sculptures in any way. It takes the form of a cross with a centrally placed bas-relief. In its centre, we see the outline of a human figure created from the empty space surrounded by a mound of human bodies. The gender of the central figure and the surrounding bodies are not given any significance by the artist. First and foremost, this representation depicts the tragedy of a single individual against the backdrop of the Ukrainian nation's enormous tragedy. The memorials in Cracow and Warsaw are linked through the presence of wheat sheaves, a reference to the "Law of Spikelets" that sanctioned the severe punishment of those found with grain, a key policy that led to the tragedy of the Ukrainian Famine.[88] The monument's location at an Orthodox cemetery is also significant, especially given its proximity to graves dedicated to the soldiers of the Ukrainian National Republic. The shape of the monument is not a traditional cross but a Cossack one (also known as the cross pattée), characteristic of military graves in Ukrainian culture. This atypical (in term of its shape) architectural solution could be mis-read as reflective of the artist's desire to emphasize the Christian nature of the burial, whereas in fact it gestures to the aforementioned military graves, thus bestowing a higher, national significance onto the memorial in its Orthodox cemetery setting.

These two Polish Holodomor monuments only slightly reference the visual culture of Great Famine remembrance as established in the diaspora. Rather, they draw from the Ukrainian memory canon while remaining, first and foremost, artistic and individual expressions of the Holodomor as understood by those who created them. These memorials differ from those in Ukraine primarily in terms of their aims. Built

---

[88] The decree "Pro okhoronu maina derzhavnykh pidpryiemstv, kolhospiv i kooperatyviv ta zmitsnennia hromads'koï (sotsialistychnoï) vlasnosti" ["On Safekeeping Property of State Enterprises, Collective Farms and Cooperatives and Strengthening Public (Socialist) Property"] of August 7, 1932, colloquially called the 'Law of Spikelets'. See: Valentina Kuryliw, "The Ukrainian Genocide–the Holodomor, 1932–1933: A Case of Denial, Cover-Up, and Dismissal," in *Teaching about Genocide: Insights and Advice from Secondary Teachers and Professors*, vol. 1, ed. Samuel Totten (Lanham–Boulder–New York–London, 2018), p. 57.

Fig. 35. The Holodomor monument in Warsaw, Poland (2009)

abroad, these initiatives should not be viewed in terms of the Ukrainian culture of Holodomor remembrance but in the context of the broadly conceived politics of Polish memory.

The approaching eightieth anniversary gave rise to a long-awaited memorial in Toronto, an important centre of Ukrainian emigration. In 2011, the so-called "Bell of Memory" monument was built on the grounds of St. Mary's Ukrainian Catholic Church in Mississauga, which neighbours Toronto. The unveiling of the bell, which was funded by Eugene (Ewhen) Kostruba, was attended by representatives of Toronto's Polish and Italian diaspora. The commemoration included first-hand accounts of Holodomor survivors Fedir Strohyj, Mykola Latyshko, and Vira Kanareyska.[89] The pedestal underneath the monument bears an inscription in both Ukrainian and English:

> The Ukrainian Holodomor of 1932–33 remains one of the most horrific crimes ever committed against humanity. Orchestrated by a totalitarian communist regime, it took the lives of approximately ten million people and threatened to destroy the ethnic backbone of the Ukrainian nation.
>
> We cherish the memory of the innocent victims of the Holodomor and strive to reveal their truth so that the world will never again have to face a similar tragedy. Ukraine remembers. The World recognizes.

Over time, noticeable changes in the visual representation of the Holodomor outside of Ukraine have taken place. In the last decade in particular, the memorials are often not original works intended to embody the ideas of a specific "community of memory," but rather are connected to Ukraine. Memorials in Germany, Brazil, Paraguay, and Argentina, among other countries, were often inspired by, or a copy of, already existing monuments. A similar process of replication can be observed in Ukraine.

3.5 Holodomor museum exhibitions in Canada

Museum exhibits that relate the story of the Holodomor are significant factors in the creation of its memory culture. As museum expositions were being organized under Viktor Yushchenko's presidency in Ukraine, two similar efforts were made in North America. The first was a thematic exhibition organized in 2008 in Hamilton, ON; the second was part of a 2014 exhibit on genocide at the Canadian Museum for Human Rights in Winnipeg, MB. Both exhibits were educational in keeping with the role of contemporary museums that realize their mandates through interaction with the public.[90]

---

[89] "N.N. Ukrainian Genocide Remembered," *Novyi shliakh*, № 47 (December 1, 2011), p. 1.

[90] Marcin Szeląg, "Edukacja głupcze! Zadania muzeum na początku XXI wieku," in *Muzeum XXI wieku. Teoria i Praxis*, eds. Elżbieta Kowalska and Elżbieta Urbaniak (Gniezno, 2010), p. 177.

3.5.1 The museum exhibition in Hamilton

The first museum exhibition in Canada created to relate the story of the Ukrainian Holodomor was opened on the occasion of the Holodomor's seventy-fifth anniversary at St. Vladimir Ukrainian Orthodox Cathedral in Hamilton, ON, on the initiative of the parish priest, Rev. William [Wasyl] Makarenko. The exhibition took six weeks to produce and consists of thirty-four richly illustrated display panels created using archival documents, press sources from the 1930s, and witness accounts. The ceremonial opening of this museum exhibition took place on November 20, 2008, with guests including representatives of numerous Ukrainian organizations as well as local authorities. In press interviews, Orysia Sushko, who had been responsible for assembling the exhibit, emphasized that the museum intended to expand its collection with artifacts and testimonies of Holodomor survivors living in Canada.[91]

The museum's collection contains a letter written by Kateryna Yushchenko, then First Lady of Ukraine, and addressed to the Ukrainian community involved in the creation of the museum:

> Awareness of the historical importance of the Holodomor is a route to oneself, an aspiration to grasp one's own identity. And this is the route we shall follow until all historical facts are examined, all survivor testimonies of still living witnesses are recorded, the names of all victims are honored, and until we tell everyone in the world about the Soviet communist regime's crimes.[92]

The fact that the exhibition in Hamilton utilized display boards prepared by the International Charitable Fund Ukraine 3000, presenting reproductions of museum content (documents, photographs, graphs, postcards, maps, etc.), was likely, at least in part, the reason for the First Lady's interest.

The museum display in Hamilton presents four fundamental contexts for understanding the genocide-by-famine: Ukraine before the Holodomor, the Holodomor's Genesis, the Holodomor's Progression, and International Recognition. The museum is fundamentally educational in its aims and oriented, from inception, toward both the Ukrainian community and Canadians in general, despite its location in the Metropolitan Wasyly Learning Centre adjacent to the St. Vladimir parish. *The Hamilton Spectator* wrote: "These museums teach you about man's inhumanity to man on the negative side. On the positive side,

---

[91] *Ukrainian Voice*, March 23, 2009, p. 8.

[92] Fragment of a letter addressed to the Museum in Hamilton by Kateryna Yushchenko, November 20, 2008. The Holodomor Museum in Hamilton collections.

you get amazing stories of survival."[93] A museum space can thus constitute the ideal environment for shaping individual identity and patriotic attitudes. Exhibitions of this type are designed to bring knowledge of the Great Famine to present and future generations, presenting the starvation terror as aimed at the annihilation of Ukrainian agricultural, cultural, and traditional folk values.

3.5.2 The Canadian Museum for Human Rights in Winnipeg

The Canadian Museum for Human Rights (CMHR), which opened in Winnipeg, MB, in September 2014, features an exhibition devoted to selected examples of genocide in the history of humankind, including the Holodomor. This museum functions, in my view, as a "site of conscience." Museums of this type are dedicated to historical events considered to be crimes against humanity as well as to violations of human rights. Museums thus conceived focus on reflection, contemplation, and discussion.[94] The creation and functioning of such museums is based on three principles: the recreation of a "place of memory" (in addition to the building of monuments and memorials) aimed at producing a unique emotional experience for the visitors; the creation of a space for dialogue rather than a simple ascertainment of facts; and providing opportunities for participation in socially significant projects.[95] A museum as a site representing conscience aims not only to recount a given event but may be intended to give rise to the sensations of empathy, mourning, and understanding.

The CMHR in Winnipeg was the vision of Israel Asper, a media magnate and politician who initiated the project in 2000 but died three years later, before its completion. The museum took fourteen years to complete and was built in an atmosphere of conflict and misunderstanding among various ethnic groups over the specific subjects to be explored. As Nadine Blumer noted:

> Analysis of how histories of violence are represented and received in cultural institutions such as museums and memorials is frequently framed in terms of conflict and hierarchies or competitions of suffering. (…) In Canada, for example, this question of a "pure" victim category versus a "pure" perpetrator category has resulted in long-standing ten-

---

[93] *The Hamilton Spectator*, December 1, 2008, pp. 1, 4.

[94] Carol S. Jeffers, "Museum as a Process," *The Journal of Aesthetic Education* 37, № 1 (2003), p. 109.

[95] Liz Ševčenko, "Sites of Conscience: Reimagining Reparations," *Change Over Time* 1, № 1 (2011), pp. 6–33.

> sions between Jewish and Ukrainian communities and has framed at least part of the background of conflicts that have played out in the CMHR's development. [96]

Following the protests of numerous Canadian ethnic organizations (not only Ukrainian), CMHR agreed to give space and recognition to the Holodomor and other traumatic historical events. The CMHR set up a partnership in July 2012 with Ukraine's National Museum, the Memorial in Commemoration of Famine Victims in Kyiv. In a press statement, the CMHR's Stuart Murray stated that this partnership would help bring the story of the Holodomor to a broader audience for the benefit of generations to come. The CEO of the Kyiv-based organization responded with a similar statement about positive aspects of international cooperation with the CMHR, underscoring that the comprehensive study of Famine as a phenomenon could help prevent such events in the future.[97]

The building housing the Canadian Museum for Human Rights, designed by the American architect Antoine Predock, rises up like a steel mountain enshrouded in glass. The museum comprises ten permanent viewing halls, of which the largest carries the name "Canadian journeys" and is devoted to the history of human rights in the country. Among other subjects covered in the exhibitions are the Holocaust and the post-war development of human rights movements, as epitomized in the Universal Declaration of Human Rights written by the Canadian lawyer John Peters Humphrey in 1948. An additional gallery – "Expressions" – is dedicated to temporary exhibits. The exhibition about the Holodomor is located on the same level as the Holocaust viewing hall.[98]

The gallery named "Breaking the Silence" explores the role of secrecy and denial in atrocities from around the world. It includes a focused examination of the Ukrainian Holodomor, the Armenian Genocide, the Holocaust, the Rwandan Genocide, and the Srebrenica Genocide in Bosnia. The centrepiece is a digital study table that presents images and documents related to mass human rights violations. [99]

This interactive table allows visitors to access materials related to a massive cross-section of human rights violations, and in particular,

[96] Nadine Blumer, "Expanding Museum Spaces: Networks of Difficult Knowledge at and Beyond the Canadian Museum for Human Rights," *Review of Education, Pedagogy, and Cultural Studies* 37, № 2–3 (2015), pp. 125–46.

[97] "CMHR Deals with Holodomor Group," Winnipeg Sun, July 5, 2012, http://www.winnipegsun.com/2012/07/05/cmhr-deals-with-holodomor-group.

[98] Norbert K. Iwan, "Kanads'kyi Muzei Prav Liudyny," *Ukrainian People*, February 11, 2017, http://ukrainianpeople.us/канадський-музей-прав-людини/.

[99] Canadian Museum for Human Rights. Galleries, accessed February 1, 2021, https://humanrights.ca/exhibition/galleries.

video of first-hand accounts. One of the testimonies comes from Maria Firman, a Holodomor survivor who describes how her mother was beaten to death by a Soviet officer for gathering stalks for soup. These recordings come from the archives of the Ukrainian Canadian Research and Documentation Centre in Toronto. A theatre linked with the viewing hall features a short documentary film that analyzes media coverage of the Holodomor at the time of its occurrence and demonstrates how media can be manipulated to distort or hide violations. The viewing hall includes the sculpture "Bitter Memories of Childhood." Designed by Anatolii Haidamaka and cast by Petro Drozdovsky, the statue of a girl is intended to encourage visitors to remember that breaking the silence around human rights violations is crucial if children are to have a chance of growing up healthy in freedom and dignity. A film about the Holodomor constitutes an essential educational element in this part of the gallery, and in fact, the rest of the exhibition complements the film.[100]

The Holodomor exhibit at the Canadian Museum for Human Rights in Winnipeg is narrative or interpretative in character, meaning that the collection serves to convey complex notions about genocide to the visitor. Speaking broadly, we are not dealing exclusively with a presentation of artifacts, but with their instrumental treatment directed at disseminating a specific content. The narrative remains closely connected to the exhibits, placing them in a historical context for better comprehension and an appropriate (according to the curator's intention) interpretation of their symbolism. Such exhibitions face a formidable task in trying to convey a challenging and even depressing message to visitors. They can provoke varied and extreme emotional states (such as empathy, compassion, shame, embarrassment, regret, or anger). Communicating such content is further complicated by the impossibility of doing so appropriately while using contemporary narrative schemes or metaphors. Therefore, those tasked with creating such spaces often reach for images of a better known, in some ways comparable, historical event, and in particular, models based on American Holocaust memory culture. As Nicole Anne Ritchie notes,

> The gallery app continues to state that, if people are silent, if they do not take it upon themselves to self-educate, if they do no listen or read, they are creating conditions in which violations can be repeated. (...) But, "when people dare to break the silence," when we present enough of

[100] Jeremy Maron, "Covering the Holodomor: Memory Eternal. Misinformation and Deception Play a Crucial Role in Mass Atrocities such as the Holodomor," Canadian Museum of Human Rights, accessed February 1, 2021, https://humanrights.ca/story/covering-the-holodomor-memory-eternal.

> the right persevering affect, we can cause change, we enable success. In the centre of the gallery, the words 'remember and demand' in multiple languages rotate on a screen, reinforcing the bringing of the past into the present for a better future led by one's taking a stand and demanding action.[101]

Therefore, educating future generations is seen here as crucial in understanding and preventing human rights violations.

I would also apply this statement to the museum in Hamilton, as it also aims to educate future generations. In both cases, the creators are convinced that it is necessary to educate the next generation of conscious Canadian citizens by informing them about human rights violations. In fact, these institutions had very different budgets, which is why their possibilities for persuasion via museum narrative are different. The CMHR tells the story of the Holodomor as does the Hamilton museum, but thanks to the technological capabilities of the CMHR, its methodology is much more effective.

3.6 Conclusions

Holodomor memorialization in the diaspora has thus undergone transformations in both form and content that are related to changes in the memory communities themselves: their generational composition and ever-deepening assimilation.

Initially, diasporic "communities of memory" did not set out to engage the viewer in emotionally experiencing the Holodomor tragedy. Instead, through the memorials they funded, the communities sought to encourage intellectual reflection on the subject of genocide and the causes and consequences of this event in the history of the Ukrainian people. They then crowned their efforts, so to speak, with the construction of monuments – Holodomor "places of memory." In the last decade we see the narrative stage of development in museum exhibitions created in Canada (especially the CMHR).

The "places of memory" commemorating the Great Famine of 1932–33 (the Holodomor) established in the Ukrainian diaspora in the West during the first fifty years following the tragedy were primarily religious in character until the start of the 1980s when commemorations began to assume a more secular nature. This difference speaks to the motives of the people engaged in cultivating the memory of the Great Famine. It can also be said that both religious and secular initiatives

---

[101] Nicole Anne Ritchie, "Queering Museums: Questions of Space, Affect, and the (Non) Normative," (MA thesis, University of Toronto, 2015), p. 81.

stemmed from varied needs and ideas about how this memory could be cultivated within the public space.

Successive anniversaries of the Holodomor created opportunities for the building of monuments abroad. Starting with the sixtieth-anniversary commemorations, numerous initiatives emerged to build monuments as indication of a given Ukrainian community's participation in remembering the genocide. At the beginning of the twenty-first century, Ukrainian diplomatic missions sought to draw the attention of their host countries to this major event in Ukraine's history and to connect Ukrainians with other nations that have experienced genocidal trauma.

Chapter IV

Forms of Holodomor Commemoration in Ukraine 1990–2016

Holodomor monuments and places of real and symbolic burial of its victims cannot be fully understood without the historical, political, and social contexts surrounding their creation. The politics of memory in Ukraine is not the subject of my research but it is of interest to the extent that it impacts our understanding of the "community of memory" behind a given monument, including its motivations and ideas and what the monument was meant to embody. I would highlight here that places of mass burial constitute a specific form of Holodomor commemoration. The time frame of this chapter's discussion begins with Ukrainian independence and continues through the events of 2016. As a result, I will not consider current initiatives because I believe it is too early to fully evaluate this chapter of Ukraine's history.

I turn first to those aspects of the politics of memory that were characteristic of independent Ukraine and related to the cultivation of Holodomor memory and how this shaped both its community and its culture of memory. In this context, working through the trauma of the Great Famine in the public sphere can be considered a process that could result in Ukrainian society's liberation from post-communist myths and the beginning of a new era both in its politics of memory and for its social consciousness that is now Ukrainian rather than post-communist or post-colonial. I will also discuss how the symbolic image of the Great Famine (Holodomor) was transformed in post-Soviet Ukraine in the context of Ukrainian society's struggle to come to terms with its Soviet legacy.

I would like to reflect on the approaches of successive governments of an independent Ukraine toward commemoration of the Great Famine. Of particular interest are the processes by which the Ukrainian culture of Holodomor memory was constituted and specifically, the decisions of individual Ukrainian presidents, civic initiatives, and public debate.

4.1 Between *Acting Out* and *Working Through*: The Holodomor in Ukraine during *Perestroika*

Dominick LaCapra, in his consideration of how societies cope with traumatic experiences of the past, differentiates between two non--binary processes: *acting out* and *working through*. In the first case we are talking about a suspended process in which the individual or society is condemned to acting out the traumatic experience. Working through trauma, in turn, opens up the possibility of coming to terms with it and perhaps returning to life as it once was or a life that allows for a new beginning. While this process does not result in cessation of mourning on either the individual or public levels, it invests the suffering with meaning, promotes understanding of the complexity of the historical situation, and shapes the ability to represent this event in the public sphere symbolically.[1]

The experience of mourning the trauma of the Holodomor became possible in Ukraine only toward the end of the 1980s. At that time, the understanding of the Holodomor established in the diaspora made its way to Soviet Ukraine as a kind of weapon in the fight with the collapsing communist regime.[2] The message conveyed by the narrative about the Great Famine suited the Ukrainian national democrats. Nonetheless, years of consistent Soviet propaganda had strongly affected the world view of Ukrainians. The society of post-communist Ukraine found itself confronting the problem of memory revision. Many people found it difficult to depart from the previously held system of values and to adopt a new social discourse. In this way, the Ukrainian diaspora's achievements in investigating the historical events, then referred to as "white spots," became less a reference point than a source of knowledge, and even a model for describing issues ignored or obscured in the Soviet historical discourse.

Ukraine's socio-political situation at the turn of the 1990s can be framed to some extent as an explosion of diverse and divergent memories. Individual memory of the communist past, including the Holodomor, was suddenly released from the confines of family histories into public life, where it began to play a significant role. Allan

---

[1] Dominick LaCapra, "Trauma, Absence, Loss," *Critical Inquiry* 25, № 4. (Summer, 1999), pp. 696–727.

[2] Andrea Gratsiozi, "Usvidomliuvannia Holodomoru," *Krytyka* 7, № 12 (2003), pp. 18–20.

Megill has already noted that memory takes on a special significance for communities whose identity is threatened. Memory can be reconfigured to support the preservation of the unity of a community.[3] The period under discussion was indeed decisive for a burgeoning Ukrainian identity, and remembrance of the Holodomor experience was a key building block.

Pierre Nora calls this time in Europe a time of "rediscovered memory."[4] However, in the case of memory of the Great Famine (indeed, of any memory previously cultivated by the Ukrainian diaspora), I am inclined to see this period from today's perspective as a time of "prosthetic memory," which obscures the authenticity of witness recollections and promotes macabre images of human downfall and the devaluation of Christian values when faced with death by starvation. On the one hand, successive governments of an independent Ukraine could have saved both effort and expense in constructing a national version of history by integrating diaspora models of enduring traditions, as compared to some other Soviet republics. On the other hand, there was little room at the time for truth about the communist past that was being unearthed by Ukrainians. The symbolism of the Holodomor as promoted by the North American diaspora was directly transplanted onto Ukrainian soil, as evidenced by the withdrawal of a Soviet textbook on the subject "The History of Ukraine" and the substitution of a history by Orest Subtelny, an American/Canadian historian of Ukrainian background.[5]

The symbolic beginning of this period of re-evaluation of Ukraine's historical narrative can be dated with the publication in the journal *Literaturna Ukraïna* [Literary Ukraine] on July 16, 1987, of an article that mentioned the Great Famine several times, emphasizing that it was a widely known fact. Even the Central Committee of the CPU could no longer stop the conversation about the Great Famine.

On November 2, 1987, Mikhail Gorbachev gave an address at the Kremlin on the subject of the seventieth anniversary of the October Revolution, featuring a traditional Stalinist presentation of the methods employed by the Party on the path to a better tomorrow. Gorbachev did not mention the famine in his speech.[6] Volodymyr Shcherbytsky, the First Secretary of the Central Committee of the CPU, could not follow

---

[3] Allan Megill, "History, Memory, Identity," *History of the Human Sciences* 11 (1998), pp. 40–2.

[4] Pierre Nora, "Czas pamięci," transl. Wiktor Dłuski, *Res Publica Nowa*, № 7 (2001), p. 37.

[5] Peter A. Rudling, "Memories of 'Holodomor' and National Socialism in Ukrainian political culture," in *Rekonstruktion des Nationalmythos? Frankreich, Deutschland und die Ukraine im Vergleich*, ed. Yves Bizeul (Göttingen, 2013), pp. 227–58. Cf. Orest Subtelny, *Ukraine: A history* (Toronto, 1988); Orest Subtelnyi, *Ukraïna. Istoriia* (Lybid, 1991).

[6] Liudmyla Hrynevych, "Vid zaperechuvannia do vymushenoho vyznannia: pro mekhanizm vkhodzhennia temy holodu 1932–1933 rr. v ofitsiinyi publichnyi prostir u SRSR

in Secretary General Gorbachev's footsteps; the commission formed by the US Congress to study the Famine was beginning to publicize its research results. On December 25, 1987, Shcherbytsky gave a public speech and mentioned the events of 1932–33 in Soviet Ukraine. For the first time in fifty-five years, a member of the Politburo of the Communist Party of the Soviet Union broke with the Stalinist taboo and uttered the banned word "famine." From this moment, historians gained greater access to the archives related to that period of history.[7]

In subsequent years, materials about the Great Famine, such as reprints of archival documents[8] and academic articles,[9] regularly appeared on the pages of communist newspapers and magazines. Finally, in the resolution *On the Famine of 1932–1933 in Ukraine and the publication of related archival documents* (January 26, 1990), the Central Committee of the CPU declared that the cause of the Great Famine was collectivization policy and the low level of land cultivation in the Soviet Union.[10] Nonetheless, from year to year, the subject of the Famine and the responsibility of the Communist Party and its members for its occurrence was actively exploited in the struggle for social influence by oppositional political movements, and in particular, *Narodnyi rukh Ukraïny* (People's Movement of Ukraine, NRU). Its media messaging, along with that of a series of other newspapers that expressed similar

---

ta URSR naprykintsi 1980-kh rr.," *Problemy istoriï Ukraïny. Fakty, sudzhennia, poshuky* 18 (2008), p. 235.

[7] Stanislav Kul'chyts'kyi, "Do otsinky stanovyshcha v sils'komu hospodarstvi USRR u 1931–1933 rr.," *Ukraïns'kyi istorychnyi zhurnal*, № 3 (1988), pp. 15–27.

[8] See Ruslan Pyrih, "Povernennia pravdy," *Radians'ka Ukraïna*, March 27, 1990; M. Panchuk and S. Dibrov, "20-Z0-e. Dokumenty, fakty, svidetel'stva," *Kommunist*, № 4 (1990), pp. 70–84; "Holod 1932–1933 rokiv na Ukraïni. Svidchat' arkh. dok.," introd. Ruslan Pyrih, *Pid praporom leninizmu*, № 8 (1990), pp. 64–86; F. Rudych, "Svidchat' dokumenty. Holod 1933-ho. Rezultaty doslidzhen'," *Radians'ka Ukraïna*, December 3, 1990.

[9] Cf. Stanislav Kul'chyts'kyi, "Iak tse bulo. Chytaiuchy dokumenty stvorenoï pry konhresi SShA Komisiï po holodu 1932–1933 rr. na Ukraïni," *Pid praporom leninizmu*, № 23 (1990), pp. 79–86; Stanislav Kul'chitskii, "Tragediia, kotoroi moglo ne sluchit'sia," *Pravda Ukrainy*, October 16, 1988; Stanislav Kul'chyts'kyi, "Trydtsiat' tretii," *Sil's'ki visti*, June 12, 1988; T. Derev'iankin, "Kolektyvizatsiia," *Pid praporom leninizmu*, № 13 (1989), pp. 50–5; № 14, pp. 38–44; Volodymyr Maniak, "Holod: chomu i iak. Rozdumy nad rukopysom Knyhy-Memorialu '33-ii: Holod'," *Sil's'ki visti*, July 11, 1989; V. Savel'ev, "V poiskakh istiny. K voprosu o prichinakh goloda 1932–1933 gg. na Ukraine," *Pravda Ukrainy*, July 8, 1989; V. Vasil'ev, "30-ie gody na Ukrainie," *Kommunist*, № 17 (1990), p. 80; Heorhii Kasi'anov, "Ukraïna, 1933-ii," *Pid praporom leninizmu*, № 5 (1990), pp. 65–70; Ruslan Pirog, "V chëm prichina goloda na Ukraine v 30-kh godakh?," *Izvestiia TsK KPSS*, № 9 (1990), pp. 130–1; S. Bibik and A. Protsenko, "Tragicheskaia stranitsa istorii Ukrainy," *Pravda Ukrainy*, September 8, 1990; Vasyl' Marochko, "Holod na Ukraïni (1931–1933 pp.). Prychyny ta naslidky," *Problemy istoriï Ukraïny. Fakty, sudzhennia, poshuky* 1 (1991), pp. 59–68.

[10] Dmytro Viedienieiev and Dmytro Budkov, *Zaruchnytsia hlobal'noho protystoiannia. Trahediia Velykoho Holodu 1932–1933 rr. v Ukraïni v konteksti „kholodnoï viiny" 1945–1991 rokiv* (Kyiv, 2013), pp. 173–5.

political views, actively promoted this strategy. The editorial board of *Literaturna Ukraïna* played an especially prominent role in this respect.[11] The fundamental aim of authors publishing in this newspaper was to write in detail about those aspects of Soviet policy in Ukraine that were previously unknown and omitted from academic research. These articles did not merely confirm the Famine as historical fact or blame Stalin's politics but rather stressed the culpability of the entire Communist Party and its regime.

An article by Volodymyr Maniak and Lidiia Kovalenko entitled *Pamiat' ne proshchaie* [Memory does not forgive], which was published in *Literaturna Ukraïna* on August 2, 1990, resounded broadly with Ukrainian society. The article included an announcement of the imminent publication of a nationwide compilation of Famine victim recollections. In addition to the recollections of the victims, which they or their children or grandchildren documented, the editorial board received letters from Ukrainian residents outraged by the idea of the book. These letters appear in the article alongside witness recollections with an extraordinary effect: the creation of a cross section of opinions on the subject of the Great Famine that existed concurrently in Ukrainian society of the day. The discussion that had been confined to the private sphere up until then had suddenly been unleashed in the public domain. On the one hand, the publication included a story about starving farmers eating weeds to survive while working on a collective farm in a village near Vinnytsia in 1933; on the other, it brought forth the account of Olha Stakhova, a retired communist activist from the village of Katsmaziv in the Vinnytsia Oblast, who participated in the collectivization of her local area. In her opinion, all of the kurkuls received just punishment: "One should have no mercy for the enemy," her letter states, adding, "the stronger person wins."[12] Many explained this ideological pluralism with a lack of sufficient knowledge about matters related to the collectivization of Ukrainian peasantry. It seems, however, reaction depended more on the background of the narrator or witness. One cannot expect dramatic recollections about the life of an oppressed and starving peasant in 1933 from a party activist.

The issue of the Famine addressed on the pages of *Literaturna Ukraïna* was one of the more frequently discussed topics in Ukraine prior to the break-up of the Soviet Union and the final dismantling of the communist monopoly on power and ideology. The paper's contributors were

[11] See Svitlana Kostylieva, "Tema holodu 1932/1933 r. u dzerkali hazety 'Literaturna Ukraïna' doby horbachovs'koï hlasnosti," in *Holodomor 1932–1933 rokiv iak velychezna trahediia ukraïns'koho narodu. Materialy Vseukraïns'koï naukovoï konferentsiï. Kyïv, 15 lystopada 2002 r.* (Kyiv, 2003), pp. 236–42.

[12] Volodymyr Maniak and Lidiia Kovalenko, "Pamiat' ne proshchaie," *Literaturna Ukraïna*, August 2, 1990.

scholars and social activists of an orientation leaning to the right, whose input into this most sensitive of subjects for post-communist society represented a departure from the way of thinking characteristic of the previous system. Moreover, starting in Gorbachev's time, this newspaper became, in a sense, a forum for the Ukrainian opposition in its struggle against compromises with Russia. Indeed, *Literaturna Ukraïna* can itself be interpreted as a specific kind of "realm of memory." As the press organ of the *Natsional'na spilka pys'mennykiv Ukraïny* [National Writers' Union of Ukraine], the newspaper focused particular attention on the problems of collective memory and essentially conveyed in print form models for remembering the Great Famine that had been created and cultivated by the Ukrainian diaspora.

One element of *working through* the Soviet experience was the Communist Party's eventual acknowledgment of its active role in the events of the 1930s in Ukraine. This party position meant the opening of doors to numerous formerly off-limits Soviet archives. For the first time, scholars were able to conduct archival research of documents that, directly or indirectly, dealt with the famine tragedy in Ukraine. A team of Ukrainian scholars affiliated with the Central Committee of the CPU, headed by Ruslan Pyrih, discovered sensational documents about this period in the party archives. For the results of this research to be published, however, approval of the Politburo was still required. A heated meeting took place, with Volodymyr Ivashko, the First Secretary of the CPU at that time, concluding there was no point in delaying the matter. As a result, in the fall of 1990, a collection entitled *Holod 1932–1933 rokiv na Ukraïni. Ochyma istorykiv, movoiu dokumentiv* [The Famine of 1932–1933 in Ukraine. Through the Eyes of Historians, in the Language of Documents] was published.[13]

Memorials marking actual grave sites (burial places) were initially most often realized with the involvement and enthusiasm of private funders and organizations.[14] These symbolic markers often overlapped with places deemed as real mass burial sites by local communities. In the works of Oleksandra Veselova, as well as in the first catalog of Ukrainian "places of memory" of the Holodomor compiled by Anna Kaminsky, we can see that, at the beginning of the 1990s, symbolic crosses were erected and symbolic graves created in cemeteries in places of mass burials.[15]

---

[13] Ruslan Pyrih, compilation, *Holod 1932–1933 rokiv na Ukraïni. Ochyma istorykiv, movoiu dokumentiv* (Kyiv, 1990).

[14] Oleksandra Veselova, "Uvikopomnennia zahyblykh vid holodnoho moru," in *Holod – henotsyd 1933 roku v Ukraïni. Istoryko-politolohichnyi analiz sotsial'no-demohrafichnykh ta moral'no-psykholohichnykh naslidkiv. Materialy Mizhnarodnoï naukovo-teoretychnoï konferentsiï na vidznachennia 65-richchia trahediï ukraïns'koho narodu, Kyïv, 28 lystopada 1998 r.*, eds. Stanislav Kul'chyts'kyi [et al.] (Kyiv–New York, 2000)," p. 229.

[15] Anna Kaminsky, ed., *Erinnerungsorte an den Holodomor 1932/33 in der Ukraine*, revised by Ruth Gleinig, and Ronny Heidenreich (Berlin, 2008)

As newly established "places of memory," they served as moral recompense for the absence of graves marking the Great Famine's nameless victims.

Fig. 36. Monument on a Holodomor mass grave in the village of Tarhan, Kyiv Oblast, Ukraine (1988)

The first such site to be marked and maintained can be found in the village of Tarhan in the Volodarka Raion of Kyiv Oblast. The idea to build a Holodomor monument at a burial site of the victims came from Oleksandr Ushyns'kyi, who had gone to work in the village after graduating with an agricultural degree. Initially, the project was to simply tidy up the cemetery, but in that process the locals showed Ushyns'kyi a mass grave into which the bodies of the village's Famine victims had been thrown. This revelation led him to propose the construction of a monument on the site. The monument depicts the figure of a woman who symbolizes the tragedy of the Ukrainian mother and, more broadly, of the entire nation. Oleksandra Ovdiiuk and Alisa Maslo, the village's two oldest residents, tried to identify those buried in the mass grave. These efforts established that some 360 people who could be identified by name were likely buried at the site. A plinth for the monument was built in May 1988, into which a letter to future generations was placed. The letter is to be read publicly in 2032. The monument was officially unveiled on July 24, 1988.

This "place of memory," the only such place in Ukraine at the time, was visited in 1990 by the participants of an academic Holodomor research conference in Ukraine. Years later, Ushyns'kyi described the experience as follows:

> Several dozen militia cars drove up to the cemetery with a column of buses behind them, which pulled up all along the length of the village street. As they got out, they attached Ukrainian national symbols to trees and slowly headed for the cemetery. Thousands of people assembled that day at this holy place. They all walked up, made the sign of a cross, lit candles, took photographs and video-filmed the monument. Father Ioan, one of the leaders of the Ukrainian Autocephalous Orthodox Church, said a memorial prayer. Then Ukrainian patriots, colleagues, and foreign guests took to the stage. Among them were: Ivan Drach; an American scholar of the Ukrainian Holodomor, James Mace; a member of the US Congress Commission; American-Ukrainian barrister Marian Pavlo Kots, who was the first to finance a book in Ukraine about the Holodomor; as well as the great advocates of historical justice, Volodymyr Maniak and Lidiia Kovalenko-Maniak.
>
> I stood on the side behind the monument to hear the patriotic speeches. I realized that this was the crown jewel of my nation, and I felt proud for the renewal of the Ukrainian question and the beginning, at long last, of awaited independence... I saw how the secretary of the Volodarka party committee and a Ukrainian woman from the Cossack village of Medvyn in the Bohuslav raion, Maria Shabelnyk, lit a candle and, together with the chairman of the executive committee, Volodymyr Volianskyi, made the sign of a cross three times. Amen! Ukraine is rising from its knees. We have found the courage to announce to the world that we, Ukrainians, promise on the grave of victims of Stalinism to overcome our inferiority complex, and demand the renewal of historical justice and a Christian commemoration of the victims of the famine-genocide in Ukraine.[16]

In August of the same year, another key event for the burgeoning culture of Holodomor memory in Ukraine took place. The writer Oleksandr Kolomiiets, combining the resources of the *Ukraïns'kyi fond kul'tury* [Ukrainian Cultural Foundation], Ukraine's artistic elite and Orthodox clergy, succeeded in having ground consecrated for a monument to the victims of the Great Famine on the banks of the River Sula near Lubny in Poltava Oblast, with the local population creating a mound on which the memorial cross was placed.[17] The pursuit of historical justice and the search for those responsible for the Holodomor tragedy thus gave way to a desire to materialize the traces of this extermination. Questions about the causes and the perpetrators were replaced by the question of how best to commemorate the Holodomor in the public sphere.

---

[16] Oleksandr Ushyns'kyi, "Pro vshanuvannia pam'iati zhertv holodomoru 1932–1933 rokiv v selakh kyïvshchyny. Pershi pam'iatnyky zhertvam henotsydu," *Problemy istoriï Ukraïny. Fakty, sudzhennia, poshuky* 18: *Holod 1932–1933 rokiv – henotsyd ukraïns'koho narodu* (2008), p. 410.

[17] Viedienieiev and Budkov, *Zaruchnytsia hlobal'noho protystoiannia*, pp. 175–6.

4.2 Ambivalence of social memory or "non-memory" in the context of memory of the Holodomor in the early 1990s

The declaration of independence by Ukraine in August 1991 heralded a new era in the life of the Ukrainian people. This would, seemingly, also open new possibilities for studying and publicizing the facts about the origins of the Great Famine of 1933. However, the opportunity was not taken advantage of fully. The newly independent Ukrainian state came into being under unprecedented international circumstances. Constructing the elements of its own state apparatus (administration, army, police, currency, etc.) was relatively easy, but liberation of the Ukrainian elites from a sense of dependence on Russia involved greater effort. The attention of society and the government was consumed, on the one hand, by the collapse of the Communist Party, the temporary ban on its activity in Ukraine, and the almost immediate eradication of the written legacy of the communist period, and – on the other hand – a deepening economic crisis.

Ukraine is still torn asunder in the realm of its memory culture. The problem, resulting largely from a lack of reflection on its communist past, has dogged independent Ukraine since 1991, and neither Leonid Kravchuk, nor Leonid Kuchma, during their respective terms in office, were able to unify the memory of Ukrainian society, divided by divergent historical experiences.[18]

The Ukrainian culture of memory has a dual character as a result of a series of political actions (and inactions), functioning in parallel and nearly independent of one another. Since the mid-1990s, the culture of memory in Ukraine serves as one of the main arenas of confrontation between two major political camps – post-communist and national-liberal.[19] The differences are readily apparent in the terms they employ in relation to World War II: while Ukraine's strongly Sovietized East still refers to the Great Patriotic War, the nationalist West has adopted the more neutral "German-Soviet War," which positions Ukraine as only an object of conflict.[20] Attempts to reconcile both views of history with hybrid conceptualizations of memory that encompass the whole of Ukraine have been made, for instance, by presenting World War II

---

[18] Mykola Riabchuk, "Kul'tura pam'iati ta polityka zabuttia," *Krytyka*, № 1–2 (2006), http://krytyka.kiev.ua/articles/s.7_1-2_2006.html.

[19] Stefan Troebst, *Postkommunistische Erinnerungskulturen im östlichen Europa. Bestandsaufnahme, Kategorisierung, Periodisierung / Postkomunistyczne kultury pamięci w Europie Wschodniej. Stan, kategoryzacja, periodyzacja* (Wrocław, 2005), p. 37.

[20] Iurii Slyvka, "Ukraïna v Druhii svitovii viini. Natsional'no-politychnyi ta mizhnarodno-pravovyi aspekty," *Ukraïna. Kul'turna spadshchyna, natsional'na svidomist', derzhavnist'*, № 3–4 (1997), p. 19.

as the apogee of tragic events rather than a conflict between "good" and "evil."[21] Regardless of how the facts are manipulated, however, it seems impossible for the memory of the war to serve as a uniting force. There is also a generational component to this divide that was formed largely during Soviet times. Perceptions of the Holodomor and of World War II, including the Holocaust, among Ukraine's oldest and middle generations is, to a great extent, an effect of the way history was taught in the Ukrainian SSR.[22] Finally, the politics of memory practised by state authorities over the last two decades are also part of this equation. Memory of the Great Famine was the most frequently exploited element of national history in the struggle to shape a unified or unifying identity.

Two different conceptualizations capture the essence of the social and political context in which Holodomor memory culture was shaped and what the "places of memory" of this event actually embodied in the 1990s. The first is known as "social ambivalence in historical memory"; I use a second, known as social (non)memory.

Mykola Riabchuk has questioned whether the memory culture furthered social consolidation or deepened social ambivalence in historical memory, an approach that resonates with Tetiana Zhurzhenko.[23] "Social ambivalence" is understood here as the parallel belief in mutually exclusive values characteristic of society in a stage of transformation, where a clash between two political cultures and two models of social, economic, and even linguistic behaviors takes place.[24] Its role can be positive, protecting individuals from psychic traumas and society from dramatic conflicts. Nevertheless, this ambivalence sustains "a state of ailment, favours social stagnation, and creates the illusion of a form of social compromise, some "third way" that, in reality, leads only to a "third world."[25] In the case of Ukraine, the fact that being a Russian-speaking Ukrainian is still standard in the country's eastern regions is one example of the effects.[26] On the level of politics, this ambivalence is seen in the conscious stance of political activists signaling their political views and past models.[27]

---

[21] Troebst, *Postkommunistische Erinnerungskulturen im östlichen Europa*, p. 42.

[22] Ibid., p. 41.

[23] Cf. Mykola Riabchuk, *Vid Malorosii' do Ukraïny: Paradoksy zapizniloho natsiietvorennia* (Kyiv, 2000); Tatiana Zhurzhenko, "Commemorating the Famine as Genocide: The Contested Meanings of Holodomor Memorials in Ukraine," in *Memorials in Times of Transition*, eds. Susanne Buckley-Zistel and Stefanie Schäfer (Cambridge, 2014), pp. 221–41.

[24] Riabchuk, *Vid Malorosii' do Ukraïny*, p. 280.

[25] Ibid., p. 281.

[26] Mykola Riabchuk, "Mizh hromadians'kym suspil'stvom i novym etatyzmom (Stanovlennia demokratiï i (chy) rozbudova derzhavy)," *Ukraïna. Kul'turna spadshchyna, natsional'na svidomist', derzhavnist'*, № 2 (1995), p. 204.

[27] Riabchuk, *Vid Malorosii' do Ukraïny*, pp. 282–3.

Such ambivalence is typical of any nation accustomed to the hard paternalism of the state. Ukraine emerged from the collapse of the Soviet Union rather than a war of liberation. Independence was thus "gifted" to Ukraine by history, along with a pre-determined territory demarcated by borders.[28] The late national awakening of Ukrainians, their unfinished process of forming a national consciousness and the consequent separatist tendencies of the various regions, fostered the deepening of this ambivalence. Moreover, at the outset of its state independence, Ukraine largely lacked that which is considered a foundation of Western European democracies – a civil society. Its population had to develop certain new attitudes,[29] changing its ways of thinking and the interpretation of its new reality.[30]

As a newly post-communist state, Ukraine, at the turn of the 1990s, was torn not only between the values of state paternalism and the free market, or between communist authoritarianism and liberal democracy, but also between a traditional Soviet identity and a new Ukrainian one – between, on the one hand, an Empire's "superior," "more prestigious" language, and on the other, a culture and regenerating language of the nation's own "inferior," predominantly rural forefathers.[31] Over the decades, many Ukrainian citizens had been convinced by the Soviet narrative of "the bloodthirsty nature of Ukrainian bourgeois nationalism," identified first and foremost with Western Ukraine and the "Banderites." At the end of the 1990s, a mere 13 percent of those surveyed saw nationalist beliefs as a positive trait in an election candidate, while 67 percent considered them to be a serious flaw (with the remainder having no view on the subject).[32] At the same time, from the moment it gained independence the Ukrainian state explained its need for sovereignty with reference to historical justice and the age-old yearning of Ukrainians for independence.[33] Support and expansion of the Ukrainian national historical narrative became an important current in the shaping of the modern nation. In line with the Ukrainian constitution (chapter 1, art. 11): "The State promotes the consolidation and development of the Ukrainian nation, of its historical consciousness, traditions and culture, and also the development of the ethnic, cultural, linguistic and religious identity of all indigenous peoples and national minorities

---

[28] Włodzimierz Pawluczuk, *Ukraina. Polityka i mistyka* (Cracow, 1998), p. 51.

[29] Andrzej J. Madera, *Ukraina na rozdrożu. Między Rosją a Europą* (Rzeszów, 2000), pp. 68–9.

[30] Oksana Zabuzhko, "Filosofiia i problema kul'turnoï prytomnosti natsiï," *Ukraïna. Kul'turna spadshchyna, natsional'na svidomist', derzhavnist',* № 2 (1995), p. 21.

[31] Riabchuk, *Vid Malorosiï do Ukraïny*, p. 285.

[32] Ibid., p. 287.

[33] Iaroslav Isaievych, "Problema pokhodzhennia ukraïns'koho narodu. Istoriohrafichnyi i politychnyi aspekt," *Ukraïna. Kul'turna spadshchyna, natsional'na svidomist', derzhavnist',* № 2 (1995), pp. 3–17.

of Ukraine."[34] This is why the restoration of memory, referred to as "filling in the blanks" in the discourse of *perestroika*, was given such weight in projects aimed at reviving Ukrainian identity. It was a natural reaction to the silencing, stigmatization, and uprooting of Ukrainian memory and the grafting on of a "Soviet historical consciousness." It bears stating that belief in the significance of collective memory was key for this period. At the same time, it is evident that the role of the past in the construction of the future was overestimated. Recent experiences of the communist past turned out to be the more significant ballast for transformations of cultural identity than the history of exile, martyrology, and "historical enemies." The vision of the past created by representatives of both younger and middle generations has not moved beyond anti-imperialist discourse.

On the level of state decisions, the process of decommunization was in progress: archives were opened, works by scholars from diaspora communities were promoted, and a new subject – "History of Ukraine" – was added to university and school curricula. Despite this, the politics of memory during the first decade of Ukrainian independence was national in content but Soviet in form, speaking to an unwillingness on the part of the Ukrainian government to break with the communist past. The authorities seemed to vacillate between arrangements with Russia and the national idea of Ukraine. The lack of clear goals of the politics of memory at that time only deepened the identity crisis and nostalgia for the former system among many Ukrainians.[35] The matter of the Great Famine remained primarily the domain of academic and artistic elites – in other words, of those who were positioning themselves as the revisionists of Soviet heritage. Let us recall that on December 11, 1990, Ukrainian politician Taras Chornovil, then editor of the newspaper *Moloda Ukraïna* [Young Ukraine] and a city councillor

Fig. 37. Taras Chornovil visiting the Holodomor monument in Los Angeles, US, in 1991

[34] Quoted after: Constitution of Ukraine, https://www.wipo.int/edocs/lexdocs/laws/en/ua/ua013en.pdf.

[35] Iuliia Zernii, "Derzhavna polityka pam'iati v Ukraïni. Stanovlennia ta suchasnyi stan," *Stratehichni priorytety*, № 3 (2008), p. 43.

in Lviv, visited Ukrainian "places of memory" in Los Angeles during a visit to the United States.[36]

It is also possible to look at the Ukrainian politics of memory of this time through the prism of Piotr Kwiatkowski's (non)memory concept. For him, non-memory (also called forgetfulness or white spots) is not limited to irreversible and complete loss of knowledge about specific fragments of the past reality. This concept refers to content that has been retained with the help of available methods of preserving the past (family memory), is relatively easy to recover (rebuild), and is essential for the "community of memory" and valid for the entire society (nation). In his opinion, non-memory can have both active and passive forms. Active non-memory is an example of the politics of memory, when the authorities use available tools to create a specific image of the past. And passive non-memory arises when the present generation does not make the effort to commemorate and thus loses something important from its own past.[37]

(Non)memory emerges as a result of either neglect or the planned erasure of a memory of specific events from the collective consciousness. When considering the communist period in the context of the Great Famine, we refer to the active generation of (non)memory of this event. The memory of the Holodomor was neglected, generations of witnesses were silenced, and its interpretation as a genocide was negated; at most, it was presented as an intermediary stage in the modernization of the Soviet countryside in the 1930s. Iwona Irwin-Zarecka underscores that, as a political act, (non)memory is a deliberate action.[38] At stake is the profound disavowal of the value of a given event or individual, consequently determined unworthy of remembrance.

At present, (non)memory appears to be an instrument in the meting out of historical justice. From this perspective, the symbolic punishment will encompass, paradoxically, the memory of communism. The issue is rooted in the fact that only the omission of certain facts from Ukraine's past can sustain the narrative of its victimization by the communist system. The Hungarian scholar Richard S. Esbenshade describes contemporary cultures of memory in post-communist countries precisely as "remembering through (non)memory." In his opinion, this carries with it the great risk of repeating the project of social amnesia that engulfed Europe after World War II, the effects of which

---

[36] *Svoboda*, № 12 (January 18, 1991), p. 5.

[37] Piotr Kwiatkowski, "Społeczne tworzenie niepamięci," in *Asymilacja, akulturacja, dyskryminacja. Wokół problemów zachowania tożsamości mniejszości narodowych i etnicznych w Polsce*, ed. Lech Nijakowski (Warsaw, 2009), pp. 91–128.

[38] Iwona Irwin-Zarecka, *Frames of Remembrance: The Dynamics of Collective Memory* (New Brunswick–New Jersey, 2009), p. 127.

these contemporary memory cultures are convinced they are eradicating through their efforts.[39]

Vladyslav Hrynevych wrote that the game played on both sides of the memory field became a daily matter for Ukrainian authorities in the 1990s. Both the left and the right could, in equal measure, enjoy President Leonid Kuchma's support for their endeavors.[40] Depending on the political situation, Kuchma chose whatever best suited him from different versions of Ukraine's history (the Soviet or the national one). As Andrew Wilson puts it, the President:

> called for the best bits of Soviet Ukrainian history to be combined with the best bits of the Ukrainophile version, shorn of awkward elements like the Purges or the OUN, to create a 'single national idea'. As this task is not yet complete, Kuchma has roamed far and wide in his historical discourse, praising Hrushevsky in Kyiv one minute and tearfully pledging eternal friendship with Russia in Sevastopol the next.[41]

In George Grabowicz's opinion, this form of politics was maintained through a compromise of Ukrainians with their conscience and dignity.[42] His near radical claim completely dismisses a series of positive initiatives undertaken by the government at that time. Nevertheless, on the other hand, all of these actions can be justified by the necessity of consolidating Ukrainian society. In the meantime, the politics did not lead to integration and caused even greater discord in society. It is thus worthwhile to examine them.

The process of nationalizing Ukraine's political and cultural space during the 1990s was neither complete nor even systematic, although shaping the nation was part of the order of the day for state authorities. Years of independence created a discourse of "necessary memory" that was accepted by both participants in, and commentators on, Ukrainian socio-political life. The nationalization of the school history program was one outcome of this situation. Changes in Ukraine's national symbolism and canon of public holidays and political rituals, which reflected the approved (by politicians) version of national history, followed the same trajectory, albeit less successfully.[43] It must be pointed out, however, that a sense of shared national identity that could legitim-

[39] Richard S. Esbenshade, "Remembering to Forget: Memory, History, National Identity in Postwar East-Central Europe," *Representations* 49 (1995), pp. 72–96.

[40] Vladislav Grinevich, "Raskolotaia pamiat'. Vtoraia mirovaia voina v istoricheskom soznanii ukrainskogo obshchestva," *Neprikosnovennyi zapas* 40–41, № 2–3 (2005), accessed July 30, 2020, http://magazines.russ.ru/nz/2005/2/gri24.html.

[41] Andrew Wilson, *The Ukrainians: Unexpected Nation* (New Haven–London, 2015), p. 222.

[42] Hryhorii Hrabovych, "Ukraïna. Pidsumky stolittia," *Krytyka*, № 11 (1999), p. 7.

[43] Sofiia Hrachova, "Pam'iat', kontrpam'iat' i polityka," *Krytyka*, № 11 (2006), https://krytyka.com/ua/articles/pamyat-kontrpamyat-i-polityka.

ize the existence of this young nation in the historical narrative did not become the only, or even the dominant, unifying idea over the course of this decade.

Despite significant social changes and the publication of numerous documents and memoirs, society's short-term reflection on the experience of communism and in particular, of repressions, did not result in a uniform view of the Soviet past among Ukrainians. Part of Ukrainian society minimized the harm inflicted by the Communist Party or viewed it as a historical necessity. The campaign conducted in the press and on television with the goal of restoring memory highlighted the approaches of different political circles to this issue. Some saw it as a chance to shape Ukrainian national identity by displacing the cornerstones of the memory of the "Soviet people": the Great Patriotic War, the myth of the Soviet Union's achievements in the fields of science and technology, and its global superpower status. Opponents of this approach assert that a rejection of the USSR's legacy is impossible and also unnecessary. Others believe it should be replaced with alternative images that can be accepted as "immemorially Ukrainian." For some, this approach intensifies the yearning for an imagined, ahistorical past, an epoch of stability and normality. As Svetlana Boym wrote, "this mass nostalgia is a kind of nationwide midlife crisis; many are longing for the time of their childhood and youth, projecting personal affective memories onto the larger historical picture and partaking collectively in a selective forgetting" of the communist system's cruelty toward its own citizens.[44]

Works on the subject of Ukrainian identity that deal with this period utilize various terms to describe this state of affairs, identifying it as Soviet, pro-Russian, Little Russian, East Slavic, multi-ethnic, non-ethnic, or weakly ethnic.[45] Despite the array of names (which speaks to their inadequacy), there is no doubt that the majority of citizens, particularly in the east and south of the country, did not adopt an exclusively Ukrainian identity, preferring other forms of self-identification.

This rejection of a Ukrainian national identity went hand in hand with the denial of a Ukrainian historical narrative, the fact of its existence, its raison d'être, and the national and patriotic ideas it embodied. Peter Rogers, in an article based on his conversations with secondary school teachers and pupils in Ukraine's eastern regions,[46] reveals the disillusionment of local residents with the state's politics of memory.

---

[44] Svetlana Boym, *The Future of Nostalgia* (New York, 2002), p. 58.

[45] Zabuzhko, "Filosofiia i problema kul'turnoï prytomnosti natsiï," p. 202.

[46] For more detail on the research outcomes see Peter Rogers, "Understanding Regionalism and the Politics of Identity in Ukraine's Eastern Borderlands," *Nationalities Papers* 34, № 2 (2006), pp. 157–74.

He notes that the respondents were particularly dissatisfied with the lack of consideration in the school history curriculum for their singular historical experience as well as cultural and familial ties with Russia. It bears noting that half of the respondents – the secondary school pupils – were born and raised in independent Ukraine.[47] Generally, this phenomenon is explained by the absence of effective means to fight the post-Soviet ideological legacy. It can also be explained by the ineffectualness of the nationalization project in Ukrainian society and by the consequences of the manipulative politics of post-Soviet Ukrainian governments, which intentionally cultivated an ambivalent historical memory to maintain social division and use it for their own benefit.[48]

Admittedly, there are other factors besides state politics in the areas of education and culture that impact the development of Ukrainian historical memory, including family communication and personal experience. Nevertheless, all historical narratives that differ from the national one are tied to a greater or lesser degree with the official narrative about the history of Ukraine and Ukrainians. Additionally, the dearth of non-nationalist historical symbols lacks an appropriate infrastructure; they cannot function on the same level as the state's historical narrative, which is backed by state holidays and social rituals, and permeates all levels of education. It is thus possible to surmise that alternative versions of history in Ukraine emerged at that time as grassroots reactions to "top-down" politics.

To summarize, it appears that slogans proclaiming the importance of historical truth to the rebirth of Ukrainian society's spiritual potential were seized upon eagerly. While various social circles treated them differently, they shared the common conviction that restoring historical truth would bring both liberation and prospects for the future. The revival of memory was even considered a condition for the building of a future in Ukraine. This ambivalent consciousness, the unsteady balance of two opposing cultures, could not last long without social resonance.

Despite the inconsistent politics of Holodomor remembrance in the public sphere and the insufficient support for academic research during the presidencies of both Leonid Kravchuk and Leonid Kuchma, quite a bit was done. For example, the foundations for establishing a Ukrainian Holodomor research culture were laid, the search for the mass graves of those who had perished in the Great Famine was initiated, and numerous social initiatives sprung up to collect and document the recollections of surviving witnesses.

---

47 Ibid., pp. 160–1.

48 See Taras Kuzio, "History, Memory and Nation Building in the Post-Soviet Colonial Space," *Nationalities Paper* 30, № 2 (2002), pp. 241–64.

State documents from the 1990s referred to the "holodomor" in the lowercase, or as the "famine-genocide" (likewise lowercase), which was also true for the media. The genocidal nature of the Holodomor was underscored in public discourse already in the mid-1990s. Still, the event's historical significance and the necessity of its commemoration were reduced to the exclusive contexts of state-building and the Ukrainian nation's moral rebirth through dissociation from its communist past.

It bears remembering that Leonid Kravchuk understood the weight that the subject of the Holodomor carried in condemning the communist leadership and the opportunity it offered him to dissociate himself symbolically. Providing support for the national democrats in their struggle with the communist past became a priority. According to Georgiy Kasianov, this was a well thought out and effective tactic aimed at strengthening presidential power, which was weak at that time.[49]

The politics of memory concerning the Holodomor was realized then by the national democratic camp with the support of politically like-minded media. The presidential decree issued by Leonid Kravchuk in March of 1993 on the occasion of the Great Famine's sixtieth anniversary set the parameters for a whole range of top-down initiatives:

> It is of utmost importance that we should be able to properly honour those murdered through hunger in every oblast, every raion, city, town, and in each village of our now independent homeland, by raising crosses and other signs of remembrance, cleaning up the cemeteries, and celebrating Memorial services. It is our fundamental duty to remember our mothers and fathers, brothers and sisters, who died in the famine-genocide. Our youth should know and remember the heinous crime that the communist clique committed against the Ukrainian nation.[50]

To mark this anniversary, a series of monuments were erected. Monuments to the victims of the Holodomor were unveiled in virtually all larger cities in Ukraine – in the center of Kyiv, in Kherson and Kharkiv, Chervonohrad in the Lviv Oblast, in the Luhansk Oblast and in Odesa, in the Vinnytsia and Chernihiv oblasts as well as in Lubny (on the Zazhura hill).[51] The cemeteries of most towns and villages were tidied up and efforts were made to identify the graves (whether real or symbolic) of the Famine victims.

Oleksandr Ushyns'kyi notes the significance of Holodomor monuments to the national revival in Ukraine at the turn of the 1990s:

---

[49] Heorhii Kasi'anov, *Danse macabre. Holod 1932–1933 rokiv u politytsi, masovii svidomosti ta istoriohrafiï* (1980-ti – pochatok 2000-kh) (Kyiv, 2010), p. 42.

[50] Quotation after: Veselova, "Uvikopomnennia zahyblykh," p. 233.

[51] Ibid., p. 237.

> The unveiling of monuments is of major historical significance, forcing Ukrainians to reflect on the bitter pages of their most recent history, on who we actually are on this sacred, fertile land, what it is that we desire, what kind of Ukraine we are planning to build and, finally, whether we can oppose everything that is anti-Ukrainian and which has accumulated in the course of the criminal communist regime.[52]

In reality, these resolutions and statements resulted from the situation at the time and were only declarative in character. The governments of the day and both presidents – Kravchuk and Kuchma – performed the absolute minimum of undertakings when it came to the politics of memory of the Holodomor. State-level announcements were an example of unprecedented political popularism, although there were admittedly a few initiatives that came to fruition in terms of creating places of remembrance. Nonetheless, starting with the sixtieth anniversary, in 1993 – the national remembrance of the victims of the Great Famine, hitherto expressed through spontaneous commemorative actions, was given a defined, institutionalized framework that enabled work through state institutions. From that time, monuments were most frequently raised on the occasion of the Holodomor's anniversaries, with each anniversary producing another opportunity to symbolically encapsulate the event, now packaged in an appropriate form. Monuments to the victims of the Great Famine of 1932–33 were established in every oblast, and today one stands in every larger Ukrainian village. The construction and unveilings of monuments, symbolic crosses and other symbols took place in a simultaneously religious and patriotic atmosphere.[53]

The monuments to the Great Famine of 1932–33 raised in the 1990s and at the onset of the twenty-first century constituted serious competition for the monuments to the "Patriotic War," both in terms of their number and their growing significance for the collective memory and modern identity of Ukrainians.[54] While the connotations of monuments to the Great Famine, particularly in the 1990s, in large part echoed the visual culture of those connected to the war, over time the designs in-

---

[52] Ushyns'kyi, "Pro vshanuvannia pam'iati zhertv holodomoru," p. 413.

[53] Oleksandra Veselova, "Uvichnennia pam'iati zhertv holodomoru-henotsydu 1932–1933 rokiv v Ukraïni," *Ukraïns'kyi istorychnyi zhurnal*, № 2 (2004), pp. 434–41.

[54] Monuments to the Great Patriotic War constituted one of the most pertinent means of Soviet propaganda in shaping the 'myth of victory over fascism.' From the end of the 1940s right up until the collapse of the USSR, thousands of monuments were unveiled in each of the Soviet republics commemorating the victims of the war. At least one was to be found in every village from which soldiers set off for the front, not to mention towns and cities where dozens of such monuments can be found. In this way the Great Patriotic War was to be omnipresent within the memory of the 'Soviet people.' Cf. Grinevich, "Raskolotaia pamiat'"; Natal'ia Konradova and Anna Ryleva, "Geroi i zhertvy. Memorialy Velikoi Otechestvennoi," *Neprikosnovennyi zapas* 40–41, № 2–3 (2005), accessed July 30, 2020, http://magazines.russ.ru/nz/2005/2/ko16.html.

creasingly came to rely on religious symbolism. As a result, the monuments erected in Ukraine differ from those created by the Ukrainian diaspora, which (with the exception of crosses raised beside Orthodox churches) were influenced by Western European and American visual culture of the Holocaust. Until the end of the 1990s, there were no monuments commemorating the Great Famine that united the national and diaspora traditions of remembrance.

4.3 The role of the Ukrainian diaspora in North America in initiating the construction of the Holodomor monument in Kyiv

The literature on the Holodomor often states that only a few monuments were constructed under the presidency of Leonid Kravchuk, even though the very significant monuments in Kyiv and in Lubny were solemnly unveiled during that time. It is also not generally known that the initial design and prospective location of the monument in Kyiv were different than those we know today.

With the return of independence to Ukraine, the role of the Ukrainian diaspora in the context of Holodomor remembrance was primarily supportive, including financially, in educational endeavors as well as academic and social projects designed to study historical materials and gather witness testimonies. Several individuals who made significant contributions to popularizing the subject deserve recognition here. Marian Kots (1922–2011) is certainly one such person. This patron of Ukrainian culture in the US financially supported, among other endeavours, the Association of Researchers of the Famine-Genocide of 1932–33 (since 1998, the Association of Researchers of Famines in Ukraine) and served as its council's representative in the diaspora. He also financed the publication of academic works and conference materials and supported monument construction projects. The Association's founder, Lidiia Kovalenko-Maniak, underlined Kots' role in a conversation with the editorial board of the journal *Suchasnist'* [Contemporaneity] in 1993:

> We have a close relationship with many enthusiasts in the diaspora. In the first place, I want to mention a publisher from the United States, Marian Kots – a true promoter and a representative of the Association in the diaspora who, in 1983, organized a commemoration in memory of the victims of the Ukrainian Holodomor in his countries [US and Canada] that is remembered by people there to this day.[55]

[55] Volodymyr Kulyk, "'My zatialysia: polyniv ne bude...'. Pro Asotsiatsiiu doslidnykiv holodu-henotsydu 1932–33 rokiv v Ukraïni rozpovidaie ïï holova Lidiia Kovalenko--Maniak," *Suchasnist'* 381, № 1 (1993), p. 94.

An obituary written by Oleksandra Veselova mentions that Marian Kots founded M-P Kots Publishing,[56] which published first-rate works on the subject of the Great Famine, including the first volume of a three-volume bibliography of the Holodomor that is an invaluable research source to this day as it contains works published in the diaspora and unknown to Ukrainian researchers.[57]

Kots was an advocate for the building of a Holodomor monument in the Ukrainian capital.[58] It was on his initiative that a competition for the project's design was organized in 1992. The competition was open only to architects and sculptors of Ukrainian nationality. The following announcement was printed in the major newspapers of the time, including in the Canadian *Ukraïns'kyi holos* [The Ukrainian Voice]:

> The somber sixtieth anniversary of these tragic events is nearing. We are confronting the fact that, to date, there is no monument to the victims of this unbelievable act of genocide in Kyiv, even though one exists in distant Winnipeg.
>
> Let justice prevail. The dead need to be memorialized, and we, the living, need to deeply reflect on this crime of Bolshevik totalitarianism.
>
> Thousands of people in Ukraine and beyond its borders think that such a monument must be created in the capital of independent Ukraine, in Kyiv. These hopes must be fulfilled.
>
> The All-Ukrainian Association of Researchers of Famines in Ukraine has supported the initiative of its council member and a Ukrainian civic activist in the United States of America, Mr. Marian Kots, and is announcing a competition for the best monument design.
>
> (...) The monument must be integrated with a memorial building (..), where all can pay homage before the Eternal Flame to the memory of those who had starved.[59]

It was from this announcement that Bohdan Kowal learned about the competition; the son of Roman Kowal, he had assisted his father in the construction of the Holodomor monument in Winnipeg unveiled in 1984, which his father had also designed. He entered his own design for the competition (ID 030658), including sketches, a wooden model of the proposed monument and a short explanation.

The author proposed a granite monument that would in places appear to be cracking. For Kowal, the cracked appearance was to symbolize

[56] Oleksandra Veselova, "Viddanist' Ukraïni. Trudy i dni Mariiana Kotsia," *Problemy istoriï Ukraïny. Fakty, sudzhennia, poshuky* 20 (2011), pp. 325–34.

[57] Stanislav V. Kul'chyts'kyi, Olha F. Botushans'ka, and Volodymyr Motyka, eds., *Holodomor v Ukraïni 1932–1933 rr. Bibliohrafichnyi pokazhchyk*, compilation Larysa M. Bur'ian, and Inna E. Rikun (Odesa–Lviv, 2001).

[58] Veselova, "Viddanist' Ukraïni," pp. 325–34.

[59] *Ukraïns'kyi holos*, August 3, 1992.

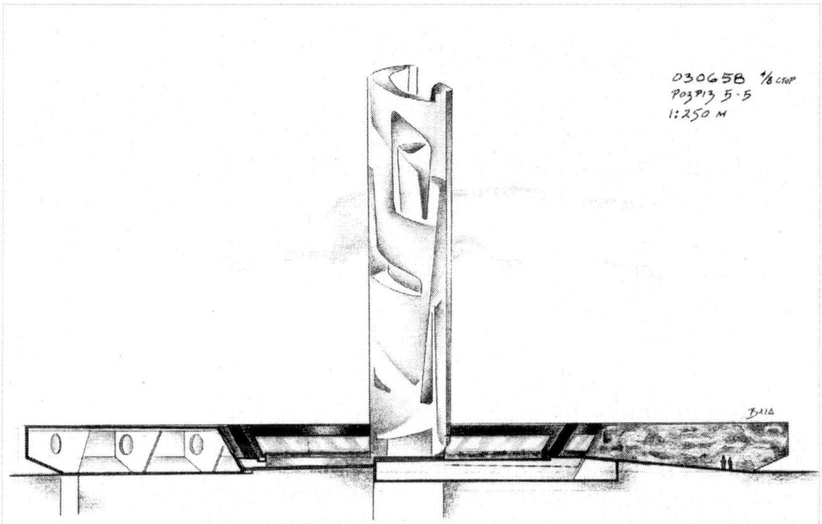

Fig. 38. Bohdan Kowal's design proposal of the Holodomor Memorial

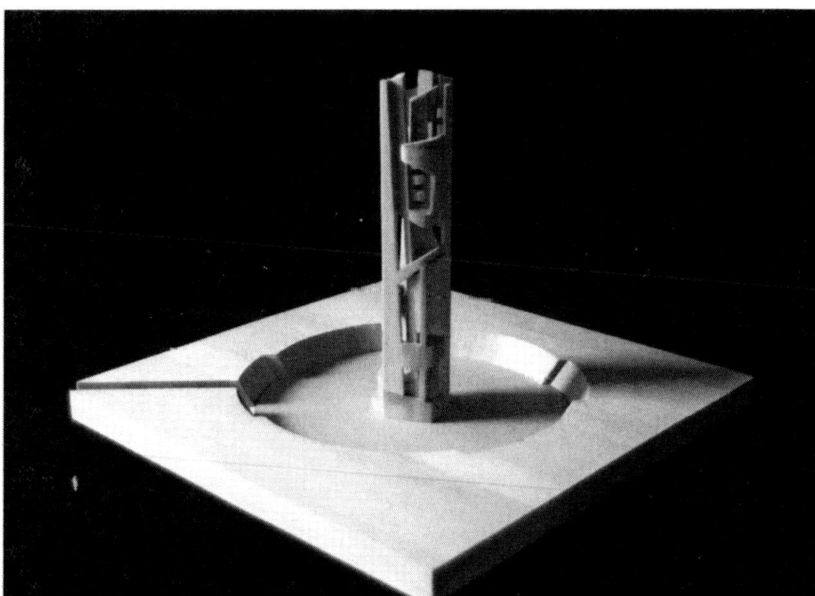

Fig. 39. Bohdan Kowal's model of the Holodomor Memorial design

the rupture in the stone veil of silence that communism had placed around its act of genocide against the Ukrainian nation, as well as the potential for surviving this trauma and moving forward.[60] Kowal noted that, in preparing his design for the competition, he realized that a nation's maturity can be measured by how it publicly commemorates the historical experiences of greatest significance to its own identity. The monument that he designed was to be a tangible sign of the end of the national mourning process.

In 1993, when the competition for the Kyiv monument was announced, several monuments commemorating the Holodomor were being built or officially unveiled in Ukraine, including in Bila Tserkva, Lubny, several villages and in Kyiv itself, beside St. Michael's Golden-Domed Monastery. These monuments were not intended to bring closure to the process of mourning, however, but to provide places to facilitate the national experience of mourning. Bohdan Kowal's design was thus far ahead of its time since the mourning process was only just beginning in independent Ukraine.

On January 30, 1994, Bohdan Kowal received a letter from Marian Kots informing him that the jurors had exercised their right to not select a winner and instead gave a commendation to seven designers, with each receiving a monetary prize and a diploma of participation. Along with the letter, Marian Kots enclosed a cheque for $500 USD.[61]

Although Kowal's design received the first commendation, it was never realized and remained in obscurity. Several years later, a monument complemented by a Hall of Memory was built in Kyiv on the basis of assumptions similar to those behind the Ukrainian-Canadian artist's design. Other designs drawn up for the competition were likewise forgotten, although some were used as illustrations in publications. For instance, fragments of the monument design that received a third-place commendation, by Ukrainian sculptor Roksolana Kardynalovsky (1929–2018), were used a decade later (in 2003) on the cover of a special issue of the monthly *Nashe zhyttya / Our Life*. In its commentary on this issue's publication, the newspaper *Svoboda* pointed out, "The cover features sculptures by Roksolana Kardynalovsky that constitute part of a monument to the victims of the Holodomor (the monument's design was sponsored by Marian Kots from the US)."[62]

I see in this decision not to build the monument the quintessence of the perception of the Holodomor at the time by the "communities

---

[60] Interview with Halyna and Bohdan Kowal, Winnipeg, November 17, 2017 (the author's private collection).

[61] The letter in the possession of the addressee.

[62] L[ev] Khmel'kovs'kyi, "Spetsiial'nyi vypusk zhurnalu "Nashe zhyttia" – iliustrovana entsyklopediia Velykoho holodu," *Svoboda*, № 10 (2004), p. 18.

of memory" in Ukraine and the most influential decision makers of the politics of memory. Unlike the Ukrainians abroad, Ukrainian society had not yet undergone a national mourning. The monument, which was finally unveiled in 1993 in the center of the Ukrainian capital, was an expression of the urgent need for Ukrainian society to start the mourning process in earnest, and this need would not be satisfied by Bohdan Kowal's winning project. The monument unveiled in Kyiv in 2008 ("The Candle of Memory") embodied an understanding of the Holodomor and the perceived role of mourning for those who had died during the famine in the national revival of Ukrainians.

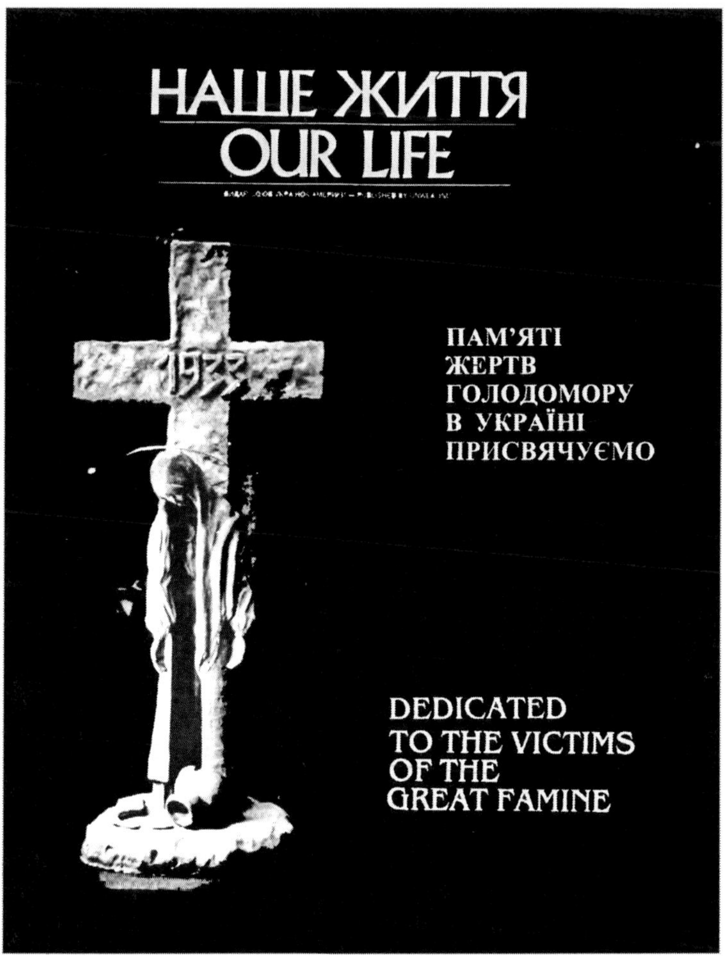

Fig. 40. Cover of the monthly Nashe zhyttia / Our life *(No. 11, 2003) featuring a fragment of Roksolana Kardynalovsky's design for Marian Kots' monument competition in 1992*

4.4 The Holodomor in the politics of memory from the mid-1990s to 2004

Some consider the two-term and ten-years-long presidency of Leonid Kuchma a worthy continuation of his predecessor's governance, while for others, it was a regression from previously initiated politics of renouncing the communist past. I would agree with the analysis of Volodymyr Kravchenko, who views Kuchma's politics as characterized by a demonstrative departure from a nationalist and romantic idea of statehood in favour of a territorial and state-based one and the abandonment of a pro-western stance for the sake of maintaining a balance between Russia and the West, as well as the partial rehabilitation (reanimation) of the Soviet past.[63]

It is important to note that Kuchma accomplished a fair amount in terms of commemorating the Great Famine. Notably, Kuchma's administration included a number of historians, among them Yurii Lytvyn, Dmytro Tabachnyk, and Volodymyr Tkachenko. According to Vasyl Marochko, this group had a bearing on the indecisive nature of the politics of memory in terms of commemorating the Holodomor as an act of genocide and the Ukrainian justice system's avoidance in declaring a position on the issue.[64] Between 1994 and 1998, while the subject of the Holodomor became the priority of certain civic organizations and individual historians, state institutions preferred to assume the comfortable position of observer and did not extend financial support to any project dealing with the subject. On October 26, 1998, the Ukrainian government headed by Prime Minister Valerii Pustovoitenko adopted resolution № 1696, "*Pro 65-i rokovyny Holodomoru v Ukraïni*" ["On the sixty-fifth anniversary of the Holodomor in Ukraine"], which enumerated a series of actions in connection with commemorating this sorrowful anniversary. In contrast to his predecessor, however, President Kuchma distanced himself, only specifying the means of commemorating the event, setting in motion an official ritual of memory by designating a memorial day in honour of its victims. On November 26, 1998, Kuchma signed a resolution that established the fourth Saturday of every November as the Day of the Victims of the Great Famine in Ukraine,[65] also proposing that flowers be laid in "places of memory" on the occa-

---

[63] Vladimir Kravchenko, "Boi s ten'iu. Sovetskoe proshloe v istoricheskoi pamiati sovremennogo ukrainskogo obshchestva," *Ab imperio*, № 2 (2004), p. 340.

[64] Vasyl' Marochko, "Holodomor-henotsyd 1932–1933 rokiv v Ukraïni. Politychnyi dyskurs," *Istorychna pam'iat'*, № 30–31 (2014), p. 54.

[65] "Pro vstanovlennia Dnia pam'iati zhertv holodomoriv. Ukaz Prezydenta Ukraïny vid 26 lystopada 1998 roku № 1310/98," *Uriadovyi kur'ier* (November 28, 1998), p. 4.

sion.[66] The social ritual of laying wreaths had until then been tied to the successive anniversary commemorations of the "Great Patriotic War."[67]

In the meantime, the cultural landscape of post-Soviet Ukraine was being filled with more monuments and recognition of mass burial sites. For the anniversary in 1999, the President assigned tasks related to the Holodomor's commemoration to specific ministries, as reflected in the government documents from that time. In this context, it is worth noting the resolution of the Ukrainian Verkhovna Rada from November 28, 2002, entitled *"Pro 70-ti rokovyny Holodomoru v Ukraïni"* ["On the seventieth anniversary of the Holodomor in Ukraine"]. It marks the first time that Holodomor commemorations focused on condemning the genocidal policies of the communist authorities along with honouring the memory of its victims. The approach drew the attention of the general public and the academic community, both in Ukraine and abroad, to the issue of the Holodomor.[68] The series of resolutions includes ideas that are particularly relevant to this discussion, including the creation of a museum under the jurisdiction of the United Nations and the building of a monument in Kyiv along with many other regional centers:

> III. To instruct the Ukrainian Cabinet of Ministers to devise, approve and secure the realization of a plan of action aimed at commemorating the seventieth anniversary of the Holodomor 1932–33 in Ukraine. First and foremost, the plan's framework needs to:
> 1. Establish a state centre for the study of the causes and consequences of famines in Ukraine.
> 2. Prepare and publish books in memory of the victims of the Holodomor 1932–33 with registers of all those who were killed across Ukraine's oblasts, raions and villages.
> 3. Run a competition for the best design for a memorial in honor of the victims of the Holodomor in Ukraine 1932–33 with a view to its construction in Kyiv.
> 4. **Also ensure the building of monuments to victims of the Holodomor abroad in cooperation with the Ukrainian diaspora.**
>
> (…)

---

66 During the presidency of Leonid Kuchma, the name of this day was changed three times: from 1998 the name used was Day of Remembrance of the Holodomor, referring to the victims of the Great Famine of 1932–1933; in 2000 the name was changed to Day of Remembrance of the Holodomor and Political Repression; in 2004, the name was changed once again to Day of Remembrance for the Victims of the Holodomors and Political Repressions. In 2007, President Viktor Yushchenko changed the name of that day to The Day of Remembrance of the Holodomors, the name that remains valid today. The term Holodomor was extended to include the famine in the 1920s, the Great Famine of 1932–1933 and the post-war famine of the 1940s.

67 Stepan Bandera, "Istorychna amneziia," *Polityka i kul'tura* 127, № 44 (2001), p. 41.

68 *Vidomosti Verkhovnoï Rady Ukraïny (VVR)*, № 51 (2002), p. 377.

VII. To recommend to the Ukrainian Ministry of Foreign Affairs:
1. To engage in actions internationally aimed at recognizing the Holodomor in Ukraine during 1932–33 as a genocidal state policy against the Ukrainian nation.
2. To initiate the recognition of the Holodomor of 1932–33 in Ukraine as an act of genocide against the Ukrainian nation by the international community.
3. To propose to the United Nations General Assembly that the victims of the Holodomor in Ukraine during 1932–33 be commemorated with a minute's silence before commencing one of its meetings.
4. To support the creation of an international Holodomor museum under the aegis of the UN.[69]

Of particular interest here is the fourth point of section III of the resolution, which signals the continuing importance of the Ukrainian diaspora, with its experience of building Holodomor monuments, to Ukraine's developing culture of memory. In the same year, Leonid Kuchma issued a proclamation on the occasion of the Day of Remembrance for the Victims of the Holodomor,[70] in which he gave his interpretation of the historical facts constitutive of the Holodomor and announced the creation of a monument (memorial) in Kyiv:

> I am convinced that a great memorial to the victims of the Holodomor should be built in Kyiv. Monuments are needed in all of the country's regions. This should not be a formality – testimony to the deep respect for the dead and the eternal remembrance of this tragic page from history – but first and foremost, it must be a symbol of the immortality of our nation. I believe that the Ukrainian Verkhovna Rada should make an assessment and scholars should carry out their investigations.[71]

Various communities in the Ukrainian diaspora had raised the need for a major monument to the Holodomor that could be central to the national historical narrative in Ukraine. This need was articulated only toward the end of the 1990s by those affiliated with the Association of Researchers of the Famine-Genocide of 1932–33. In 1998, participants of the conference "*Holod-henotsyd 1933 roku v Ukraïni*" ["Famine-genocide 1933 in Ukraine"], which took place in Kyiv, developed the rationale for Holodomor commemoration and presented the government with a petition to fund a museum and monument: "*Holod 1933. Henotsyd ukraïns'koho narodu*" ["Famine 1933. The Genocide of the Ukrainian

[69] Ibid.

[70] Ukaz prezydenta Ukraïny "Pro vstanovlennia Dnia pam'iati zhertv holodomoriv," November 26, 1998, https://zakon.rada.gov.ua/laws/show/1310/98#Text.

[71] "Zvernennia Prezydenta Ukraïny do ukrains'koho narodu u zv'iazku z Dnem pam'iati zhertv Holodomoru ta politychnykh represii," *Nad Buhom*, accessed April 2, 2019, http://nadbuhom.pl/art_0850.html.

Nation"].[72] The numerous monuments that had been funded across the entire country as well as in its capital provided additional impetus.[73]

In addition to the resolution of the Ukrainian Verkhovna Rada from November 28, 2002, calling for a design competition for a monument to victims of the Holodomor, it is worth recalling President Leonid Kuchma's proposals from a directive dated December 6, 2002.[74] These initiatives came to fruition a year later when the Verkhovna Rada resolved to initiate the building of a national history museum that would memorialize not only those who died in the Famine but also those deported *en masse* to the interior of the USSR, as well as other victims of Stalinist repressions. The national competition for its design was announced in 2003 and attracted twenty-one entries. A meeting of the competition committee took place on September 17, 2003, during which it was unexpectedly decided that the site proposed by the city was not suitable for a museum dedicated to such tragic historical events and that it ran counter to the recommendations of the Ukrainian authorities about building a museum to the victims of the Holodomor and of other political repressions. A decision to void the competition and announce another, this time of international scope, was also made at this meeting.[75] In order to bring this abortive attempt at building a monument in the Ukrainian capital to a close, the monetary award of 10,000 hryvnia initially intended for the winning design was divided instead among the creators of the top five designs, with the respective works receiving commendations.

After the competition's results were announced, a lengthy article about the selected designs and the jury's decision appeared in *Holos Ukraïny* [The Voice of Ukraine], which also discussed tendencies in monumental sculpture as revealed by the submitted designs. Volodymyr Priadka, a Ukrainian artist without a personal stake in the competition, summarized its results and the ensuing discussions over the designs as follows:

> I am not a participant nor a jury member in this competition, so I can openly say that I do not accept artistic solutions that attempt to "imagine through horror" national tragedies. For no artistic expression – either

[72] Oleksandr Hrytsenko, *Prezydenty i pam'iat'. Polityka pam'iati prezydentiv Ukraïny* (Kyiv, 2012), pp. 223–4.

[73] Vitalii Ohiienko, "Memorial'na polityka vshanuvannia pam'iati zhertv Holodomoru 1932–1933 rr. v Ukraïni," *Hileia. Naukovyi visnyk* 61 (2012), pp. 72–7.

[74] Rozporiadzhennia prezydenta Ukraïny "Pro dodatkovi zakhody u zv'iazku z 70-my rokovynamy holodomoru v Ukraïni", December 6, 2002, https://zakon.rada.gov.ua/rada/show/393/2002-%D1%80%D0%BF.

[75] Kor. "OM," "De i iakym bude Memorial henotsydu ukraïntsiv ta chomu vtrutylys' sluzhbovtsi?" *Obrazotvorche mystetstvo*, № 4 (2003), p. 84.

> in sculpture or painting – can convey the horror and gloom of death by starvation from the 1930s to those alive today. Moreover, they leave a negative impression. The naturalism of the events, the horrific images, and hunched over and crucified figures, cannot say anything about those terrible times. Those who did not live through it cannot imagine anything like it. (…) I believe that a memorial church must also be built in Kyiv, where anyone can come at any time to remember their kith and kin and to pray for them. It would be fitting for the church to be dedicated to the Holy Virgin Mary. (…) If we build monuments like those we have seen in this competition, we will not solve the problem and society will continue to be dissatisfied.[76]

In the journal *Obrazotvorche Mystetstvo* [Visual Arts], a short item was printed along with the designs selected by the jury, but without identifying the artists. I recognized one of the submissions, known to me from discussions around the design of the monument in Chicago in 1993. It is a sculpture by Anatoliy Kushch entitled "*Velyka rana*" ["The Great Wound"].[77] Initially, it was to stand in Chicago, but it did not meet the expectations of the local Ukrainian diaspora community. It was subsequently entered into the later annulled competition in Kyiv in 2003, as well as into a 2008 competition organized by Viktor Yushchenko, where it was again not selected as the winning design.

Fig. 41. Anatoliy Kushch's Holodomor monument design, made out of bronze (1993)

[76] V[olodymyr] Pidvysots'kyi, "Subota skorboty (Holodomor)," *Holos Ukraïny*, № 221 (November 22, 2003), pp. 1–5.

[77] "Pam'iatnyk berestets'kii bytvi khotily pokryty zolotom," accessed 30 July 2020, https://gorohiv.rayon.in.ua/news/18525-pamiatnik-v-berestechku-hotili-pokriti-zolotom.

With the advent of 2004, another government directive to organize a design competition for a Holodomor museum was issued. In April 2004, Oleh Smal offered his emotional opinion on the potential design of the monument on the pages of *Dzerkalo tyzhnia* [The Mirror of the Week]:

> I fear the appearance of the monument on Volodymyr Hill in Kyiv, but not because it will disturb the harmony of the place. After all, we have enough talented architects and sculptors capable of subtly incorporating the planned monument into its surroundings. The worst that can be expected from this structure is disrespect for the emotions that it is expected to evoke. Thousands of people will walk by the cross daily, lovers will use it as a meeting spot, retirees will walk their dogs... A devaluation of the images that should be evoking a nearly cathartic state. (...)
>
> Yes, the Holodomor is a tragedy of the entire nation, but it was aimed, first and foremost, at the Ukrainian peasant. Villages died out and cities introduced ration cards, isolating themselves from the hungry reminiscent of the medieval citadels during the plague epidemic. And the Ukrainian peasant fell on this fertile land that had fed him for centuries. Why is this memory not immortalized somewhere in a field of wheat, far from tarmacked roads and noisy cities? Perhaps there it would be most appropriate to erect that crystal temple of remembrance and sorrow.[78]

In his conclusion he argues that the means of immortalizing the memory of the Holodomor's victims would speak to Ukrainian society's current state: "The issue of investigating and commemorating the memory of victims of the Holodomor is possibly the most important test of our nation's ability to develop and exist in the future."[79]

The results of the competition were announced in 2005. More than fifty submissions were entered. The jury awarded the first prize to the brothers Roman and Dmytro Seliuk. The young team's design for the monument and the museum was both modest and low budget. The monument was to take the form of a cross, standing seventeen meters in height and finished with a copper wheat sheaf in its centre. The plan included an annual sowing of wheat around the monument, to be harvested and gathered into stacks each autumn. The museum, in turn, was to be located in an existing building that belonged to the city and was falling into disrepair, approximately one hundred metres from St. Michael's Golden-Domed Monastery where a monument had been built in 1993.[80]

---

[78] Oleh Smal', "Simnadtsiat' metriv horia," *Dzerkalo tyzhnia*, № 15 (April 16, 2004), p. 17.
[79] Ibid.
[80] Andrii Saichuk, Iryna Diachenko, and Serhii Ieromenko, "Memorial zhertvam Holodomoru. Tsina pytannia," *Podrobnosti*, November 16, 2008, accessed July 30, 2020, http://podrobnosti.ua/566586-memoral-zhertvam-golodomoru-tsna-pitannja.html.

As it turned out, Ukraine's new president, Viktor Yushchenko, thought that the winning design did not represent the tragedy of the Ukrainian people with sufficient majesty.[81] In his directive from November 4, 2005, on respecting the memory of the famine victims in Ukraine,[82] the head of state authorized the government to resolve the issue of building a monument and museum. A new team was formed that was to choose a new design and ensure the project's implementation. The chosen location for the entire architectural complex was a grove that was previously planted in memory of the Famine's victims and funded by the President. The competition was announced the following year, thus paving the way for the President's vision for national Holodomor remembrance.

4.5 The most significant Holodomor "places of memory" from the period of the Viktor Yushchenko presidency

Beginning in 2005, the politics of memory in Ukraine enters a qualitatively new stage. Viktor Yushchenko had already emphasized in his address as the new president the weight that he would place on cultivating the memory of his country's dramatic past under communist totalitarianism. The head of state treated the victory of the Orange Revolution as a unique opportunity to sever ideological ties with Russia and create a single (homogeneous) Ukrainian nation, united by shared memory and the condemnation of the Soviet legacy.[83] The Ukrainian government's politics of memory from 2005 to 2010, despite inconsistencies, can indeed be classified as an attempt to impose a Ukrainian historical narrative, a move needed to legitimize the forces that gained power following the Orange Revolution. Their methods resonated with the anti-Orange movement, which, in turn, started to deploy historical narra-

---

[81] "Kalynovyi hai na zhadku pro Holodomor," *Ukraïna moloda*, № 42 (March 5, 2005).

[82] The term *Holodomor* was until a certain moment reserved exclusively for the Great Famine of 1932–33. From the mid-1990s historical works started to appear in which this designation was used in relation to other famine situations within Soviet Ukraine. It is also important to note that the last Saturday of November, which we have become accustomed to viewing as a Day of Remembrance of the Holodomor, unequivocally points in its formulation in Ukrainian to the commemoration on that day of all victims of all the Soviet famines that occurred in Ukraine. (The Day of Remembrance of the Holodomors). See Linina Odynoka, Liudmyla Prykhod'ko, and Rostyslav Romanovs'kyi, compilation, *Holodomory v Ukraïni 1921–1923, 1932–1933, 1946–1947. Materialy do bibliohrafiï dokumental'nykh publikatsii* (Kyiv, 2005).

[83] Iaroslav Hrytsak, "Holokost i Holodomor. Vyklyky kolektyvnii pam'iati," *Krytyka*, № 1–2 (2011), pp. 159–60.

tives in its propaganda that were consistent with the eastern Ukrainian experience of the past.[84]

With his assumption of power, Viktor Yushchenko found himself between two opposing forces. On the one side, his allies – the national democrats – expected him to make a decisive break with the Soviet ideological legacy. At the same time, he sought to improve his image among those who had voted for other candidates in the presidential election. As often happens when a politician wants to appease two opposing political groups, Yushchenko's popularity suffered among both camps. The dissatisfaction of the national democrats was related primarily to the fact that President Yushchenko had not removed the cornerstone of the Soviet historical narrative, namely the Great Patriotic War, from the national cultural canon. Doing so would have been more than just problematic, however, given his family's experience. As Yushchenko often reiterated during his election campaign, his father fought in the ranks of the Red Army against the fascist onslaught and was sent to Auschwitz as a prisoner of war. After the election, Ukrainians heard about this in numerous presidential addresses, which rendered impossible the removal of Victory Day from the calendar of state holidays.

Yushchenko tried to alter the holiday's significance, adding a modified version to the nationalized narrative of Ukraine's history. In his interpretation, the Great Patriotic War was a tragedy rather than a victory of communist ideology. The subject of the sacrifices incurred, invariably bound to the Ukrainian national historical narrative, allowed for this war to be "assimilated" into the framework of the official politics of memory. In its most radical nationalist version, it was not one part but the entire Ukrainian nation that fell victim to the war, finding itself on different sides of the barricades as a result of a historical collision. The narrative of the suffering of Ukrainians who fought on the Soviet side only confirmed this perception of the war.[85]

Presenting the war as a national tragedy gave the president hope for the realization of his dream of national unity through the reconciliation of historical memory. In an address to the Ukrainian people on May 9, 2007, Yushchenko included both the relentless fight of Red Army combatants and that of the Ukrainian Insurgent Army among a series of wrongs suffered by Ukrainians as a result of the war and called on both sides for reconciliation. The president repeated this appeal subsequently, but no such reconciliation took place.

Yushchenko felt responsible for shaping perceptions about the past held by Ukrainian citizens. With this in mind, he announced a series

---

[84] Zernii, "Derzhavna polityka pam'iati v Ukraïni," pp. 46–51.

[85] Slyvka, "Ukraïna v Druhii svitovii viini," p. 31.

of resolutions demonstrating the head of state's official position on every fundamental question concerning Ukraine's history. In 2006, on the strength of government resolution № 927 dated July 5, 2006, *Ukraïns'kyi instytut natsional'noï pam'iati* [Ukrainian Institute of National Remembrance (UINR] was established. Its aims included focusing society's attention on its own history and disseminating objective facts in Ukraine and around the world; realizing state policy and coordinating efforts to reconstruct and preserve the national memory of Ukrainians; and ensuring the comprehensive study of the stages of Ukraine's twentieth-century struggle to achieve statehood.[86]

The institute became operational on March 3, 2007, with Ihor Yukhnovsky stepping into the role of its first head (until 2010). The expectation was for the UINR to concentrate on researching the history of Ukrainian liberation struggles and the martyrdom of its people. In the first phase of its existence, the Institute examined those social issues that the authorities deemed relevant for contemporary politics of memory. As a result, its initiatives included the rehabilitation of Ukrainian Insurgent Army soldiers and granting them the status of combatants for an independent Ukraine. However, the subject that came to dominate public discourse was the Great Famine.

President Yushchenko facilitated the signing of a resolution that declared the Great Famine in Ukraine of 1932–33 an act of genocide against the Ukrainian people.[87] From this moment, we can speak of a "decalogue" of the Great Famine's "community of memory" forming in the public sphere. Indeed, Yushchenko never hid the fact that the Holodomor was to act as a binding agent in his politics of memory, unifying the inhabitants of Ukraine into a modern Ukrainian nation. He also did not limit himself to declarations. A series of his decisions were meant to socially reinforce the belief that the Holodomor should be commemorated as a Stalinist act of genocide against the Ukrainian nation. Among other measures, the president called for the criminal prosecution of those who publicly refute the Holodomor. In a series of official speeches, he repeated the comparison of the Holodomor to the Holocaust. In this context, his attempts to have the Holodomor recognized as an act of genocide by the Israeli government, something he promoted during an official state visit in 2007, were met with considerable controversy.

---

[86] Kabinet Ministriv Ukraïny, Postanova vid 5 lypnia 2006 r. N 927, Kyïv "Pro zatverdzhennia Polozhennia pro Ukraïns'kyi instytut natsional'noï pam'iati," https://zakon.rada.gov.ua/laws/show/927-2006-%D0%BF.#Text.

[87] Ukaz prezydenta Ukraïny № 250/2007 "Pro zakhody u zv'iazku z 75-my rokovynamy Holodomoru 1932–1933 rokiv v Ukraïni," March 28, 2007, https://www.president.gov.ua/documents/2502007-5688.

Wilfried Jilge interprets such actions as examples of the struggles of "victim-nations."[88] More specifically, one element of renouncing the communist past in Europe was the "reproduction" of ever new genocides that cast the nation as victims in a national history.[89] The Ukrainian president's motivation behind these decisions even became the subject of discussion at a conference in Toronto in 2008 on the seventy-fifth anniversary of the Great Famine. For Mykola Riabchuk, Yushchenko was driven by emotion that flowed from his identity and values: "President Yushchenko is sacrificing, in fact, certain electoral "dividends" for the sake of moral principles he believes are crucial for the whole nation."[90] According to Georgiy Kasianov, however, entirely pragmatic considerations (namely, the president's self-promotion on the international stage) were explanation enough.[91]

The essence of Yushchenko's initiatives in relation to the Holodomor was developing the foundation of a Holodomor-genocide conception, as framed by the Act on the Great Famine in Ukraine 1932–33, and seeing the draft legislation pass through the parliamentary process. The president personally presented his proposal to the Verkhovna Rada, while Ihor Yukhnovsky, then the president of UINR, introduced it at the first sitting. Yukhnovsky relied on the definition of genocide adopted by the UN in 1948 (in the Convention on the Prevention and Punishment of the Crime of Genocide) to establish the genocidal and national characteristics of the Great Famine of 1932–33. Differences of opinion and the need to define a specific position with respect to the proposal led to postponement of this sitting. In the meantime, members of the pro-Russian opposition, the Party of Regions (*Partia Rehioniv*), proposed an alternate draft of the act. The party's vice-chairman, Yevhen Kushnaryov, insisted that their proposal did not negate the tragic nature of those events despite asserting that it was not a case of genocide.

On November 28, 2006, activists in front of the Verkhovna Rada building associated with the pro-presidential party Our Ukraine (*Nasha Ukraïna*) handed out wheat sheaves tied with black ribbon to the parliamentarians. Yukhnovsky, who was present in the chamber as a People's Deputy of the People's Movement of Ukraine (*Rukh*) party, requested that a discussion of the draft legislation be added to the agenda. His motion did not find support, caused considerable indignation among left-

---

[88] Vil'frid Il'he, "Zmahannia zhertv," *Krytyka*, № 5 (2006), pp. 14–7.

[89] Kasi'anov, *Danse macabre*, pp. 56–7.

[90] Mykola Riabchuk, "Holodomor: The Politics of Memory and Political Infighting in Contemporary Ukraine," *The Holodomor of 1932–33. Papers from the 75th-Anniversary Conference on the Ukrainian Famine-Genocide*, University of Toronto, November 1, 2007, special issue of *The Harriman Review* 16, № 2 (November 2008), pp. 3–9, https://holodomor.ca/wp-content/uploads/2020/04/Harriman-Review-Holodomor-75th-Nov-2008.pdf.

[91] Kasi'anov, *Danse macabre*, pp. 56–7.

-wing and Party of Regions representatives, and appeared sure to fail if brought to a vote. Parliamentary Speaker Oleksandr Moroz reminded the deputies of the President's priority to discuss the draft wording and proposed that Yukhnovsky's motion be brought to a vote.

In the ensuing discussion, the Ukrainian right (Viacheslav Koval from the Our Ukraine party and Oleksandr Turchynov from the Yulia Tymoshenko Bloc) argued that any attempt to avoid the restoration of historical justice made a mockery of the memory of millions of compatriots martyred in a genocide aimed at the destruction of a nation. The matter was brought to a head with a declaration that the vote would test the maturity of both the nation and its representatives.[92] Opponents of the presidential act were likewise prepared for a fight. The communist Petro Tsybenko shifted the discussion to ethics and conscience, accusing his opponents of lacking the moral right to condemn their forebears and avoiding responsibility for their own crimes. Tsybenko emphasized that other parts of the Soviet Union had suffered famine at that time and that consequently it was not a genocide of the Ukrainian nation but an all-Soviet tragedy. Moreover, he described the situation arising from the ineffective lobbying of the act in the Verkhovna Rada as political blackmail on the part of President Yushchenko.[93]

Ultimately, inclusion of this point in the day's agenda passed in a second vote by a small margin (mainly due to party discipline among socialists loyal to their leader, Oleksandr Moroz). A compromise was reached to extend the discussion to both proposals tabled in the Verkhovna Rada, which differed primarily in one regard – the use of the word "genocide." After a break, Verkhovna Rada returned to the debate during the evening session of November 28, 2006. As it happened, both proposals were rejected. A conciliatory solution was proposed by Moroz, who introduced amendments softening the grandiose language of the act's draft and eliminating the term "genocide". The following day, on the strength of seven votes, the Verkhovna Rada ratified Act № 376-V "On the Great Famine 1932–1933 in Ukraine."[94]

At this time, emotions were running high due to the building of memorials and monuments memorializing the victims of the Great Famine in Kyiv and a suburb of Kharkiv. While the construction of the monument and museum in Kyiv, in which the president was personally engaged, generated little controversy (the design fulfilled the expectations and intentions of the government at the time), the public discussion

---

[92] Stenohrama rankovoho zasidannia VRU 28 lystopada 2006 roku, http://static.rada.gov.ua/zakon/skl5/2session/STENOGR/28110602_36.htm.

[93] Ibid.

[94] Zakon Ukraïny "Pro Holodomor 1932–1933 rokiv v Ukraïni," *Vidomosti Verkhovnoï Rady Ukraïny (VVR)*, № 50 (2006), https://zakon.rada.gov.ua/laws/show/376-V.#Text.

triggered by the situation in Kharkiv was markedly different. The first point of contention was the proposed location in the centre of the city, which was opposed on the grounds that a cross in memory of the Great Famine's victims had been erected in the municipal Youth Park in 1989 (this park was established during communist times in a place where the bodies of people who starved during the Holodomor were allegedly buried). An alternative location for the new monument was proposed in close vicinity to the city, in the town of Cherkaska Lozova. The monument was ultimately unveiled on November 19, 2008, during a ceremony attended by President Yushchenko. In the centre of the monument's composition is a family. It is worth noting that a controversial element of the design was the figure of a man gazing eastward, in Russia's direction. The hands of the man, crossed across his chest, in turn, have been variously interpreted, including as a threatening gesture directed at the powers in the Kremlin.[95]

Descriptions of Yushchenko's politics of memory in literature about the Holodomor completely skip over the fact that the first Holodomor museum in Ukraine was established during his time in power. Its creation, in a small town away from the bustle of the capital city, was not related to any anniversary commemorations and is an artistic expression of how the theme of genocide can be represented in a museum space.

The museum is located in the Medzhybizh Fortress, the former residence of the Sieniawski and Czartoryski families, and was opened on October 4, 2008, with President Yushchenko in attendance. Specifically, it is an installation commemorating the victims of the Great Famine, distinguished for being the first thematic museum exhibit dealing with the Holodomor in Ukraine. Its concept and creation were the work of Mykola Mazur, a well-known Ukrainian artist.[96] The exhibit is interpretative in character, like other thematic exhibits. It does not merely display artefacts but treats them instrumentally to convey specific messages. The narrative is closely connected to the objects, providing a historical context intended to make them easier to understand and properly interpret (that is, according to the author's intention).

The museum features six installations, each consisting of a white plaster sculpture, farming-themed artefacts, as well as copies of archival documents and photographs. Each exposition constitutes a closed whole, although they are ordered chronologically, with visitors first

[95] Tatiana Zhurzhenko, "'Capital of Despair': Holodomor Memory and Political Conflicts in Kharkiv after the Orange Revolution," *East European Politics & Societies* 25 (2011), pp. 604–10.

[96] For more on the history of the museum's construction see Anatolii Trembits'kyi, ed., *Muzei pam'iati zhertv Holodomoru na Khmel'nychchyni 1932–1933 rokiv (do 5-richchia vid dnia stvorennia)* (Khmelnytskyi, 2013).

introduced to the period of the 1930s and the situation of Soviet Ukraine during collectivization, including the repressions that followed for those who refused to join the collective farm.

Notably, the featured objects are not the agricultural tools of those who survived the Holodomor; their role, rather, is to symbolize the agricultural nature of Ukrainian society and the rural character of the Holodomor. The objects and the story they tell are part of an effort to depart from clichés in representing the Holodomor in a museum. At stake here is the artist's desire to overcome the limitations of language that become apparent in efforts to express traumatic human experiences and to find alternative means of representing fundamentally incommunicable experiences.

The six installations were built in chronological succession, with their creator giving their work a specific logical dimension: each subsequent installation following from the previous. To a large extent, the museum is an artistic expression of a certain textbook truth about events now called the Holodomor. The exposition cannot be deemed precise enough to warrant the status of a historical museum, and at the same time, its creators did not leave emotional space for visitors to add to the narrative. The visitor moves within a dedicated symbolic space of rooms adapted for this purpose. Nothing is left to supposition and there is nothing to be read between the lines. The historical aspect is conveyed as a supplement to artistic representations through captions underneath the numerous exhibited artefacts. It is impossible to determine, in fact, whether all of the artefacts fit the chronology of the exhibit. As a result, it is difficult to call this chamber of memory a work of art, and even harder to count it among museums of the Great Famine (as it is nevertheless called). It is simply one take on already well-known historiographic facts that highlights the ample information already in the public sphere. The installations in Medzhybizh Fortress can be compared to a performance based on real events, which lends an engaging appearance to the Ukrainian nation's past. Given its character, the exhibition is most expressive as a testament to the politics of memory at the time of its creation and as an example of a place that transmits the Holodomor's prosthetic memory; it speaks to the conceptions of the Holodomor of its creators and local society.

The premises of the theory of prosthetic memory were laid out by Alison Landsberg in her book *Prosthetic Memory: The Transformation of American Remembrance in the Age of Mass Culture* (2004). The concept describes the processes of memory, including the acquisition of prosthetic recollections in the framework of consuming a cultural industry's goods and in contact with mediated representations of the past. According to Landsberg, by using both technology and empathy, we can cross individual boundaries of experience. Technologies utilized by mass culture

Fig. 42. Installation "Tragedy of Maternity" in the Museum of Holodomor Memory in Medzhybizh, Ukraine

Fig. 43. Installation "Regime of 'Black Boards'" in the Museum of Holodomor Memory in Medzhybizh, Ukraine

allow individuals to find a place for themselves in collective history and interweave their history with that of the Other.[97]

The approach to the narrative of the Holodomor as told in the museum hall of the memorial in Kyiv is similar. Its means of recounting the experience engage successive generations through Holodomor study while distancing us from its historical dimension, related through historical facts. Both museums discussed here are "realms of memory" that call on both the cognitive and the axiological sphere. They synthesize content that forms memory and conceptualization, impacting the means of remembering victims of communist crimes in both individual and collective dimensions, consequently shaping the national and social identities of various "communities of memory." These exhibition spaces do not easily allow for debate or multiple interpretations about a single phenomenon, artifact, or installation. The presented facts are substantiated through archival sources, and only those that have already attained academic consensus are included. Ambiguity, presentation of unverified information, and hypotheses are all avoided, with the museum serving the educational role of shaping its public and nurturing patriotic attitudes. In a visit to such a museum, the young can identify with an event's heroes (for instance, the witnesses narrating their story through visual identification), taking in stimuli and recollections linked to situations in which they would never find themselves otherwise. This is an important aspect of prosthetic memory: the enabling of the transmission of experiences beyond the limits of time, culture, or politics. The participants of museum lessons experience to some degree a simulation of emotions felt by the victims of the Holodomor that collide with their sense of safety, of which they become aware with relief. This combination gives rise to an impulse that can inspire ethical consideration and interpretations of the Holodomor.

Both museums (Medzhybizh and Kyiv) established during the Yushchenko presidency embody the way memory of the Holodomor resonated in the public sphere at the time, constituting in a sense the symbolic essence of memory politics and its tangible evidence. They represent its positive aspect, which less successful moves in the field of memory politics can obscure. The significance of President Yushchenko's politics of memory can be overshadowed, for instance, by the boundless support for some often absurd decisions around commemorating the Great Famine. To give one example: on May 25, 2009, the Ukrainian Security Services launched an official investigation to establish the Holodomor of 1932–33 as an act of genocide, which was

---

97 Alison Landsberg, *Prosthetic Memory: The Transformation of American Remembrance in the Age of Mass Culture* (New York, 2004), p. 25–8.

completed in November of the same year and led to the Prosecutor General of Ukraine issuing an indictment in January 2010. On January 13, 2010, after hearing the case, the Kyiv Court of Appeals found Joseph Stalin, Vyacheslav Molotov, Lazar Kaganovich, Pavel Postyshev, Stanislav Kosior, Vlas Chubar, and Mendel Khatayevich posthumously guilty of genocide as defined in Art. 442 § of the Penal Code of Ukraine. After much publicity, the court then dismissed the case due to the accused being deceased.[98] The absurdity of the undertaking, in my opinion, discredited the government, since it painted the authorities as being less interested in saving the country's economy than in correcting historical wrongdoings. Such initiatives cast a shadow over a series of very important actions for the cultivation of the Holodomor's memory. Consequently, the subject of the Great Famine did not fulfill its collective and consolidating function. Perhaps the overemphasis of the President's commemorative efforts, instead of uniting society, more than likely contributed to deepening internal antagonisms. Ukrainians subconsciously divided themselves into those who fully accepted the new doctrine of the Holodomor-genocide and those who negated this new historical narrative about the Great Famine, either for ideological reasons (the pro-Russian left), or out of a desire to take a stand against the politics of memory of that time.

4.6 The Great Famine of 1932–33 and the politics of memory since 2010

Viktor Yanukovych's moves in historical policy while holding the top political post in Ukraine were predictable in principle. He was already the second "pro-Russian" president, after Kuchma, and thus forecasts predicted the return of ambivalence and a radical halt to his predecessor's extensive commemorative politics. Key to Yanukovych's politics were the anniversary commemorations of the "Great Patriotic War" on May 9, 2010, followed by the disbanding of the Ukrainian Institute of National Remembrance and the eightieth-anniversary commemorations of the Great Famine in Ukraine.

First, a court in Donetsk overturned President Yushchenko's resolutions to posthumously confer the title of Hero of Ukraine on Stepan Bandera and Roman Shukhevych, substantiating its decision with the fact that neither ever held Ukrainian citizenship. On December 9, 2010,

[98] "Postanova apeliatsiinoho sudu m. Kyieva u kryminal'nii spravi za faktom vchynennia henotsydu v Ukraïni v 1932–1933 rokakh," Kharkivs'ka pravozakhysna hrupa, February 1, 2010, http://khpg.org/index.php?id=1265039604.

UINR was dissolved by a presidential decree, only to be created anew with a resolution of the Cabinet of Ministers of Ukraine (January 12, 2011). Valeriy Soldatenko took over as head of the institution, with his communist past causing much anxiety in some quarters.

Among the manifestations of ties to the Soviet past, the commemorations of Victory Day in 2010 in Luhansk involved decorating the town with posters featuring Stalin, on the initiative of Communist Party representatives. In Zaporizhzhia, a bust of Stalin was reported in front of the Communist Party headquarters. A scandal broke and the local public prosecutor's office was asked to intervene. The bust turned out to be an element of the building façade and consequently could stay in place without approval of the authorities. The central authorities, meanwhile, remained ambiguous in their comments on the subject.

The Victory Day parade in Kyiv to a great extent recalled the times of Leonid Brezhnev. The issue here is not President Yanukovych's intention to negate specific images of the past and replace them with others. A succession of his decisions in the field of historical policy reveals rather his complete indifference toward all things Ukrainian. The pompous parades marking May 9th anniversaries did not stem from a desire to fight the Ukrainian right but from an unexamined acceptance of Soviet heritage and a need to reconstruct a former reality.

An event took place in Kharkiv in 2013, on the eve of the eightieth anniversary of the Holodomor, that was symptomatic of the state of unsettled historical consciousness among Ukrainians at that time and the dependent relationship of the cultivation of memory about past events of national significance and the political views of those in power. Local authorities were debating whether to dismantle the monument to the Great Famine in Cherkaska Lozova. Ultimately, it was left standing.[99] Under Yanukovych, therefore, the dominant narrative sought if not to openly dismiss the Great Famine as a historical fact, then certainly to lessen its relative weight and impact on Ukraine's history, which made his policy of remembrance different from Kuchma's.

The fundamental aim of Yanukovych's politics of memory was not to practise a specific politic but rather to seek approval from the Kremlin. This was most apparent in the President's speech given on the occasion of the eightieth anniversary of the Holodomor. At a time when a sizeable part of Ukraine's citizens opposed his policies and were joining the Euromaidan movement, the President officially questioned whether the Great Famine was a genocide or nothing more than a natural disaster. Listening to his speech, one might have been left with the impression that Ukraine in the 1930s had been unexpectedly struck by

---

[99] See more: Zhurzhenko, "'Capital of Despair'," pp. 604–10.

an act of nature (a hurricane perhaps, or a flood) that resulted in millions of fatalities. The President also added that, despite their emaciation during the Famine, Ukrainians also contributed to the victory in the Great Patriotic War. His failed attempt to depoliticize the Famine came across as a veiled bow in Moscow's direction via acknowledgment of the famine in Povolzhye (the Volga Region), Russia, during the 1930s.[100] President Yanukovych skillfully relayed the position of the Russian authorities in terms of negating the Holodomor's status as a genocide, adding a personal touch in speaking of brotherhood. The societal reaction to the speech would have been predictable had it not been for the "Revolution of Dignity," in the context of which the President's actions receded to the background.

Tadeusz Olszański evaluated the politics of Viktor Yanukovych less harshly in 2013 when he wrote:

> Ukrainian authorities today do not promote, as it is sometimes claimed, a Soviet or Russian (neo-imperialist) identity politics. They are searching for their own narrative, somewhat in the dark (for the leading intellectuals who could develop it are now part of the opposition), and striving to harmonize conflicting visions of national history so as not to antagonize any large social group (except for the radical nationalists) ahead of the 2015 presidential elections.[101]

From today's vantage point, his analysis can be deemed too far a stretch. Olszański sees Yanukovych as the successor of Kuchma's politics, which was not the case. To start, Yanukovych was not speaking of a "harmonized" version of national history. What is more, during a sitting of the OSCE Parliamentary Assembly in September 2011, President Yanukovych claimed that the Great Famine was not a genocide of Ukrainians but instead affected multiple nationalities and was aimed at a class, rather than a national opponent.

It should also be underlined that despite initially withdrawing Ukrainian state financing for the Holodomor monument in Washington, DC, in 2013 Yanukovych decided to financially support this initiative that his predecessor, Viktor Yushchenko, very much wanted to realize. The diaspora newspaper *Homin Ukraïny* published a copy of an announcement from Hanna Herman, a Party of Regions People's Deputy, stating that the Government of Ukraine had approved the selection of a competition commission that had been created under the previous

---

[100] "Ianukovych ne vvazhaie Holodomor henotsydom," produced by Oleksii Obukhov, November 26, 2010, YouTube video, 0:32, https://www.youtube.com/watch?v=YlIcu8zwmK0.

[101] Tadeusz A. Olszański, *Miejsce UPA w Wielkiej Wojnie Ojczyźnianej. Dylematy polityki historycznej Ukrainy* (Warsaw, 2013).

administration. President Yanukovych was to commit two million dollars of Ukraine's state budget to this end.[102] This was to remain, however, the only act of his presidency related to creating a "place of memory" of the Holodomor.

In October 2013, the sociological group *Reitynh* [Rating] conducted a social research poll of two thousand Ukrainian citizens on the statement "the Holodomor was an act of genocide against the Ukrainian people."[103] According to the collected data, 66 percent of those polled agreed with the statement, 22 percent did not consider the Holodomor to be a genocide, and 12 percent held no views on the subject. The rise in the percentage of those who saw the Holodomor as a genocide is worth highlighting; only two years previously, this opinion was shared by 58 percent of respondents. Affirmative replies were given by more than 80 percent of respondents living in Ukraine's western, northern, and central regions, more than 50 percent of those from the east of the country, and around 40 percent of residents from the Donbas region and Ukraine's south. A clear increase was observed across all regions of Ukraine. The Holodomor was considered a genocide by almost 90 percent of the people who voted for Oleh Tyahnybok, Yulia Tymoshenko, and Arseniy Yatsenyuk in the previous election, 80 percent of those who voted for Vitali Klitschko and Petro Poroshenko, more than 50 percent of Viktor Yanukovych's supporters, and – perhaps most surprisingly – around 40 percent of those who voted for the communist candidate, Petro Symonenko. The research team also noted that the Great Famine was considered a genocide by 90 percent of the Ukrainian-language speakers, and by 60 percent and 40 percent of bilingual and Russian-language speakers, respectively. Moreover, 68 percent of respondents with higher education agreed with the thesis, along with 79 percent of urban dwellers and 60 percent of rural inhabitants (regardless of region). These results can be seen as a harbinger of the growing need among Ukrainians to assert their dignity, fuelled by the desire to engage with their national history apart from politics.

The overthrow of Yanukovych took place in February 2014. The accompanying dramatic challenges to the integrity of Ukraine's borders, the annexation of Crimea, and the declaration of self-proclaimed republics in the east of the country naturally pushed Holodomor commemoration initiatives to the background. Moreover, it is certainly too early to evaluate the politics of memory during the leadership of President Poroshenko (2014–19). Georgiy Kasianov has shared his reflections on this

[102] "Memorial Holodomoru v Vashynhtoni," *Homin Ukraïny*, May 24, 2013.

[103] See the detailed report: "Dynamika stavlennia do Holodomoru, lystopad 2013," Sotsiolohichna hrupa "Reitynh," accessed April 2, 2019, http://ratinggroup.ua/files/ratinggroup/reg_files/rg_holodomor_ua_112013.pdf.

subject, noting that the social rituals to commemorate the Holodomor had not changed since the time of Viktor Yushchenko. He emphasized that the Holodomor in the Ukrainian politics of memory was presented as evidence that Russia is Ukraine's eternal enemy. Thus, commemoration of this event was extremely timely.[104] Regarding the emergence of Holodomor "places of memory" in Ukraine, the Holodomor was not an essential element of the politics of memory in Poroshenko's time. It should also be remembered that as a result of the war with Russia, cultivating the memory of new heroes became important for the Ukrainian authorities. Nevertheless, President Petro Poroshenko returned to the idea of building a Holodomor Museum in the Ukrainian capital. Toward the end of November 2016, a parliamentary committee was set up to this end, and a state-owned company was created to oversee the museum's construction.[105]

In a speech on the occasion of Holodomor Memorial Day, then President Poroshenko underlined the importance of the undertaking as a part of the already existing museum complex. He asserted that to fittingly commemorate the event, the museum exposition should meet the highest standards of modern museology.

An architectural design for the museum was developed by a group of Ukrainian architects from the company "Project Systems" (Kyiv, Ukraine, Chief Architect Andrii Myrhorodskyi), in cooperation with a leading European studio, "Nizio Design International" (Warsaw, Poland). For the architects, the starting challenge in the design was to take into account the tectonics and landscape of the slopes of the Dnipro valley in the vicinity of Kyivan Cave Monastery, a place of exceptional significance in the history of Ukraine. The museum building is situated on an axis leading toward the existing "Candle of Memory" monument to the victims of the man-made famine in Ukraine. The building's architectonic design encapsulates the idea of revealing the intentionally concealed truth about the Great Famine. The hidden history is to be remembered not only through the tectonic layers covering the building and the architectonic intervention of hiding the body of the building underground but also through a change in the vegetation growing on an earth-covered roof. The distinctive break in the rooftop that shifts half of it into the symbolic dimension is intended to demonstrate how human action can lead to revealing and declassifying crimes. The monumental entrance to the museum building, located on

---

[104] Heorhii Kas'ianov, *Rozryta mohyla: Holod 1932–1933 rokiv u politytsi, pam'iati ta istorii (1980-ti – 2000-ni)* (Kharkiv, 2019).

[105] Mariia Ivashchuk, "Proekt muzeiu Holodomoru," *The Village*, August 1, 2017, accessed July 30, 2020, http://www.the-village.com.ua/village/city/city-news/260765-proekt-muzeyu-golodomoru.

the side of the "Candle of Memory," is a gateway leading to the earth's depths and to the truth that will be revealed at the exhibition. Using the scenery and an array of artistic and architectonic means, the designers intend to arouse emotions and reflection about the tragedy that took place in Ukraine. The exhibition's design presupposes the construction of a two-part narrative. Its premise is that it will supplement the already existing museum located under the "Candle of Memory" memorial (See also 5.6 The memorial in Kyiv (2008)).

The museum plan also provides for a separate exhibition space for temporary thematic exhibitions, a conference hall, a room for educational projects, library, as well as archival and research centres.[106]

In the new concept, I see two issues important to the memorialization of the Holodomor. The first is the transformation of the memorial into a research and educational institution. The second is that this is not the conception from ten years ago. In fact, the project, intended to be completed before the ninetieth anniversary of the Holodomor, may reflect the politics of memory of President Volodymyr Zelensky.

4.7 Is it possible to end the mourning?

Summarizing my deliberations on the politics of memory in Ukraine, I cannot omit the answer to a fundamental question that I asked myself at the very beginning of my research: what exactly is being commemorated in Holodomor "places of memory" in Ukraine? While looking for an answer to this question in the empirical material, I concluded that each of the "communities of memory" commemorates only the elements of the collective image of the Holodomor that are important to it at that moment. In recent years in Ukraine, the need to end the mourning process has come to the fore, and I think I can deviate from my original intentions here to discuss this issue. Therefore, I will discuss the question of *working through* the Holodomor experience at "places of memory" in Ukraine. I will also consider why it is not possible to build an ideal monument, or in other words, why a monument will always be a defective form of commemorating a trauma, regardless of its artistic value.

In the context of *working through* Holocaust experiences, Dominick LaCapra writes that we must come to terms with the existence of open

[106] See "The Project of the Second Part of the National Museum 'Holodomor Victims Memorial' Was Presented to President of Ukraine Petro Poroshenko," November 23, 2018, accessed July 30, 2020, https://holodomormuseum.org.ua/en/news/the-project-of-the-second-part-of-the-national-museum-quot-holodomor-victims-memorial-quot-was-presented-to-president-of-ukraine-petro-poroshenko/.

wounds but need to resist their power to absorb the whole of a given person's existence and deprive them of agency.[107] For Ukrainian society, the experience of belated grief over the event is of primary importance to *working through* the trauma of the Holodomor.

Discussion about collective *working through* Holodomor trauma constitutes the beginning of cultural and social change as it reveals the individual and social belief that memory contains important gaps, or "blank spots," to state it differently. Collective memory of a society does not preserve significant parts of its members' experience, which thoroughly influence the shape of their identity and therefore require critical reflection, reinterpretation, and restoration of the event's falsified or erased image.

As research on the commemoration of the Holodomor as a "realm of memory" in Ukraine shows, in the first years of independence this topic was clearly abused by Ukrainian politicians. In the first decades of Ukraine's independence, discussions of the Holodomor as genocide were avoided because of Ukrainian-Russian economic relations and dependence, and falsified versions of history were circulated (the results of natural disaster, local supply difficulties, economic crisis throughout the Soviet Union, etc.). The first Ukrainian authorities seemed afraid to take a stance on this matter so as not to appear as nationalists similar to those of the diaspora in the West. These tensions are reflected in the visual culture of the Holodomor as is evident in the religious or mourning symbols at the turn of the twentieth and twenty-first centuries. In the symbolic layer of the monuments, the question of culpability for the Holodomor was avoided. It is, on some level, understandable. Apart from potential international conflict, there was the risk of fuelling internal conflicts. However, after the events of 2014 (when these fears became a reality), Holodomor commemoration was further relegated to the background, placed among the many Ukrainian "realms of memory," and recalled only on anniversaries, making it more difficult to find closure in the mourning process. However, the process of decommunization initiated in the last few years in Ukraine resulted in the belief that the memory of the Holodomor was falsified.

Belief in the falsification of identity prompts introspection and a peeling of the layers of memory, including visiting places actually connected with death by famine. The lack of acceptance of the politicization of the Great Famine, the desire to understand this phenomenon, locating the stories of one's forebearers in the context of these events (whatever side they were on), can provide the impulse to work through the Great Famine's trauma. These processes can thus provide a space for

---

[107] Dominick LaCapra, *History in Transit: Experience, Identity, Critical Theory* (Ithaca–London, 2004), pp. 106–43.

negotiation and discussion on how to *work through* the communist past without eliminating the extremes of emotions that often accompany the process (from nostalgia to victimization), which could ultimately lead to its demythization. This process is becoming more difficult now that only a few true witnesses of the event are still alive. At the same time, the problem of inheriting trauma that is yet to be worked through is felt ever more keenly. While the trauma of the Holodomor cannot be healed, its symptoms can be lessened by *working through* the event.

The work of memory in this instance necessitates recourse to the memory of others (representatives of other "communities of memory" or perpetrators), or alternatively to the mediums of memory (for example, to real places) that help to order the reworked content. The process of belated national grief does not guarantee that the regained memory will not deepen the void and sense of incomplete identity. Nevertheless, the search for a "true" memory about the Great Famine of 1932–33 may turn out to be key in *working through* the social trauma caused by the experience on the one hand, and its multi-layered (non) memory on the other.

In my opinion, the crucial factor for experiencing delayed social mourning in Ukraine in the context of the commemoration of the Holodomor is to recover the actual burial places and keep alive the memory at these places. Of course, monuments and memorials also play an important role in this process, but not the most significant. It is, therefore, worth examining them more closely.

4.8 Conclusions

This chapter shows the processes by which the Great Famine gained social significance and evolved into the Holodomor. I have considered here various aspects of the policy of remembrance from the time of *perestroika* to the presidency of Viktor Yanukovych. As I have shown, the activities of the authorities and social initiatives of various "communities of memory" aimed at commemorating this event in the public space do not indicate the existence of a uniform and purposeful state policy. Rather, they reflect the fragile condition of the Ukrainian state at the time and the complicated process of creating a contemporary Ukrainian identity that would not be based on foreign values.

At the beginning, the Ukraine of Leonid Kravchuk (1991–94) stuffed the Soviet inheritance into "the sack of social amnesia." During the Kravchuk presidency, the term "(non)memory" was applied to the highly selective admission of voices from the victims' generation as well as the unreflective transplantation onto Ukrainian ground of the Great Famine motif as cast by the Ukrainian diaspora in North America.

Leonid Kuchma's presidency (1994–2005), in turn, is an example of ambivalence of social memory. A president who was elected on the strength of votes cast in the country's eastern regions did not set any regional preferences for his politics. Moreover, his desire to rise above existing divisions led to, among other things, a willingness to substitute a revision of the ambivalent legacy of the Soviet times with permission to hold mutually exclusive values. Remembrance of the Holodomor under Leonid Kuchma was cultivated in an opportunistic and selective manner and treated as an element of the country's domestic political game.

Subsequently, Viktor Yushchenko (2005–10) was elected president of an "orange Ukraine" – effectively only one part of the nation. Nevertheless, he felt it his duty to be the leader of the entire Ukrainian nation. The memory of the Great Famine served as a point of connection, especially since some areas that voted for Yushchenko's main rival, Yanukovych, were particularly hard hit during the Famine. The Holodomor's revived memory was seen as an opportunity to consolidate Ukrainian society. Under Yushchenko, it seemed that these were not merely the speculations or illusions of specific political forces; the concept appeared realistic. In the short term, the identity of being a nation-victim of communism created distance from the communist legacy, and in the long term it enabled complete separation from it. The insistence of the government at the time on recognizing the Great Famine as an act of genocide, however, only entrenched existing social divisions in Ukraine. In other words, a unique chance to arrive at the memory of the Great Famine and in so doing, come to grips with the past, was usurped by the "Holodomor" project. As Ukraine's president, Yushchenko legitimized interpreting the Holodomor as a "Ukrainian Holocaust," as Western diaspora circles had long done. Enraptured by the power of Jewish memory about the Holocaust, he believed that the tragedy of the Great Famine united Ukrainians across the country in the same way diverse Jewish circles are brought together in remembering the Shoah. Among the lasting effects of Yushchenko's policy, one should note those related to the culture of memory of the Holodomor, among them, the creation of museums, the construction of nationally important memorials, and the identification of unmarked burial places of the victims. Undoubtedly, he was the only president of Ukraine who made the Holodomor the core of his politics of memory.

During Viktor Yanukovych's term in office (2010–14), (non)memory involved negating the established image of the Great Famine of 1932–33. Since total negation was impossible for objective reasons, given the broad public knowledge of irrefutable proof of the Famine, the authorities resorted to specific discursive strategies to fundamentally reinterpret it: on the one hand, they negated the discriminate and national character of the Holodomor, while also diminishing its scope and juxtaposing it with other rural disasters across other parts of the Soviet Union during the Stalinist period.

In the following years, the Holodomor continued to be present in the public space and in the politics of memory of Ukrainian presidents. The social rituals that were created in the first years of Ukraine's independence were continued. None of Yushchenko's successors has relinquished their support for the commemoration of the Holodomor. It is also a fact that the Holodomor is an essential but not the most important element of the symbolic canon that shapes Ukrainian national identity.

Chapter V

Holodomor "Places of Memory": Iconology Analysis

This chapter is dedicated to the iconological analysis of a selection of seven Holodomor monuments: one in Lubny (1993), three in Kyiv (1993, 2002, and 2008), and one each in Edmonton (1983), Winnipeg (1984), and Washington, DC (2015). Each memorial speaks to the historical moment of its creation. These monuments will be discussed in chronological order, starting with the fiftieth anniversary of the event, when the first competition for the design of a Holodomor monument was announced (1982). Two of the competition's winning monuments now stand in Canada. Earlier initiatives were local and community-based in character. The Lubny monument to the victims of the Holodomor was the first to be built in Ukraine. The monuments in the Ukrainian capital have their own tradition, while the monument in Washington, DC, is an example of an initiative financed by Ukraine yet built in another country. The chosen monuments will be discussed in terms of the circumstances around their creation, the "community of memory" to which they are linked, and finally, their messages.

5.1 The monument in Edmonton (1983)

In 1983 in Edmonton, on the initiative of Bohdan I. Shulakewych and the Ukrainian Canadian Professional and Business Club (UCPBC) of Edmonton, a competition for the design of a commemorative monument to the victims of the Holodomor was announced. What made it exceptional was that, for the first time, it involved a location in the city centre – directly in front of the City Hall – donated by resolution of a city council along with a commitment to maintain this "place of memory" in perpetuity as the property of the city and its residents.[1] It was

[1] "Misto podaruvalo zemliu," *Ukraïns'ki visti,* May 25, 1983, p. 3.

the first completely secular initiative which was able to achieve publicity thanks to the involvement of the local Ukrainian community. The competition is also of interest for resulting in not one but two monuments: in Edmonton (built in 1983) and Winnipeg (1984).

Lydia and Bohdan I. Shulakewych recalled the behind-the-scenes process of the monument's construction. The idea to erect a Holodomor monument emerged from a meeting of the Ukrainian Canadian Congress (UCC) in Edmonton in 1982, led by Dr. Melety Snihurowych. Mr. Shulakewych points out that the diasporic community active in the UCC at that time immigrated predominantly from Galicia and had not experienced the Holodomor first-hand. With time, Dr. Bohdan Krawchenko, whose parents came from eastern Ukraine, joined the UCC Committee. His role was to act as a substantive advisor. Dr. Yar Slavutych, who joined the project later still, enriched the committee with his knowledge of Slavic studies, history, and poetry. His recollections of the Holodomor were published in a cover story of *Alberta Report* magazine (October 31, 1983).

Lydia and Bohdan I. Shulakewych underscore that the key goals in building a Holodomor monument on the occasion of the fiftieth anniversary were to commemorate the tragedy through a tangible monument, to publicize the subject of the Holodomor among successive generations of Ukrainian-Canadians, and to educate the non-Ukrainian community. Mrs. Shulakewych was particularly involved in realizing the latter aim by involving in the commemorations other ethnic groups and their representatives. By working with the political powers of the Province of Alberta (including in the choice of the site and financial commitment to its maintenance), she engaged them in recognizing the tragedy. The committee also succeeded in gaining the attention of national English-language media to publicize matters connected with the project's realization.[2]

The announcement of the competition was sent to twenty-one architects and artists, with only some of them submitting designs. Dr. Melety Snihurowych, then head of the UCC, led a jury comprised of Iwan Keywan (artist), George Chernenko (architect), Frits Pannekock (historian), and Barbara Johnston (cultural advisor). They awarded a prize to three artists and recognized three others with awards of merit.[3] Some sources note that Georg (Hryhory) Kruk submitted his design after the deadline.[4] The list of winners and commendations was announced in several Ukrainian-language periodicals:

---

[2] Interview with Bohdan I. and Lydia Shulakewych, Toronto, November 19, 2017 (the author's private collection).

[3] *Novyi shliakh*, September 10, 1983, p. 1.

[4] *Ukraïns'kyi holos* 73, № 42 (1983), p. 2.

Winners:
1. Ludmilla Temertey – Montreal
2. Roman Kowal – Winnipeg
3. Bohdan Alexander Shulakewych – Edmonton

Highly commended:
1. Yarema Shulakewych – Edmonton
2. Miroslaw Opyr – Edmonton
3. Mike Andrews – Edmonton
4. Georg Kruk – Munich (late entry)

The jury's task was difficult given that the monument was expected to meet the needs of not only the Ukrainian community but of other communities in, and visitors to Edmonton. In a word, it needed to be aesthetically attractive as well as able to convey the Holodomor's dramatic essence.[5] In the end, the jury chose as the winner the bold, modernist design of Ludmilla Temertey, which she named "The Broken Life Cycle." The monument design, in the shape of a circle made from polished aluminum and eight feet in height, was intended to symbolize a human life broken in an unnatural way. The circle features hands made of steel, deformed and outstretched in a gesture of pleading for salvation or cessation of suffering. Words of explanation and dedication are inscribed in three languages (Ukrainian, English, and French): *Eternal Remembrance. In memory of many millions of Ukrainians who perished in the genocidal great famine inflicted upon Ukraine by the Soviet Regime 1932–33. Let us all stand on guard against tyranny, violence and inhumanity.*[6]

The interpretation of the symbolism of Temertey's design provided on the City of Edmonton website reads as follows:

> Temertey's sculpture symbolizes the scar on humanity left by authoritarian political regimes, and more specifically on the Ukrainian people by Josef Stalin. It was commissioned by the Canadian Ukrainian Committee to commemorate the lives lost and acknowledge a little known and poorly understood event in world history. (…)
>
> The sculpture invites examination of the histories constructed by Soviet Russia and allows members of the larger community to show solidarity against injustices committed against humankind. On the base of the artwork is inscribed, "Let us all stand on guard against tyranny, violence and inhumanity."[7]

[5] *Homin Ukraïny*, November 23, 1983, p. 5.

[6] M. D., "Edmontons'kyi pam'iatnyk zhertvam holodu v Ukraïni," *Novi dni* 34, № 404 (1983), p. 14.

[7] "Holodomor (Ukrainian Famine of 1933 Memorial) by Ludmilla Temertey," City of Edmonton Public Art Collection, accessed February 1, 2021, http://edmontonpublicart.ca/#!/details/82.

Fig. 44. Ludmilla Temertey's monument installation in Edmonton, Canada (1983)

This was to be Temertey's only monument; she was already a well-established artist whose work is dominated by genre paintings, studies of Ukrainian folk costumes, and portraits. She did not return to the subject of the Holodomor or to sculpture.[8]

Temertey was clear about her motivation for working in a completely different medium and on a theme that diverged from her usual

[8] Karpo Rohonovs'kyi, "Khudozhnytsia Liudmyla Temertei," *Novi dni* 34, № 398 (April 1983), pp. 16–8.

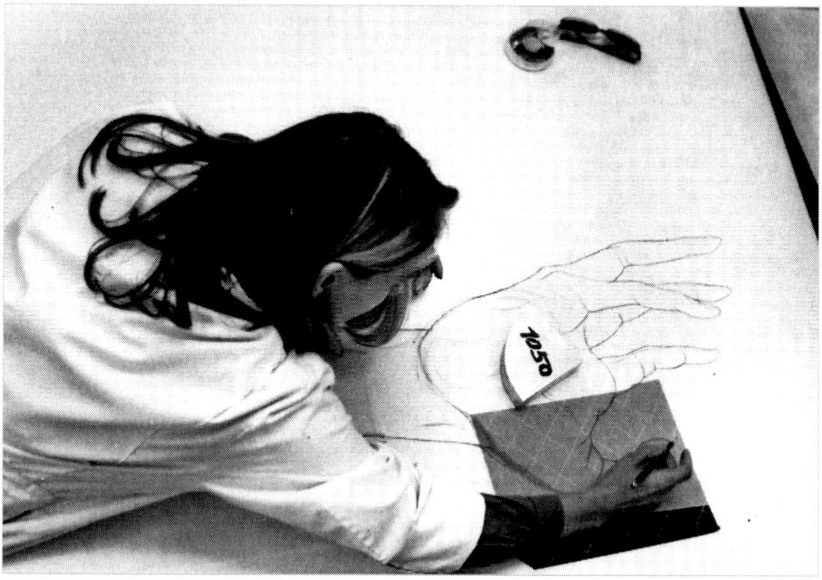

Fig. 45. Ludmilla Temertey sketching the design for the monument "The Broken Life Circle" (1983)

artistic interests. From an article published in the newspaper *Homin Ukraïny*, we learn that the artist's mother was a Holodomor survivor.[9] In another interview, she recalled: "I understood how much I was defined by my parents' history, even though I did not live through it. (…) I wanted to honour those silent victims of this heinous crime against humanity (…) my family and their indomitable spirit (…) survivors of the Holodomor."[10]

The artist did not include any personal references in the proposal she submitted to the competition. However, in a 1983 interview for the magazine *Promin / Promin'* [Ray], Temertey explained the symbolism of her design:

> This monument symbolizes the devious twist of a political ideology and the intense range of human suffering and defiance in the face of its gargantuan power, without condoning the perpetrators of this heinous famine, or those who chose "not to see" […]. The circle represents this

[9] *Homin Ukraïny*, November 23, 1983, p. 5.

[10] "Dity tykh, khto perezhyv Holodomor: Interv'iu z Liudmyloiu Temertei," *New Pathway Ukrainian News*, September 15, 2015, accessed July 30, 2020, https://www.newpathway.ca/діти-тих-хто-пережив-голодомор-інтерв/; "UCRDC Interviews Child of Holodomor Survivors," Ukrainian Canadian Congress, November 14, 2015, accessed July 30, 2020, https://www.ucc.ca/2015/11/14/ucc-enewsletter-november-2015/.

> Life Cycle being torn by an unnatural – force: Emaciated hands resist, grasp and beg for an end to their neglected human condition. There is a nobility in life that we confer only upon dying, I elect to do homage to that indomitable spirit that lives on in the aftermath [...].[11]

In a private interview, Temertey mentions that she designed the sculpture to be made of aluminum because the competition rules stipulated that the monument was to be made of materials that the artist could guarantee for fifty years. Since she wanted a material that would reflect the sun to further enhance the symbolic nature of the transition to a new life, she chose aluminum. She mentioned that if she were to realize the design as a sculpture, she would have chosen crystal glass as the most appropriate material. In discussing her motivation and artistic inspiration, Temertey indicated that the monument is meant to honour

Fig. 46. The unveiling of the monument in Edmonton, Canada (1983)

[11] "Vybraly plan pam'iatnyka / Monument design picked," *Promin / Promin'*, № 11 (1983), pp. 7 (Ukr.), 16 (Eng.).

survivors who managed to preserve their humanity despite experiencing the collapse of values and morality in the face of genocide. The monument also provides some closure to her family's Holodomor experience, a form of working through loss by means of its symbolic and non-literal representation.[12]

It is rarely mentioned that this monument, besides the inscription of dedication, was at one point intended to feature a fragment from Dante's *Divine Comedy*, and more precisely from "Hell" (song 33, lines 37–39): "When I awoke, before the dawn, amid their sleep I heard my sons (...) weep and ask for bread."[13] The quotation from Dante's masterpiece was intended to stir reflection, stimulate imagination, and generate compassion for victims of the Holodomor, feelings not contingent on knowledge (which might be absent), but on emotions. Canadian art historian Daria Darewych asserts that Temertey's monument speaks in universal symbols that are understandable to every viewer.[14]

The initiative to erect a monument met with various forms of opposition from the beginning. As soon as Edmonton's city council designated a plot of land for its installation, Councillor Gerry Wright made public his concern over the city's decision to build a monument commemorating the fiftieth anniversary of the Holodomor in the centre of Edmonton. His fears were mainly related to the possibility of Soviet authorities seeing it as an act of provocation by the Canadian government, potentially leading to international conflict.[15] The initiative was in fact opposed by the Soviet Embassy in Canada. In an official letter, Soviet representatives stressed that building this monument would worsen Soviet-Canadian relations and distort the actual picture of agricultural collectivization in the Soviet Union.[16]

Interestingly, voices of opposition were also heard within Ukrainian circles, although in this case in relation to the jury and its work. Letters appeared in the Ukrainian press that criticized the selected design and proposed alternative solutions. One such letter, sent to the newspaper *Novyi shliakh* and signed S. Lantukh, criticized the rationale behind the jury's choice:

---

[12] Interview with Ludmilla Temertey, Toronto, November 26, 2017 (the author's private collection).

[13] Dante Alighieri, *The Divine Comedy: Hell, Canto XXXIII*, accessed July 30, 2020, https://ebooks.adelaide.edu.au/d/dante/d19he/canto33.html.

[14] Dariia Darevych, "Holodomor iz perspektyvy mystetstva," *Krytyka*, № 7–8 (2008), pp. 31–3.

[15] *Ukraïns'kyi holos*, May 9, 1983, p. 1.

[16] Olena Koval'chuk and Tamara Marusyk, *Holodomor 1932–1933 rr. v USRR i ukraïns'ka diaspora Pivnichnoï Ameryky* (Chernivtsi, 2010), pp. 126–7; Petro Tron'ko [et al.], ed., *Na skryzhaliakh istoriï. Z istoriï vzaiemozv'iazkiv uriadovykh struktur i hromads'kykh kil Ukraïny z ukraïns'ko-kanads'koiu hromadoiu v druhii polovyni 1940–1980-ti roky* (Kyiv, 2003), pp. 675–84.

> I simply lack the words to express my protest over the design for the monument commemorating the victims of the Great Famine in Ukraine that is to stand before City Hall in Edmonton. If I may comment, the monument will speak to no one. It amounts to nothing more than a transferring of the modernist-symbolic art of degradation and "monstrosity" into the sphere of immortalizing our national events. For those afflicted with a symbolic fever, the terrible and unforgettable tragedy of Ukraine in 1933 may be expressed symbolically. Surely the sign of the hammer and sickle, under which our brothers and sisters groan and suffer, along with half the world – serve as a sufficient reminder of the Ukrainian victims under communist rule and they would forewarn generations of Canadians of the Communist threat. It would be interesting to see the remaining monument designs. Perhaps there were some among them that fulfilled the role of both a monument and a warning? In any case, for me, this monument will mislead not only the Ukrainian community of Edmonton, but in all of Canada.[17]

In a December issue of the newspaper, another critical letter appeared. Liashenko was negatively inclined toward the monument's entire concept but especially regarding the symbolism of the extended hands:

> The question is what will the raising of arms upward mean? Upraised arms can signal: submission to the enemy, voting at a meeting, saying goodbye to friends departing on some train, boat or other form of transportation, or hello on their arrival. If someone had seen or experienced the tragedy of the Ukrainian people, where on the sidewalks of industrialized cities lay dead mothers with their tiny children in various horrific poses, and other Ukrainians like them of every age. (…) In no way does this monument design fit. A monument has to be constructed in accordance with the truth. Without any excessive fantasies. The truth that took place in Ukraine cannot be replaced by a fantasy. The monument should reveal the truth to the entire civilized world, if it can be considered as such.[18]

Criticisms of Temertey's design touched on how the Holodomor should be remembered and whether it is possible to create a monument that meets expectations of an entire community. Discussions centred on how to memorialize the victims appropriately. Worth noting is that negative reaction to modernist monuments and their abstract symbolism is not uncommon. It is impossible to portray loss literally, but given the impossibility of fully representing trauma figuratively, abstract forms offer the richest breadth of expression. Temertey's monument is an homage to survivors like her mother, who despite her traumatic

---

[17] *Novyi shliakh*, № 39 (September 24, 1983), p. 5.
[18] *Novyi shliakh*, № 49 (December 3, 1983), p. 5.

past, found the inner resources to move past bitterness and appreciate life. The artist has said that it also suggests a millstone twisted by a superhuman force, a form symbolically connected to the quern and the grain confiscated during the Holodomor, an interpretation that has received less attention.[19] Perhaps this is symptomatic of the processes that "places of memory" undergo over time, in which some elements of the symbolism are forgotten, while others are nurtured by successive generations of memory communities.

This first monument to the Holodomor located in a public space was unveiled on October 23, 1983, in a ceremonial and solemn atmosphere. In a report prepared years later for UCRDC in Toronto, Mr. Shulakewych describes the participants at the event, who were gathered on the premises of Edmonton's Main Library, which faces City Hall and Churchill Square. Joining representatives of various Ukrainian organizations and their flag-bearers were delegates of various ethnic groups, clergy, judges, and other VIP guests. At least fourteen representatives of ethnic communities participated, among them Poles, Hungarians, Latvians, Lithuanians, Estonians, Koreans, Metis, East Indians, Italians, and members of the Jewish community. Several judges of Ukrainian heritage were present: Justice Russell Dzenik, Justice Peter Greschuk, and Citizenship Judge Rudolf Pisesky, along with their families. The artist Ludmilla Temertey and her family came from Montreal – Raissa (Ludmilla's mother) and Kost' (James Temerty, Ludmilla's brother).[20]

Ukrainian-Canadians ensured that representatives of other Canadian minority communities were present during the unveiling. The procession of about eight thousand people made its way to the front steps of City Hall, with the dignitaries settling on the prepared dais. They included Ukrainian Catholic Bishops of the Eparchy of Edmonton – Most Rev. Neil Savaryn and Most Rev. Demetrius M. Greschuk (Auxiliary Bishop), Ukrainian Orthodox Church Archbishop Boris Yakovkevych, Archbishop Joseph N. MacNeil representing the Roman Catholic community of Alberta, and Rabbi Haim Kemelman representing the Jewish community of Edmonton.[21]

Mayor Laurence Decore pronounced October 23, 1983, "as a day of remembrance of the victims of Ukraine famine." Among the Alberta Government's representatives were Hon. Julian G. J. Koziak, MLA, Minister of Alberta Municipal Affairs, and Hon. Bill W. Diachuk, MLA,

---

[19] Interview with Ludmilla Temertey, Toronto, November 26, 2017 (the author's private collection).

[20] Edmonton's Holodomor Monument (1983), Report by Bohdan I. Shulakewych (HM Project Manager), October 1, 2018, The Ukrainian Canadian Research & Documentation Centre Archive, Toronto, Canada, pp. 1–15.

[21] Ibid.; Petro Savaryn, *Z soboiu vzialy Ukraïnu: Vid Ternopillia do Al'berty* (Kyiv, 2007), p. 230.

Fig. 47. Holodomor monument in Edmonton, Canada (1983) today

Minister Responsible for Workers' Health, Safety and Compensation. The Federal Government was represented by Don F. Mazankowski, MP for Vegreville, Alberta. Representing UCC National (from Winnipeg) was John Nowosad, President. Also present were John Kushnir, President of UCC Calgary, along with a busload of participants from that city, and Stefan Romaniuk, President, UCC Lethbridge. Representing the US was Hon. David Schwartz, US Consul General for Canada. In addition, there were about ten other politicians on the podium.[22]

---

[22] Ibid., p. 231.

Dr. Peter Savaryn, Q.C., Chancellor, University of Alberta, was the Master of Ceremonies, while Dr. Bohdan Krawchenko, Director of CIUS at the University of Alberta was the keynote speaker. A short religious service – *Panakhyda* and blessing of the Holodomor monument, was co-celebrated by the Ukrainian Catholic and Ukrainian Orthodox hierarchs, assisted by their clergy. The assemblage was addressed by Dr. Melety Snihurowych, President of UCC Edmonton, followed by Hon. Jacques Blais of the Federal Government, Premier of Alberta Hon. Peter Lougheed, and Mayor of Edmonton Laurence Decore. After the monument's unveiling, a simple wreath of blue "forget-me-nots" was placed at its base by Dr. Yar Slavutych, a survivor of the Holodomor, accompanied by two boys. The wreath was designed to remember and honour those who perished from hunger in the far-off land – Ukraine in 1932–33. The ceremony concluded with singing of the Ukrainian and Canadian anthems, led by the Kashtany vocal group.[23]

The monument in Edmonton's urban space was the first instance of moving beyond Ukrainian diaspora circles in cultivating memory of the Holodomor, and it also inspired Ukrainian communities in Toronto and Winnipeg to create similar monuments.

5.2 The monument in Winnipeg (1984)

The Winnipeg monument[24] was designed by the second prize winner of the Edmonton competition, the Ukrainian-Canadian sculptor Roman Ivan Kowal.[25] It was officially unveiled on June 24, 1984, near Winnipeg's City Hall. Its construction was spearheaded by the Winnipeg branch of the Ukrainian Canadian Committee (today's Ukrainian Canadian Congress), and the monument presently belongs to the city.

Roman Ivan Kowal (1922–2004) was a creator of chiefly sacral, monumental and/or decorative works. Besides the monument in question, he was also responsible for the stained glass work at St. Michael's Church in Winnipeg (Transcona); the mosaic at the Holy Family Ukrainian Catholic Church in Winnipeg; stained-glass window at St. Andrew's Church in Winnipeg; the stained glass and interiors of

[23] Edmonton's Holodomor Monument (1983), Report by Bohdan I. Shulakewych, pp. 1–15.

[24] "Pam'iatnyky zhertvam Holodomoru, vstanovleni v Kanadi," accessed April 3, 2019, http://canada.mfa.gov.ua/ua/ukraine-ca/holodomor-remembrance/holodomor-remembrance-canada/holodomor-remembrance-canada-monuments.

[25] Liuboslav Hutsaliuk, "Roman-Ivan Koval'," *Obrazotvorche mystetstvo*, № 1 (2004), p. 45; Iaroslav Rozumnyi, "Ukraïns'kyi mytets' zhyv i tvoryv u Kanadi (Pam'iati Romana-Ivana Kovalia)," *Mystets'ki obriï* 7 (2004) [2005], pp. 408–10; Myroslav Shkandrii, "Mystetstvo Romana Kovalia," *Zakhidnokanads'kyi zbirnyk*, № 5 (2008), p. 423.

Holy Ghost Ukrainian Catholic Church in Beausejour, Manitoba; and the mosaics at both St. Mary the Protectress Ukrainian Catholic Church in Winnipeg and the Ukrainian Orthodox Cathedral of St. John the Baptist in Edmonton. He also made the coat of arms bas-reliefs on the Main Post Office building in Winnipeg and the bas-reliefs on the Taras Shevchenko monument in that city. Together with Sviatoslav Hordynsky, he produced the iconostasis at Sts. Vladimir and Olga Ukrainian Catholic Cathedral in Winnipeg. Working with architect Victor Deneka, he also decorated the interiors of several Orthodox churches in Winnipeg and across Western Canada.[26]

In the centre of Roman Kowal's composition entered into the competition is the figure of a mother and child, cast in bronze. The entire monument stands 4.5 metres tall, with a base made of black granite. In terms of its expressive content, emphasis is placed on loneliness and isolation from any external help during the Great Famine of 1932–33. Unlike in other monuments, the figure of the woman with her child as portrayed by Kowal is not crying but rather, lowers her head in the face of an inescapable situation. She is alone in a trap from which there is no exit. She holds her child close, shielding it with her right arm from the walls that surround and are closing in on them.

In writing about the Winnipeg monument, Myroslav Shkandrij emphasized that in devising the concept, Kowal recalled the testimony of a militiaman involved in the arrest of a woman accused of cannibalism. The account shocked the artist and stayed with him for years.[27] Another source of Roman Kowal's artistic inspiration may have been the sculptures representing everyday life in the Ukrainian village before World War II that were exhibited in Munich in 1947. Whether this young art apprentice, who lived in Munich from just after the war until 1948, actually attended this important artistic event for the Ukrainian diaspora is a matter of speculation. The exhibition catalogue included a sculpture entitled "Holod" [Famine] by Antin Pavlos. Some art historians have interpreted this terracotta sculpture as depicting everyday life on collective farms and the experience of famine as a natural disaster. It may be that this work is the first post-war attempt to represent the Great Famine in sculpture.[28] The exhibition catalogue states:

---

[26] Volodymyr Popovych and Roman Senkus, "Kowal Roman-Ivan," *Encyclopedia of Modern Ukraine*, updated 2013, http://esu.com.ua/search_articles.php?id=9165; Alexandra Hawryluk, "Mosaic and stained glass: the art of Roman Kowal," *The Ukrainian Weekly*, № 9 (March 3, 2002), http://www.ukrweekly.com/old/archive/2002/090226.shtml; Basil Rotoff, Roman Yereniuk, Stella Hryniuk, *Monuments to Faith. Ukrainian Churches in Manitoba* (Winnipeg, 1990), pp. 97–8, 102–3, 124–5, 172–3.

[27] Shkandrii, "Mystetstvo Romana Kovalia," p. 423.

[28] Sviatoslav Hordyns'kyi, *Kruk, Pavlos', Mukhin. Try ukraïns'ki riz'biari* (Munich, 1947), p. 17.

"The most important is man and his tragedy, and more precisely the tragedy of a mother who stands with an exhausted child staring into a distance from which she already no longer expects rescue."[29]

A photograph of this sculpture appeared on the cover of the journal *Novi dni*.[30] The winning entry for the monument in Edmonton was published in an earlier issue.

This sculpture could have inspired Kowal. He did not experience the Holodomor personally (he came from Eastern Galicia, which was within Polish borders at the time of the Famine). He learned of the Famine from press reports and from the first-hand accounts of people he

Fig. 48. Sculpture entitled Holod *by Antin Pavlos presented at the 1947 Munich exhibition*

Fig. 49. A model of Roman Kowal's Holodomor monument (1983)

[29] Ibid., p. 18.

[30] *Novi dni*, № 405 (November 1983).

met later, already in the diaspora. He commented on his conceptualization of the monument as follows:

> It occurred to me that women suffered from famine the most. It was they who were always responsible for preparing meals. When food ran out, it was they who had to contend with the pleas of children. I know that the responsibility for the evil done lies with the regime that later tried to sweep the course of events under the carpet. One day, the idea to represent the regime in the form of pincers came to me. I imagined a suffering mother with a child next to her, asking for food. The competition jury liked the idea.[31]

According to the artist's son, Bohdan Kowal, his father believed he could convey the essence of the tragedy most successfully through the image of a mother and child enclosed in a tight, constricting space of totalitarian power. In his view, no one before or since has been able to tell the tragedy of the Holodomor so simply, without resorting to the shock value of human suffering and drama or excessive tears and pathos, as is frequently encountered in monumental sculpture of the Ukrainian diaspora.[32]

Kowal's design was brought to the attention of Winnipeg City Council by Harry Dmytryshyn, the head of the Holodomor Committee, established in 1982, which also included Peter J. Manastyrsky, John Baluta, Dr. Walter Lebedin, Oksana Rozumna, Lesia Szwaluk, Marijka Diakiw, George Holowka, Stan Jaworsky, Rustislav Surrowy, and Ron Bryk. The monument was to be the pinnacle of civic actions undertaken to commemorate the Holodomor's fiftieth anniversary in Manitoba. In October 1983, a large demonstration took place on the grounds of the Manitoba Legislature, which included a ceremonial memorial service conducted over a mock coffin with the inscription "7 million." Marijka Diakiw, a member of the Holodomor Committee, recalled that some five thousand people took part in the gathering, which was covered in the *Winnipeg Free Press* and *Winnipeg Sun* newspapers.[33] In the memory of the city's residents, the last event to similarly move the Ukrainian community of Winnipeg had been the unveiling of the Taras Shevchenko monument in 1961. *Svoboda* wrote:

> The decision to honour the millions of victims of the Holodomor from 1932–33 in Ukraine, which was planned and sadistically organized by Moscow, was the result of a mass, thousands strong demonstration that

[31] Shkandrii, "Mystetstvo Romana Kovalia," p. 424.

[32] Interview with Halyna and Bohdan Kowal, Winnipeg, November 17, 2017 (the author's private collection).

[33] Peter J. Manastyrsky, "30-year anniversary of Holodomor monument in Winnipeg," *Ukrainian Winnipeg*, January 20, 2015, http://www.ukrainianwinnipeg.ca/30-year-anniversary-of-holodomor-monument-in-winnipeg/.

> resonated with us and others on an anniversary of this greatest tragedy of the Ukrainian nation. It took place on October 9, 1983 under the direction of the Winnipeg branch of the Ukrainian Canadian Committee and with the support of all the Orthodox churches and organizations. The overwhelming success of this national manifestation and the understanding shown to the Ukrainian community by city authorities and the government of Manitoba persuaded the demonstration's organizing committee to take steps to ensure that the memory of the Great Holodomor's victims would not dissipate with the demonstration, but be given permanence first and foremost by means of a suitable and proper monument that would constantly remind Ukrainians and their compatriots what Moscow is capable of, and what those who suffer from the delusion of cooperation with Moscow, or of having its protection, can expect. The committee then decided to undertake efforts to include complete information about the Ukrainian Holodomor in Manitoba's educational curricula and to bring this historical fact into full light among the professional and intellectual circles of our compatriots through appropriate publications. Following the full agreement of both the Provincial and National Office of the Ukrainian Canadian Committee, the organizing committee behind the October 9 demonstration along with representatives of all Ukrainian organizations commenced a series of consultations and proceeded to seek permission and a plot of land from local authorities for the monument's construction, and to seek an artist capable of creating the monument and the funding necessary for its construction as well as the realization of the committee's future plans.[34]

Kowal's design was ultimately selected outside of the competition. Halyna Kowal recalled that her husband, Roman Ivan, entered the Edmonton competition reluctantly, only agreeing at her insistence. To date, several of his other designs had not been realized, while another artist's design was chosen for the Edmonton monument. Harry Dmytryshyn, meanwhile, saw this as a splendid opportunity to have a monument built in Winnipeg by a local artist.

According to Peter Manastyrsky, the monument was to stand in front of the Manitoba Legislative Building, but this idea was dropped as a result of a dispute between government employees and representatives of the Ukrainian community over the Holodomor's status as an act of genocide. The Ukrainian diaspora in Canada did not present a united front on this issue, with a pro-communist group denying the Great Famine had occurred. In the end, permission was granted for the monument to be erected before Winnipeg's City Hall. A foundation was established to fund the monument,[35] which raised $118,330 CAD,

---

[34] Komitet Pobudovy Pam'iatnyka Holodomoru Ukraïny u Vinnipehu, "Vinnipeh buduie pam'iatnyk zhertvam holodomoru v Ukraïni," *Svoboda*, № 35 (February 24, 1984), p. 6.

[35] A. K., "U Vinnipehu plianuiut' vidkryttia pam'iatnyka zhertvam holodu," *Svoboda*, № 78 (April 26, 1984), p. 1.

Fig. 50. A fragment of sculpture for the Holodomor monument in Winnipeg, Canada (1984)

of which $65,683 CAD was spent on the monument itself.[36] The artist's son, who helped realize his father's design, has claimed that this amount was in fact insufficient and that certain details of the monument were inadequately finished.[37]

Dr. Peter Savaryn emphasized in his memoirs that the Embassy of the Soviet Union in Canada protested the construction of this monument. In several letters to local government authorities, the Soviet ambassador claimed that the initiative was nationalist in character and a distortion of historical reality, depicting the Soviet Union in a bad light. These letters, in Savaryn's opinion, used aggressive communist rhetoric and presented Canada's Ukrainian community as a dangerous ethno-religious community.[38]

---

[36] *Propam'iatna knyha: U pam'iat' ponad 7,000,000 ukraïntsiv holodom zamuchenykh Moskvoiu / Commemorative Book: In Memory of Over 7,000,000 Ukrainians Starved to Death by Moscow* (Vinnipeh, s.d.), p. 59.

[37] Interview with Halyna and Bohdan Kowal, Winnipeg, November 17, 2017 (the author's private collection).

[38] Savaryn, *Z soboiu vzialy Ukraïnu*, pp. 232–3.

Fig. 51. Roman Kowal with his work

Bohdan Kowal stated that his father had intended to use bronze for the Winnipeg monument but eventually chose a more expensive material – African granite – and also added a base in the shape of a trident (*tryzub*). Halyna Kowal recalled that her husband feared possible sabotage by communists who were boycotting the event. At night, volunteers took turns guarding the monument.[39] Accounts from those years indicate that a significant portion of Ukrainian-Canadians affiliated with the communists denied the Great Famine had occurred and thus did not consider it an act of genocide, but it is difficult to determine today the real extent of the opposition. Approximately three thousand people attended the monument's unveiling on Sunday, June 24, 1984.

[39] Interview with Halyna and Bohdan Kowal, Winnipeg, November 17, 2017 (the author's private collection).

Fig. 52. The installation of the monument at Winnipeg City Hall (1984)

The solemn, commemorative unveiling was attended by Metropolitans Maxim and Andrew and representatives of community organizations of different generations as well as Ukrainian cultural organizations that provided musical interludes. Harry Dmytryshyn ensured that a minute of silence was observed for the victims. The numerous speeches delivered on the occasion met with the approval and loud applause of those present:

> The speakers enthusiastically accepted the idea of building a monument as a reminder of totalitarian Moscow's ruthlessness. They thanked the Ukrainian community for enriching the city with yet another monument and noted its symbolic warning against the tragedy of a holocaust* of any kind, and especially one as great as the one in 1932–33 in Ukraine, ever repeating in any country in the world.[40]

[40] Anatol' Kurdydyk, "U Vinnipehu vidkryly pam'iatnyk zhertvam Holodomoru," *Svoboda*, № 125 (July 3, 1984), p. 1.

Thus, a primary aim of the monument's construction was to serve as a warning against Muscovite totalitarianism. This message linked the monument to the guiding principle of Temertey's design for the Edmonton monument. Consequently, it is tempting to conclude that this was how the cultivation of Holodomor memory was perceived by the whole of the Ukrainian diaspora in Canada on the occasion of its fiftieth anniversary, given that two out of the three designs distinguished by the competition accented this very theme.

As mentioned, the monument in Winnipeg differed in some details from the design submitted to the competition. One of them is the inscription that in the end was included in three languages: English, French, and Ukrainian. It reads: "This monument was erected to commemorate the fiftieth anniversary of the famine-genocide in Ukraine in 1932–33, and to the eternal memory of over 7,000,000 innocent victims of forced starvation: the result of a ruthless procurement policy decreed by the Soviet Government in Moscow."

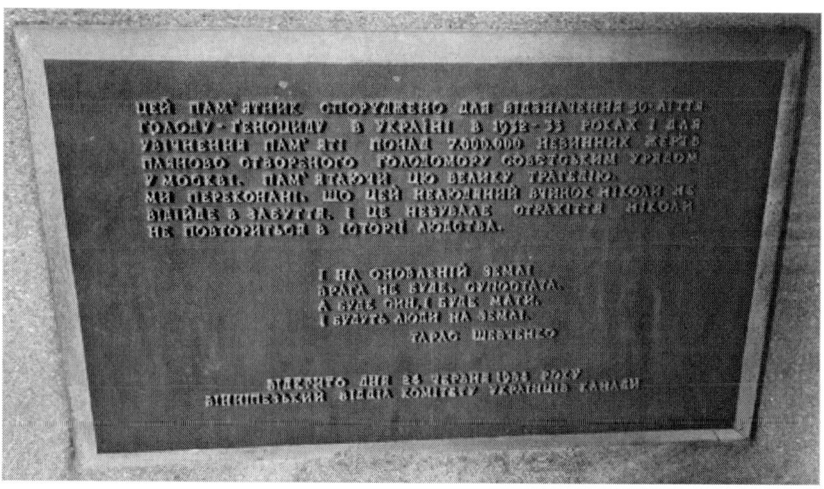

Fig. 53. The inscription on the monument in Winnipeg, Canada (1984)

Halyna Kowal recalled that the idea for the inscription came from the monument construction committee and was not an element of Kowal's concept. She also mentioned the difficulty in choosing a verse to complement the inscription. Opinions were divided: some favoured an excerpt from an English poet, while others favoured a Ukrainian text.[41] In the end, the monument's plinth features the final quatrain

[41] Interview with Halyna and Bohdan Kowal, Winnipeg, November 17, 2017 (the author's private collection).

from a work by Taras Shevchenko translated into English by the unidentified author:

On a renewed and blessed Earth
All evil deeds shall disappear,
And mothers there shall be, and, sons,
And truth shall reign upon the Earth.[42]

І на оновленій землі
Врага не буде, супостата.
А буде син, і буде мати,
І будуть люди на землі.[43]

According to George Yurii Shevelov and Grzegorz Igliński, this work by Shevchenko is constructed on the semantic contrast of opposing notions: between persecutors, the selfish oppressors who serve only their own interests, and people who selflessly fight for the truth and aim for the triumph of humanity and regeneration of the world.[44] The inclusion of this evocative and prophetic motif illuminates how the tragedy of the Great Famine of 1932–33 is understood by the "community of memory" that created this "place of memory" in Winnipeg and how this understanding is formally reflected in the monument. Two fragments of the inscribed verse – its first and last lines – are especially significant here: "On a renewed and blessed Earth / … / … / And truth shall reign upon the Earth!" In this way, by upholding the memory of the Holodomor, Ukrainians in the "free world" can tell the truth about the Holodomor. In this light, the memory of the Holodomor is

---

[42] It is worth noting that at that time, existed a well known literary translation by the Soviet translator Irina Zheleznova: Wine was a potion Galileo / And Archimedes never drank; / Into the paunches of the monks / Streamed holy oil…. You, prophets, freely / Spread o'er the world and bags of grain / Gave to its wretched kings…. No gain / The corn the kings have sown will bring them, / For beaten down by hailstorms stinging / 'Twill be…. Before they are conceived / The princelings they will die, and leave / The earth reborn, with its inhuman, / Brute foes of man forever gone. / But mothers there will be, and sons– / Aye, here on earth there will be humans! // St. Petersburg, September 24, 1860 (translated by Irina Zheleznova). Taras Shevchenko, *Selected Works: Poetry and Prose* (Moscow, 1979), p. 279.

[43] There is also a literal translation of the verse: "And on the reborn earth / There will be no enemy, no tyrant / There will be a son, and there will be a mother, / And there will be people on the earth." Myroslav Antokhii, Daria Darewych, Marko Robert Stech, and Danylo Husar Struk, "Shevchenko Taras," *Internet Encyclopedia of Ukraine*, updated 2004, http://www.encyclopediaofukraine.com/display.asp?linkpath=pages%5CS%5CH%5CShevchenkoTaras.htm.

[44] Grzegorz Igliński, "Romantyczne posłannictwo Słowa. 'Ni Archimedes, ni Galileusz…' Tarasa Szewczenki jako przykład liryki profetycznej," in *W kręgu kultury ukraińskiej*, ed. Walenty Piłat (Olsztyn, 1995), pp. 31–44; George Yurii Shevelov, "The Year 1860 in Shevchenko's Work," in *Shevchenko and the Critics*, ed. George S. N. Luckyj (London, 1980), pp. 329–30.

purifying and defines a sense of being Ukrainian for successive generations of those born and raised outside Ukraine's borders.

The leaflet and commemorative stamp for distribution on the occasion of the unveiling are also worth noting.[45] Designed by Marijka Diakiw, the leaflet contained an official interpretation of Kowal's sculptural work[46] that describes the monument as symbolizing an undefeated Ukraine, even if one severely tested by history: "The monument and its trilingual inscription in the Ukrainian, English, and French languages will remind us and our fellow citizens of blood-soaked Ukraine."[47] One interpretation that concurs with that expressed in the leaflet posits that the two stone slabs are reminiscent of an open coffin, with the woman and her tightly clinging child clasped within. The woman with all her strength tries to postpone the inevitable.[48]

Winnipeg's Ukrainian community saw the monument's construction as a means of declaring that the Holodomor was a punishment for Ukrainian struggles for independence. As one of the articles announcing the monument's construction states:

> The monument to the victims of the Holodomor in Ukraine in the very heart of Winnipeg is not a question of honour for our whole community nor for each of us individually. It is to be unveiled at a specific moment and will constitute a permanent reminder of Ukraine and of those murdered by the Muscovite executioner through the brutal Holodomor for the love of their native land and their struggle to live as free men. We are counting on the help of Winnipeg's Ukrainians in raising this sign together as another great deed for Ukraine.[49]

The monument construction committee modified Roman Kowal's concept to correspond with their notions of what needed to be communicated to viewers, both Ukrainian and non-Ukrainian. The monument thus reflects the dialogue between a community and the artist who belonged to it. The concurrence of their respective visions (presumed given the lack of community opposition to Kowal's design) was possible because the sculptor referenced traditional symbols while also leaving room for personal interpretation. For some, the woman featured on the monument represents Ukraine embracing all of the Holodomor's victims; for others, she is a famine-stricken mother in despair, seeking

---

[45] Kurdydyk, "U Vinnipehu vidkryly pam'iatnyk," p. 4.

[46] Manastyrsky, "30-year anniversary."

[47] Kurdydyk, "U Vinnipehu vidkryly pam'iatnyk," pp. 1, 4.

[48] "Istoriia stvorennia pam'iatnyka Holodomoru u Vinnipezi," *Ukrainian Winnipeh*, May 1, 2017, http://www.ukrainianwinnipeg.ca/kowal.

[49] Komitet Pobudovy Pam'iatnyka Holodomoru Ukraïny u Vinnipehu, "Vinnipeh buduie," p. 6.

salvation. These interpretative possibilities follow, in my mind, from the fact that Kowal built the monument to honour the dead rather than the survivors, as was the case with Temertey's work.

The designs distinguished in the 1983 Edmonton monument competition evoke three aspects of the Holodomor: the closing off and isolation of Ukraine from sources of potential external aid, the enormity of the number of victims, and the inexpressibility of the experience due to the crime's horrific, dramatic nature. The monumental representation of the Holodomor from this period is typified by projects that sought to immortalize Holodomor victims for all time. It is important to note, however, that there is one monument (in Edmonton) that refers to the generation of survivors and their children. In these monuments, the question of who was responsible for the tragedy and the desire to punish the perpetrators are pushed aside. At the forefront is the heated discussion about how to commemorate, recollect, and remember the Holodomor. As these generations pass on, changes in the perception and understanding of the symbolism of these "places of memory" will follow; they will be interpreted anew and they will be forgotten, with other monumental interpretations of the Holodomor raised by successive generations of memory communities.

The "communities of memory" that negotiated the means of Holodomor remembrance among themselves at this time imposed their own sensibilities onto the event. They were convinced that the world would not be safe absent the overthrow of communist power. In point of fact, Holodomor monuments created during the 1980s were free of traces of Soviet political culture but not of North American and West European models and clichés, on the basis of and alongside of which they arose. Given the absence of an existing, official and socially accepted Ukrainian culture of Holodomor memory, the Ukrainian diaspora found itself referencing another genocide widely represented in Western culture, namely, the Holocaust. While the public symbolization of the Holodomor trauma, made possible through the creation of "places of memory" in Edmonton and Winnipeg, was intended to bestow the deaths of millions of Ukrainians with social significance, it also became a focus of the Ukrainian diaspora's activities for decades to come.

5.3 The memorial in Lubny (1993)

The first monument to the Holodomor to be built in Ukraine is the so-called "Mound of Sorrow" located near the town of Lubny in Poltava Oblast, close to the Mhar Transfiguration Monastery. Shaped like a bell, the monument was unveiled on September 11, 1993, to mark the sixtieth anniversary of the Great Famine in Ukraine on the initiative of the writer Oleksii Kolomiiets and the Ukrainian Cultural Foundation [*Ukraïns'kyi fond kul'tury*].

An open letter by Kolomiiets on the subject of building a monument to coincide with the sixtieth anniversary commemorations was published on January 4, 1990, on the pages of *Literaturna Ukraïna* and a few other national newspapers. Kolomiiets lived through the Holodomor as a child in his hometown of Kharkivtsi in Poltava Oblast. He addressed his letter to Borys Oliynyk, the head of the Supreme Council of People's Deputies of the Ukrainian SSR in 1991. Historical consensus points to Oliynyk as raising the issue of the famine's genesis during his address at the 19th All-Union Conference of the USSR Communist Party in 1988: "Given that persecution in our republic began long before 1937, it is still necessary to explain the causes of the 1933 famine, which claimed the lives of millions of Ukrainians, and to name those responsible for this tragedy."[50] While Kolomiiets does not refer in his letter to Oliynyk's remarks, he was convinced that, as a poet, Oliynyk was filled with love for his nation and would want to be a patron of the monument.[51]

In his letter, Kolomiiets shares his reflections on what the monument should look like and the Ukrainian national traditions it should evoke:

> What should a monument dedicated to millions of famine victims resemble? Most of them were peasants who attracted little attention even when alive. They lived as they suffered and in suffering gave up their lives. They don't really need a monument. They can, and we, aware of how many have died, will draw upon ourselves the eternal curse by remaining idle.
>
> There simply must be a monument! What kind of monument – that is what we must ponder, searching for answers in our nation's history, in its mercy, goodness and unfathomable wisdom.
>
> Let us look into Ukraine's distant past. It is heavily marked with flashes of battles for its freedom and future. The nation's best sons perished in these battles, countless people died and were buried in mass graves. The whole of the Zaporozhian Cossack Army while defending constructed a monument. Every warrior tipped a hatful of earth on the grave – and a high burial mound grew on the steppe, a monument for the ages. A monument that defies time. Look at the heart of Ukraine: centuries past? And monuments to Cossack glory arise…why not drink in the custom of the masses?
>
> Why not raise a huge burial mound – a grave to Ukraine on the steppe, on the richest soil? So that all can see and remember. The poverty endured by a nation that, living on such land, was forced to starve

[50] "Borys Oliinyk pomer na 82 rotsi zhyttia," *Ukraïna Moloda*, April 30, 2017, http://www.umoloda.Kyiv.ua/number/0/2006/111161/.

[51] Dmytro Ianko, "Memorial narodnoï skorboty i pam'iati," *Dnipro*, № 3–4 (2004), pp. 88–99.

> to death. Anyone from among the millions-strong Ukrainian nation can be the monument's hero. Let everyone consider it their holy duty to repent before those starved to death. How to break the curse – never forget them and never allow a similar outrage to happen on Ukrainian soil!
>
> Let everyone bring to this burial mound at least a fistful of soil as their contribution to a monument made by the entire nation.
>
> Everything passes. Even stone and iron deteriorate with time. But soil is like life itself – eternal, and eternal shall be this monument raised by all Ukrainian people. So I think. And so I believe.[52]

Kolomiiets' letter was published along with Oliynyk's reply. In responding to the appeal, the poet evaluates the Famine as an event that wreaked havoc on the Ukrainian nation and inflicted long-term social, economic, and psychological consequences. From a reading of both letters, it would seem that the Famine was purely a social phenomenon that took place in a political and economic void.

> The famine took the best of our people. Those who did not follow the order of the day and did not inform on their brothers, those who did not go to wrench the last morsel from the starving mouths of children, who did not know how to trade and wheel and deal, steal, and murder in order to survive.
>
> The famine of 1933 in Ukraine became one of, if not the most terrible of events to take place in a system of cannibalistic selection, when all were talented, wise, courageous, more dignified, more humane and more moral as they disappeared into labour camps. Taught a lesson and, finally, murdered by starvation. These were planned attacks on our nation's genetic reserves. We must be deeply aware of the irreversible damage they inflicted on our culture, science, economy, how they bled dry the historical development of the nation, and what a yoke they placed on its psyche.[53]

In concluding his letter, Oliinyk encouraged readers to submit their proposals and ideas regarding the monument's form and location.

> Our forefathers built mounds to bury their compatriots with their hands and caps. These burial mounds have survived as monuments for centuries. Let us also raise mounds on the broad steppe of beloved Ukraine – a monument to famine victims on the most fertile soil, and likewise eternal. Let it reach the silent cosmos and teach our descendants how to live in harmony with tradition on this simultaneously holy and sinful earth. There is no need for statues nor idols. Idols fall. The earth is eternal. This monument has to become truly national. Let us reach together for the horizon and find for it the most prominent place in our Ukraine.

---

52 Ibid.

53 Quoted after: Ibid.

> Together, we shall consult and devise when and how we shall raise this mountain with our hands, who shall have the honour of building it, what we will sow on its sacred slopes and what trees we shall plant on it, what pathway we shall tread, and who shall be among the first to pay their respects. All of us together. For we have no right to ruin this.[54]

These letters are appeals to society to become involved in commemorating the Holodomor and a proposal for how this could be accomplished. They present a poetic vision steeped in Ukrainian tradition of paying homage to the Great Famine within the public sphere. In his letter, Kolomiiets references the tradition of Cossack graves and military burial mounds. This could be read as stemming from the desire to present the event outside the expressive framework characteristic of Ukrainian monumental art at the turn of the 1990s. The appeal resonated broadly in the Ukrainian daily press. Newspapers that published it received a multitude of letters not only from within Ukraine but also from the Ukrainian diaspora. The monument's proposed form of a burial mound gained broad acceptance, while the issue of its location generated many different proposals.[55] On the question of the monument's designer, poet and People's Deputy Ivan Drach proposed in 1992 that the future monument be designed by the well-known Ukrainian sculptor, Ivan Kavaleridze.[56]

The mound in Lubny was raised in 1990 using soil brought in from all of Ukraine's regions. That same year, a cross was placed and consecrated on the mound. The monument's construction was organized by a committee formed for this purpose by the Ukrainian Cultural Foundation, with the aforementioned Borys Oliynyk at the head. The Foundation received eight amateur monument design proposals as well as two by professional teams (Volodymyr Priadka, Anatoliy Ihnashchenko). Ultimately, architect Ihnashchenko's design, symbolically titled "Bells of the World," was selected. The bell was placed on a twelve-metre wooden cross and was cast in Dnipropetrovsk at the Metal Constructions Production Plant.[57] Anatoliy Ihnashchenko, in turn, built the monument that was to crown the mound in 1993.

This monument stands out from among others in Ukraine not only because it was the first. It is remarkable for superbly illustrating the birth of the visual culture of the Holodomor in Ukraine. The creators of Holodomor monuments were deeply rooted in the previous epoch

---

[54] Ibid.

[55] Volodymyr Tatarenko, "Vyroste Kurhan Skorboty [Reportazh z hromad, pomynannia zhertv holodomoru]," *Literaturna Ukraïna*, August 16, 1990, pp. 1–2.

[56] Volodymyr Koroliuk, "I vdariat' dzvony pam'iati [Pro sporudzhennia memorialu "Holodomor-33" na Poltavshchyni]," *Literaturna Ukraïna*, March 25, 1993, p. 1.

[57] Ianko, "Memorial narodnoï skorboty i pam'iati," pp. 88–99.

Fig. 54. Holodomor monument in Lubny, Poltava Oblast, Ukraine (1993)

and often had experience working on monuments to Soviet heroes. The biography of the architect behind the Lubny monument, Anatoliy Ihnashchenko (1930–2011), is of interest in this context. His output included both monuments to significant individuals and events in Ukrainian history as well as communist monuments. Three monuments that he designed in Soviet times were demolished in 2016 as part of a campaign to decommunize public spaces in Ukraine or as a result of military engagement in the east of the country. One of them was a monument to the Chekists that had stood at Lybids'ka ploshcha in Kyiv since 1967. Made from red granite, the monument was nine metres high and featured the faces of two Cheka officers in high relief atop a rectangular base.

Fig. 55. The Cheka monument in Kyiv, Ukraine (1967) before demolition in 2016

The second of the demolished (in 2015) monuments commemorated the Bolshevik commander Mykola Shchors and was built in Chernihiv in 1977. Ihnashchenko also had monuments connected to World War II in his portfolio, having been part of the team that built a monument at Babyn Yar in Kyiv in 1976, as well as one at the peak of the Savur-Mohyla, constructed in 1967 and positioned at a strategic height (277.9 metres above sea level) on the Donets Ridge, about ten kilometres south of the town of Snizhne and around ten kilometres from the border of Donetsk Oblast (in Ukraine) with Rostov Oblast (in Russia). During World War II, it became part of the German defence line

"Mius-Front," passing back and forth between the Germans and Russian in the summer of 1943, finally to be captured and held by the Red Army in August of that year. In 2014, after the outbreak of war in eastern Ukraine, Russia-backed separatists took control of the ridge. Control of the ridge meant control of the plain below for a distance of tens of kilometres. The Ukrainian Army won back the ground on August 9, but it was retaken by the separatists on August 26. During the fighting, the obelisk was destroyed. Control of this ridge has taken on a symbolic significance for both sides in the conflict, similar to the way it did during World War II.

Fig. 56. Monument to soldiers killed in combat in 1943 on the peak of Savur-Mohyla, Ukraine (1967)

The monument at Babyn Yar is an example of Soviet monumental art, setting aside any political aspects of its construction and failings. Later monuments commemorating, for instance, the extermination of the Romani during World War II were designed specifically for Babyn Yar but erected in other Ukrainian towns.[58] With the onset of the 1990s, the artist thus felt the need to design a monument in the shape of a bell precisely for Babyn Yar. As he recalled in an interview, the fifteen-metre-tall bell was to have been unveiled at Babyn Yar, but the idea did not find financial support, even if it were to honour the partisans who died during World War II. A year later, Ihnashchenko proposed a monument in the shape of a bell dedicated not to the victims of the war but to those of the Great Famine.

Ihnashchenko's design for the Holodomor monument in Lubny envisioned a bronze bell in a shape reminiscent of the globe and supported by a pedestal resembling a cross in form. In addition, the image of Our Lady of the Sign with the infant Jesus in her arms was to be emblazoned on the bell to emphasize that women and children were the first to starve to death. The monument was made from much cheaper cast iron, and funds were lacking for including the image of the Mother of God. During its installation it turned out that the monument obscured the view of the area, in particular that of the nearby monastery. Consequently, and without the sculptor's permission, its height was reduced by five metres.[59]

As it stands, the monument appears as a mighty bell with thirty smaller bells attached to its lip. An inscription reads: "The Holodomor -1933: when one person departs – an entire world dies with them. When millions head off into the abyss – a whole galaxy then becomes extinct." These words were taken from a speech given by Oliynyk on August 12, 1990, at a patriotic gathering connected with the building of the memorial mound. He apparently said: "They say that when a man dies a whole world departs with him. What is there to say when millions die? It means that an entire enormous world community is heading for extinction and that a gaping hole appears in the space of memory through which oblivion enters."[60]

Borys Oliynyk wrote a poem to mark the unveiling of the monument, which contains an interpretation of the premises behind the monument placed on this symbolic memorial grave:

[58] "Komu zavazhav pam'iatnyk 'Zakam'ianila kybytka' v Babynomu Iaru?," *Biblioteka Holokostu*, accessed April 3, 2019, https://sites.google.com/site/lohocoust/babin-ar/komu-zavazav-pam-atnik-zakam-anila-kibitka-v-babinomu-aru.

[59] "Reportazh pro pershyi memorial zhertvam Holodomoru," *5 Kanal*, November 22, 2008, https://www.5.ua/suspilstvo/reportazh-pro-pershyi-memorial-zhertvam-holodomoru-video-36326.html.

[60] Quoted from Ianko, "Memorial narodnoï skorboty i pam'iati," pp. 95–6.

На цій горі, на пагорбі печалі,
Де все болить – від квітки до хреста,
– Ідуть дощі вдовиними плачами…
На цій горі, на пагорбі печалі,
Німіє слово і мовчать уста.
Гірка сльоза пече, як сіль чумацька.
Стоять в жалобі схилені Лубни.
І монастир – як оберіг козацький…
І дзвін вола безмовно: «Пом'яни!»
Страшне число у нелюдській напрузі
Пропалює світи до глибини:
У тридцять три розіп'ято Ісуса.
У тридцять третім на земному прузі
Розіп'ято мільйони без вини.
Ми відспівали їхні чисті душі.
Вони нас не спалили у клятьбі.
Вони – простили. Але пам'ять душить:
Чи маєм право ми простить собі?
…На цій горі, на пагорбі печалі,
З небесної святої чистоти
Ідуть дощі вдовиними плачами.
Спадає плащаницею мовчання.
І тільки дзвін волає: «Не прости!»

On this mountain, on this hill of sorrow,
Where everything is in pain – from the flower to the cross,
– Rains come down like a widow's weeping …
On this mountain, on this hill of sorrow,
The word goes silent and the lips are still.
A bitter tear burns like sea salt.
The town of Lubny is bowed in mourning.
And the monastery – like a Cossack talisman …
And the bell silently cries out: "Remember!"
A terrible number with inhuman intensity
Burns worlds to the depths:
At thirty-three Jesus was crucified.
In thirty-three, on the face of the earth
Millions of innocents were crucified.
We sang lamentations for their pure souls.
They did not burn us with curses.
They – forgave. But memory suffocates:
Do we have the right to forgive ourselves?
…On this mountain, on this hill of sorrow,
From heavenly holy purity
Rains come down like a widow's weeping.
A shroud of silence descends.
And only the bell cries out: "Do not forgive!"[61]

[61] Translated by Taras Koznarsky.

The highlighted fragments clearly indicate that the "community of memory" was not ready at the time to *work through* the Holodomor trauma toward an end to the process of social mourning. The monument in Lubny was intended as a beginning to the long and bumpy road of adjusting to the loss. It is also worth noting that the artist indicated that this place is important for cultivating the memory of World War II ("widow's weeping"), and that from then on it would be given a new, completely different social sense. The first Holodomor monument in Ukraine is an example of creating the Ukrainian "symbolic dominion" by displacing Soviet symbolism from public space. The new "community of memory" gives this place a new sense corresponding to its emotional needs. The space once associated with the "community of memory" of the Great Patriotic War is, through new rituals (not secular, but religious in terms of form), adapted to the goals of the new "community of memory", which begins to exercise symbolic care over it.

The monument's unveiling was attended by Leonid Kravchuk, then President of Ukraine (and head of the Supreme Council of the Ukrainian SSR shortly before), as well as Mykola Zhulynsky, Deputy Director of the Ukrainian Academy of Sciences. In his speech, President Kravchuk illuminated the idea behind the monument:

> I want to say that people come here not only to bow their heads in regret. They will come here to grow stronger and to follow the path of independence, the way of sovereignty. We will create our own state. We will create it in the name of the nation. This is not easy. It will be difficult since we have many problems that we need to resolve together. (...)
>
> We have come here not only to bow down in regret and honour those who died in the Holodomor, but also to grow stronger and to swear an oath in this place that we will never stray from this path.

Many of the addresses given on this occasion commented on the accompanying weather, with the falling rain referred to as nature's tears, shed for Ukrainians lost to the Famine.[62]

In the autumn of 2008, the idea to renovate the monument was raised, with Ihnashchenko expressing interest in participating in the project. His perception of the Great Famine had changed, along with what of the event should be immortalized; he did not wish to return to what he could not create the first time around, but rather wanted to add symbols evocative of farm work to the monument, namely grain, sickles, and harrows.[63] Ihnashchenko wanted to emphasize the social origins of the victims rather than the religious experience of belated

[62] Volodymyr Koroliuk, "Dzvin na Hori zazhury. Vidkryttia Memorialu skorboty pid Lubnamy," *Literaturna Ukraïna*, September 16, 1993.

[63] "Reportazh pro pershyi memorial."

national mourning. We see here an example of the reinterpretation of the symbolism of a work carried out by its author under the influence of a new social understanding of the Holodomor. Ihnashchenko's proposed modifications reflect changes that had taken place in the discourse on the social understanding of the Holodomor between the beginning of the 1990s and the end of the first decade of the twenty-first century in independent Ukraine.

5.4 The Monument at the Church of St. Michael in Kyiv (1993)

In the same year as the Lubny monument, the most recognizable Holodomor monument in the world was unveiled in Kyiv, beside St. Michael's Golden-Domed Monastery. Its official unveiling took place on September 12, 1993, with its construction tied to the commemorations of the sixtieth anniversary of the Great Famine. At the time, its construction was overshadowed by the monument in Lubny, the subject of several years' discussion, which had been unveiled the previous day.

The commemorations began in the square in front of St. Sophia's Cathedral with a somber march that proceeded in the direction of St. Michael's Cathedral, where the monument to the memory of the victims of the Great Famine of 1932–33 was to be unveiled. As in Lubny, the ceremonies were attended by then president Kravchuk, who stressed in his speech that it was the first time Ukrainian citizens could ceremoniously and publicly honour the memory of the Holodomor's victims: "The Holodomor's anniversary is being nationally observed for the first time, established to honour the eternal memory of the murdered millions of innocent Ukrainian farmers and to draw attention of the world's community to this event."[64]

The monument was designed by Mykola Kysly and the sculpture was made by Vasyl Perevalsky. As in many cases, the personal motivations of people involved in creating the monument had significance. Perevalsky's family came from Cherkasy, where they suffered from both repressions and famine during the 1930s. Perevalsky recalled:

> – The village of Bubniv was poor (…). – People lived there thanks to animal grazing and fishing in the Dnipro river, without noblemen, since these were Cossack villages from the start. But division reached the village and some "kulaks" had to be stripped of land. And so my grandfather lived his old age in someone else's cottage. He didn't survive the famine, even though relatives helped as they could. With time they also persecuted my father – for being the son of a *kulak*. (…)[65]

---

[64] *Literaturna Ukraïna*, September 16, 1993, p. 2.

[65] Snizhana Lysenko, "Cherkashchanyn Vasyl' Pereval's'kyi stvoryv usesvitn'ovidomyi symvol Holodomoru," November 20, 2012, accessed July 30, 2020, http://uman.info/ua/

The monument in question is a square stele made from grey granite with the shape of a cross cut out of its centre; within this cross-shaped space stands a female figure, formed in metal, with the cut-out shape of a child with outstretched hands nestled within her. The earth on which the monument stands was brought from all regions of Ukraine, including the Autonomous Republic of Crimea.[66] According to the official interpretation, the female figure, in reference to Orthodox iconography, "symbolizes (…) a mother with outstretched arms with a dead child on her bosom."[67] Both figures are framed by the cross to highlight the martyrdom of death and annihilation during the Holodomor.

Fig. 57. Holodomor monument in Kyiv, Ukraine (1993)

news/cherkashchanyn-vasyl-perevalskyy-stvoryv-usesvitnovidomyy-symvol-golodomoru--1540.html.

[66] Oleksandra Veselova, "Pam'iatni znaky i pam'iatnyky zhertvam Holodu-henotsydu 1932–1933 rr. v Ukraïni," *Problemy istoriï Ukraïny. Fakty, sudzhennia, poshuky* 13 (2005), p. 434.

[67] M. Miroshnychenko, "Smertiu smert' podolavshy," *Literaturna Ukraïna*, September 16, 1993, p. 1.

The symbolism contained in this monument has been analyzed in other works. Johan Dietsch [Öhman], in one of his articles on the culture of memory in Ukraine, cites an interpretation of one of the Holodomor monuments situated in Kyiv:

> This monument, erected in central Kyiv, is inspired by the Danish artist Bertel Thorvaldsen's famous statue of Christ welcoming the children. The symbolic meaning is a saviour who also welcomes the children who died during the Famine.[68]

The author of the interpretation compares the Holodomor monument at St. Michael's Orthodox Church in Kyiv to a sculpture made by Bertel Thorvaldsen – one of his most famous works – located at the Church of Our Lady (Vor Frue Kirke) in Copenhagen. The cathedral was built in the classicist style; its interior is fairly stark, and the sculpture in question, made from white marble, is found at the main altar. This comparison is certainly underpinned by the Protestant cultural background of its author, where the figure of Jesus Christ constitutes the foundation of iconography. In an Orthodox context, however, it is the cult of the Virgin Mary that dominates, which is incomparably less significant in Protestant churches. In Orthodox culture, the monument's associations would evoke the Marian cult. If the analysis of this Holodomor monument were to stop at the iconographic level, Dietsch's interpretation would seem apt to the degree that it addresses the religious form of Holodomor commemoration. Since my goal is to surmount conventional interpretations of art works as exemplified by Holodomor monuments, I am interested in finding a meaning that connects it with the culture of Holodomor commemoration.

Indeed, while Holodomor iconography relies on universal Christian symbolism, it is still deeply rooted in Orthodoxy. To return to the monument in question: on the pre-iconographic level, we observe a figure with delicately etched female features, suggested by the shape of the head, the sleeves of attire reminiscent of the traditional clothing of married Ukrainian women, and the inscription of a child's figure within it. Both figures appear within a cross, partially filling its interior. On the iconographic level, we note that the female form recalls two canonical representations of the Virgin Mary: The Virgin Orans icon (Oranta) and the Icon of the Protection (Pokrova). The first refers to representations of the Virgin Mary in a praying pose, with raised and outstretched

[68] Johan Dietsch [Öhman], "From Famine to Forgotten Holocaust: The 1932–1933 Famine in Ukrainian Historical Cultures," in *Echoes of Holocaust: Historical Cultures in Contemporary Europe*, eds. Klas-Göran Karlsson and Ulf Zander (Lund, 2003), p. 241.

Fig. 58. The Bertel Thorvaldsen Christus sculpture at the Cathedral in Copenhagen, Denmark (1833)

arms that symbolize a redeemed soul in Christian iconography. One of the variants of the Orans image is the representation of Our Lady of The Sign, which shows Mary in the orans position with the Infant Jesus nestled in her womb and likewise in a praying pose. A similar image can be found in Saint Sophia Cathedral located a few minutes' walk from the Holodomor monument. The Icon of the Protection (Pokrova), in turn, evokes images of the Virgin Mary covering God's people with a shawl in a gesture of protection. The image is deeply rooted in Ukrainian culture.

Perevalsky himself confirms that this painting was actually an inspiration for him to create this monument:

In 1993, when Ukraine was preparing to organize the sixtieth anniversary of the Holodomor at the state level for the first time, I was the secretary of the Union of Artists of Ukraine. The Union was entrusted with coming up with the emblem for the participants' ribbons. I proposed my own design – a graphic cross at once symbolizing a martyr's death and eternal life. Against the background of the cross – a suffering mother symbolizing mother–Ukraine, and the Virgin Mary with a child at her

Fig. 59. Icon of Our Lady of the Sign from Yaroslavl, Russia (12th–13th century)

> breast. The female figure evokes a well-known twelfth-century icon, "The Great Panagia." The union's leader, Volodymyr Chepelyk, liked the idea, and together we proposed it as an option for the memorial that no one had been able to conceptualize. The architect Mykola Kysly determined how to convey this image in stone, but there was a shortage of granite. We then prepared the memorial plaque from material available at the Union of Artists. We barely made it to the announcement of the Holodomor commemorations themselves.[69]

The icon known also as the *Yaroslavl Theotokos*, or Great Panagia, is a depiction of the Holy Mother and is dated back to the twelfth or thirteenth century. The icon was discovered in 1919 by conservation workers at the Transfiguration Cathedral in Yaroslavl, Russia, and is found today at the Tretyakov Gallery in Moscow.[70] In Orthodox iconography, this image most often features the Virgin Mary with a Child, and less often without. In the first case, the Infant Jesus is depicted at his mother's bosom, mysteriously supported and seemingly defying the law of gravity. As a rule, his countenance is that of a grown man: he holds a Gospel scroll and extends his right hand in a blessing. When Mary is depicted without Jesus, she appears in the pose and gesture of prayer.

An iconological analysis of this monument allows for the rejection of faulty interpretations of its central image and the identification of those iconographic features that are unique and characteristic for Ukrainian Orthodoxy and that were significant in the mid-1990s, when the monument was unveiled in Kyiv. Despite its similarity to the image of the Intercession of the Theotokos and setting aside the fact that this image has been used in visual representations of the Holodomor, I do not interpret it through this particular Marian icon. Instead, I see its image of a woman as a reference to the canonical image of the Virgin Orans and Our Lady of the Sign, albeit in an artistic, non-canonical interpretation designed to enhance and strengthen the Holodomor's historical context. The Virgin Orans presumably never lowers her arms – she is untiring in prayer. Worth noting here is the Ukrainian expression "to drop one's hands" (corresponding to the English expression "to throw up one's hands", although the Ukrainian phrase signals less frustration than resignation to fate, the cessation of one's struggle). Representing the Ukrainian mother in an orans pose but with lowered hands is deeply symbolic of the fate of Ukrainians during the Holodomor, when they were left to fend for themselves and condemned to death by starvation, imprisoned within state borders (hence the sculpture's enclosure of the figure within the shape of a cross rather than another configuration).

---

69 Lysenko, "Cherkashchanyn Vasyl' Pereval's'kyi."

70 Nikodim Kondakov, *Ikonografiia Bogomateri*, vol. 2 (Sankt-Peterburg, 1915), pp. 110–1.

> People brought soil to go under the monument from all over Ukraine and everything was covered in tears and candle wax. After the anniversary passed, the stele just disappeared one night. It turned out it was moved to a courtyard as a result of restoration work at St. Michael's Cathedral. A scandal broke out, and Hryhorii Omelchenko, then mayor of Kyiv, ordered it to be returned to its place. It stands there to this day, and religious passersby often bow down in front of it as if before an icon.[71]

The monument was moved to one of Kyiv's parks during reconstruction on St. Michael's Golden-Domed Monastery. According to members of the Association of Researchers of the Famine-Genocide of 1932–33, it stood there merely as an adornment in the park at the time, which speaks to the relative indifference of society towards the Holodomor during the mid-1990s. With time, however, it was possible to restore it to its original location.[72]

The design put forth by Perevalsky and Kysly references religious themes from a secular perspective, which would become a characteristic feature of Holodomor remembrance in independent Ukraine. Social rituals of remembrance in the public space had yet to develop, with broadly understood homegrown traditions and culture as the reference point for artists. Consequently, secular symbols (at times even folk, or primeval) can be found alongside sacral ones on Holodomor monuments. This degree of *semiotic volunteerism* allows for the creation of a complex, albeit fragmentary, image of loss on the basis of symbols understood as Ukrainian by engaged "communities of memory." The lack of Holodomor iconography at this time was compensated for by the use of sentimental symbolism relating to individual experience (by referencing the experience of losing a loved one rather than the political aspect and mass scale of the genocide). The artist's aim was to convince the viewer that the trauma of the Holodomor was their personal loss, and that this "place of memory" should function as a kind of secular shrine where one can honour Ukrainians struck down by the Famine. In summary, it is worth noting that over time these artistic quests led to the emergence of a specific canon of iconographic images unequivocally associated with Holodomor remembrance based on certain such motifs and symbolic collages.

---

[71] Lysenko, "Cherkashchanyn Vasyl' Pereval's'kyi."

[72] Veselova, "Pam'iatni znaky," pp. 434–41.

5.5 The monument on the grounds of MAUP in Kyiv (2002)

The monument in question came about in the context of discussions about the need for a Holodomor monument in the capital to mark the seventieth anniversary of the Holodomor and the competitions during Leonid Kuchma's presidency that failed to arrive at a winning design. Borys Krylov's and Oles Sydoruk's monument to the victims of the Great Famine is located far from the city centre, on the grounds of the Interregional Academy of Personnel Management (*Mizhrehional'na akademiia upravlinnia personalom*, MAUP),[73] one of Kyiv's post-secondary institutions. It was unveiled on November 15, 2002, during the All-Ukrainian Academic Conference on the Hunger Plague.

It would be an exaggeration to say that this monument had a significant impact on the formation of Holodomor memory in Ukraine. Nevertheless, it constitutes an attempt to link to the historical policies of the presidency of Leonid Kravchuk, who was a member of the Academy's Supervisory Board. This monument thus needs to be interpreted in the context of the already existing sculpture garden on the academy's grounds on the one hand, and as an element of the historical policy of a specific Holodomor "community of memory" on the other.

The MAUP sculpture garden was established gradually through the addition of successive works from the workshop of Krylov and Sydoruk. The idea behind its creation is outlined on the institution's website and reveals the motivations of the Academy while also suggesting how the garden should be interpreted:

> The truth is that MAUP enjoys the reputation of being the biggest and the best among Ukrainian private universities, to which we should also add – "the most patriotic." The Academy has set as its task the education of not only specialists armed with the newest knowledge, but of spiritually and harmoniously developed individuals – true patriots. Only a harmoniously developed personality, with total love for the homeland and respect for other cultures and religions, can become Ukraine's stately architect, a spiritually enriched person prepared to realize their lofty ideals. At MAUP we stress that we are preparing future Ukrain-

[73] The Interregional Academy of Personnel Management (MAUP) was founded in 1989 in Kyiv and was the first private institution of tertiary education in Ukraine. The academy runs twenty degree courses with 62 specialist options. It is geared towards the education of social psychologists and managers of various rank. The academy was under the patronage of the president of Ukraine – first Leonid Kravchuk, then Viktor Yushchenko. MAUP supported the Orange Revolution, including the protests of the 5 *Kanal* journalists against limitations in freedom of speech. However, Viktor Yushchenko turned down the award of an honorary PhD from the academy after the academy authorities started to publicly express anti-Semitic and xenophobic views.

> ian elites. This would be impossible without incorporating nationalist-patriotic elements. Thus, among the many tasks the academy sets for itself, the issue of nationalist and patriotic upbringing of the young is highly ranked.[74]

I would like to consider the monument on the grounds of MAUP in the context of both the creative output of Sydoruk and Krylov and its placement in a university sculpture garden. Sydoruk and Krylov currently have four monuments commemorating the Great Famine in Ukraine in their portfolios. They realized all of these designs jointly, with each constituting a unique and different conceptualization of the Holodomor. Their first monument on the theme was the monument on the grounds of MAUP, unveiled in 2002; the other three were unveiled in 2008 in various places within Kyiv Oblast. Notably, their subsequent monuments are conceptually markedly different from the first. The monument in the village of Velykyi Krupil is in the form of a cross overlaid with the dates 1932 and 1933; the monument in the village of Andriivka resembles the Orthodox Eucharistic bread – *prosphora*; and in Vyshhorod, the monument is reminiscent of the monument in Edmonton.[75]

The monument in the MAUP garden was unveiled during a conference on the subject of the Famine. The publication of the conference proceedings that followed, in addition to papers delivered, included photos from the unveiling and speeches given on the occasion by social and political activists. Some of the same individuals were also present at the unveiling of the first Holodomor monument in Ukraine in Lubny, namely, Levko Lukianenko, Borys Oliynyk, and by then former President of Ukraine – Leonid Kravchuk. Of note is also the fragment of a poem by Borys Oliynyk, entitled "*Bilia Mhars'koho monastyria,*" [Next to the Mhar monastery] that was written to mark the Lubny unveiling and is featured on the monument unveiled in Kyiv:

Страшне число
у нелюдській напрузі.
Пропалює світи до глибини:
У тридцять три розіп'ято Ісуса.
У тридцять третім на земному прузі
Розіп'ято мільйони без вини.

A terrible number with inhuman intensity.
Burns worlds to the depths:

[74] "Zberehty istorychnu pam'iat'," Mizhrehional'na Akademiia upravlinnia personalom, accessed April 3, 2019, http://maup.com.ua/ua/monuments.html.
[75] On mentioned monuments see: "Tvorcha maisternia Sydoruka ta Krylova," accessed July 27, 2020, https://www.tms.kiev.ua/?section=monuments&lang=ua.

At thirty-three Jesus was crucified.
In thirty-three, on the face of the earth
Millions of innocents were crucified.[76]

The inscription is important in so far as it links the incongruent symbols used in this monument. From Christian symbols we find an angel and a bell, from folk symbolism – embroidery, from sepulchral art – the shape and arrangement of individual elements of the work, and in terms of direct references to the Great Famine – three wheat sheaves and an empty grain sack.

The published volume of conference proceedings includes the creators' interpretation of the monument's symbolism and of elements of the social perception of the Great Famine, and the appropriate means of public commemoration prevalent at the time. For the viewer, a key element of the composition is the white marble angel standing atop and over a black marble slab. Firstly, its contrasting colour makes it stand out to passersby. Were it not for elements of folk embroidery used to adorn the plinth, the monument would look even more like a piece of

Fig. 60. The Holodomor monument on the grounds of MAUP in Kyiv, Ukraine (2002)

[76] Translated by Taras Koznarsky.

nineteenth-century cemetery sculpture than a memorial to a twentieth-century genocide. In describing the monument's concept on the cover of the published conference proceedings, however, the volume's editor notes only a seemingly unremarkable element of the architectonic composition, namely, the three sheaves of wheat bound with barbed wire and symbolically placed in an empty sack of grain, all made of bronze and laid in the centre of the black slab, in front of the bell and below the overlooking angel.

In his speech, Prof. Georgy Shchokin, the Dean of the Academy, noted the bell as a key element of the composition:

> We must not forget about it, and we all have a duty before our deceased countrymen, who did not live long enough to fully experience life, or love, or even their own breath. We shall carry this debt until the name of every victim and of every executioner is known. We shall be reminded of this daily by the tolling of the bell of the memorial monument to the innocent victims of the world's worst genocide.[77]

Former President Leonid Kravchuk's address, in turn, emphasized the following:

> Commemorating the immortal memory of the innumerable and righteous victims of the Holodomor in Ukraine in the 1930s, we are only now unveiling a memorial to victims of the Holodomor on the grounds of the MAUP. Historical justice and conscience deems that such a sign should stand in every Ukrainian village, for so many of their inhabitants died while so many simply disappeared without a trace.[78]

This monument is a fitting example of how the Holodomor figured in the public domain at the time of its seventieth anniversary. It was a bottom-up initiative and an attempt to stop time, since no monument had been constructed in the centre of the capital but rather only on the grounds of an institution that includes a former Ukrainian president as its patron and by referencing the memorial aesthetics and iconography of his presidential tenure.

The MAUP monument is symbolically linked to the one in Lubny not only through Borys Oliynyk and Leonid Kravchuk but also through its iconography. It utilizes Christian symbolism (the bell and the angel) in combination with sepulchral architectural features (the shape and material of the tomb) and the folk ornamentation of the plinth. For the "community of memory" linked to the Association of Researchers of Famines in Ukraine, time seems to have stood still, with the same sym-

---

[77] *Holodomor 1932–1933 rokiv iak velychezna trahediia ukraïns'koho narodu. Materialy Vseukraïns'koï naukovoï konferentsiï Kyïv, 15 lystopada 2002 r.* (Kyiv, 2003), p. 5.
[78] Ibid., p. 7.

bolic forms of mourning and understanding of the Holodomor being deemed appropriate despite Ukraine's entry into the second decade of its independence.

5.6 The memorial in Kyiv (2008)

The National Museum of the Holodomor-Genocide is, for a variety of reasons, associated with Viktor Yushchenko, Ukraine's president from 2005–10. To begin with, it can be said to mark the historical policy of his presidency, acting as a kind of manifesto that stands out in the context of his other undertakings in the "realm of memory" politics and the "de-Sovietization" of Ukrainian national identity (and not only because of the impetus with which the memorial museum was created). Second, the degree of the President's personal involvement in the work on this memorial is well known and included concrete suggestions of symbolic solutions as well as rejection of those that did not align with his vision.[79] Nevertheless, the memorial-museum is the end product of many years of collective effort on the part of academics, social activists, and various political powers, formed on the basis of general perceptions and fundamental knowledge of the historical events surrounding the Holodomor. Already in 2002, former presidents Kravchuk and Kuchma made it clear that a Holodomor museum must be built in the Ukrainian capital. It was only in 2004, however, that the idea for its construction gained an influential patron in the person of President Yushchenko, who put a stop to earlier attempts and embarked on an entirely new commemorative undertaking.

When the law on "The Great Famine in Ukraine of 1932–1933" (*Zakon Ukraïny "Pro Holodomor 1932–1933 rr. v Ukraïni"*) was ratified in 2006,[80] recommendations to build the Holodomor museum were repeated in the body of that document. It addresses primarily the planned construction of a museum to the famine victims, and not the commemoration of political repression in Soviet Ukraine – as had been the case previously. This change was a sign of the times in which the act was formulated and ratified, for we can already speak at that point – as Georgiy Kasianov has written – of the rise of the Holodomor as a project of President Yushchenko's politics of memory. In final form, the monument and museum were to honour victims of famines that struck Soviet Ukraine in succession in the 1920s, 1930s, and 1940s.

---

[79] Vitalii Ohiienko, "Vizual'na kul'tura pam'iatnykiv zhertvam holodomoru v Ukraïni," *Hileia. Naukovyi visnyk* 65 (2012), pp. 114–9.

[80] Zakon Ukraïny "Pro Holodomor 1932–1933 rokiv v Ukraïni," Vidomosti Verkhovnoï Rady Ukraïny (VVR), № 50 (2006), p. 504, https://zakon.rada.gov.ua/laws/show/376-V.#Text.

A competition to design the memorial and museum was announced in spring of 2006, which attracted entries from seventeen artistic teams from all over Ukraine.[81] Designs that had been submitted to earlier contests, including that of Anatoliy Kushch (ID 194511) and Roksolana Kardynalovsky (ID 105555), were also entered into the competition.[82] The winning design (ID 555557) was by a team headed by a Kyiv architect, Anatolii Haidamaka. In some of his public comments, he emphasized that the monument as ultimately constructed corresponded only in 70 percent to the submitted design. He also noted that in its final form the monument was the result of cooperation between then President Viktor Yushchenko, Deputy Prime Minister Ivan Vasiunyk, and Director of the Ukrainian Institute of National Remembrance Ihor Yukhnovsky.

The original assumptions of the design are worth examining since changes made during the course of construction may reveal a drive to create a specific image of the past and vision of the Great Famine. In its initial variant, the monument resembled more of a bell tower, a chapel of memory, which may have been influenced by the proximity of the planned site to the Kyivan Cave Monastery – the most important centre of Orthodox pilgrimage in Ukraine. Its decorative elements were exclusively Christian in their symbolism, without the use of pagan symbols characteristic of Ukrainian folk culture. It was a monument refined in its simplicity, its task being to recall an important event in the history of Ukraine in contrast to another nearby monument dedicated to the "Great Patriotic War."

Museum construction was split into two distinct stages, starting with the raising of the monument and only then, with its form in the foreground, proceeding to the building of the museum. By 2017, due to the lack of public funds, only the first part of the plan had been realized, including: the sculptures of the mourning angels and of the little girl with stalks of wheat, the querns, the "Candle of Memory" monument and "the black plaques" behind it, the Hall of Memory (located underground), as well as the Viburnum Grove [*Kalynovyi Hai*]. The architectonic compositions are fundamentally and strongly individualized but are joined together with the common denominator of a "memorial to Holodomor victims." Phase two of construction is to be completed by 2023, with the design prepared by the Polish architectural firm, "Nizio Design International".[83]

---

[81] "Vseukrainskii otkrytyi konkurs na luchshii proekt Memorial'nogo kompleksa pamiati zhertv golodomorov v Ukraine," *Format Market*, accessed April 3, 2019, http://archunion.format-maket.com.ua/golodomor-06-001.shtml.

[82] Ibid.

[83] "Mirosław Nizio projektuje Muzeum Ofiar Wielkiego Głodu w Kijowie," InfoArchitekta, accessed March 31, 2019, https://www.infoarchitekta.pl/artykuly:4-projekty:17748-

The existing memorial can be approached from several sides. One can arrive from the direction of the *Arsenalna* subway station, passing by the monument to soldiers of the Great Patriotic War. One may also enter from the side of the Kyivan Cave Monastery. Guides, however, commence their tours on Lavrska Street, where one encounters the figures of two kneeling angels, their arms crossed over their chests and the sculptures' surface decorated with crosses. The stone path leading from the angels to the "Candle of Memory" monument is bumpy and described by the guides as the "domain of memory"; it is intended to symbolize Ukrainian *chornozemy* (areas of fertile black earth). At around the halfway point to the entrance underneath the monument, there is a little square surrounded by round, flat stones that resemble querns. Ukrainian researcher Vitalii Ogiienko suggests a possible dual interpretation of this site's symbolism. On the one hand, its shape recalls a clock face – the clock of history – while on the other, it corresponds to the daily number of famine losses (some 24,000 people per day).[84] This interpretation is substantiated by the number of stones (twenty-four) and the arrangement of two per place. Querns were among the agricultural implements confiscated during the famine years. The monument's initially Christian conceptualization and its close proximity to the Cave Monastery complex also makes possible a comparison of the stones to *prosphora* – the unleavened bread used in the Orthodox Church for the rite of Transubstantiation, and a cross adorned with sheaves of wheat is etched into the middle of each stone.

In the centre of this symbolic stone circle is a sculpture of a little girl, officially entitled "Bitter Memories of Childhood." The girl holds five stalks of wheat as a symbol of the "Law of Spikelets" that criminalized the gleaning of as little as a few stalks. She stands on a stone plinth that resembles with its shape the surrounding stones. It is difficult to reject a Christian interpretation of this part of the monument given the girl's central placement, which can be interpreted as the death of a child laid down in sacrifice by Ukrainians on the altar of history. Certainly, the largest group of famine victims were infants and young children. The plinth is inscribed in gold letters with the title of a poem by Taras Shevchenko, "*I mertvym, i zhyvym, i nenarodzhenym zemliakam moïm v Ukraïni i ne v Ukraïni moie druzhnieie poslaniie*"[85] [To my fellow-countrymen, the dead, the living, and as yet unborn, in Ukraine and not in Ukraine, my

miroslaw-nizio-projektuje-muzeum-ofiar-wielkiego-glodu-w-kijowie.html; https://holodomormuseum.org.ua/arkhitekturnyj-proekt-muzeiu/.

[84] Ohiienko, "Vizual'na kul'tura."

[85] Reference is to the poem written in 1844 but only published in 1859. Original poem in Ukrainian: Taras Shevchenko, *Zibrannia tvoriv: u 6 t.*, vol. 1, *Poeziia 1837–1847* (Kyiv, 2003), pp. 348–54.

brotherly appeal].[86] Outside of its broader context, the fragment should be understood as a warning and a reminder. Notably, visitors to the monument often leave sweets and candy rather than flowers. The custom of taking food to cemeteries to leave on the graves of dead relatives is an established part of Orthodox tradition. Does this mean that those who stop here recognize the cemetery symbolism of the site, which in turn prompts practices taken from other aspects of life? Or does this type of symbolism simply occur to them as the most appropriate form of remembering this event in Ukraine's history? It is impossible to answer these questions unequivocally and comprehensively. We remain in the realm of the author's intention and the viewer's reception, with the latter always supposing the monument's intent and bestowing it with their own sense.

Behind the statue looms an imposing white monument in the shape of a candle, commonly referred to as the "Candle of Memory." It rises to a height of more than thirty metres, with its surface made to look like a traditional Ukrainian embroidered cloth (*rushnyk).* The fabric pattern is celebratory, like white-threaded embroidery on a white backcloth (similar to the *rushnyks* employed in traditional wedding ceremonies). The cross-stitch pattern is also a symbol of Ukrainianness. Tourist guides at the monument often comment on the varied size of the crosses adorning the tower, with the small ones said to symbolize children and larger ones, adults. Their shape is also reminiscent of bees, which evoke traditional Ukrainian culture and the country's rural landscape. Four black crosses are placed around the monument at even distances, resembling barbed wire. Additionally, golden storks are trapped within the crosses, or crucified on them. The stork is very important in Ukrainian folk culture, symbolizing the comfort of the home. These birds are unequivocally associated with the landscape, peace, and prosperity of areas they inhabit. The colour gold signals the riches of the Ukrainian countryside, often used to contrast with elements representing the situation during and after the Holodomor in Ukraine. The crucified storks are, in my interpretation, a signal of the former world's annihilation, its irretrievable loss. The individual figures of birds that are freed of the cross, in turn, are a sign of hope and Ukraine's restoration following years of oppression.

The composition is a mix of folk and Christian symbols. The latter appear to be used in a more artistic and symbolic fashion rather than as unequivocal references to Orthodoxy, the faith of most Holodomor victims. It is a refined symbolism, emptied of religious meaning; the monument's creators utilized the Christian treasure trove of symbols

[86] English translation from: Taras Shevchenko, *"Song out of Darkness": Selected Poems*, transl. Vera Rich (London, 1961), pp. 74–80.

Fig. 61. The "Candle of Memory" and sculpture "Bitter Memories of Childhood" in Kyiv, Ukraine (2008)

just as they did folk and pagan ones, with the sole intent of making certain meanings and compositional assumptions understandable to the widest possible circle of visitors.

The museum hall located beneath the "Candle of Memory" can be viewed in terms of the inspiration it draws from other "places of

Fig. 62. The "crucified storks" at the Kyiv Memorial

memory" dedicated to similarly traumatic events. For instance, as is also the case at Yad Vashem, visitors here encounter a list of victims: in Kyiv the names are illuminated on the exhibition's walls, and in Jerusalem they are read out. The effect is similarly moving. As well, the listing conveys the scale of the Holodomor, rendering its victims as more than mere numbers in an administrative index, but as individuals with names who once lived and perished during the Great Famine.

Fig. 63. Exhibition at the National Museum of the Holodomor-Genocide, Kyiv, Ukraine

The Kyiv museum accentuates the contrast between the world "before" and "after" the Holodomor. Prior to entry into the main hall, visitors may look at a display of old family photographs of Ukrainian peasants in festive costume, which arouses curiosity given the initial lack of historical context for the photographs. Only the surnames of the photographed subjects are provided, and it is difficult to discern the curator's intent. The various agricultural tools exhibited around the room can similarly be provocative. Among other possibilities, they are likely meant to symbolize the agricultural nature of Ukrainian culture and traditional forms of work among Ukrainian peasants. Both strategies aim to arouse empathy by personifying the victims of the Holodomor.

In the centre of the hall is an altar in the shape of a glass coffin filled with grain, surrounded by stone columns adorned with the image of the tree of life. Significantly, the images are not identical representations of this common Ukrainian pagan symbol; each has the characteristics of one of eight regions of modern-day Ukraine that had been devastated by famine in 1932–33. Above the altar, a pagan straw protectress doll hangs to ward off evil spirits. This is not the result of artistic indecisiveness, in my opinion, meaning an artist who cannot decide on the fundaments of a work's symbolic layer. It is rather a deliberate extensive mix of symbols of "genuine Ukrainian culture" that, by appearing in one place, lead to confusion, and even disapproval.

On the wall as the backdrop of this eclectic scenery, together with the names of Holodomor victims, documents about the Great Famine are displayed. The light in the rooms is dim, making examination of the artefacts challenging at best.

In analyzing museums of totalitarianism, Anna Ziębińska-Witek concludes that a narrative museum does not stop at presenting a collection of artifacts that relate to history. Rather, it utilizes the expositions to construct a story that develops over time and uses historical context to help visitors better understand the artifacts and their significance. Narrative is understood here as an attempt to create a visual historiography by linking together visual components (i.e., photographs, films), artifacts, and textual elements (i.e., labels, documents) by way of elucidating the exhibition's general context. An exhibition usually has a predetermined trajectory, with visitors following a set direction, viewing the displayed items from a beginning through culmination to the conclusion. When well-structured, this type of exhibition not only makes an intellectual impact, but also – and perhaps more so – an emotional one. Instead of simply registering disparate facts, visitors enter a three-dimensional story that exceeds the temporal and spatial framework of the events in question. The emotional force of such representation is comparable to that of novels, fine arts, and feature films that prompt empathy or identification with victims.[87] As Robin Ostow emphasizes, a museum visitor needs merely to attend to the presented events as a participant led by an interpreter.[88]

The entire body of the exhibition is subordinated to a specific conceptualization of the remembered event: it is used to tell a particular story of the Holodomor as an act of genocide against a nation. The artifacts have been selected for their symbolic value and logically relate to the exhibition's theme. Museum visitors can examine the presented genocides through four access points: 1) their origin, which in the Holodomor's case means the growth in Ukrainian nationalism that Stalin wanted to crush; 2) details about the violation of rights, such as the arrest or execution of people found to be hiding food during the Great Famine by the Soviet police; 3) attempts to deny or distort know-

[87] See Anna Ziębińska-Witek, *"Totalitaryzm w nowych muzeach historycznych," in Historia Polski od-nowa. Nowe narracje historii i muzealne reprezentacje przeszłości*, eds. Robert Kostro, Kazimierz Wóycicki, and Michał Wysocki (Warsaw, 2014), pp. 29–31.

[88] Robin Ostow, "Remusealizing Jewish History in Warsaw. The Privatization and Externalization of Nation Building," in *(Re)Visualising National History. Museums and National Identities in Europe in the New Millennium*, ed. Robin Ostow (Toronto–Buffalo–London, 2008), p. 160.

ledge of the events, as was the case with the refutation of the Famine's intentional character by Soviet officials; 4) efforts to break the silence around human rights violations, as happened in Winnipeg at the beginning of the 1980s with initiatives connected to the Holodomor's fiftieth-anniversary commemorations.

Fig. 64. A part of the installation "The Tree of Life" in the National Museum of the Holodomor-Genocide, Kyiv, Ukraine

The emotional engagement of the viewer is a distinguishing aspect of this exhibition. The unconventional perspective on the Holodomor requires an examination of the past, empathy with the victims, reflection, and in the end, the transformation of clichéd views of the event. Despite its narrative and interpretative character, we can speak here of the creation of new experiences inspired by the Great Famine rather than of a reproduction. Museums aspire to a more realistic representation of the Holodomor experience, which is why visitors are condemned to a play of symbols and imagination that, as with all forms of trauma representation, risk appearing inappropriate, unreal, or disrespectful of human suffering.

The Holodomor exhibition is framed to produce a credible account of events from the communist past, encouraging a new framework for understanding Ukraine's history through immersion in and confrontation of historical wrongs. The following strategies serve this aim: the inclusion of survivor accounts, 1930s press photographs, and recollections of foreigners who visited Soviet Ukraine during the Holodomor; the juxtaposition of the official Soviet narrative about the situation in Ukraine with reports of foreign and diaspora journalists; and the use of art installations to embody national mourning symbolically. The museum encourages visitors to "enter" the past, so to speak, ensuring contact with authentic artifacts, performance, and survivor accounts. The goal is not so much to tell the history of the victims but the history of this event as a violation of human rights, an act of genocide and extermination.

The experience of the Holodomor is understood here as the 'sensation' and internalization of historical events through testimonies, traces, and images. In a museum context, it emerges also through encounter with narrative and other forms of representing the past. Notable is the intuitive and sensual character of such exhibitions. These spaces leave little room for diversity or multiplicity of interpretation. The history of the Holodomor is less so the point as inscribing the museum as an institution into national memory politics where Ukraine figures as a nation-victim of communism and emotions are stirred that prompt visitors to identify with the victims, reflect on Ukraine's past, and perhaps position familial history against this backdrop.

On leaving the exhibition hall, there is a sense of insufficiency of basic information about the Great Famine. That said, it is important to remember that this monument was devised as a symbolic foyer to the museum proper that is to stand next to it. The "Candle of Memory" was conceived as a temple of memory expressive of an artistic concept rather than as a place of education. It is thus hardly surprising that it does not fulfill an educational function; in addition, the symbolic layer is so dominant that visitors would have trouble absorbing any factual knowledge about the Great Famine. On leaving the hall, visitors can once again look at the photographs displayed in the entryway, although this time in terms of their negatives, a symbol of a lost world registered by the camera but not allowed to "develop" into a future. A bell has also been placed here, which can be struck by anyone who visits. It was initially to hang above the altar, but the idea was discarded during construction. In its present location, the bell can be seen as symbol of the lament for the deceased that is characteristic of Ukrainian folk tradition. Next to it is a staircase leading to a hallway of "black plaques": marble slabs inscribed with names of places in famine-ravaged areas that currently enumerate more than six thousand towns and villages, with the list being continually expanded.

The Viburnum Grove part of the complex is also worth note. Founded by Viktor Yushchenko as a symbol of national rebirth and of hope for better times, it is not yet fully established. Initially, trees were planted there by important dignitaries on the occasion of various events, but at present new trees are planted infrequently. The majority of guides finish the tour of the site with a moment of silence for those who died in the Holodomor. A minute of silence is also observed by foreign guests, including official delegations from other countries.

On my first visit to this memorial site, I did not perceive it as the greatest "place of memory" of the Great Famine, as is its reputation. I was more intrigued by the people who, like me, were trying to find themselves in this space filled with the memory of the Holodomor and to shake off this veneration of human suffering as a national good. It seemed to me that Ukrainians, as a victim-nation, seeking to reassure or rather convince themselves of the significance of events like the Great Famine, need "places of memory" that can serve as a form of a temple. Such places have the task of kindling an emotional relationship with national history and require from the visitor only the contemplation of the past's image as represented by an artefact, a sculpture, or an artistic installation. In this instance, the viewer is not a co-creator of the exposition who undertakes a subjective interpretation of what has been presented, but a consumer from whom nothing more is expected than presence and engagement with the vision of the past on offer. It was only with time that I came to believe that this is a place for the veneration of suffering to a much lesser degree than it is a temple designed to cleanse contemporary Ukrainians – Ukrainians lost in a mass of symbols of the past, which are not always clear, legible or understandable, and who want to spend time in a place dedicated to an event they know little about and identify with even less.

Notably, while the steps leading to the main entrance go down into the depths of earth, as if "into the land of the dead," at the end of the exhibition, on route to the "black plaques," the staircase leads visitors upward, from darkness into the light of day. This metaphor of passage, of cleansing through immersion in the suffering of forebearers and learning the truth about the nation's past, is a strategy implemented to support the understanding of the Holodomor's significance for Ukrainian national identity. The museum complex that is to stand in the monument's shadow is essentially meant to build on this idea.

From the perspective of the politics of memory, it is symptomatic that the Holodomor museum building, planned from the very beginning, will begin construction some ten years later. The new museum is to fill in the historical context and explain the complex and eclectic symbolism of the installation. Its primary goal is to convey to visitors the genocidal character of the Holodomor. I believe it will be the culmination of many years of effort on the part of Ukraine to draw the world's attention to the issue of the Great Famine and to the Kremlin's particularly repressive policies in relation to Ukraine. It is also an attempt to enter a new level of telling the story of the Holodomor at a site of its memory by departing from the post-communist rhetoric of injustice and the sacralization of national suffering and taking up the mantle of saving the memory of the Holodomor from oblivion.

5.7 The monument in Washington, DC (2015)

At the time of the seventy-fifth anniversary commemorations of the Holodomor, the most important initiative of the Ukrainian diaspora in North America was the construction of a Holodomor monument in the United States capital of Washington, DC. Efforts to build a monument were initiated in 2006; it was to be based on a design selected by independent jurors in an international competition.

On October 13, 2006, the US Congress passed and President George W. Bush signed an act to authorize the Government of Ukraine to establish a memorial on federal land in the District of Columbia to honour the victims of the manmade famine that occurred in Ukraine in 1932–33.[89] It was to stand between North Capitol Street NW, Massachusetts Avenue NW and F Street NW, and the realization of the project was entrusted to the US National Park Service agency. The monument was built with the close cooperation of the governments of the United States and Ukraine. Many years were needed to obtain the permissions required to build on

[89] Public Law 109–340 109th Congress, October 13, 2006. An act to authorize the Government of Ukraine to establish a memorial on Federal land in the District of Columbia to honor the victims of the manmade famine that occurred in Ukraine in 1932–1933), https://www.govinfo.gov/content/pkg/PLAW-109publ340/pdf/PLAW-109publ340.pdf.

the very desirable site and to arrive at a design agreeable to the city's urban planners. The ground of the construction site was consecrated on December 2, 2008, and a memorial service was celebrated in the presence of Ukraine's first lady, Kateryna Yushchenko, the hierarchs of the Ukrainian churches abroad, and representatives of various diaspora organizations.

At the beginning of 2009, an article by the Ukrainian-American journalist Rostyslav "Ross" Chomiak (1936–2015) appeared in the daily newspaper *Svoboda*. Its author asks Ukrainian-Americans a key question: what is the expected impact of building the monument in Washington? In his view, a monument designed to commemorate only the Holodomor would not achieve the aims of the Ukrainian community. He thought it impossible to organize a demonstration of more than fifteen thousand participants at the monument's planned site, as had been the case during the Holodomor's fiftieth-anniversary commemorations in the US:

> In truth, the monument will not be ours. For Americans, the construction of yet another monument in Washington is impossible. Exceptions do happen (like the Martin Luther King Monument, for example) and there are cases of special requests from other countries – Ukraine in this instance. Only two years ago, the Congress agreed to Ukraine's request to erect a monument in Washington as a reminder of the horrendous Holodomor – a genocide of the Ukrainian people at the beginning of the 1930s. The monument was to stand on federal grounds in the capital, which is why two years have passed on reaching agreement on its placement (…) After arrangements with various commissions responsible for the capital's aesthetics, Ukraine received a triangular plot of federal land close to the main railway station and the postal museum – almost opposite Columbus Circle. It isn't a bad location, and much better than the one where the monument to victims of communism stands (in order to see it, you have to walk on foot for several blocks as parking there is challenging). One can forget about the significant events to be supposedly organized around the planned monument.
>
> This triangle of land is situated next to the city's main thoroughfares – Massachusetts Avenue and North Capitol Street, where heavy traffic is the rule. People cannot congregate there in a way that does not block traffic. During the site's consecration on December 2 there were not that many people present, so everyone managed to fit in the space. On the fiftieth anniversary of the Holodomor in 1983, fifteen thousand of the American Ukraine gathered on the National Mall, however. Such a number cannot be assembled at the planned Holodomor monument. During the consecration ceremony celebrated by the bishops and clergy of the Catholic and Orthodox Churches, and during speeches by the wife of the President of Ukraine – Kateryna Yushchenko, Ukrainian diplomats, Holodomor survivors, lawyers and high-ranking civil servants, thanks to whom it was possible to obtain the ground on which to build

the monument, I was reminded of the words of Taras Shevchenko from his poem "Beyond the Ravine, Another Ravine" (*Za bairakom bairak*):

> They heaped up the earth
> And went home,
> And no one remembers.
> Three hundred of us comrades,
> pure as glass, perished here!
> And the earth does not receive us.[90]

> (...) In a word, I am personally not convinced that there is a need for a Holodomor monument in Washington. Am I against the painful truth of the Holodomor?! To the contrary, I wholeheartedly agree with making the crime of genocide committed in 1932–33 known. But a mute monument will not achieve that![91]

In Chomiak's opinion, the monument would not have broad social resonance. For him, of much greater importance was to publicize the subject of the Holodomor through mass media, culture, and the arts:

> Almost none of the monuments in Washington attract public attention. This is why I think that it is not worth counting on the memorial in Washington in helping to publicize the Holodomor. All the more so given the absence of public discussion on the building of a Holodomor monument in the American capital. To compare, the subject of the Shevchenko monument during the fifties and sixties resulted in dozens of articles and reports in *Svoboda*. This time around, all of these undertakings lack transparency on the principle of – as they say in Kyiv – "we'll come to some kind of arrangement."
>
> All of this was done by Ukraine, even though the leader of the UCCA chaired the monument construction committee and lobbied Congress to obtain a plot for it. The Ukrainian government, meanwhile, played a supportive role. All of this is murky when the whole of the diaspora is working toward transparency in Ukraine. A reputable academic research centre dedicated to studying this terrible crime would constitute a persuasive Holodomor monument. (...)
>
> In my opinion, therefore, we should shout out about the Holodomor, write academic works, and make hard-hitting films (the recent films *Katyn* and *Soviet Story*, directed by Polish cinema master Andrzej Wajda and Latvian Edvins Snore, respectively, come to mind). While a monument of granite or bronze next to the railway station in Washington, even with a long text in the languages of its makers, will convey little, I'm afraid. One can only hope that the competition for the monument's

[90] George G. Grabowicz, "Consideration of the Deep Structures in Shevchenko's Works," in *Shevchenko and the Critics*, ed. George S. N. Luckyj (London, 1980), p. 493.

[91] Rostyslav L. Khomiak, "Iaka efektyvnist' nashykh pam'iatnykiv u Vashingtoni?" *Svoboda*, № 1 (January 1, 2009), p. 5.

> design will be transparent, and not akin to the way Soviet Russians hid the truth about the Holodomor for 75 years.[92]

Chomiak's article, quoted here, is crucial for many reasons. First, it is a significant voice in the social debate on commemorating the loss suffered by the Ukrainian people during the Holodomor era. Second, to strengthen his argument, he refers to an essential component of the Holodomor's culture of memory, the poetry of the national bard Taras Shevchenko (his monument is also in the US capital). His aim is not to convince the reader that the venture is pointless but to think about how best to implement it. I believe a similar dilemma plagued the Canadian Ukrainians in the process of constructing the Edmonton monument. It can be summed up by the critical question: How best to mark and commemorate loss?

The dead leave a void behind them, so creators of memorials face a perennial challenge which designers of previous Holodomor monuments and memorials addressed in various ways: how to produce the physical expression of emptiness. Memorials that spring up after tragedies are created by those preoccupied with grief. Then time passes, memories fade. The memorial in Washington was intended to halt the progressive process of forgetting if not so much for Rostyslav Chomiak's generation, then for subsequent generations.

The building of the Washington Holodomor Memorial took almost as long as the Bound Brook Memorial Church, with different consequences. Political events did not influence the process of building the Memorial Church, made possible by contributions from the faithful. In the case of the Washington Holodomor Memorial, much had changed from the moment in 2006 when permission was granted to begin work and its opening in 2015. Russian aggression in the east of Ukraine has given the Holodomor Monument in Washington a different symbolic meaning than was initially planned.

In February 2020, the Kibel Gallery School of Architecture, Planning and Preservation, organized an exhibition titled *Making the Holodomor Memorial: Context and Questions*. On one of the boards discussing the idea of building a monument to the Ukrainian genocide in the US capital, the authors of the exhibition wrote:

> The Holodomor memorial reminds us of what horrors can result when a powerful aggressor subdues a weaker neighbour. Because Congress sanctioned the memorial on American soil, it can be seen as a call for US solidarity with Ukraine today as it again faces Russian aggression.[93]

---

[92] Ibid., p. 11.

[93] "Making the Holodomor Memorial: Context & Questions," accessed February 1, 2021, https://arch.umd.edu/events/making-holodomor-memorial-context-questions.

Starting in 2009, work on realizing the monument, including the design competition, began in cooperation with the Ukrainian Ministry of Culture and Tourism. The competition commission included among its jurors eminent art historians and diaspora artists Bohdan Urbanovych – a Washington-based architect (US); Daria Kulchytska – an iconographer from Cleveland (US); and Radoslav Zhuk – a Montreal-based architect (Canada).

In 2009, *Svoboda* reported that the Ukrainian Cabinet of Ministers had designated 5 million hryvnia for the construction of a Holodomor monument in Washington, with its unveiling planned for the end of 2010.[94] Toward the end of 2009, the Ukrainian Ministry of Culture and Tourism announced a competition for the design of the Washington Holodomor monument.[95]

Fifty-two submissions were received. A twenty-two-member jury comprised of Ukrainian nationals, and Ukrainians from the United States and Canada, narrowed the submissions to five finalists:

- "Destroyed Sphere" by Oleksandr Diachenko
- "Field of Wheat" by Larysa Kurylas
- "Ritual Cloth" by Boris Danyluk
- "Tear Drops on a Wheat Field" by Iulii/Lev Synkevych
- "Shooting Hands" by Igor/Liudmyla Grechanyk[96]

The Ukrainian press indicated that first place had been awarded to Ukrainian architect Oleksandr Diachenko. His design proposed a sculpture in the shape of a cracked globe, or of a bread loaf with a thick slice cut off:

> A sphere was to sit on the plinth, a symbol of harmony, but with a part cut off, representing its violation and the world's ruin; or else a slice of bread, so inaccessible to those who were starving to death. The granite's vivid red surface was to suggest one more association – of a bloody wound. The text on one side of the plinth was to read in Ukrainian and English: "To the memory of the millions of Ukrainians who died as a result of the man-made famine in 1932–33." Another inscription stating "The disappearance of a people destroys the world's integrity" was intended to encapsulate the monument's essence.[97]

---

94 "Vydileno 5 mln. hrn. na pam'iatnyk zhertvam Holodomoru u Vashingtoni," *Svoboda*, № 43 (October 23, 2009), p. 2.

95 "Konkurs na krashchyi proekt pam'iatnyka zhertvam Holodomoru v Ukraïni 1932–1933 rokiv u m. Vashynhtoni (SShA)," Ukrainian National Memory Institute, October 23, 2009, accessed July 30, 2019, http://www.memory.gov.ua:8080/ua/announce/detail/74.htm.

96 Alla Rogers, "Holodomor Memorial in Washington: A progress report," *The Ukrainian Weekly*, № 49 (December 5, 2010), pp. 14, 26.

97 Oleksandr Diachenko, "Ukraïns'kyi pam'iatnyk dlia Vashynhtona," *Ukraïna. Nauka i kul'tura* 35 (2009), pp. 73–5.

Nevertheless, the undertaking was put on hold. In 2010, the new government of Ukraine announced its position on the issue of a monument in the US and stopped financing its construction with Ukrainian taxpayers' money. The initiative was then taken up by the American government. At this time, it was decided that the monument should be built on its designated plot according to the design by Larysa Kurylas, a Washington-based American architect of Ukrainian descent. Her project proposal had been awarded second place in the competition. The competition's winner, Oleksandr Diachenko, did not hide his disappointment and in an interview expressed the hope that his monument would, one day, be realized in another place:

> After I had won the competition, there was a presidential election [in Ukraine] and the new president in a matter of a few months announced that there had been no Holodomor in Ukraine. When the subject became current again after a few years, who won the competition was forgotten. The design of a Washington architect who came in second was realized instead. This is the story as affected by political changes. (…) As for my proposal, I would like it to be realized one day. If not in Washington, this Holodomor monument could stand in many places. It could even be built in Ukraine.[98]

Fig. 65. Oleksandr Diachenko's design for the Holodomor monument in Washington, DC, US

---

[98] "Skul'ptor Diachenko kazhe, shcho ioho pam'iatnyk zhertvam Holodomoru vartyi uvahy," *Ukrinform*, June 7, 2016, https://www.ukrinform.ua/rubric-culture/2030647-skulptor-dacenko-kaze-so-jogo-pamatnik-zertvam-golodomoru-vartij-uvagi.html.

On October 1, 2013, the Ukrainian Embassy in the US received permission to start building the monument. In the end, Larysa Kurylas' design received partial funding from Ukraine.[99]

At the centre of the National Holodomor Memorial is a bronze bas-relief sculpture titled "Field of Wheat." Across thirty feet, highly articulated wheat heads and stalks gradually fade and practically disappear, symbolizing confiscation of the wheat. In this dynamic transition from left to right, the projecting wheat field finally intersects the sculpture's datum plane and crosses into negative space. The negative space not only symbolizes the emptiness left by the lives lost in the Holodomor, but also reflects the artificiality of the famine. As the recess steadily deepens and the famine grows more extensive, "HOLODOMOR 1932–1933" emerges at the base of the wheat stalks in ever bolder relief.

The sculpture is placed within arm's reach to encourage both visual appreciation of the wheat and facilitate a tactile experience, which has resulted in the burnishing of the bronze surface's high points.[100] This is

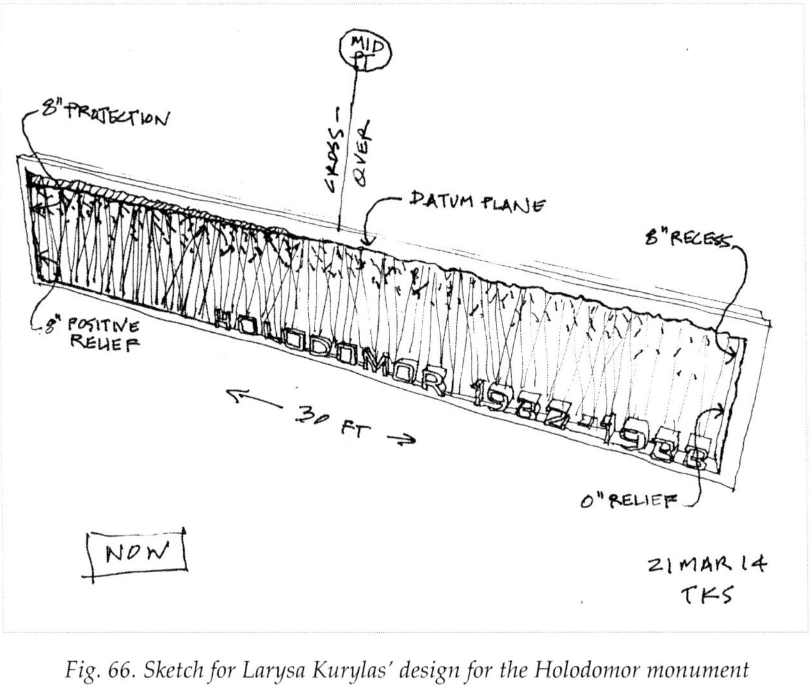

Fig. 66. Sketch for Larysa Kurylas' design for the Holodomor monument in Washington, DC, US

[99] "Memorial Holodomoru v Vashynhtoni," *Homin Ukraïny*, May 24, 2013.

[100] "National Holodomor Memorial 'Field of Wheat'," The Kurylas Studio, accessed February 1, 2021, https://thekurylasstudio.com/memorials/holodomor-memorial-field-of-wheat/.

a recurring theme in earlier monuments as found in the works of Anatoliy Kushch.

Larysa Kurylas is the first artist to draw attention to the non-physical destruction caused by the Holodomor. To symbolize the Soviet regime's attack on Ukrainian culture and the Ukrainian cultural elite, she included granite panels on the back of the "Field of Wheat" that feature a geometric pattern derived from a folk-inspired textile pattern created by the prominent Kyiv artist Vasyl Krychevsky in 1933.

Fig. 67. Design for woodblock printed textile by Vasyl Krychevsky (1933)

The result abstractly evokes barbed wire, alluding to the Ukrainian border, which was deliberately sealed by the government, preventing farmers from leaving in search of food and journalists from entering to report on the famine.[101] The choice of the prototype is worth considering. Krychevsky was an artist associated with Ukrainian national symbols from the times of the Ukrainian National Republic and had designed the first banknotes and securities in 1918. Krychevsky died in exile in Venezuela but was buried in the cemetery in South Bound Brook. Larysa Kurylas explained her choice in an interview for *Our Life* magazine:

[101] Ibid.

Fig. 68. The back of the Washington Holodomor Memorial

> There is a pattern of his that I abstracted a few more steps for the plaza paving. It has an angular, somewhat barbed look to it. I decided to have the stone panels on the reverse side of the sculpture etched with this abstracted Krychevsky pattern. To me, it is a visually engaging pattern, so when you look under the tree canopy there will be this interesting pattern on the sculpture wall. The pattern is also an element that clearly speaks of the attack on Ukrainian culture. As a result of the Famine, a tremendous creative potential of a generation of Ukrainians was extinguished.[102]

Kurylas collaborated with Lawrence Welker, owner of Laran Bronze Foundry in Chester, Pennsylvania, to create the sculpture bass-relief, helping her test ideas that she had designed on paper. To transform the harvested wheat into a foam pattern, they experimented with modeling software. Together they explored production methods and refined the memorial project.

Fig. 69. Three-dimensional model of a "Field of Wheat," made of foam

The monument was ceremoniously unveiled on November 7, 2015. In a conversation with a correspondent of the broadcaster *Holos Ameryky* [Voice of America], the artist emphasized the significance to the design of the monument's location in the centre of the US capital since it was to play an informative role from the outset, broadening knowledge about the Holodomor and prompting reflection:

[102] Olesia Wallo, "Holodomor Memorial in Washington, D.C.: Interview with Architect Larysa Kurylas," *Nashe zhyttia / Our Life*, № 12 (December, 2013), pp. 18–20.

> If we want to spread knowledge about the Holodomor, then this is an excellent location. There are many passers-by here, and cars and tourist buses driving past. It is a very visible place in Washington. Some might think that when it comes to the Holodomor, its monument should stand in a quiet place, at a cemetery, so that people can stop and reflect there, meanwhile the more important role here is to disseminate knowledge about the Holodomor – which is why there could be no better spot for this monument.[103]

In an interview with *Homin Ukraïny*, Congressman Sander Levin spoke in a similar vein when describing the process of completing the monument:

> I do not consider it merely a stone. Research is needed, and discussions as well. This particular monument, very well executed I think, is informative. Sometimes a stone can provoke thought, and that is the case here. The location is also first rate as many people walk by it. It is a magnificent recollection of a human tragedy; it is a tragic but also beautiful monument. It expresses the sorrow of losing millions of people. When people see it, it will stir them to question: what is this all this about? It will be a reminder and – I hope – a lesson, which needs to be learnt from this tragedy. [104]

Indeed, the full impact of the memorial can be appreciated only years later. The monument has become the object of academic interest as an example of an innovative, modern form of commemorating mass extermination in contemporary art. In February 2020 Larysa Kurylas presented a lecture at the opening of the exhibit "Making the Holodomor Memorial: Context & Questions" at the Kibel Gallery, part of the School of Architecture at the University of Maryland.[105]

The exhibition and the lecture are closely related and even interdependent. Larysa Kurylas thoroughly presented her motivation to take up this topic in her art. It is worth noting that Larysa Kurylas was a student of James Mace and knew some Holodomor survivors personally. Before entering the Holodomor monument competition, she carefully studied the Ukrainian and diasporic traditions of commemorating this event in monumental art.[106]

---

[103] [Larysa Kurylas], "Avtor pam'iatnoho monumenta 'Pole pshenytsi' – pro vazhkyi shliakh ioho zvedennia," *VOA*, November 7, 2015, accessed July 30, 2020, https://ukrainian.voanews.com/a/kurylas-memorial/3047914.html.

[104] *Homin Ukraïny*, January 7, 2016, p. 16.

[105] Larysa Kurylas, "Making the Holodomor Memorial: Context and Questions," Kibel Gallery Lecture Spring 2020, youtube video, 1:18:45, https://www.youtube.com/watch?v=kaoZTuRLOUE&feature=emb_title.

[106] Ibid.

Fig. 70. The Holodomor monument in Washington, DC, US (2014)

The artist assumes the existence of many interpretations of her work. In her opinion, everyone will grasp the symbolism but will add to it their own understanding.

By design, memorials invite spectators to step out of their daily routine, to pause, reflect and perhaps consider their present actions in light of the past. Memorials are conceived to accommodate both individual and small group contemplation. Kurylas in fact changed the initial concept design to add a bench where one could sit and contemplate the Memorial. The space in front of the sculpture is mostly paved, which allows for group gatherings as well, an important aspect of the Memorial as commemorations take place at least annually.[107]

"Field of Wheat" encourages tactile engagement: visitors nestle candles and flowers within the spaces of the large letters. Although in a busy public place, the memorial is restrained and private. The work successfully navigates its urban context, contributing to the US capital's cultural landscape.

The intentions of the Washington Holodomor monument's creator coincide with those of numerous Ukrainian diaspora organizations. I maintain that the fundamental goal of diasporic "communities of memory" in current efforts to build Holodomor monuments is to transfer knowledge about the genocidal nature of the event to future generations. Part of this desire is to warn against the ideology and consequences of communism (and of other forms of totalitarianism). The intended audiences are no longer those who experienced the Holodomor first hand or who were raised on familial experiences and recollections of the Holodomor. These monuments, along with many educational initiatives, are aimed at members of all nationalities.

5.8 Conclusions

In writing about Holodomor monuments and memorials, I reflect on their significance and seek to understand the artist's message as conveyed through various symbols. I have not set out to evaluate these "places of memory" or select those that I believe most appropriately represent this tragic event. I am interested in the creative process: the way an artist comprehends and interprets the historical event on which his work's conceptualization is based.

As "places of memory," monuments to the victims of the Great Famine (Holodomor) do not merely commemorate history by means of the information and symbols they contain, but also preserve, reconstruct,

[107] Wallo, "Holodomor Memorial in Washington, D.C."

and transform it. The monuments in Ukraine's capital city make clear the manner in which the interpretation of the Holodomor evolved in the public sphere of independent Ukraine. In the case of the memorial unveiled on the square adjacent to St. Michael's Church in the early 1990s, we can speak about the replacement of communist symbols with religious ones (symbols still rooted in Russian Orthodoxy, it could be argued). It should be noted that a monument created by a sculptor from the Ukrainian diaspora and financed by a diaspora sponsor was erected at the same time. The memorial, constructed in 2003 on the grounds of MAUP, reinterprets the symbols present in the first Ukrainian Holodomor monument in Lubny (Poltava Oblast). Indeed, the two monuments share the same circle of initiators and sponsors, and bear the same inscription, a quatrain composed for the unveiling of the Lubny monument. The individuals involved in realizing these monuments played secondary roles on the Ukrainian political scene. On the other hand, the "Candle of Memory" monument, erected during the presidency of Victor Yushchenko, reflects a rejection of the Holodomor concept developed in the first decades of independence and the emergence of a new concept for Ukraine that draws on symbols used by diaspora "communities of memory" in the mid-twentieth century to commemorate the Holodomor.

The monuments of North American artists from the Ukrainian diaspora analyzed here show that the monuments and memorials established in the West tend to use multiple symbols, sometimes even abstract and modern ones. Monuments are intended to highlight the tragedy of Ukrainians to the people of the diaspora's host countries. On the other hand, artists from the Ukrainian diaspora, who are themselves at some length from the historical context, have been tasked with encapsulating all of what is known about the Great Famine 1932–33 in their memorials. When built abroad, these monuments are notable for a certain distance they maintain from folk traditions, in which Ukraine is, after all, strongly rooted. Therefore, some of them can seem alien to the average audience, incomprehensible in both form and content, and are treated by traditional Ukrainian diaspora communities with some distance.

Chapter VI

Visual Culture of the Holodomor

In considering the new official Ukrainian ritual of commemorating the Holodomor, born from antagonism toward all things previously deemed 'Soviet," I wonder whether such memory practice merely imitates the post-communist aesthetic of reacting to past harms and filling in the "blank spaces." Moreover, I am interested in whether the visual culture of the Great Famine is still intentionally restricted to conveying national ideas related to understanding the famine as a genocide of the Ukrainian people carried out by the Soviet regime. In my opinion, after more than thirty years of independence and despite numerous negative outcomes of Ukraine's incoherent memory politics, certain symbols common to Holodomor monuments can be ordered into a new and relatively recognizable, standard memorial thesaurus. A canon for representing and exploring the human suffering in the USSR of the 1930s is forming in sculpture and architecture, poetry, music, and literature. I am also interested in the relationship between the Holodomor's symbolic interpretations by diaspora architects and artists from Ukraine.

Previous chapters explored the historical, political and social contexts in which numerous Holodomor memorials and monuments arose, taking into consideration their geographic location. The subject of this chapter is less the monuments that were erected in Ukraine and abroad than the processes of symbolizing the Holodomor in these memorials. The primary purpose of this chapter is to consider the symbolic motifs that have shaped the visual culture of the Great Famine 1932–33 (Holodomor). Here I will discuss the visual representations of the Holodomor created by artists living outside Ukraine prior to the first monuments being erected. In the concluding section, I will discuss the iconographic motifs that make up the visual culture of the Holodomor, both in Ukraine and the diaspora.

6.1 The iconography of symbolic burial sites and cemetery monuments

Trauma studies employ many definitions and terms for symbolic and real places of mass execution. The ascribing of various philosophical concepts from a purely theoretical domain to a practical sphere leads to a range of oversimplifications. The unique nature of real and symbolic burial sites is of particular significance to the memory culture of a traumatic event. Within an urban or rural environment an actual place reminds us of the Holodomor's facticity, while the sheer number of such sites signals the magnitude of the devastation wrought by the Holodomor in the Ukrainian countryside.

A considerable number of such marked sites have been established in Ukraine. In 2009–10, in the framework of the criminal proceedings No. 475 "On the crime of the Holodomor," 857 mass graves of Holodomor victims were identified.[1] In 2018, an interactive map became available that uses a search engine to access information about a given location (the number of people buried, monument description, and the story of how the location became "place of memory").[2]

These places reveal the mass and dramatic nature of the Holodomor. Their restoration and identification are currently the most telling manifestations of the public mourning of the Great Famine. Given their location, real places of burial do not require the additional provision of the history of the event, for they are, as places, also witnesses to the Holodomor.

In the case of Holodomor memorials at cemeteries, I discern two tendencies: first, they are places where actual burial sites may be present, albeit unmarked, in which case symbolic graves are created there; and second, as a cemetery is seen as the most suitable place for honouring those who died of starvation, the monuments raised there are not linked to a real place of burial, but rather denote all victims of the famine understood either generally, or in the context of local history. In the second case of symbolic sites, namely, monuments erected in cemeteries but unrelated to any actual burial place of famine victims, it is crucial to understand the essence and specifics of established cemetery monuments in their connection to the history of the local community.

In the context of commemorating the Great Famine, symbolic places of burial located at cemeteries serve as the symbolic grave of all victims. The most common marker of these symbolic spaces at Ukrainian

---

[1] Cf. Mykola Herasymenko, ed., *Holodomor 1932–1933 rokiv v Ukraïni. Materialy kryminal'noï spravy № 475* (Kyiv, 2014).

[2] "Mistsia masovoho pokhovannia zhertv Holodomoru-henotsydu,". Holodomor Museum, accessed February 25, 2020, https://map.memorialholodomor.org.ua/.

cemeteries in places struck by the Famine of 1932–33 are cenotaphs – symbolic, empty graves devoid of human remains. Their function is primarily commemorative and cultural. They are often substitutes for non-existing graves as a symbolic recompense to the dead.[3] Since cenotaphs simultaneously express loss and gain – the death of the individual for the life of the nation[4] – they are most readily associated with military cemeteries. In the case of the Great Famine, however, they do not symbolize heroes and warriors, but rather denote the Ukrainian nation's torment.

Of interest here is the overlap in Ukrainian collective memory between the Great Famine symbols and those of the anti-religion campaign and the Great Terror. A "place of memory" at the cemetery in Dniprovske (Verkhnodniprovsk Raion, Dnipropetrovsk Oblast) underlines this point most eloquently. In its construction, the local architect, Oleksii Bloha, incorporated a crucifix that once crowned the dome of a local Orthodox church desecrated by the Bolsheviks in Stalin's time. In Snizhkiv, Kharkiv Oblast, in turn, a symbolic grave for the victims of the Great Famine was created where the cemetery chapel stood before being destroyed by the Bolsheviks in the 1930s.

The mass-scale construction of monuments to the Great Famine victims has created a specific symbolic canon of so-called "cemetery sites," which combines the symbolism of Holodomor monuments with sepulchral culture. It is not only the architectonic forms of these monuments that are of interest here. Cemetery memorials to the Holodomor take the form of a stela or an obelisk, and most frequently of a cross made of wood, stone, or metal alloys (particularly cast iron). The different materials used to make the crosses are matched by differentiation in their form, which follows artistic and regional variants. Village crosses made out of stone (not necessarily only those connected with the Holodomor) are often prime examples of naïve art, created by anonymous craftsmen with their nevertheless visible stylistic characteristics.[5] Cemetery crosses that commemorate Holodomor victims are decorated with wheat sheaves or placed on a symbolic burial mound.

---

[3] Oleksandra Veselova, "Uvichnennia pam'iati zhertv holodomoru-henotsydu 1932–1933 rokiv v Ukraïni," *Ukraïns'kyi istorychnyi zhurnal*, № 2 (2004), pp. 50–67; Oleksandra Veselova, "Uvikopomnennia zahyblykh vid holodnoho moru," in *Holod – henotsyd 1933 roku v Ukraïni. Istoryko-politolohichnyi analiz sotsial'no-demohrafichnykh ta moral'no-psykholohichnykh naslidkiv. Materialy Mizhnarodnoï naukovo-teoretychnoï konferentsiï na vidznachennia 65-richchia trahediï ukraïns'koho narodu, Kyïv, 28 lystopada 1998 r.*, eds. Stanislav Kul'chyts'kyi [et al.] (Kyiv–New York, 2000), pp. 218–42; Oleksandra Veselova, "Pam'iatni znaky i pam'iatnyky zhertvam Holodu-henotsydu 1932–1933 rr. v Ukraïni," *Problemy istoriï Ukraïny. Fakty, sudzhennia, poshuky* 13 (2005), pp. 434–41.

[4] Susan-Mary Grant, "Raising the Dead: War, Memory and American National Identity," *Nations and Nationalism* 4, № 11 (2005), pp. 509–29.

[5] Jacek Kolbuszewski, *Cmentarze* (Wrocław, 1996), pp. 90–1.

Fig. 71. Symbolic burial mound to memorialize Holodomor victims, Chetvertynivka, Vinnytsia Oblast, Ukraine

This may be related to the fact that contemporary cemeteries, according to Kolbuszewski, are governed by a conventionalized cemetery subculture, which impacts their appearance, aesthetic and philosophical content, eschatological expression, and consequently, the form of grasping the problematics of death. This subculture is a variant of contemporary popular culture with which it shares the aesthetics of kitsch. The appearance of contemporary cemeteries is its most obvious manifestation. Their generic style is dictated by the monumental stone masons who produce the gravestones.[6] Individualized graves were thus replaced with the schematic products of monumental stonemasonry companies that promoted successive designs and trends in sepulchral craft characteristic of an industry rather than an art.[7] Aesthetically speaking, in my opinion, these monuments blend into their surroundings as opposed to resembling other monuments, for instance, those

[6] Ibid., p. 237.
[7] Ibid., p. 244.

Fig. 72. The Holodomor monument in Pohrebyshche, Vinnytsia Oblast, Ukraine

in urban centres. They often look just like the monuments on the surrounding graves, with only their inscription betraying the purpose of their presence at a local cemetery.

The ornamentation of cemetery monuments is often folk (vernacular) in character, inspired by embroidery and sculpture. These gravestone symbols can be compared to tattoos: just as the sign on a body is unique (including in its meaning), headstones at each such site differ according to region. These symbols are alike in lending themselves to multiple interpretations, which explains the magnitude of meanings, often quite different or even opposing, that they can generate. A large number of headstones are decorated with traditional cemetery flower motifs (carnations and lilies) or the image of a willow tree. Carnations, lilies, and roses are emblems of the Virgin Mary ("rose without thorns").[8] Sometimes replacing the rose, red carnations can symbolize the blood of Christian martyrs.[9] As James Hall has pointed out, in western iconography, lilies in the scene of the Last Judgment symbolize the

[8] James Hall, *Illustrated Dictionary of Symbols in Eastern and Western Art* (New York, 1994), pp. 149, 143, 157.

[9] Ibid., pp. 143, 157; Diane Apostolos-Cappadona, *A Guide to Christian Art*, foreword Gabriele Finaldi (London, 2020), pp. 198–200.

Fig. 73. The Holodomor monument in Snizhkiv, Kharkiv Oblast, Ukraine (1990)

innocent,[10] and local stone masons have included them on the symbolic graves of the Famine's innocent victims. The willow, in turn, appeared as a symbol of mourning in European funereal culture toward the end of the nineteenth century.[11] In Western Christian iconography, the willow signified tears shed in grief and over the dead. And in Ortho-

[10] Hall, *Illustrated Dictionary of Symbols*, p. 149.

[11] Ibid., p. 161.

dox Christianity and Judaism, the willow (*Salix Babylonian* in Latin) is strongly associated with mourning in biblical references.[12] In traditional Ukrainian funereal art, another symbol that is often found on the tombs is the traditional motif of a tree as a symbol of eternal life and a metaphor for the road to the afterlife.[13]

It is noteworthy that in the case of Holodomor monuments in cemeteries, Marian symbols and symbols related to justice in Western Christianity appear. Moreover, the carnation is not present in Orthodox Marian iconography, but it is associated with Soviet funereal culture. In the cases of local Holodomor "places of memory" as discussed here, I believe that the symbolism is sundry. And there is even an awkward balancing act by local artists between kitsch and art.

6.2 Iconographic motifs in monuments and memorials

In my deliberations, I see the monument as a "catalyst" – a place of engagement that evokes within its surroundings certain "time loops" that play out in the imagination of incidental passersby. The "catalyst" is equivalent here to a symbol in its broad understanding, namely a representation with a known, established and, moreover, unchanging meaning, the external form of which gives rise to our emotions. In looking at a symbol, we instantly associate it with certain facts, remembered from experience or other sources of knowledge, which impacted the creation of its semantic layer. Thus, a cross symbolizes the torment of Christ since a cross became the instrument of his suffering.[14]

The external form of this semantic layer lies in the artist's purview. Of utmost importance is the ability to communicate with the audience by encapsulating an idea in a form that someone who does not regularly deal with art can assimilate.[15] The form of such a monument is to direct the viewer's associations toward the particular, symbolized event and, additionally, to arouse specific emotions, as intended by the artist, in the process.

As Maciej Lewandowski writes, misunderstandings between the artist (creator) and the recipient of a work "most frequently arise from ambiguity of form, and more precisely from the coexistence in a given form of various elements that can be variously interpreted when

[12] Apostolos-Cappadona, *A Guide to Christian Art*, p. 208.

[13] Serhii Shapravs'kyi, "Traktuvannia osnovnykh elementiv pravoslavnykh kladovyshch z pozytsii khrystyians'koï symvoliky," *Naukovi zapysky [Natsional'noho universytetu Ostroz'ka Akademiia]. Seriia: Istorychne relihiieznavstvo* 5 (2011), pp. 220–30.

[14] Maciej Lewandowski, "Rzecz o pomnikach," *Przeszłość i Pamięć*, № 4 (1998), p. 4.

[15] Mykola Mozdyr, *Ukraïns'ka narodna memorial'na skul'ptura* (Kyiv, 1996), pp. 105–6.

considered separately. These elements are the texture, material, composition, and means of artistic expression, which we may call style."[16] In addition, the majority of architectonic metaphors are conjectural and mixed, and most often based on anthropomorphic figurations.[17] In architecture, a symbol designates a sign or an object that represents another object or concept. The information conveyed by a symbol is determined by a socially agreed-upon code. Experience of symbols causes an emotional reaction, most often subconscious, due to the contrast between the object's relative simplicity and the potential complexity of the meanings it conveys.[18] In art, symbols function on many different planes, depending on the beliefs and customs that inspire a given artist. Symbolic images can easily take on different meanings among different peoples; rarely, in art at least, do they possess a permanent, unchanging semantic core, independent of social and religious contexts.[19]

It is important to understand that in the phenomenon of the visual culture of the Holodomor there is considerable variation in visual design and distinction in addition to the specifics of Ukrainian and diasporic "communities of memory," although dominant visual themes have nonetheless emerged. Many Holodomor monuments abroad do not occupy innately resonant or meaningful Famine-related locations, nor are they located in the highly visible public spaces of major monuments, with the majority located in local parks, Orthodox or Catholic cemeteries or parish grounds, and peripheral urban locations. Varied in scale and cost, most were modest commissions managed by local grassroots community groups. Private donations constituted the majority of funding, usually supplemented by limited amounts of local government support. The intended audience was nearly always local, defined, and delimited by geography, budget, and/or ambition. Several involved the participation of visual artists in their development and execution, but by no means all. These monuments in the diaspora communities of cities or towns with few physical traces of Famine history constitute the public visualization of either the Holodomor or Ukrainian memory/identity within the crowded multicultural landscape of the respective countries. In Ukraine, however, due to the lack of visual designs associated with commemorating social loss at the level of official rituals, different forms of commemoration were created simultaneously. Regardless of the size of the budget (dependent on the ambitions of

---

[16] Lewandowski, "Rzecz o pomnikach," p. 5.

[17] J. Krzysztof Lenartowicz, *O psychologii architektury. Próba inwentaryzacji badań, zakres przedmiotowy i wpływ na architekturę* (Cracow, 1992), p. 198.

[18] Ibid., p. 199.

[19] James Hall, *Dictionary of Subjects and Symbols in Art*, introd. Kenneth Clark (New York–London, 2018), p. xii.

local governments), they were to distinguish the memory of this event from other competing memories in Ukraine (especially in the first decade of independence).

The most resonant examples of monuments have been discussed in the previous chapter, analyzed in terms of iconology. But the ideas that inspired various "communities of memory" to create particular monuments warrant consideration here. In retrospect, monuments to the victims of the Great Famine are not neutral, nor non-ideologized. They are more than artwork aimed at memorializing the victims of the Holodomor. Their creation was accompanied by the need to understand the incurred loss and to vest it with meaning. Despite the significant differences that divide the "communities of memory" in Ukraine and in the diaspora as discussed earlier, and which concern the different historical and social contexts of the formation of Holodomor "places of memory," visual culture is characterized by a common iconography.

Anastasiia Honcharenko identifies a series of iconographic motifs that dominate Ukrainian monumental sculpture at the turn of the twenty-first century. In discussing the representation of the Holodomor in Ukrainian visual culture, she points to images of the Intercession of the Theotokos (the Protection of Our Lady), a starving child, the Cossack cross, grain, wheat sheaves, cranes, and hands reaching toward the sky. She omits, however, bells, Orthodox crosses, burial mounds, and angels. Honcharenko also identifies the iconographic motifs characteristic of representations of other traumatic events. On this basis, one may conclude that Ukrainian monumental stone masonry of this period relies on the same symbols to memorialize the victims of the war in Afghanistan, the "Great Patriotic War," and Stalinist repressions including during the Holodomor and of the Ukrainian underground.[20]

Moreover, Holodomor "places of memory" are conventional in form, their purpose being to symbolize a traumatic event and arouse empathy. These monuments and memorials, both in Ukraine and abroad, are thus characterized primarily by an aesthetic of martyrdom and mourning, which can involve locating the monument in the vicinity of Orthodox sites of worship and with attendant religious symbolism of cupolas, bells, crosses, and the number "33" (referencing both Christ's age and the year of the Famine in Ukraine). In other words, Holodomor visual culture in Ukraine and the diaspora is represented by vernacular monumental projects that perpetuate visual clichés of Ukrainianness, both at home and abroad.

[20] Anastasiia Honcharenko, "Komunikatyvna funktsiia 'istoṙychnoï pam'iati' v ukraïns'kii monumental'nii skul'pturi 1990-kh–2000-kh rr.," *Visnyk Kharkivs'koï derzhavnoï akademiï dyzainu i mystetstv. Mystetstvoznavstvo, arkhytektura,* № 8 (2014), pp. 57–9.

Another problem encountered by the "communities of memory" with respect to the visual culture of the Holodomor comes down to this – the presentation of human suffering as a work of art is extremely difficult. As in the case of the memories of the Holodomor generation, it is not possible to reflect the entire tragedy of the victims, the suffering of the survivors, and the guilt of the inert witnesses. The choice of symbols (iconography) is the result of how the Holodomor is perceived by an individual community and what, in the history of that event, is of utmost importance to them or worth relaying for posterity. The analysis of numerous Holodomor monuments around the world suggests the existence of several patterns in this respect: rich in sentimentalism (symbols of longing for the lost world that was before the Holodomor), exaggerated monumentalism (gargantuan size of the monuments), and a strong affect (symbols of high emotional impact).

It is necessary to discuss several crucial symbolic images chosen by the authors of Holodomor monuments, regardless of location. One of them, in my opinion, is the image of a woman (Marian iconography in the sacral version, a mother in the secular version) with a child, or with a family. It is the most developed image and historically has the longest tradition in the visual culture of the Holodomor. Other significant images include hands, angels, crosses, circles, and bells. This does not mean that I find other images less powerful as far as their impact on the recipients is concerned. I consider the symbols in question as the most affective and comprehensible, constituting the essence of Holodomor iconography.

6.2.1 Mother and child(ren)

The first artistic representation of the Holodomor is generally attributed to Victor Cymbal [Viktor Tsymbal] (1901–68), a Ukrainian-Argentinian artist. His oeuvre includes the painting *Rik 1933* [The Year 1933], which, I would argue, left a serious mark on the shape of the visual culture of the Holodomor.

Cymbal is a recognized Ukrainian artist and diaspora socio-political activist.[21] Born in Stupychne (currently in Cherkasy Oblast), he began his art studies at Kyiv Art School. In 1917, he joined the Sich Riflemen Halych-Bukovyna Kurin and remained in combat until November 1920. In the years 1920–22 he was a prisoner-of-war in camps located in Poland. He later settled in Prague, where he began art studies at the

---

[21] Petro Mehyk, "Viktor Tsymbal (1901–1968)," *Notatky z mystetstva,* № 10 (1970), pp. 47–52.

Ukrainian Studio of Plastic Arts. In the years 1928–60 he lived in Buenos Aires, Argentina. Cymbal spent his last years in New York and was buried at the Ukrainian cemetery in South Bound Brook.

In the years 1933–34, while living in Argentina and mainly involved in advertising art, he was also working on the painting *The Year 1933*. It was first publicly displayed in Galleria Müller in Buenos Aires during an exhibition of Cymbal's works in 1936. The exhibition, as recounted by his wife, Tatiana Mikhailovska-Cymbal, evoked a strong public reaction, and the local press published favourable reviews.[22] However, Sviatoslav Hordynsky noted that the broader public had the chance to see the painting only in 1956, during an exhibition of Cymbal's works in Galleria Rose Mari. He notes that, after the first exhibition in 1936, Argentinian art critics criticized Cymbal's detachment from his native culture since the exhibition did not include any works addressing issues important to "Cymbal as a Ukrainian."[23]

In the Ukrainian-language paper *Ukraïns'ke slovo* [Ukrainian Word] published by "Prosvita" society in Argentina, Hryhorii Goliian wrote a short review, in which he described *The Year 1933* as an example of mysticism in the artist's oeuvre.[24] The same opinion was offered by Yuriy Tys, who published his impressions of that exhibition in the paper *Vyzvol'nyi Shliakh* [Liberation Way]. In his opinion, the artist, with his typical symbolism, represents starving Ukraine with a woman holding a child. Both figures have no eyes and float between heaven and earth.[25] Sviatoslav Hordynsky stressed that *The Year 1933* provoked a strong public response after the 1956 exhibition and prompted protests from Argentinian communists.[26] However, it seems that the Cymbal painting was not originally designed to have any political significance. The artist focused on its moral aspect, but the understanding of the essence of the Holodomor he proposed was so moving that it naturally provoked a strong public reaction, including a political one.

In Daria Darewych's opinion, it is the first artistic representation of the Holodomor in the form of a suffering woman and her child.[27] It is also worth mentioning that in 1948 in Munich, another artist of Ukrainian origin, Antin Pavlos, completed his sculpture *Holod* [*Famine*], which he presented during an exhibition the same year.

---

[22] Tetiana Mykhailivs'ka-Tsymbal, *Spohady (Moie zhyttia na emigratsiï)*, ed. Julian Serediak (Buenos Aires, 1984), pp. 83–5.

[23] Sviatoslav Hordyns'kyi, ed., *Viktor Tsymbal: maliar i hrafik* (New York, 1972), p. 12.

[24] Hryhorii Holian, "Viktor Tsymbal," *Ukraïns'ke slovo*, November 28, 1956, quoted after: Mykhailivs'ka-Tsymbal, *Spohady*, pp. 127–8.

[25] Iurii Tys, "Viktor Tsymbal," *Vyzvol'nyi Shliakh*, № 1 (111) (1957), pp. 104–10.

[26] Hordyns'kyi, ed., *Viktor Tsymbal*, pp. 16–7.

[27] Dariia Darevych, "Holodomor iz perspektyvy mystetstva," *Krytyka*, № 7–8 (2008), pp. 31–3.

Fig. 74. Victor Cymbal's painting The Year 1933

Undoubtedly, in Holodomor iconography, both of these works initiated the practice of representation of the Holodomor through images of women and children. Pavlos' sculpture remains less widely known. In 1978, Wasyl Hryshko published the first edition of the book *Ukraïns'kyi Holokost* using Cymbal's painting as the cover art.[28] Later it was copied in other publications on the Holodomor.

In the Cymbal painting, the figures of the woman and the child are floating between heaven and earth, which relieves the artist from hav-

[28] Vasyl' Hryshko, *Ukraïns'kyi "holokost", 1933* (New York–Toronto, 1978).

ing to declare whether it is a secular or religious painting, whether it depicts a mother and a baby or Madonna and Child. On the other hand, in monument representations, that image clearly evolved and started to develop in two directions. Some artists have presented a woman with a dead child (children), while others have gone further and present an entire family. Yet others present a woman as Madonna and employ Marian iconography. The woman is never alone though, as she is always presented as a mother.

Ukrainian scholar Oksana Kis stresses that in traditional Ukrainian culture, 'mother' holds the highest position in the hierarchy of social values. In popular consciousness, her image is surrounded by a halo of sanctitude.[29] In *Mala entsyklopediia Ukraïny* [The Concise Encyclopaedia of Ukraine] published in the mid-1950s in Buenos Aires, Professor Yevhen Onatsky wrote that the cult of mother found its reflection in folk culture, as evidenced in numerous rites in which the mother figure plays a key role. For Ukrainians, the image of the Mother of God is a symbol of ideal maternity. For them, Mother also means Motherland, as is clear from the national literary legacy.[30] Indeed, the monumental representations of the Holodomor, by employing the image of mother, remain within the scope of traditional national values and folk tradition. Of special note is the symbol of the "crying/bereaved mother" that aims to either emphasize the magnitude of the tragedy and its pain and suffering,[31] or present Ukraine as a living being fighting to survive.

The representation of Ukraine as a woman and mother is frequently reproduced in both folk and religious variations, including in the interpretation by Yevhen Onatsky. In Ukraine, that image dominates, reinforced by means of presenting the figure of a woman dressed in folk costume and holding a baby, placed in front of a sizeable cross or bell, as in the case of the Bilopillia monument (2008) in Sumy Oblast of northeastern Ukraine designed by Viktor Stukan, in Brovary in Kyiv Oblast (2008) and in Strohanivka in Zaporizhzhia Oblast, in Kryvyi Rih and Dovhalivka in Vinnytsia Oblast. In several cases, the female figure is inscribed on a cross.

The presumption of the Holodomor's national and Ukrainian association is conveyed, for example, by the monument to the Great Famine in Chicago. It belongs to a group of monuments that are remarkable in terms of utilized symbols. At first glance, it resembles a pieta, but on closer inspection the crying figure under the cross is not the Virgin Mary but an emaciated Ukrainian mother in folk attire mourning over her starved child. This interpretation of the monument is supported by

---

[29] Oksana Kis', *Zhinka v tradytsiinii ukraïn'skii kulturi* (Lviv, 2012), pp. 194–5.

[30] Ievhen Onats'kyi, ed., *Mala entsyklopediia Ukraïny*, vol. 7 (Buenos Aires, 1960), pp. 934–5.

[31] Larysa Skoryk, "Znaity symvol," *Obrazotvorche mystetstvo*, № 3 (1990), p. 8.

Fig. 75. The Holodomor monument in Frontivka, Vinnytsia Oblast, Ukraine

the dates on the cross and the words of the Ukrainian Autocephalous Orthodox Church metropolitan, Mstyslav: "Let us pray, brothers and sisters, for the warmth of a long-awaited sun to warm the weathered Ukrainian soil." A black marble stele inscribed with the phrase "sin of the century" completes the monument.

Consequently, besides national and religious symbols, another recurring element is that of the suffering family, especially of women and, most of all, of children. A large number of monuments depict starvation-disfigured human bodies – mostly women and children but also entire families. We see them in monuments in Los Angeles, Canberra, Cracow, and Warsaw. Figures of dead or starving children on Holodomor memorials symbolize the Great Famine's dramatic consequences for Ukraine, which have been underlined frequently in historiography. The artistic intention behind these compositions is to arouse empathy and compassion toward the defenceless, often abandoned children. The task of these monuments is to overwhelm the onlooker, who then has no need to learn more about the Holodomor or experience it independently in one's own way.

It should be noted here, however, that monuments that present images of suffering children are created by people for whom the Holodo-

Fig. 76. The Holodomor monument in Yakymivka, Vinnytsia Oblast, Ukraine

mor is part of acquired knowledge, or of post-memory, and for a similarly positioned audience. In the image of a mother (parent) bending over her deceased children, I see a symbol of hope destroyed, a lost future for millions of Ukrainians. The metaphor fulfills the function of a warning for generations who do not know the essence of Soviet totalitarianism.

In this context, the monuments in the suburbs of Kharkiv and in Winnipeg warrant special consideration, primarily because all of the figures are alive. The Winnipeg monument depicts only a mother and a child. The memorial in Cherkaska Lozova, near Kharkiv, was designed by the sculptor Oleksandr Ridnyi and portrays an entire family. Of interest here is the female figure and the children represented on the monument. Overwhelmed by the suffering of her family, the woman raises her hands in prayer, while the terrified children cling to their parents. It seems as if they are standing over a chasm rather than on the middle of a hill, and that their fate is sealed. Taken together, the work speaks to the enormity of human suffering and despair caused by the Holodomor.[32] The monument stands out from the sentimental Holodomor monuments and differs from them considerably. It echoes Soviet monumental art depicting civilian victims of the "Great Patriotic War."

Fig. 77. The Holodomor monument in Cherkaska Lozova, Kharkiv Oblast, Ukraine (2008)

All those monuments share one common feature: the depicted figures are inert, seemingly accepting their fate.

6.2.2 Hands

Hands are another symbol that can be interpreted both as religious and secular. In the case of the Holodomor monument in Cracow, the creator of which is Professor Stefan Dousa, the hands are intertwined with

[32] Tatiana Zhurzhenko, "'Capital of Despair': Holodomor Memory and Political Conflicts in Kharkiv after the Orange Revolution," *East European Politics & Societies* 25 (2011), p. 625.

faces with blurred features. In his opinion, the symbolism of hands is a significant symbol of national martyrdom both in Ukrainian and local (Polish) visual cultures:

> In the simple expression of a cry for help, the gesture shows the hopelessness of the situation. The hand gesture is legible for both secular people and Christians.[33]

However, Dousa adds that the symbolism of hands played a complementary role in his design:

> In this case, there is a church and an associated parish community. The figure of a woman emerged from conversations with Holodomor survivors. This mother is the epitome of a mother who was seen as a rock, who was to provide food and help survive, who was to provide hope for the next day.[34]

Yevhen Onatsky emphasized that hands in Ukrainian culture symbolize hard work and generosity. They may also symbolize passiveness, the failure to provide help.[35] The hand motif plays a particularly important role in the monument in Edmonton (1983) and in Cracow (2008), as well in some other projects that have yet to be finalized.

Unrealized monuments in which the hands motif was envisioned are relevant to this discussion. The design that came third in the Edmonton monument competition in 1982/83 represents a middle ground between the Temertey and Kowal respective architectonic proposals. Submitted by Bohdan Alexander Shulakewych, it depicts a pair of hands raised upwards, aligned at the wrist and with palms opening outwards. The artist, who was a student at the University of Lethbridge in Alberta at the time, explained its symbolism as follows: "The two hands extended toward Heaven has a double meaning: the request for Divine eternal help and also for the immediate assistance of nourishment for a starving nation."[36] The Holodomor is represented as an event that is still in progress, present in the past and in the future, since the plea is addressed as much to the living as it is to timeless greater forces. This entry is also worth mentioning as evidence of the Ukrainian community's engagement in symbolizing the Holodomor on the occasion of its fiftieth anniversary, which was not limited to artistic circles.

Ivan Keywan, who highly rated the design, commented in his review:

---

[33] Interview with Stefan Dousa, Cracow, April 16, 2020 (the author's private collection).

[34] Ibid.

[35] Ievhen Onats'kyi, ed., *Mala entsyklopediia Ukraïny*, vol. 13 (Buenos Aires, 1964), p. 1636–8.

[36] Bohdan Ihor Shulakewych's letter to the author, November 20, 2017.

> A figure with hands extended to God and people stretched through a heavy masif, symbolizing the brutal occupation of Ukraine by the Moscow-Bolshevik regime. Under the same massif, the Ukrainian people were crushed, but not conquered. This is a totally symbolic composition that affects its audience with strong emotional language.[37]

Igor and Liudmyla Grechanyk's unrealized monument titled "Rostochok" or "Shooting Hands," submitted for the 2009 Washington monument competition (and among the five finalists), is another interesting case. A pair of bronze hands is prominently featured in the composition. The gesturing of the hands implies asking or begging for an offering, for alms, for food. The hands are weathered; the wrists are thin with sinew and blood vessels near the surface. As Alla Rogers writes: "Throughout time hands have held a fascination for artists for their complexity, sculptural qualities and ability to convey emotion separate from the human face."[38]

Fig. 78. A model of Bohdan A. Shulakewych's monument design (1983)

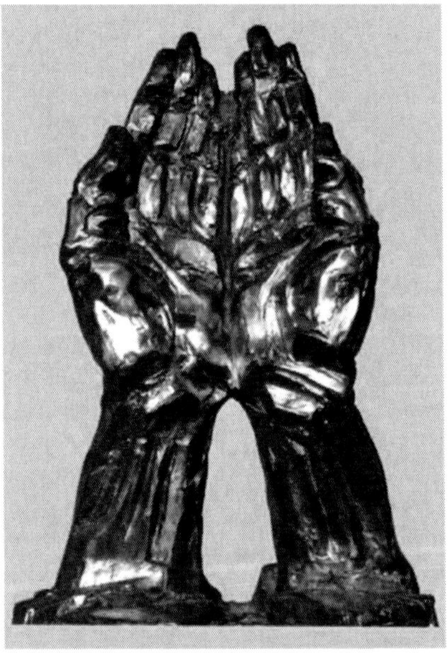

Fig. 79. A model of Igor and Liudmyla Grechanyk 's monument design (2009)

---

[37] Ivan Keywan's letter to Bohdan I. Shulakewych, June 21, 1983 (in the author's private collection).

[38] Alla Rogers, "Holodomor Memorial in Washington: A progress report," *The Ukrainian Weekly*, № 49 (December 5, 2010), pp. 14, 26.

In Ukraine, a hand-motif monument was erected in the village Berezanka, Mykolaiv Oblast.

Fig. 80. Monument in Berezanka, Mykolaiv Oblast, Ukraine (2007)

Notably, Eastern Christian symbolism dominates the monuments despite the variety of nationalities and denominations represented by Famine victims. Significantly, this applies to monuments built in Ukraine and those abroad. For example, the three monuments to the victims of the Holodomor in Poland are all found in places connected with Orthodoxy or Greek Catholicism. In Warsaw, a monument in the shape of a cross is located at an Orthodox cemetery, in Cracow it adorns the wall of a Uniate church, while in Lublin, it stands next to a local Orthodox church. An analogous state of affairs can be observed in North America. In South Bound Brook, NJ, St. Andrew Memorial Church was funded by the local Ukrainian community connected to the Ukrainian Orthodox Church.[39] In addition, the Holodomor monuments

[39] Olena Koval'chuk and Tamara Marusyk, *Holodomor 1932–1933 rr. v USRR i ukraïns'ka diaspora Pivnichnoï Ameryky* (Chernivtsi, 2010), pp. 118–9.

in the United Kingdom are mainly located on the grounds of Orthodox churches or on properties belonging to Orthodox parishes.

The location of a memorial on the territory of an Orthodox church gives society a chance to participate in honouring the victims and symbolically experience the long-deferred national mourning in the public sphere. Indeed, the monuments at such sites most commonly depict a cross. A number of similar monuments have been erected both in the United Kingdom and Australia.

6.2.3 Cross

In Ukraine, the cross is one of the most frequently employed symbols. A large number of the monuments are reminiscent of tombstones. Vitalii Ogiienko perceives them as an expression of a grassroot initiative to commemorate the Holodomor.

> Monuments in the style of tombs, crosses, the presence of memorial objects and their visual representations in the symbolic practices of the Holodomor confirm the spontaneous nature of the Holodomor practices, which are literally understood as remembering the starving. The Ukrainian embroidered cloth (*rushnyk*) also fulfills a funereal function – a very important attribute that is repeatedly used at various stages of the funeral rite, in particular, they are tied to grave crosses. This *rushnyk* hangs until it fades completely. Soviet funeral attributes such as wreaths are often used.[40]

The UCRDC website features a catalogue of Ukrainian monuments to the Holodomor that was developed by Ogiienko. In analyzing such materials, as well as the materials included in Anna Kaminsky's catalogue, I notice one fundamental pattern. Cross-shaped monuments dominate the landscape of Ukrainian villages, rather than cities.[41] They are erected in cemeteries but also in the centres of municipalities. To a large degree, I agree with Ogiienko about the somber nature of Holodomor commemoration in Ukraine. I also notice in it a continuation of the perception of the Holodomor as an element of broader Soviet repressions and terror, frequently referred to as the "Ukrainian Golgotha," as in the case of the monument in Horodske in Zhytomyr Oblast (2009). It is worth remembering that during the presidency of Leonid Kuchma monuments were often designed to commemorate the Great

[40] Vitalii Ohiienko, "Vizual'na kul'tura pam'iatnykiv zhertvam holodomoru v Ukraïni," *Hileia. Naukovyi visnyk* 65 (2012), p. 119.

[41] Cf. Ibid.; Anna Kaminsky, ed., *Erinnerungsorte an den Holodomor 1932/33 in der Ukraine*, revised by Ruth Gleinig, and Ronny Heidenreich (Berlin, 2008)

Fig. 81. The Holodomor monument in Skomoroshky, Vinnytsia Oblast, Ukraine

Terror, the famine of 1921–22, the Great Famine 1932–33, and the post-war famine in the years 1945–47.

By far the most popular iconographic motif used in monuments to the victims of the Great Famine, however, is the cross – a symbol of Christianity and, more precisely, of the Passion of Christ, redemption, and finally, Resurrection. It functions in this sense in Holodomor memorials, thus investing the tragedy with a Christian significance. The cross aligns Christian values with those suffering and thereby counters the oppression of the atheist Stalinist state.[42] In various forms, this

[42] Apostolos-Cappadona, *A Guide to Christian Art,* p. 231; Mozdyr, *Ukraïns'ka narodna memorial'na skul'ptura,* p. 11.

symbol is featured on nearly every monument, ranging in scope from a tiny cross on a map that is part of the monument in Windsor, to the entire monument taking its form. In diaspora contexts, cross-shaped monuments to the victims of the Great Famine were often constructed near Orthodox churches (for example, the monuments in London and Canberra). In Ukraine, in turn, they were erected in places where churches, chapels, or cemeteries had stood before their destruction. Many of these churches are being rebuilt, with the monuments taking on a new significance by virtue of their proximity. At St. Michael's Orthodox Cathedral in the heart of Ukraine's capital of Kyiv, Famine victims are memorialized with a monument showing a female figure on a cross with a dead child in her womb. In monumental architecture, the allegory of Ukraine depicted as a woman inscribed into a cross is encountered as often as comparisons between Christ's age at the time of his crucifixion (33) and the year of the genocide in Ukraine, which figure in poetry on the subject.

Fig. 82. The Holodomor monument in Obodivka, Vinnytsia Oblast, Ukraine

The Orthodox cross on these monuments is meant to signal the Holodomor's national, Ukrainian character. It excludes, however, from the community of victims the members of other nations and denominations who lived in 1930s Soviet Ukraine. The aim, however, is not to exclude but to contrast the inhuman (evil) face of the Holodomor's perpetrators with the victims' innocence and defencelessness through reference to Christian (Orthodox) symbolism. Minority communities may also call for the memorialization of their ancestors' deaths by starvation.

Fig. 83. The Holodomor monument in Lublin, Poland (2015)

Monuments reminiscent of tombstones have been erected in Melbourne (1983), Budapest (2006), Munich (2008), Lublin (2015), Lohvytsia in Poltava Oblast (2009), Boiarka in Kyiv Oblast (2005), Piatykhatky in Dnipropetrovsk Oblast (1999) and Mariupol in Donetsk Oblast (2004). In Alexander Etkind's opinion, tombstone monuments as a commemoration of genocide constitute a refusal to reflect upon the commemorated event. A plain stone covering a mass grave is synonymous with challenging the recipient, an expression of the powerlessness of the author or the "community of memory" in the face of the terrifying suffering of millions of innocent victims of totalitarianism.[43] Yevhen Onatsky maintains that in traditional Ukrainian culture, a stone is a symbol of a burden perceived as guilt.[44] In fact, it is much more probable that the tombstone monuments are erected for pragmatic reasons (their low cost being the most important factor). Nevertheless, not unlike the cross monuments, due to their large number, in the public space they constitute testimony to the mass nature of the Famine. They are the artistic evidence of the fact that starvation occurred in all of the locations where these symbolic signs have been erected.

6.2.4 Angel

Among religious and mourning symbols, an important role is played by the representation of an angel, which, in Ukrainian culture, is mainly present as a guardian angel.[45] The angel is another frequently occurring religious symbol found on monuments to Famine victims. Representations of angels, particularly in the aesthetics of mourning, have become the subject of numerous analyses of late. Various explanations of current interest in these celestial beings have been offered.[46] As Matilde Battistini noticed, in Byzantine art angels commonly hold a banner, golden rod and a globe, symbols of the power of God. And the votive images of guardian angels are a recurrent motif in sacred Christian art.[47]

It seems, however, that the angels on Ukrainian monuments are depicted in a manner inconsistent with Orthodox iconography connected

---

43 Alexander Etkind, *Warped Mourning: Stories of the Undead in the Land of the Unburied* (Stanford, 2013), pp. 172–96.

44 Ievhen Onats'kyi, ed., *Mala entsyklopediia Ukraïny*, vol. 5 (Buenos Aires, 1959), pp. 584–5.

45 Ievhen Onats'kyi, ed., *Mala entsyklopediia Ukraïny*, vol. 16 (Buenos Aires, 1967), p. 2125.

46 For more on the subject of the depiction of angels and their symbolic role in art see Rosa Giorgi, *Angels and Demons in Art*, ed. Stefano Zuffi, transl. Rosanna M. Giammanco Frongia (Los Angeles, 2003).

47 Matilde Battistini, *Symbols and Allegories in Art*, transl. Stephen Sartarelli (Los Angeles, 2005), p. 150.

Fig. 84. The Holodomor monument in Khmelnytskyi, Ukraine (1998)

to Ukrainian culture. These angels resemble those found in Catholic cemeteries and found even more frequently in the Protestant areas of Western Europe. Erected in urban spaces, and yet still associated with graveyard aesthetics, as in Khmelnytskyi and Zhytomyr, their impact on the emotions and imagination of the recipients is even stronger. In such places the affect has the power to create the impression of being in a cemetery rather than in a bustling city centre. Passersby encounter them suddenly, and even when in a hurry, feel compelled to reflect on them.

The angels may speak to the rebirth of religion following the collapse of communism, or else a fascination with religious matters and the spiritual world, signalling the rejection of limiting human life to its visual and material aspects. Theologically grounded, the motif takes on an additional secular expression in bypassing the existence of hell. These angels take those who died in the hellish torment experienced here on Earth straight to heaven, and, with increasing frequency, they pity and mourn the deceased as humans would. As a symbol of taller-than-human standing on the ladder of spiritual development, the angel is a divine envoy to the living.[48]

For example, the angel figures at a Holodomor memorial in Kyiv and on a monument in the centre of Zhytomyr are shown crying over those killed by the Stalinist regime, resembling tombstone monuments.

Fig. 85. The Holodomor monument in Zhytomyr, Ukraine (2006)

[48] Hall, *Illustrated Dictionary of Symbols*, pp. 113–4.

Fig. 86. Figures of angels in front of the Holodomor memorial in Kyiv, Ukraine

These monuments are meant to symbolize the public experience of national mourning as an element of *working through* the social trauma caused by the events of the Holodomor as well as the years of amnesia and inability to cultivate the memory of the victims that followed.

The angel symbolizes a state of existence higher than that of man and fulfills the role of God's messenger. He may be either a protective presence or a force of vengeance.[49]

However, among the Holodomor monuments known to me, I did not encounter the use of the image of angels of vengeance. However, if we assume that the term 'vengeance' will be understood as a reminder of the ignored genocide, then the angel depicted on the monument in Khmelnytskyi definitely can also be read in such semantic categories.

6.2.5 Bell

The symbol of the bell, widely employed by artists in designing Holodomor monuments, is an inseparable element of Christian temples.[50] On Holodomor monuments it becomes a symbol of the living historical memory of a nation that recalls its past. One example is the memorial in Lubny (Poltava Oblast), the work of architect Anatoliy Ihnashchenko, which was unveiled in September 1993. Shaped like a bell with a cross, its centre features small bells in a number corresponding to the number of Ukraine's regions. A similar mound was subsequently constructed in Mykolaiv, which differs from the Lubny memorial in its regional folk motifs.

According to Yevhen Onatsky, in traditional Ukrainian culture the bell also serves as a symbol of important news, including bad news, or as a warning.[51] In my opinion, artists interpreted it similarly in the post-communist aesthetics of martyrdom in Holodomor "places of memory."

The largest number of bell-shaped monuments or those incorporating a bell as an element of their structure, similar to the one in Kyiv, were erected during the term of President Viktor Yushchenko. These can be found in Konotop in Sumy Oblast; Valky in Kharkiv Oblast; Nizhyn in Chernihiv Oblast; Teofipol in Khmelnytskyi Oblast; Bashtanka in Mykolaiv Oblast; Malyn in Zhytomyr Oblast; Borodianka and Sokolivka in Kyiv Oblast; and Novoukrainka in Kirovohrad Oblast.

---

49 Battistini, *Symbols and Allegories in Art*, p. 150.

50 Hall, *Illustrated Dictionary of Symbols*, pp. 56–7.

51 Ievhen Onats'kyi, ed., *Mala entsyklopediia Ukraïny*, vol. 3 (Buenos Aires, 1958), pp. 337–8.

Fig. 87. The Holodomor monument in Mykolaiv, Ukraine (1993/2008)

Fig. 88. The Holodomor monument in Konotop, Sumy Oblast, Ukraine (2008)

Fig. 89. The Holodomor monument in Nizhyn, Chernihiv Oblast, Ukraine (2007)

6.2.6 Circle

The circle is an important religious and secular symbol. Like a sphere, it is a symbol of the heavens and of God himself.[52] As mentioned earlier, the first monument employing this motif was unveiled in Edmonton (1983) and designed by Ludmilla Temertey. The twisted, broken circle personifies a life fragmented by unnatural forces, while the hands emanating outward seem to be resisting, grasping at life and beseeching their inhuman tormentors. In their gesture of pleading for help, the outstretched arms are endlessly expressive. Another example of a monument that uses a circle motif is the work of Canadian artist Oleh Lesiuk, called "A Nation's Memory," located at St. Joseph's Ukrainian Catholic

[52] Onats'kyi, ed., *Mala entsyklopediia Ukraïny*, vol. 5, pp. 679–80.

Church in Oakville, ON, Canada. This monument incorporates eight key themes in Ukrainian history including the Holodomor. The circle is also sometimes present as a quern-stone, as in the monument in the village of Bilmanka in Zaporizhzhia Oblast, and in the municipalities of Andriivka and Vyshhorod in Kyiv Oblast.

Rounded breads and wheat sheaves are also motifs characteristic of Holodomor monuments. In the Christian world, they are *substances* that are transformed into the *body* of Christ, and thus constitute a symbol of man's spiritual renewal.[53] On Holodomor monuments, however, these symbols express other meanings. Their semantic load is not sacral.[54] The use of this motif is an artistic symbol of the consequences of the so-called "Law of Spikelets" that forbade the starving from taking even the stalks left behind in the field after harvest. These symbols are featured on monuments in Kharkiv and the village of Kapustyntsi (in the Yahotyn Raion of Kyiv Oblast).

It is intriguing, therefore, that the circle is present among Holodomor symbols in so many fashions – as quern-stones, prosphora, and symbolic bread, the circle of life or the circle of history. Similarly, the bell is used as a liturgic symbol or as a folk metaphor. In the same manner I perceive the mingling of the secular and the sacral in the case of the female figure.

Most certainly, in their juggling between Christian and funereal symbolism, these monuments are designed to maintain a state of national melancholy. Their fundamental purpose is to show that the Holodomor was a genocide in a metaphysical sense rather than to legally justify this claim. At stake is convincing the viewer of the scale and magnitude of the suffering and atrocities, conveying that the Holodomor was an act of annihilation aimed at the very core and future of Ukrainian culture given its agricultural character.

The iconography of the Holodomor cannot be divided simply and uniformly, e.g., into religious, national, or folk motifs. Ultimately and very conventionally, it is possible to divide iconographic motifs into the religious and secular, but my analysis of the visual culture of the Holodomor in Ukraine and in the diaspora shows the two elements as closely intertwined. In my view, the symbolism of individual monuments depends on the perception of the Holodomor among members of a given community. Of utmost importance is not the act of remembering the victims nor creating material, tangible proof of their memory, but rather underscoring Ukraine's particularly dramatic and tragic

---

[53] Hall, *Illustrated Dictionary of Symbols*, pp. 142–3.

[54] On the traditional significance see Hall, *Illustrated Dictionary of Symbols*, pp. 1–4, 89; Shapravs'kyi, "Traktuvannia osnovnykh elementiv pravoslavnykh kladovyshch," pp. 304–5.

Fig. 90. The Holodomor monument in Oakville, Ontario, Canada

fate (relative to other Soviet republics) and expressing a sense of connection to the victims and of being part of this history (which is especially significant for the Ukrainian diaspora in North America).

6.3 Holodomor monuments: From inspiration to replication

Over time, besides symbols unequivocally associated with the Holodomor, the memory canon of the Great Famine began to include well-known monumental conceptualizations of this tragedy. Currently, we may even speak about "ready to use" visual representations of the subject evidenced in the replication of certain iconographic motifs, and even fragments of certain monuments, across the whole of Ukraine and abroad.

Considering the most frequently used iconographic motifs in Holodomor representations based on the exemplified monuments, along with the evolving process of copying favoured monumental images, several aspects of Holodomor remembrance come into play here: the aesthetics of monuments, the iconographic motifs most accepted by memory communities, and the needs of said communities with respect to commemoration. The most important questions that need to be posed are: which specific motifs are being replicated? What is the aim behind replicating a monument? And finally, which needs of a memory community are satisfied as a result?

Examples of replicas abound. For instance, the monument in the Ukrainian town of Smile (Sumy Oblast) is extraordinarily similar in composition to the one in Windsor, ON, Canada. The monument in Vyshhorod is similar to the one in Edmonton, Canada.

I will turn now to a consideration of two of the most significant conceptualizations of the Holodomor, which have been replicated in many places worldwide and are often seen as emblematic of the event, namely, the monument built in 1993 beside St. Michael's Orthodox Church in Kyiv, designed by Vasyl Perevalsky, and the 2008 "Bitter Memories of Childhood" statue by Petro Drozdovsky that is an element of the Holodomor Memorial Museum in Kyiv. My observations suggest that the first of these monuments was copied particularly in places connected with the religious practices of a memory community (in front of a parish hall or a church), possibly stemming from the placement and spiritual symbolism of the original. Petro Drozdovsky's sculpture in front of the memorial museum, in turn, has been replicated chiefly in secular places (museums, near important government buildings, and occasionally in cemeteries), even though it evokes the sacred connotation to almost the same degree as Perevalsky's work.

Fig. 91. The Holodomor monument in Windsor, Ontario, Canada

Fig. 92. The Holodomor monument in Smile, Sumy Oblast, Ukraine

Fig. 93. The Holodomor monument in Vyshhorod, Kyiv Oblast, Ukraine

6.3.1 Replicas of Vasyl Perevalsky's sculpture

The sculpture designed by Perevalsky was the first monument to the Holodomor to stand in the centre of Kyiv. Copies and replicas of this monument can be found in Ukraine and many other places in the world. For instance, a remarkably similar monument was raised in the village of Litky, Kyiv Oblast, in 2008, with the only difference being that it was made out of red marble. In other instances, only the central element of the Kyiv monument is replicated, namely, the image of the mother with outstretched hands and a child at her breast. This is the case of the monument unveiled in 2008 in Munich, Germany, on the grounds of the Cathedral of the Intercession of the Mother of God and St. Andrew. The stone monument features the image of mother and child from the Kyiv monument, along with an inscription in Ukrainian that reads: "To the memory of the millions of victims of the Holodomor in Ukraine 1932/33."

Fig. 94. The Holodomor monument in Litky, Kyiv Oblast, Ukraine (2008)

A monument to the victims of the Holodomor by Alistair Pierson and unveiled in the English town of Rochdale on November 20, 2009, is also clearly influenced by the Kyiv monument. A note in the diaspora newspaper *Svoboda* reports:

> The sculptor Alistair Pierson has immortalized the most tragic event in Ukraine's history – the Holodomor of 1932–33. The one-and-a-half-metre high monument in the shape of a cross depicts a mother with outstretched hands with a child in her bosom, whose arms are also out-

Fig. 95. The Holodomor monument in Munich, Germany (2008)

Fig. 96. The Holodomor monument in Rochdale, England (2009)

> stretched. A bilingual inscription reads: "Holodomor – 1932–33: Ukrainian Famine, an Act of Genocide.[55]

Pierson gives the stele the shape of the cross and does not cut out any space from the stone. The mother and child are positioned at the finial of the cross.

An artistic take on the Kyiv monument can be found in North Battleford, Saskatchewan, Canada, where a monument to the Holodomor was funded in 2008 and installed in a permanent location in 2014.[56] The sculpture features the figures of the mother and child and does not include a cross.

The image of the Kyiv monument was also used as a motif in monuments in Clifton, US, in 2010, Toronto, Canada, in 2011, Edinburgh, Scotland in 2017, and Leicester, England, in 2018.

The commemorative plaque dedicated to the memory of Holodomor victims that was mounted on the wall of Buenos Aires Metropolitan Cathedral in 2008 (Argentina), for example, is a faithful copy of the monument in Kyiv.

These monuments reference the original to varying degrees and in some cases are true to it in all but their dimensions. Exact copies of Perevalsky's monument were unveiled in Encarnación (Paraguay) and Curitiba (Brazil). The monument in Encarnación – a slightly smaller version of the Kyiv monument – stands in the Plaza de Armas, next to a bust of Taras Shevchenko (1814–61) that was likewise funded by the local Ukrainian community. In Brazil, a similar (though once again smaller) monument was built on the initiative of Vitório Sorotiuk (who commissioned it from a local stone mason) and is on display in a Ukrainian park in Curitiba (state of Paraná).

In a private interview, Sorotiuk related that the Kyiv monument had left him so affected during one of his visits to Ukraine that he decided to have a copy made. The work was undertaken based on sketches by a local monumental stone mason in Curitiba. Sorotiuk emphasized that the Ukrainian community in Brazil needed a Holodomor monument but did not have the means to organize a competition or realize a winning design. The structure of Perevalsky's monument, meanwhile, allowed for a copy to be made at a reasonably low cost.[57]

---

[55] o. Ievhen Nebesniak, "Pam'iatnykom vshanovano v Anhliï zhertv holodomoru," *Svoboda*, № 50 (December 11, 2009), p. 9.

[56] John Cairns, "Holodomor Monument Unveiled in North Battleford," November 25, 2014, accessed July 30, 2020, https://www.newsoptimist.ca/news/local-news/holodomor-monument-unveiled-in-north-battleford-1.1656120.

[57] Interview with Vitório Sorotiuk, Toronto, November 11, 2017 (the author's private collection).

Fig. 97. The Holodomor monument in North Battleford, Saskatchewan, Canada (2008/2014)

Fig. 98. The Holodomor monument in Mala Vovcha, Kharkiv Oblast, Ukraine (2008)

Fig. 99. The Holodomor monument in Clifton, NJ, US (2010)

Fig. 100. The Holodomor monument in Edinburgh, Scotland (2017)

Fig. 101. The Holodomor monument in Leicester, England (2018)

Fig. 102. Commemorative plaque at Buenos Aires Metropolitan Cathedral, Argentina

In an interview, Perevalsky expressed his approval of the practice of copying his monument:

> I allow anyone to do it (...). I never ask for money – I have not received a penny for any of these monuments, and I would contribute myself if there were need. It's good that the memory of the tragedy is still alive. And I think it will not be possible to cover up the matter again.[58]

These statements suggest that Perevalsky sees his design as a carrier of memory that recalls the event and popularizes the subject. Nevertheless, there are two ways to interpret the act of copying. On the one hand, it is a sign of approval for a certain artistic commemorative representation of the Great Famine, a symbolic agreement of a given memory community about how to remember this important event in their history. This is particularly significant in cases where the Ukrainian monument is replicated by the diaspora, which standardizes the perception of the Holodomor's symbolic representation among Ukrainians both at home and abroad. On the other hand, a replica can signal the withdrawal of a "community of memory" from the active effort of proposing its own ideas for commemoration that could be made by a local (not necessarily Ukrainian) artist. Since the monument at its inception was not linked to the ideas of the "communities of memory" that copy it, a risk exists that its distance from said communities will only deepen with time. In other words, such a monument is fostered, rather than adopted, by a "community of memory." Indeed, a replica is always a form of imitation that encompasses the original interpretation.

Nonetheless, the practice of copying the Kyiv monument continues apace, with a recent example unveiled in Toronto in 2018. In this case, however, of note is the use of inscriptions as an interpretive element that supplements the original sculpture's symbolism.

[58] Snizhana Lysenko, "Cherkashchanyn Vasyl' Pereval's'kyi stvoryv usesvitn'ovidomyi symvol Holodomoru," November 20, 2012, accessed July 30, 2020, http://uman.info/ua/news/cherkashchanyn-vasyl-perevalskyy-stvoryv-usesvitnovidomyy-symvol-golodomoru--1540.html.

Fig. 103. The Holodomor monument in Encarnación, Paraguay, is the meeting place of the Ukrainian community on important national holidays

Fig. 104. The Holodomor monument in Curitiba, Brazil

Fig. 105. The Holodomor monument at St. Demetrius Ukrainian Catholic Church in Toronto, Canada (2011)

6.3.2 Replicas of Petro Drozdovsky's sculpture

Faithful copies of Petro Drozdovsky's sculpture "Bitter Memories of Childhood" – the figure of a little girl that stands before the Holodomor Memorial Museum in Kyiv – have also appeared in recent years. The first copy appears to have been erected in 2007 in the village of Khoruzhivka (Sumy Oblast), the family village of former President Viktor Yushchenko.

Despite fewer possibilities for modifying the design of Drozdovsky's sculpture, certain departures from the original can still be observed. First of all, a comparison of the copies with the original reveals changes in the girl's facial features. Her expressions convey shades of sorrow, grief, hopelessness and resignation, with each version a variant of the original. The position of her hands, her clothing, and her hair, however,

Fig. 106. The Holodomor monument in Khoruzhivka, Sumy Oblast, Ukraine (2007)

remain unchanged. What is always different (and important to our discussion) are the surroundings onto which the copy is "inscribed." In a museum space, the sculpture is part of an exhibit, an artefact commemorating both the event and the forms of sculptural remembrance of the Holodomor over recent decades. At the cemetery in Khoruzhivka, the figure complements the burial space and serves as a monument on a symbolic mass grave.

Notably, the sculptor himself created copies of his work for the Canadian Museum for Human Rights and the grounds of the Manitoba Legislature, both in Winnipeg, as well as for the cities of Regina and Toronto, in the latter case as an element of a Holodomor memorial parkette unveiled in 2018.

Fig. 107. The exhibit at the Canadian Museum for Human Rights in Winnipeg, Canada (2014)

Fig. 108. The Holodomor monument on the grounds of the Manitoba Legislature in Winnipeg, Canada (2014)

For the Toronto monument, Drozdovsky considered several variations of the original. Oksana Rewa, who led the call for a monument in Toronto, emphasized in an interview that the most appropriate representation for the Toronto community was that of the little girl as it is an internationally recognized image of Holodomor commemoration. In the case of this replica, therefore, priority was given to known and recognizable iconographic motifs rather than the creation of an original

Fig. 109. The Holodomor monument in Regina, Saskatchewan, Canada (2015)

Fig. 110. The Holodomor monument in Toronto, Ontario, Canada (2018)

idea of remembrance. My conversation with Oksana Rewa led to an awareness that the process of Holodomor commemoration had reached a historical juncture. Successive post-memory generations that had inherited the trauma, although still trying to keep the memory of the tragedy alive and to commemorate it in their own way, were experiencing considerable difficulty in transferring knowledge about the event to the next generation.[59]

A "community of memory" does not need new iconographic motifs but rather redefines existing ones by investing them with meaning by virtue of placement and surrounding landscape. In Winnipeg, for example, the sculpture replica stands in proximity to other Ukrainian-themed monuments (including one of Taras Shevchenko and a monument to Ukrainian WWI internees), while in Toronto its background features elements inspired by Ukrainian folk embroidery.

[59] Interview with Oksana Rewa, Toronto, November 23, 2017 (the author's private collection).

Fig. 111. Early variant of the monument in Toronto, Canada (2018)

Fig. 112. One of Petro Drozdovsky's conceptions for the Toronto monument (2018)

Replication also points to another important change in the culture of Holodomor memory in the diaspora. The focus shifts from iconography of the statue to the inscription unique to the destination. Inscription becomes the carrier of the meaning that a community gives to the Holodomor. Iconography is relegated to the background and becomes the context for the inscriptions.

Monuments remind the living of the past in ways understandable in terms of Holodomor commemoration conventions. They say more about the generation that funds them and its understanding of the Holodomor, however, than about the importance of this historical event to a sense of identity. On the basis of the monuments discussed here, we can discern the direction of a given country's historical policy and the depth of emotion experienced by the "community of memory" that feels the need to create them.

Replication, in turn, refers to the copying of selected Ukrainian monuments abroad as a form of connection with the historical homeland; it also involves the repetition of specific iconographic motifs that have come to be associated with the culture of Holodomor memory over time and that have grown to the rank of symbolic representations of this event in monumental art as well as museum spaces. The copying of a monument popularizes the original, but it also changes its reception as an expression of a unique interpretation of the Holodomor. The replicated monument becomes a symbol in itself – a symbol of the history of remembrance, however, and not of the history of the event that it commemorates.

6.4 Do Holodomor monuments have a future?

Reflection on monuments to the Great Famine of 1932–33 and particularly on the symbolism and images conveyed in them by the "community of memory" that brought them to life, inevitably leads to the problem of "irrepresentability" of experiences such as the man-made famine. This issue arises with some frequency in the poor selection of symbols on monuments, their excesses, and the simultaneous use of multiple (and at times contradictory, for instance, Christian and secular) symbols to convey the same idea. The question arises, is the viewer ready to accept the literal nature of the visual message?

Analyzing Holocaust memorials, James Young emphasized that many Holocaust survivors believe that the searing reality of their experiences demands as literal a memorial expression as possible.[60] However, it is impossible to portray loss literally through artistic means. Experiences such as the Holodomor and the Holocaust cannot be conveyed fully in the language of art. The artists with whom I spoke while writing this book frequently said that a monument cannot tell the whole story, but it can at least stimulate the viewer to reflect, to empathize, to learn.

Regardless of whether we are talking about real or symbolic burial sites that represent the Holodomor in the public domain, one can observe two processes outside of replication that are underway in the development of the culture of memory: aestheticization and acclimatization to the monument.

When talking about the aestheticization of suffering in representations of the Holodomor, I have in mind the practice of conveying human suffering, moral decline, and loss of dignity (including cases of cannibalism) presented in "places of memory" by means of aesthetically beautiful female figures or intellectually and emotionally moving artistic installations. The act of aesthetic appreciation accompanying the viewing of museum exhibitions can leave viewers agitated, unable to distinguish whether they are moved by the symbolism proposed by the artist or by the human tragedy of loss of life, which the exhibition

[60] James E. Young, *The Texture of Memory: Holocaust Memorials and Meaning* (London–New Haven, 1993), p. 9.

presents in an artistic manner. A canonical form of historiography is not as effective in manifesting the past as contact with artefacts drawn from the mists of time and now proximate enough to touch. Bonding with the past through a multi-sensory and aesthetic experience serves in place of the sacrum, joining aesthetic, metaphysical, and cognitive experiences in a single event. In the course of a sudden aesthetic experience, what is sensually absent takes on tangible form. The experiencing of the past as something that is still emotionally present can even be similar to mystical or deeply religious experiences.[61]

But what if the monument distances us even further from the event it is supposed to commemorate? To what extent are the Holodomor monuments "visible" in the urban space? I believe they owe their recognition to the explanatory inscriptions. This is especially true for monuments outside Ukraine. But monuments in Ukraine are also subject to the inevitable processes of merging with urban development.

Frank Ankersmit sees commemoration as the "ultimate attempt to master the past and to render it innocuous forever."[62] He understands commemoration to be a form of collective memory and posits that memory converts public events into idiosyncratic personal experiences.[63] Elsewhere, he writes that a monument strives to become part of the urban landscape. It ordinarily stands somewhere in the bustling centre of a city, with absolutely nothing to remind us of the historical personality or event that is being honored. This "contextlessness" may mean that the public, insofar as it is even aware of the presence of the monument, is inclined to subsume the monument in the context of daily routines with nothing in the collective memory incorporated in stone or in bronze to resist this. It is as if the monument throws off what it represents and willingly takes part in everyday, human life. For example, the flame at the Tomb of the Unknown Soldier in Paris can evoke memories both among widows and orphans of loved ones lost in war, while at the same time evoke memories for young couples of their first meeting in its proximity. The monument is a kind of protuberance of the past in the present, a place where past and present "meet" while having their backs turned to each other. In this, the monument is the helpless victim of all that we project on it with impunity.[64]

---

[61] Elżbieta Nieroba, "Rola warstwy afektywnej w doświadczeniu muzealnym, narracja o Zagładzie we współczesnym muzeum historycznym," *Zeszyty naukowe Wyższej Szkoły Oficerskiej Wojsk Lądowych im. gen. T. Kościuszki*, № 3 (2012), p. 175.

[62] Frank Ankersmit, *Historical Representations* (Stanford, 2001), p. 166.

[63] Ibid., p. 167.

[64] Frank Ankersmit, "Commemoration and National Identity," *Textos de História* 10 (1–2) (2002), p. 26.

The first Holodomor monument in Kharkiv, located in a park that serves as a leisure destination for young people, illustrates Ankersmit's thesis. The taking of tourist and wedding photographs in a monument's shadow, as happens in Ukrainian cities, also speaks to the domestication of the monument within the surrounding urban space. In addition, Holodomor monuments prompt us to project our own personal feelings and associations with them.

An analysis of the visual representations of the Holodomor reveals certain patterns and conventions. I believe that the visual culture of Holodomor memory, born from Soviet and diaspora models, currently reflects the need to understand the loss and to invest it with meaning, and to work through the trauma by means of commemoration, regardless of a monument's location. To a large degree, it is not the act of memorializing victims and creating material. It is the tangible proof of our memory that is at stake. Undoubtedly, the religious, sacral character of the Holodomor's visual culture results, on the one hand, from the need to negate Soviet visual culture, in particular in terms of commemorating suffering in monumental art, and, on the other hand, from the desire to accentuate the ruthless nature of the atheist Soviet state that perpetrated this tragedy. The suffering of millions of Ukrainians during the Great Famine becomes, in this way, a key element of Ukrainian national martyrology and a way of settling accounts with the nation's communist past.

Holodomor monuments rarely function in abstract or negative form. The few exceptions apply to the North American diaspora. Take the monuments in Edmonton, AB, and Washington, DC. At this point, there are still no "counter-monuments" to consider. Sculptures devoid of monumentalism and direct referencing of the past do not yet exist in the Holodomor context (as they do in other contexts, as exemplified by a monument in Hamburg opposing fascism, war, and violence, which disappears into the ground). This reality signals that Ukrainians are not prepared to say farewell to the memory of the Holodomor. The need to *work through* it via traditional forms of commemoration is still very much alive.

6.5 Conclusions

This chapter describes the real dialogue between the diaspora and the Ukrainian community of Holodomor memory, a dialogue between artists in Ukraine, artists of Ukrainian origin, and foreign artists grappling with the subject of the Holodomor.

Three decades of Ukrainian independence produced a series of symbols for embodying the Great Famine in social memory, a result in part of the cultural exchange between the western Ukrainian diaspora and the independent Ukrainian state. Drawing on remembrance models of a community, known for its significant output and numerous academic achievements inspired many Ukrainian artists to create artistic and literary works to save the Great Famine from oblivion and emphasize its significance for a newly independent Ukraine. Ukraine is developing its own, individual architectonic style for Holodomor monuments capable of relating this tragic event. In recent years, monuments in Ukraine have more frequently renounced the symbolism of traditional Soviet architecture, rejecting its didacticism and inauthenticity. Using legible symbols, they are creating a legacy rich in emotional charge. The difficulty lies in the choice of a composition appropriate to martyrology. In reality, however, it is not important whether it reflects religious discourse, based on Christian symbolism, as has been common to date, or something functional, in the form of parks and gardens. Commemoration will continue to reflect the post-communist need to recall the "forgotten victims" of the system.

But this, paradoxically, does not separate them from the diaspora artists, but brings them even closer. Therefore, it is possible to distinguish a common set of symbolic signs considered by the artists as appropriate, adequate to represent the loss of Ukrainians in monumental art. Whether we speak of Ukrainian monuments copied in entirety and erected outside the country or the replication of iconographic motifs now associated with Holodomor memory culture, these representations are found in both monumental art and museum spaces and constitute a form of communication with the historical homeland.

Conclusions

Over the last several decades, we have witnessed the creation of a historical event by both those who record history and the broader public domain in modern Ukraine. The Great Famine of 1932–33 has evolved from being understood mainly in the context of the agricultural transformation of the USSR (as suggested by the Soviet historiography that did not deny the Famine altogether) to a transformational event in the formation of the modern Ukrainian nation as indicated by the country's authorities. The Holodomor has become a symbol uniting millions of Ukrainians worldwide, regardless of their individual biographical experiences. Its symbolic representation, created by the Ukrainian diaspora at a time when the subject of this Stalinist genocide was one of the greatest taboos of Soviet collective memory, is now a legacy that people can build on as they search for both historical truth and an understanding of national identity. In Ukraine, the official ritual of remembrance came about gradually, as a balancing of and departure from Soviet traditions of remembrance and imitation of other models of commemoration. The renunciation of Soviet remembrance structures and models in the cultivation of memory of the Holodomor is most apparent in the example of monuments. These differ and can be examined based on transmitted content and in relation to their producers and sponsors.

In this book, I have conceptualized the monuments as forms of memory depositories for the communities that gave rise to them and ensured their presence in the public sphere. On the one hand, my interests focused on collective memory as well as on the artists and their understandings of the event as memorialized in their sculptural and architectural works. On the other, I sought to test my research premise regarding the politicized nature of Holodomor memory culture. I have analyzed from the socio-political perspective the process of assigning extraordinary political and social significance of the Great Famine to the national identity of Ukrainians the world over. Both my iconological and discourse analyses focused on the question of whether it is possible to extract the symbols that have been assigned a particular importance through actions such as repetition in other "places of memory." Does there exist a specific symbolic language used by the artists memorializing the experience of the Famine? Is it possible to establish how the symbolic image of the Great Famine has been shaped in the Ukrainian diaspora and in independent Ukraine? And, last but not least: Do the Holodomor monuments constitute their own, non-historiographic account of that event, or do they merely illustrate its existing image, commemorating the manner in which this experience is currently perceived in the social context?

Holodomor monuments have been established worldwide for many different reasons, including individual, communal, and national ones. These reasons have significantly affected the shape and meaning of the monuments, often determining their presence or marginalization in the public sphere for which they were created. Indeed, the monuments share certain standard features (similarity of symbols), and sometimes even initiators (the same people have been involved in more than one initiative of erecting a Holodomor monument). Sometimes these features seem to be similar only virtually. Essentially, the monuments remain exceptional, individual representations of the memory of the Holodomor as commemorated in a specific time and space (a historical moment and geographic location). The objective is always the same – to honour the victims and pay homage to the survivors of the Holodomor, even as we notice particular, individual features of a "place of memory" and even when we speak about a replica or copy of an existing monument. The case studies in Chapter Six highlight the basis for such conclusions, grounded in research on the "communities of memory" and the interpretations of the Holodomor as reproduced by them, both in Ukraine and abroad.

I use the notion of a "community of memory" in my deliberations to provide a theoretical framework for outlining the social groups that initiated the creation of "places of memory" of the Holodomor in Ukraine and abroad from the 1940s onward. As a matter of fact, the activities of Ukrainian diaspora organizations and of intellectual circles in Ukraine were not, and are not, limited to the exclusive cultivation of Holodomor remembrance. Nevertheless, in the West after World War II and after the collapse of communism in Ukraine, the memory of this event played a significant bonding and community role. I thus do not identify the Ukrainian diaspora as a Holodomor "community of memory." I assume, however, that among people of Ukrainian descent there exists a supra-generational group of individuals convinced that the Holodomor was a genocide and that the cultivation of its memory requires raising the awareness of contemporary society about the consequences of a socio-political situation under which citizens are completely controlled by an authoritative ruling.

As I suggested in Chapter Two, the Holodomor "community of memory" in independent Ukraine refers to the very broad part of society that feels an affinity with the Famine's victims or perceives the Ukrainian nation as a victim of genocide. It is worth noting that the present form of the Great Famine "community of memory" results not only from its formation on territories once ravaged by famine but also in emigration and in Western Ukraine, where it became a "transplanted tradition." The driving force of this community, and in effect its core, is currently constituted by representatives of the intelligentsia. In this way, the experience of genocide at the hands of the Kremlin in the East naturally separates Ukrainians from the Soviet legacy. Some of the intelligentsia in Ukraine's eastern regions, in turn, are more comfortable describing the Great Famine not as a genocide but as a tragic event, a position closer to that of their neighbour to the north.

Studies suggest that the image of the Holodomor in the public sphere has continued to evolve throughout the years, depending on either the needs of the "communities of memory" or merely the individuals involved in its development. As discussed in Chapters Two, Three, and Four, the process of Holodomor symbolization among the Ukrainian diaspora differed from that in independent Ukraine, originating from distinct cultures of memory. In Ukraine, the memory of the Holodomor, and the rituals supporting it and providing it with social meaning, were intended to indict communist ideology for a genocidal famine, while artists reached for familiar components of Soviet monumentalism – didacticism and symbols styled on those commemorating World War II. Gradually, religious and national symbols were introduced. However, in terms of giving meaning to human suffering, something called "semiotic volunteerism" in memory studies prevailed in the public sphere. It means that this kind of commemoration is a fragmented object that helps the "communities of memory" prescribe meaning to their loss in an environment devoid of the symbolic order. The tendency to perceive or even construct public space through an intense patchwork of symbolism was vividly employed in the "Candle of Memory" by designers. The lack of a civic narrative and an analytic distance was compensated for with a sentiment-provoking composition of visual and audio media. State violence was turned into a private trauma for all Ukrainians, and a museum was transformed into a site of memory for national mourning, something like a secular church (See Chapter Five).

In the Ukrainian diaspora, on the other hand, the development of a Holocaust memory culture preceded the establishment of a Holodomor memory culture. It is worth noting here that, although the Ukrainian and Irish cultures of memory developed in a similar manner in the twentieth century, their paths rarely crossed. What they have in common is the more frequent use of religious symbolism rather than secular. (Chapter Two).

Every "community of memory" creates "places of memory" to suit its needs, and thus the monuments they fund embody disparate memories. Holodomor monuments outside of Ukraine are most often intended to convey to the viewer that the Holodomor was a genocide carried out against the Ukrainian people in the 1930s. They employ official national symbolism and underscore the scale of the disaster by including the number of its victims. The symbols chosen by artists of Ukrainian descent were designed to draw the attention of passersby in the United States, Canada, Australia, and other countries to the fact that a little known event so enormous in scale had taken place in world history. Western societies that include Ukrainian minorities know about the Holocaust and the magnitude of the Jewish tragedy, but one cannot say the same of the Great Famine of 1932–33. Thus, symbols of nation, religion, and human suffering prevail, with the first exemplified by the state's coats of arms. The use of a map of Ukraine on the monument in Windsor, illustrating the scale of the tragedy, was thus motivated.

Monuments in Ukraine have a different main theme in common. The Great Famine inhabits the collective memory of Ukrainians as a genocidal instrument of Stalinist repression that took place in the whole of the Soviet Union, although with particular viciousness in the Ukrainian SSR as a result of the mass opposition of the Ukrainian peasantry to collectivization of the countryside. As a result, there is a tendency in modern Ukraine to raise monuments that memorialize both the victims of the Holodomor and Stalinist repressions generally.

Monuments in Ukraine were most often erected to fulfill the expectations of the authorities. The result of public procurement, they were built on the occasion of successive Holodomor anniversaries. They are largely devoid of remarkable characteristics, almost as if they were cast from the same mold. There is little difference among the commemorative angels, crosses, and women with children found across hundreds of villages in Ukraine, including areas that were untouched by famine in regions that were located in interwar Poland.

Places of real or symbolic burial that commemorate victims of the Great Famine are another element of independent Ukraine's historical landscape that diverges from the Soviet model of commemoration. As a top-down attempt to involve society in the building of historical consciousness, these sites facilitate the integration of individual memories of the Great Famine into the collective memory of Ukrainians.

The "communities of memory" established in post-Soviet Ukraine were linked in pursuing proof that the Holodomor actually took place (hence the search for witnesses and authentication of burial sites) after more than half a century of silence about it in the public sphere. Key, therefore, has been establishing a place to immortalize this historical fact symbolically, express it artistically, and encourage the visitor to reflect on the Holodomor with empathy. The two museum exhibitions created in Ukraine during the presidency of Viktor Yushchenko have become such a place.

Moreover, empirical study points to one crucial feature common to Holodomor memory cultures in independent Ukraine and the diaspora that I would describe as a certain "anniversary remembrance." Each anniversary, both for the Ukrainian diaspora and independent Ukraine, has constituted a milestone in the process of shaping the symbolic image of the Holodomor. For the diaspora, consecutive anniversaries have served as stimuli for addressing the issue of the Great Famine in the public sphere of countries where Ukrainian immigrants settled. The monuments erected upon the initiative of the diaspora communities were designed to tell the story of the victims, including the failure of the international community to act, and to pay tribute to the survivors. In independent Ukraine in the early 1990s, meanings were systematically introduced into public circulation, as provided by consecutive governments of independent Ukraine and reinterpreted on every anniversary. Anniversary commemorations were used as opportunities to erect more monuments with particular visions being confirmed by the selection of winning designs in consecutive contests.

Initially, the rituals of Holodomor commemoration in the diaspora were meant as a warning, a reminder of what befell Ukrainians in the Soviet Union, punished for striving for independence. The rituals aligned with this aim were mostly religious in character. Their genesis was influenced by the culture of memory of countries where Ukrainian emigrants settled with members of these communities organizing readings, demonstrations, and exhibitions on the subject. For the Ukrainian diaspora, the subject of the Holodomor remains extremely important despite the passage of years. Commemorating anniversaries, recording the oral histories of the ever fewer Holodomor survivors, and organizing events and exhibitions are important initiatives. In independent Ukraine, some social and academic projects devoted to the Holodomor are financially supported by members of the Ukrainian diaspora.

Significantly, the passing years have altered the demographics of Ukrainian organizations abroad as well as the needs of new members in these "communities of memory." The last twenty years have seen a change in media used by activists to reach successive generations, including the young citizens of various countries of permanent residence. Educational rather than social initiatives, which held sway until the end of the 1980s, are now a main focus of diasporic activities.

Today, diaspora remembrance efforts are realized in tandem with constant dialogue with Ukrainian counterparts, as evidenced by the recurring use of certain motifs, the copying of entire sculptures and references to a mutual cultural heritage (including the important role of Taras Shevchenko's writings), as discussed in Chapter Six.

The iconological interpretation of selected Holodomor monuments discussed in Chapter Five demonstrates that the answer to whether the Holodomor monuments constitute a new epistemology is negative. They fail to create an alternative to already existing accounts of the Holodomor. I would argue they include a *working through* of current interpretations of the Holodomor as a historical event. Moreover, artists use secondary sources, except in the cases of Roman Ivan Kowal, Ludmilla Temertey, Stefan Dousa and Vasyl Perevalsky, where we can speak about drawing from the biographical experiences of friends and relatives.

In analyzing the press in historical context, it is possible to perceive the development of a Holodomor culture of memory in Ukraine as being shaped by the North American Ukrainian diaspora's conceptualization, naturally influenced by a North American culture of memory and the Holocaust in particular. In post-Soviet Ukraine of the 1990s, the culture of memory served as an instrument for the creation of a Ukrainian symbolic domain that was simultaneously modelled on Soviet aesthetics of martyrdom.

Only with the fusion of these two perspectives was I able to understand that the range of symbols represented in Holodomor monuments and considered to be canonical by certain political formations were initially created by artists and creators aiming to convey completely different ideas. For example, Vasyl Perevalsky may not have considered the connotations of a Cossack icon as has been ascribed to him in literature but merely the well-known image of Our Lady reproduced from the Marian Russian school of iconography as exhibited at the Tretyakov Gallery.

By combining critical discourse analysis with iconological analysis, I was able to separate the media transfer on the subject of a monument's symbolic assumptions from the author's conception. This turned out to be particularly significant; the media message was the more persuasive one. Such was the case with the monument in Edmonton (1983), the work of Ludmilla Temertey. In a sense, the artist created a counter monument in reverence to those who survived. On the pages of the diaspora press, however, it was criticized for allegedly falling short, reflecting the short-sighted, conservative stance of the editorial board of the newspaper *Novyi shliakh* at the time.

Conversely, the Soviet satirical press employed an array of aggressive propaganda tools (caricatures, personally directed arguments, irony) in an attempt to distort the aims of the memorial complex that was being built in South Bound Brook, NJ, at the turn of the 1960s and divert the attention of Ukrainians in the USSR from the lack of memorials for Holodomor victims in places where the events had actually occurred (See Chapters Three and Four).

The analysis of media discourse is relevant for visual culture analysis. This study advocates a broader use of discourse analysis in visual studies. Hence, we must show that problems in historical studies can, in principle, be studied more completely and more adequately when the discursive dimension is recognized.

I would like to emphasize that numerous theoretical concepts (discussed at the beginning of this study) constituted the point of departure for my empirical studies of Holodomor memory culture (Chapter One). This monograph provides examples that, when introduced into academic discourse, I hope will initiate discussion on whether we can speak about a convention of presenting genocide in monumental sculptures. The conclusions will constitute a contribution to our understanding of non-historiographic forms of looking at the past, which, in academic discourses are dominated by the analysis of the Holocaust "places of memory." Therefore, I take the position that examinations of this issue in other contexts can strengthen the field of memory studies.

The analysis presented here distinguishes similarities between Holodomor memory culture and other cultures of memory related to crimes against humanity, so widespread in the twentieth century. I also draw attention to the unique aspects of the Holodomor culture of memory, pointing to traits that differentiate it from others. It is my hope that this work will prompt broader discussion of how genocide and crimes against humanity are presented in monumental sculptures.

Bibliography

Archival documents:

The Holodomor Museum in Hamilton collections:

A letter addressed to the Museum in Hamilton by Kateryna Yushchenko, November 20, 2008.

The Ukrainian Canadian Research & Documentation Centre Archive, Toronto, Canada (UCRDC):

Edmonton's Holodomor Monument (1983), Report by Bohdan I. Shulakewych (HM Project Manager), October 1, 2018, pp. 1–15.

The Ukrainian History and Education Center, Somerset, NJ, US (UHEC):

"Holodomor commemoration and blessing of graves at St. Andrew Church and Cemetery South Bound Brook, NJ. May 6, 1973." Private video from Mykola Holovs'ko, 13:08. UHEC_2012-6-20_MP01.

Edynak Family collection, g.50.

Ukraïns'ke pravoslavne slovo / Ukrainian Orthodox Word collection.

Tsentral'nyi derzhavnyi arkhiv hromads'kykh ob'iednan' Ukraïny, Kyiv, Ukraine (TsDAHOU):

f. 1 (Tsentral'nyi komitet Komunistychnoï partiï Ukraïny (TsK KPU) (1918–1991)), op. 25 (Dokumenty zahal'noho viddilu TsK KPU (sekretna chastyna) (1968–1988 rr.)), spr. 2219, 2716, 2719, 2818.

Private archives:

Bohdan Ihor Shulakewych private archive.

Larysa Kurylas private archive.

Ludmilla Temertey private archive.

Oksana Rewa private archive.

Roman and Bohdan Kowals' private archive.

Interviews and letters (in the author's private collection):

Bohdan Ihor Shulakewych's letter to the author, November 20, 2017.

Interview with Bohdan and Lydia Shulakewych. Toronto, November 19, 2017.

Interview with Halyna and Bohdan Kowal. Winnipeg, November 17, 2017.

Interview with Liudmyla Hrynevych. Toronto, November 20, 2017.

Interview with Ludmilla Temertey. Toronto, November 26, 2017.
Interview with Oksana Rewa, Toronto. November 23, 2017.
Interview with Stefan Dousa. Cracow, April 16, 2020.
Interview with Vitório Sorotiuk. Toronto, November 11, 2017.
Interview with Valentina Kuryliw. Toronto, November 20, 2017.
Ivan Keywan's letter to Bohdan Shulakewych, June 21, 1983.

Legal Acts:

Constitution of Ukraine. https://www.wipo.int/edocs/lexdocs/laws/en/ua/ua013en.pdf.

Kabinet Ministriv Ukraïny. Postanova vid 5 lypnia 2006 r. N 927, Kyïv, "Pro zatverdzhennia Polozhennia pro Ukraïns'kyi instytut natsional'noï pam'iati." https://zakon4.rada.gov.ua/laws/show/927-2006-%D0%BF.

"Postanova apeliatsiinoho sudu m. Kyieva u kryminal'nii spravi za faktom vchynennia henotsydu v Ukraïni v 1932–1933 rokakh." Kharkivs'ka pravozakhysna hrupa. February 1, 2010. http://khpg.org/index.php?id=1265039604.

"Proclamation 5273: Commemoration of the Great Famine in the Ukraine." https://www.presidency.ucsb.edu/documents/proclamation-5273-commemoration-the-great-famine-the-ukraine.

Public Law 109–340 109th Congress, October 13, 2006, An act to authorize the Government of Ukraine to establish a memorial on Federal land in the District of Columbia to honor the victims of the manmade famine that occurred in Ukraine in 1932–1933. https://www.govinfo.gov/content/pkg/PLAW-109publ340/pdf/PLAW-109publ340.pdf.

Rozporiadzhennia prezydenta Ukraïny "Pro dodatkovi zakhody u zv'iazku z 70-my rokovynamy holodomoru v Ukraïni." December 6, 2002, N 393/2002-рп. https://zakon.rada.gov.ua/rada/show/393/2002-%D1%80%D0%BF.

"S. 2456 – 98th Congress: Commission on the Ukraine Famine Act." https://www.govtrack.us/congress/bills/98/s2456.

Ukaz prezydenta Ukraïny № 250/2007 "Pro zakhody u zv'iazku z 75-my rokovynamy Holodomoru 1932–1933 rokiv v Ukraïni." March 28, 2007. https://www.president.gov.ua/documents/2502007-5688.

Ukaz prezydenta Ukraïny "pro vstanovlennia Dnia pam'iati zhertv holodomoriv." November 26, 1998. N 1310/98. https://zakon.rada.gov.ua/laws/show/1310/98#Text.

Zakon Ukraïny "Pro Holodomor 1932–1933 rokiv v Ukraïni." (*Vidomosti Verkhovnoï Rady Ukraïny (VVR)*, 2006, № 50, st. 504). https://zakon.rada.gov.ua/laws/show/376-V.#Text.

Primary sources:

"Dity tykh, khto perezhyv Holodomor: Interv'iu z Liudmyloiu Temertei." *New Pathway Ukrainian News*. September 15, 2015. Accessed July 30, 2020.

https://www.newpathway.ca/діти-тих-хто-пережив-голодомор-інтерв/

"Speech by Archbishop Mstyslav at the dedication of St. Andrew Memorial Church (Ukrainian)." October 10, 1965. Audio, 14:41. UHEC. Accessed February 1, 2021. https://www.ukrhec.org/collections/archives/recorded-sound/speech-archbishop-mstyslav-dedication-st-andrew-memorial-church.

Stenohrama rankovoho zasidannia VRU 28 lystopada 2006 roku. http://static.rada.gov.ua/zakon/skl5/2session/STENOGR/28110602_36.htm.

"The Project of the Second Part of the National Museum 'Holodomor Victims Memorial' Was Presented to President of Ukraine Petro Poroshenko." Holodomor Museum. November 23, 2018. https://holodomormuseum.org.ua/en/news/the-project-of-the-second-part-of-the-national-museum-quot-holodomor-victims-memorial-quot-was-presented-to-president-of-ukraine-petro-poroshenko/.

Ukrainian Famine of 1932 and 1933: Hearing before the Committee on Foreign Relations United States Senate, Ninety-eighth Congress, Second Session on S. 2456. A Bill to Establish a Commission to Study the 1932–33 Famine Caused by the Soviet Government in Ukraine, August 1, 1984. Washington, 1984.

"Zvernennia Prezydenta Ukraïny do ukrains'koho narodu u zv'iazku z Dnem pam'iati zhertv Holodomoru ta politychnykh represii." *Nad Buhom*. Accessed April 2, 2019. http://nadbuhom.pl/art_0850.html.

Source editions:

Herasymenko, M., ed., *Holodomor 1932–1933 rokiv v Ukraïni. Materialy kryminal'noï spravy No 475*. Kyiv, 2014.

Koval', V., ed. *Stalins'ko-khrushchovs'ke okhvistia*, New York–Chicago, 1964.

Propam'iatna knyha: U pam'iat' ponad 7,000,000 ukraïntsiv holodom zamuchenykh Moskvoiu / Commemorative Book: In Memory of Over 7,000,000 Ukrainians Starved to Death by Moscow. Vinnipeh, s.d.

The Black Deeds of the Kremlin: A White Book. Vol. 1: *Book of Testimonies*, ed. Semen O. Pidhainy, transl. Alexander Oreletsky and Olga Prychodko, introd. George W. Simpson. Toronto, 1953; Vol. 2: *The Great Famine in Ukraine in 1932–1933*, eds. Semen O. Pidhainy, Petro P. Pavlovych, and Vasyl I. Hryshko, transl. M. Coach, J. Hladun, and Olga Prychodko, introd. Charles J. Kersten. Toronto, 1955.

Tron'ko, Petro [et al.], ed. *Na skryzhaliakh istoriï. Z istoriï vzaiemozv'iazkiv uriadovykh struktur i hromads'kykh kil Ukraïny z ukraïns'ko-kanads'koiu hromadoiu v druhii polovyni 1940–1980-ti roky*. Kyiv, 2003.

Memories and eyewitness testimonies:

Mace, James, and Leonid Heretz, eds. *Oral History Project of the Commission on the Ukraine Famine*. 3 vols. Washington, 1990.

Maistrenko, Ivan. *Istoriia moho pokolinnia. Spohady uchasnyka revoliutsiinykh podii v Ukraïni*. Edmonton, 1985.

Maniak Collection. HREC. Accessed February 1, 2021. https://holodomor.ca/resource/maniak-collection/.

Maniak, Volodymyr, and Lidiia Kovalenko-Maniak. *1933-ii: Holod. Narodna knyha-memorial*. Kyiv, 1991.

Mykhailivs'ka-Tsymbal, Tetiana. *Spohady (Moie zhyttia na emihratsiï)*. Ed. Julian Serediak. Buenos Aires, 1984.

Savaryn, Petro. *Z soboiu vzialy Ukraïnu: Vid Ternopillia do Al'berty*. Kyiv, 2007.

Ses'-Marchenko, Nina. "V'iazanka spomyniv…" In *Regensburg. Statti, spohady, dokumenty*, ed. Omelian Kushnir, 612–6. New York–Paris–Sydney–Toronto, 1985.

Velykyi holod v Ukraïni 1932–1933 rokiv. Svidchennia ochevydtsiv dlia Komisiï Konhresu SShA. 4 vols., compilation Dzheims Meis. Kyiv, 2008.

Literature and poetry:

Alighieri, Dante. *The Divine Comedy: Hell, Canto XXXIII*. https://ebooks.adelaide.edu.au/d/dante/d19he/canto33.html.

Bahrianyi, Ivan. *Chomu ia ne khochu vertatys' do SSSR?* Winnipeg, 1946.

Shevchenko, Taras. *Selected Works: Poetry and Prose*. Moscow, 1979.

Shevchenko, Taras. *"Song out of Darkness": Selected Poems*. Transl. Vera Rich. London, 1961.

Shevchenko, Taras. *Zibrannia tvoriv: u 6 t*. Vol. 1, *Poeziia 1837–1847*. Kyiv, 2003.

Press and journals:

Alberta Report (Edmonton) 1983.

American Spectator (Arlington, Vir.) 1983.

Avangard (Munich) 1948.

Congressional Record (Washington, DC) 1984.

Dnipro (Chicago, IL; Philadelphia, PA; Trenton, NJ) 1933.

Dzerkalo tyzhnia (Kyiv) 2004.

Hamilton Spectator (Hamilton) 2008.

Holos Okhtyrshchyny (Okhtyrka) 1943.

Holos Poltavshchyny (Poltava) 1943.

Holos Ukraïny (Kyiv) 2003.

Homin Ukraïny (Toronto) 1973, 1983, 2013, 2016.

Izvestiia TsK KPSS (Moscow) 1990.

Kanadiis'kyi farmer (Winnipeg) 1963.

Kommunist (Moscow) 1990.

Literaturna Ukraïna (Kyiv) 1987, 1990, 1993.

Myrhorods'ki visti (Myrhorod) 1943.

Na storozhi (Winnipeg) 1948.

Nashe zhyttia / Our Life (New York) 1953, 1973, 1993, 2003, 2013.
Novyi shliakh (Winnipeg–Toronto) 1983–84, 1989, 2006, 2011, 2015.
Novi dni (Toronto) 1983.
Oko (Montreal) 1983.
Perets' (Kyiv) 1960–61.
Pravda Ukrainy (Kyiv) 1988–90.
Promin / Promin' (Toronto) 1983.
Radians'ka Ukraïna (Kyiv) 1990.
Samostiina Ukraïna (Kyiv–New York–Chicago) 1964.
Shliakh peremohy (Munchen–Lviv) 1983.
Sil's'ki visti (Kyiv) 1988–89.
Spectator (London) 1983.
Sums'kyi visnyk (Sumy) 1943.
Svoboda (Jersey City, NJ) 1935, 1948, 1953, 1956, 1958, 1961–63, 1973, 1978, 1981, 1983–86, 1991, 1993, 1997, 2004, 2009–10, 2013.
Tarashchans'ki visti (Tarashcha) 1943.
Ukrainian Voice (Winnipeg) 2009.
The Ukrainian Weekly (Jersey City, NJ) 1933, 1956, 1982–84, 1991, 2000–4, 2006, 2008, 2010.
Ukraïna moloda (Kyiv) 2005, 2017, 2020.
Ukraïns'ke pravoslavne slovo / Ukrainian Orthodox Word (South Bound Brook, NJ) 1953, 1955, 1960–61, 1963–65, 1984.
Ukraïns'ki visti (Neu-Ulm, Detroit) 1948, 1983, 1993.
Ukraïns'kyi holos (Winnipeg) 1983, 1992.
Uriadovi dunaievets'ki visti (Dunaivtsi) 1943.
Uriadovyi kur'ier (Kyiv) 1998, 2004, 2006.
Vidomosti ieparkhiial'noho upravlinnia UAPTs u Velykii Brytanii (London) 1993.
Vidomosti Verkhovnoï Rady Ukraïny (VVR) (Kyiv) 2002.
Vil'na dumka (Sydney) 1973, 1983–84, 1997.
Vpered (Munchen) 1958.
Vyzvol'nyi shliakh (London) 1948, 1957, 1983.
Wall Street Journal (Chicago) 1983.

Catalogues and maps of Holodomor monuments, memorials and burial places:

"Holodomor monuments in Ukraine." The Ukrainian Canadian Research & Documentation Centre. Accessed February 25, 2020. http://www.holodomor-monuments.org/.
Kaminsky, Anna, ed. *Erinnerungsorte an den Holodomor 1932/33 in der Ukraine,* revised by Ruth Gleinig, and Ronny Heidenreich. Berlin, 2008.
Kushch, Anatoliy. Holodomor. Accessed February 25, 2021. http://sculptor.kiev.ua/gallery3.html.

"Mistsia masovoho pokhovannia zhertv Holodomoru-henotsydu." Holodomor Museum. Accessed February 25, 2020. https://map.memorial holodomor.org.ua/.

"Pam'iatnyky zhertvam Holodomoru, vstanovleni v Kanadi." Accessed March 23, 2019. http://canada.mfa.gov.ua/ua/ukraine-ca/holodomor-remembrance/holodomor-remembrance-canada/holodomor-remem brance-canada-monuments.

Secondary literature:

Anderson, Benedict. *Imagined Communities: Reflections onthe Origin and Spread of Nationalism*. New York, 2016.

Ankersmit, Frank. "Commemoration and National Identity." *Textos de História* 10 (1–2) (2002): 15–39.

Ankersmit, Frank. *Historical Representations*. Stanford, 2001.

Antokhii, Myroslav, Daria Darewych, Marko Robert Stech, and Danylo Husar Struk. "Shevchenko, Taras." *Internet Encyclopedia of Ukraine*. Updated 2004. http://www.encyclopediaofukraine.com/display.asp?linkp ath=pages%5CS%5CH%5CShevchenkoTaras.htm.

Apostolos-Cappadona, Diane. *A Guide to Christian Art*. Foreword Gabriele Finaldi. London, 2020.

Ariès, Philippe. *The Hour of Our Death: The Classic History of Western Attitudes Toward Death Over the Last One Thousand Years*. Transl. Helen Weaver. New York, 2008.

Assmann, Aleida. "Das Gedächtnis der Orte – Authentizität und Gedenken." In *Firma Topf & Söhne – Hersteller der Öfen für Auschwitz: Ein Fabrikgelände als Erinnerungsort?*, eds. Aleida Assmann, Frank Hiddemann and Eckhard Schwarzenberger, 197–212. Frankfurt–New York, 2002.

Assmann, Aleida. *Między historią a pamięcią. Antologia*. Ed. and postscript Magdalena Saryusz-Wolska. Warsaw, 2016.

Assmann, Jan. *Cultural Memory and Early Civilization: Writing, Remembrance, and Political Imagination*. Cambridge, 2011. https://doi.org/10.1017/ CBO9780511996306.

Assmann, Jan. *Das kulturelle Gedächtnis. Schrift, Erinnerung und Politische Identität in frühen Hochkulturen*. München, 1992.

Assmann, Jan. "Die Entdeckung der Vergangenheit. Innovation und Restauration in der ägyptischen Literaturgeschichte." In Jan Assmann, *Stein und Zeit, Mensch und Gesellschaft im Alten Ägypten*, 303–13. München, 1991.

Assmann, Jan, and Tonio Hölscher, eds. *Kultur und Gedächtnis*. Frankfurt a. M., 1988.

Augé, Marc. *Non-Places: An Introduction to Anthropology of Supermodernity*. Transl. John Howe, London–New York, 1992.

Bandera, Stepan. "Istorychna amneziia." *Polityka i kultura* 127, № 44 (2001): 41.

Battistini, Matilde. *Symbols and Allegories in Art.* Transl. Stephen Sartarelli. Los Angeles, 2005.

Bazhan, Oleh. "Initsiatyvy ukraïns'koï diaspory, pov'iazani z vshanuvanniam zhertv holodu 1932–1933 rr. u 80-ti roky." In *Holod – henotsyd 1933 roku v Ukraïni. Istoryko-politolohichnyi analiz sotsial'no-demohrafichnykh ta moral'no-psykholohichnykh naslidkiv. Materialy Mizhnarodnoï naukovo--teoretychnoï konferentsiï na vidznachennia 65-richchia trahediï ukraïns'koho narodu, Kyïv, 28 lystopada 1998 r.*, eds. Stanislav Kul'chyts'kyi [et al.], 48–52. Kyiv–New York, 2000.

Bellah, Robert N. [et al.]. *Habits of the Heart: Individualism and Commitment in American Life*. New York, 1985.

Bellezza, Simone A. "Building Memory: National Identities and Monuments in Post–Soviet Ukraine." In *Ukraine Twenty Years After Independence: Assessments, Perspectives, Challenges*, eds. Giovanna Brogi, Marta Dyczok, Oxana Pachlovska, and Giovanna Siedina, 241–64. Rome, 2015.

Bilenko, Tetiana. "Funktsional'nist' khrystyians'koï symvoliky u tvorakh ukraïns'koï diaspory XX viku." In *Literatura emigracyjna Rosjan, Ukraińców i Białorusinów*, eds. Anna Woźniak and Lubomir Puszak, 143–54. Lublin, 2001.

Bilovus, Lesia. "Tematyka Holodomoru v ukraïnomovnii periodytsi diaspory SShA iak chynnyk zberezhennia natsional'noï identychnosti," *Eminak: naukovyi shchokvartal'nyk*, № 1 (21) (2018), vol. 2: 135–40.

Blumer, Nadine. "Expanding Museum Spaces: Networks of Difficult Knowledge at and Beyond the Canadian Museum for Human Rights," *Review of Education, Pedagogy, and Cultural Studies* 37, № 2–3 (2015): 125–46. https://doi.org/10.1080/10714413.2015.1028831.

Bodnar, John. *Remaking America: Public Memory, Commemoration, and Patriotism in the Twentieth Century*. Princeton–New York, 1992.

"Borys Oliinyk pomer na 82 rotsi zhyttia," *Ukraïna Moloda*, April 30, 2017, http://www.umoloda.Kyiv.ua/number/0/2006/111161/.

Borysenko, Valentyna. *A Candle in Remembrance: An Oral History of the Ukrainian Genocide of 1932–1933*. New York, 2010.

Boym, Svetlana. *The Future of Nostalgia*. New York, 2002.

"Brazil and Paraguay Join International Action to Commemorate Holodomor Victims." *Ukrinform*, October 1, 2018. https://www.ukrinform.net/rubric-society/2549357-brazil-and-paraguay-join-international-action-to-commemorate-holodomor-victims.html.

Burke, Peter. *Eyewitnessing: The Uses of Images as Historical Evidence*. London, 2001.

Cairns, John. "Holodomor Monument Unveiled in North Battleford." November 25, 2014. Accessed July 30, 2020. https://www.newsoptimist.ca/news/local-news/holodomor-monument-unveiled-in-north-battleford-1.1656120.

Canadian Museum for Human Rights. Galleries. Accessed February 1, 2021. https://humanrights.ca/exhibition/galleries.

Charmaz, Kathy. *Constructing Grounded Theory: A Practical Guide through Qualitative Analyses*. London–Thousand Oaks–New Dehli, 2006.

Choma. Ambrosio. "História de Praça Ucrânia Curitiba." *Portal Ukrainiano*, September 21, 1999. https://www.ucraniano.com.br/pracaucrania.html.

"CMHR Deals with Holodomor Group." *Winnipeg Sun*, July 5, 2012. http://www.winnipegsun.com/2012/07/05/cmhr-deals-with-holodomor-group.

Confino, Alon. "Collective Memory and Cultural History: Problems of Method." *The American Historical Review* 102, № 5 (1997): 1386–403. https://doi.org/10.2307/2171069.

Conquest, Robert. *The Great Terror: Stalin's Purge of the Thirties*. London, 1968.

Conquest, Robert. *The Harvest of Sorrow: Soviet Collectivization and the Terror-Famine*. London, 1986.

Darevych, Dariia. "Holodomor iz perspektyvy mystetstva." *Krytyka*, № 7–8 (2008): 31–3.

Denysenko, Nicholas. *The Orthodox Church in Ukraine: A Century of Separation*. DeKalb, IL, 2018.

Derev'iankin, T. "Kolektyvizatsiia." *Pid praporom leninizmu*, № 13 (1989): 50–5.

Diachenko, Oleksandr. "Ukraïns'kyi pam'iatnyk dlia Vashynhtona." *Ukraïna. Nauka i kul'tura* 35 (2009): 73–5.

Dietsch [Öhman], Johan. "From Famine to Forgotten Holocaust: The 1932–1933 Famine in Ukrainian Historical Cultures." In *Echoes of Holocaust: Historical Cultures in Contemporary Europe*, eds. Klas-Göran Karlsson and Ulf Zander, 223–54. Lund, 2003.

Dietsch [Öhman], Johan. *Making Sense of Suffering: Holocaust and Holodomor in Ukrainian Historical Culture*. Lund, 2006.

Djebabla, Mourad. "Pamięć zaklęta w kamieniu. Czytanie pomników ofiar Wielkiej Wojny w Québecu (1919–1939) jako miejsc pamięci," transl. Kamilla Kuźmicka. In *Inscenizacje pamięci*, eds. Izabela Skórzyńska, Christine Lavrence, and Carl Pépin, 259–67. Poznań, 2007.

Domańska, Ewa. "Jakiej metodologii potrzebuje współczesna humanistyka," *Teksty Drugie*, № 1–2 (2010): 45–55.

"Dynamika stavlennia do Holodomoru, lystopad 2013." Sotsiolohichna hrupa "Reitynh." April 2, 2019. Accessed February 1, 2021. http://ratinggroup.ua/files/ratinggroup/reg_files/rg_holodomor_ua_112013.pdf.

Edensor, Tim. *National Identity, Popular Culture and Everyday Life*. Oxford, 2002.

Esbenshade, Richard S. "Remembering to Forget: Memory, History, National Identity in Postwar East-Central Europe." *Representations* 49 (1995): 72–96.

Etkind, Alexander. *Warped Mourning: Stories of the Undead in the Land of the Unburied.* Stanford, 2013.

Fairclough, Norman. *Analysing Discourse, Textual Analysis for Social Research.* London, 2003.

Fairclough, Norman, and Anna Duszak. "Wstęp. Krytyczna analiza dyskursu – nowy obszar badawczy." In *Krytyczna analiza dyskursu. Interdyscyplinarne podejście do komunikacji społecznej,* eds. Anna Duszak and Norman Fairclough, 7–32. Cracow, 2008.

Fedorak, V. "Iak vchyty istoriï v suchasnii shkoli." *Istoriia v shkolakh Ukraïny,* № 6 (2003).

Ferro, Marc. *The Use and Abuse of History: Or How the Past is Taught.* London, 1984.

"Filiia ukraïns'koho natsional'noho ob'iednannia – Toronto-Zakhid." In *Narys istoriï konhresu ukraïntsiv Kanady v Toronti,* 536–47. Toronto, 1991.

Forster, Kurt. "Monument: Memory and the Mortality of Architecture." *Oppositions,* № 25 (1982): 2–19.

Gębczyńska-Janowicz, Agnieszka. *Polskie założenia pomnikowe. Rola architektury w tworzeniu miejsc pamięci od połowy XX w.* Warsaw, 2010.

Giedion, Sigfried, Jose Luis Sert, and Fernand Lager. "Nine Points on Monumentality." In *Architecture Culture 1943–1968: A Documentary Anthology,* eds. Joan Eigen and Edward Ockman, 29–30. New York, 1993.

Gillis, John R., ed. *Commemorations: The Politics of National Identity.* Princeton, 1994.

Giorgi, Rosa. *Angels and Demons in Art.* Ed. Stefano Zuffi, transl. Rosanna M. Giammanco Frongia, Los Angeles, 2005.

Grabowicz, George G. "Consideration of the Deep Structures in Shevchenko's Works." In *Shevchenko and the Critics,* ed. George S. N. Luckyj, 481–96. London, 1980.

Grant, Susan-Mary. "Raising the Dead: War, Memory and American National Identity." *Nations and Nationalism* 4, № 11 (2005): 509–29. https://doi.org/10.1111/j.1469-8129.2005.00217.x.

Gratsiozi, Andrea. "Usvidomliuvannia Holodomoru." *Krytyka* 7, № 12 (2003): 18–20.

Grinevich, Vladislav. "Raskolotaia pamiat'. Vtoraia mirovaia voina v istoricheskom soznanii ukrainskogo obshchestva." *Neprikosnovennyi zapas* 40–41, № 2–3 (2005). Accessed July 30, 2020. http://magazines.russ.ru/nz/2005/2/gri24.html.

Grynevych, Liudmyla. "The Present State of Ukrainian Historiography on the Holodomor and Prospects for Its Development." *The Harriman Review* 16, № 2 (November, 2008): 10–20.

Halbwachs, Maurice. *Das Gedächtnis und seine sozialen Bedingungen.* Frankfurt a. M., 1985.

Halbwachs, Maurice. *Das kollektive Gedächtnis.* Frankfurt a. M., 1991.

Halbwachs, Maurice. *On collective memory*. Ed., transl., introd. Lewis A. Coser. Chicago–London, 1992.

Hall, James. *Dictionary of Subjects and Symbols in Art*. Introd. Kenneth Clark. New York–London, 2018.

Hall, James. *Illustrated Dictionary of Symbols in Eastern and Western Art*. New York, 1994.

Hall, Stuart. *Encoding and Decoding in the Television Discourse*. Birmingham, 1973.

Himka, John Paul. "War Criminality: A Blank Spot in the Collective Memory of the Ukrainian Diaspora." *Space of Identity* 5, № 1 (2005): 9–24. https://doi.org/10.25071/1496-6778.7999.

"Hirki farby Holodomoru: U Kyievi rozpovidaiut' pro khudozhnyka-emihranta Viktora Tsymbala." *Ukraïna moloda* № 076 (August 18, 2020). https://umoloda.kyiv.ua/number/3626/164/149136/.

"Histoire ukrainienne, entre génocide, makhnovtchina et pyramides." *Paper Blog*, March 22, 2014. https://www.paperblog.fr/7060673/histoire-ukrainienne-entre-genocide-makhnovtchina-et-pyramides/.

Hnatiuk, Ola. *Pożegnanie z imperium. Ukraińskie dyskusje o tożsamości*. Lublin, 2003.

Ho Tai, Hue-Tam. "Remembered Realms: Pierre Nora and French National Memory." *The American Historical Review* 106, № 3 (2001): 906–22. https://doi.org/10.2307/2692331.

"Holod 1932–1933 rokiv na Ukraïni. Svidchat' arkh. dok.," introd. Ruslan Pyrih. *Pid praporom leninizmu*, № 8 (1990): 64–86.

"Holodomor (Ukrainian Famine of 1933 Memorial) by Ludmilla Temertey." City of Edmonton Public Art Collection. Accessed February 1, 2021. http://edmontonpublicart.ca/#!/details/82.

Holodomor 1932–1933 rokiv iak velychezna trahediia ukraïns'koho narodu. Materialy Vseukraïns'koï naukovoï konferentsiï, Kyïv, 15 lystopada 2002 r. Kyiv, 2003.

Honcharenko, Anastasiia. "Komunikatyvna funktsiia 'istorychnoï pam'iati' v ukraïns'kii monumental'nii skul'pturi 1990-kh–2000-kh rr." *Visnyk Kharkivs'koï derzhavnoï akademiï dyzainu i mystetstv. Mystetstvoznavstvo, architektura*, № 8 (2014): 57–60.

Hordyns'kyi, Sviatoslav. *Kruk, Pavlos', Mukhin. Try ukraïns'ki riz'biari*. Munich, 1947.

Hordyns'kyi, Sviatoslav, ed. *Viktor Tsymbal: maliar i hrafik*. New York, 1972.

Hrabovych, Hryhorii. "Ukraïna. Pidsumky stolittia." *Krytyka*, № 11 (1999): 7.

Hrachova, Sofiia. "Pam'iat', kontrpam'iat' i polityka." *Krytyka*, № 11 (2006). https://krytyka.com/ua/articles/pamyat-kontrpamyat-i-polityka.

Hrynevych, Liudmyla. "Vid zaperechuvannia do vymushenoho vyznannia: pro mekhanizm vkhodzhennia temy holodu 1932–1933 rr. v ofitsiinyi publichnyi prostir u SRSR ta URSR naprykintsi 1980-kh rr.," *Problemy istorii Ukraïny: fakty, sudzhennia, poshuky*, 18 (2008): 232–44.

Hryshko, Vasyl'. *Ukraïns'kyi "holokost", 1933*. New York–Toronto, 1978.

Hryshko, Wasyl. *The Ukrainian Holocaust of 1933*. Toronto, 1983.

Hrytsak, Iaroslav. "Holokost i Holodomor. Vyklyky kolektyvnii pam'iati." *Krytyka*, № 1–2 (2011): 159–60.

Hrytsenko, Oleksandr. *Prezydenty i pam'iat'. Polityka pam'iati prezydentiv Ukraïny*. Kyiv, 2012.

"Hunger for Truth: Illuminating the Hidden History of the Holodomor: Symposium Commemorating the Ukrainian Genocide of 1932–1933: California State University, Fresno, Henry Madden Library," Fresno State, October 5–6, 2017, 9. Accessed February 1, 2021. http://www.fresnostate.edu/socialsciences/historydept/documents/Holodomor-Symposium-web.pdf.

Hutsaliuk, Liuboslav. "Roman-Ivan Koval'." *Obrazotvorche mystetstvo*, № 1 (2004): 45.

Ianko, Dmytro. "Memorial narodnoï skorboty i pam'iati." *Dnipro*, № 3–4 (2004): 88–99.

Ieremieieva, Kateryna. *Byty satyroiu. Zhurnal "Perets'" v sotsiokul'turnomu seredovyshchi Radians'koï Ukraïny*. Kharkiv, 2018.

Ievtukh, Volodymyr B., and Olena O. Koval'chuk, "Etnokul'turna diial'nist' ukraïns'kykh kanadtsiv. Zdobutky i problemy," *Ukraïns'kyi istorychnyi zhurnal*, № 9 (1991): 42–50.

Igliński, Grzegorz. "Romantyczne posłannictwo Słowa. 'Ni Archimedes, ni Galileusz...' Tarasa Szewczenki jako przykład liryki profetycznej." In *W kręgu kultury ukraińskiej*, ed. Walenty Piłat, 31–44. Olsztyn, 1995.

Il'he, Vil'frid. "Zmahannia zhertv." *Krytyka*, № 5 (2006): 14–7.

"In Memory of Helen Dobusz 1928–2017," Hagan-Chamberlain Funeral Home, March 23, 2019. Accessed February 1, 2021. https://hagan-chamberlain.com/tribute/details/477/Helen Dobusz/obituary.html#content-start.

"Inauguration of the Monument to Victims of the Holodomor." Consulate of Ukraine in Edinburgh, 28 November 2017. http://edinburgh.old.mfa.gov.ua/en/news/photos/2238-vidkrittya-ta-osvyachennya-pershogo-v-shotlandiji-pamjatnogo-znaku-zhertvam-golodomoru-19321933-rokiv-v-ukrajini.

Irwin-Zarecka, Iwona. *Frames of Remembrance: The Dynamics of Collective Memory*. New Brunswick–New Jersey, 2009.

Isaievych, Iaroslav. "Problema pokhodzhennia ukraïns'koho narodu. Istoriohrafichnyi i politychnyi aspekt." *Ukraïna. Kul'turna spadshchyna, natsional'na svidomist', derzhavnist'*, № 2 (1995): 3–17.

"Istoriia stvorennia pam'iatnyka Holodomoru u Vinnipezi." *Ukrainian Winnipeh*. May 1, 2017. Accessed July 30, 2019. http://www.ukrainian-winnipeg.ca/kowal.

Ivashchuk, Mariia. "Proekt muzeiu Holodomoru," *The Village*. August 1, 2017. Accessed July 30, 2020. http://www.the-village.com.ua/village/city/city-news/260765-proekt-muzeyu-golodomoru.

Iwan, Norbert K. "Kanads'kyi Muzei Prav Liudyny." *Ukrainian People*, February 11, 2017. http://ukrainianpeople.us/канадський-музей-прав-людини/.

Jeffers, Carol S. "Museum as a Process." *The Journal of Aesthetic Education* 37, № 1 (2003): 107–19.

Jilge, Wilfried. "Holodomor und Nation. Der Hunger im ukrainischen Geschichtsbild." *Osteuropa* 54, № 12, *Vernichtung durch Hunger. Der Holodomor in der Ukraine und der UdSSR*, eds. Rudolf A. Mark and Gerhard Simon (2004): 147–63.

Kalinichenko, Volodymyr, and Ielyzaveta Iatsenko. "Istoriohrafiia holodomoru 1932–1933 rokiv v Ukraïni." In *Holod – henotsyd 1933 roku v Ukraïni. Istoryko-politolohichnyi analiz sotsial'no-demohrafichnykh ta moral'no-psykholohichnykh naslidkiv. Materialy Mizhnarodnoï naukovo-teoretychnoï konferentsiï na vidznachennia 65-richchia trahediï ukraïns'koho narodu, Kyïv, 28 lystopada 1998 r.*, eds. Stanislav Kul'chyts'kyi [et al.], 15–25. Kyiv–New York, 2000.

Kasianov, Georgiy. "The Open Grave: The 1932–1933 Famine in Ukrainian Historiography, Politics, and Mass Consciousness." *Ab Imperio*, № 3 (2004): 1–37.

Kasi'anov, Heorhii. *Danse macabre. Holod 1932–1933 rokiv u politytsi, masovii svidomosti ta istoriohrafiï (1980-ti – pochatok 2000-kh)*. Kyiv, 2010.

Kasi'anov, Heorhii. *Rozryta mohyla: Holod 1932–1933 rokiv u politytsi, pam'iati ta istoriï (1980-ti – 2000-ni)*. Kharkiv, 2019.

Kasi'anov, Heorhii. "Ukraïna, 1933-ii." *Pid praporom leninizmu*, № 5 (1990): 65–70.

Katarhina, Tetiana. "Skryzhali skorboty. Zarubizhni pam'iatky Holodomoru-henotsydu 1932–1933 rr. v Ukraïni." *Kraieznavstvo*, № 4 (2013): 65–80.

Kaźmierska, Kaja. *Biography and Memory: The Generational Experience of the Shoah Survivors*. Transl. Katarzyna Maciejczyk. Boston, 2012. https://doi.org/10.1515/9781618111180.

Kis', Oksana. *Zhinka v tradytsiinii ukraïns'kii kulturi*. Lviv, 2012.

Klid, Bohdan. "The Black Deeds of the Kremlin: Sixty Years Later." *Genocide Studies International* vol. 8, no. 2 (Fall 2014): 224–35.

Kolbuszewski, Jacek. *Cmentarze*. Wrocław, 1996.

"Komitet budovy pam'iatnyka, pam'iatnyk zhertvam Holodomoru v Kanberri." In *Ukraïntsi v Avstraliï*. Vol. 2, 172–3. Melbourne, 1998.

"Komu zavazhav pam'iatnyk 'Zakam'ianila kybytka' v Babynomu Iaru?". *Biblioteka Holokostu*. Accessed April 3, 2019. https://sites.google.com/site/lohocoust/babin-ar/komu-zavazav-pam-atnik-zakam-anila-kibitka-v-babinomu-aru.

Kondakov, Nikodim. *Ikonografiia Bogomateri*. Vol. 2. Sankt-Peterburg, 1915.

"Konkurs na krashchyi proekt pam'iatnyka zhertvam Holodomoru v Ukraïni 1932–1933 rokiv u m. Vashynhtoni (SShA)." Ukrainian Institute of National Memory, October 23, 2009. Accessed July 30, 2019. http://www.memory.gov.ua:8080/ua/announce/detail/74.htm.

Konradova, Natal'ia, and Anna Ryleva. "Geroi i zhertvy. Memorialy Velikoi Otechestvennoi." *Neprikosnovennyi zapas* 40–41, № 2–3 (2005). Accessed July 30, 2020. http://magazines.russ.ru/nz/2005/2/ko16.html.

Kończal, Kornelia. "Miejsca pamięci. O niebywałej karierze pewnej koncepcji badawczej." In *Polsko-niemieckie miejsca pamięci*. Vol. 4, *Refleksje metodologiczne*, eds. Robert Traba, Hans Henning Hahn, cooperation Maciej Górny, Kornelia Kończal, 77–100. Warsaw, 2013.

Kor. "OM," "De i iakym bude Memorial henotsydu ukraïntsiv ta chomu vtrutylys' sluzhbovtsi?" *Obrazotvorche mystetstvo*, № 4 (2003): 84. https://elib.nlu.org.ua/view.html?id=6594.

Koselleck, Reinhart. *Vergangene Zukunft. Zur Semantik geschichtlicher Zeiten*. Frankfurt a. M., 1995.

Kostylieva, Svitlana. "Tema holodu 1932/1933 r. u dzerkali hazety 'Literaturna Ukraïna' doby horbachovs'koï hlasnosti." In *Holodomor 1932–1933 rokiv iak velychezna trahediia ukraïns'koho narodu. Materialy Vseukraïns'koï naukovoï konferentsiï. Kyïv, 15 lystopada 2002 r.*, 236–42. Kyiv, 2003.

Kostylieva, Svitlana. "Vysvitlennia vitchyznianoiu presoiu 70-oï richnytsi holodu 1932–1933 rr." *Problemy istoriï Ukraïny. Fakty, sudzhennia, poshuky* 11 (2004): 343–53.

Koval'chuk, Olena. "Holodomor 1932–1933 rr. v USRR i ukraïns'ka diaspora Pivnichnoï Ameryky: informatyvni aspekty," *Ukraïna XX st.: kul'tura, ideolohiia, polityka*, № 15 (2009): 172–207. http://resource.history.org.ua/publ/xxx_2009_15_2_172.

Koval'chuk, Olena, and Tamara Marusyk. *Holodomor 1932–1933 rr. v USRR i ukraïns'ka diaspora Pivnichnoï Ameryky*. Chernivtsi, 2010.

Kozak, Stefan. *Z dziejów Ukrainy. Religia, kultura, myśl społeczna. Studia i szkice*. Warsaw, 2006.

Kranz, Tomasz. "Miejsca pamięci czy pamięć miejsc? Rozważania o roli upamiętniania w przekazie społeczno-historycznym." *Przeszłość i Pamięć*, № 1 (2000): 57–63.

Kravchenko, Vladimir. "Boi s ten'iu. Sovetskoe proshloe v istoricheskoi pamiati sovremennogo ukrainskogo obshchestva." *Ab imperio*, № 2 (2004): 329–68.

Kress, Gunther, and Teo van Leeuwen, eds. *Reading Images: The Grammar of Visual Design*. London–New York, 2006.

Krylenko, Olha. "U Toronto vstanovyly memorial zhertvam Holodomoru." *Hromadske*, October 22, 2018. https://hromadske.ua/posts/u-toronto-vstanovili-memorial-zhertvam-golodomoru.

Kudela, Wiktoria. "Wielki Głód na Podolu w latach 1932–1933 w oczach dzieci." *Studenckie zeszyty historyczne* 5 (2004): 85–102.

Kudela-Świątek, Wiktoria. "From Private Memory to the Collective Image of the Ukrainian Holodomor." *Wrocławski Rocznik Historii Mówionej,* № 6 (2016): 33–65. https://doi.org/10.26774/wrhm.148.

Kudela-Świątek, Wiktoria. *Miejsca (nie)pamięci. O upamiętnianiu ukraińskiego Wielkiego Głodu z lat 1932–1933.* Cracow, 2014. https://doi.org/10.12797/9788376384344.

Kudela-Świątek, Wiktoria. "Pamięć i "miejsca pamięci" Holodomoru. Krajobraz po bitwie." *Nowa Ukraina* 5–6, № 1–2 (2008): 102–18.

Kudela-Świątek, Wiktoria. *W labiryncie znaczeń. Pomniki ukraińskiego Wielkiego Głodu 1932–1933.* Cracow, 2020. https://doi.org/10.12797/9788381382328.

Kula, Marcin. *Nośniki pamięci historycznej.* Warsaw, 2002.

Kul'chyts'kyi, Stanislav. "Do otsinky stanovyshcha v sil's'komu hospodarstvi USRR u 1931–1933 rr." *Ukraïns'kyi istorychnyi zhurnal,* № 3 (1988): 15–27.

Kul'chyts'kyi, Stanislav. *Holodomor 1932–1933 rr. iak henotsyd: trudnoshchi usvidomlennia.* Kyiv, 2008.

Kul'chyts'kyi, Stanislav. "Iak tse bulo. Chytaiuchy dokumenty stvorenoï pry konhresi SShA Komisiï po holodu 1932–1933 rr. na Ukraïni." *Pid praporom leninizmu,* № 23 (1990): 79–86.

Kul'chyts'kyi, Stanislav. "Problema holodu 1932–1933 rr. ta ïï mistse v suspil'no-politychnomu zhytti Ukraïny kintsia 80-kh – pochatku 90-kh rr." In *Holod – henotsyd 1933 roku v Ukraïni. Istoryko-politolohichnyi analiz sotsial'no-demohrafichnykh ta moral'no-psykholohichnykh naslidkiv. Materialy Mizhnarodnoï naukovo-teoretychnoï konferentsiï na vidznachennia 65-richchia trahediï ukraïns'koho narodu, Kyïv, 28 lystopada 1998 r.*, eds. Stanislav Kul'chyts'kyi [et al.]: 27–45. Kyiv–New York, 2000.

Kul'chyts'kyi, Stanislav V., Olha F. Botushans'ka, and Volodymyr Motyka, eds. *Holodomor v Ukraïni 1932–1933 rr. Bibliohrafichnyi pokaznyk,* compilation Larysa M. Bur'ian, Inna E. Rikun. Odesa–Lviv, 2001.

Kulyk, Volodymyr. "'My zatialysia: polyniv ne bude…' Pro Asotsiatsiiu doslidnykiv holodu-henotsydu 1932–33 rokiv v Ukraïni rozpovidaie ïï holova Lidiia Kovalenko-Maniak." *Suchasnist',* 381, № 1 (1993): 91–5.

[Kurylas, Larysa]. "Avtor pam'iatnoho monumenta 'Pole pshenytsi' – pro vazhkyi shliakh ioho zvedennia." *VOA,* November 7, 2015. https://ukrainian.voanews.com/a/kurylas-memorial/3047914.html.

Kuryliv, Valentyna. *Metodyka vykladannia istoriï. Kurs pidvyshchennia kvalifikatsiï vchyteliv istoriï.* Lviv–Toronto, 2003.

Kuryliv, Valentyna. *Metodyka vykladannia istoriï. Kurs pidvyshchennia kvalifikatsiï vchyteliv istoriï. Navchal'nyi posibnyk.* Kharkiv–Toronto, 2008.

Kuryliw, Valentina. *Holodomor in Ukraine, the Genocidal Famine 1932–1933: Teaching Materials for Teachers and Students.* Toronto, 2015.

Kuryliw, Valentina. "The Ukrainian Genocide–the Holodomor, 1932–1933: A Case of Denial, Cover-Up, and Dismissal." In *Teaching about Genocide: Insights and Advice from Secondary Teachers and Professors*. Vol. 1, ed. Samuel Totten, 49–60. Lanham–Boulder–New York–London, 2018.

Kuryliw, Valentina. *The Unknown Genocide: Holodomor in Ukraine 1932–1933*. Toronto, 2008.

Kutsevych, Vadym. "Evoliutsiia khramobuduvannia v poselenniakh ukraïns'koï diaspory." *Ukraïns'ka akademiia mystetstva* 21 (2013): 87–96.

Kuzio, Taras. "History, Memory and Nation Building in the Post-Soviet Colonial Space." *Nationalities Paper* 30, № 2 (2002): 241–64. https://doi.org/10.1080/00905990220140649.

Kwiatkowski, Piotr. "Społeczne tworzenie niepamięci." In *Asymilacja, akulturacja, dyskryminacja. Wokół problemów zachowania tożsamości mniejszości narodowych i etnicznych w Polsce*, ed. Lech Nijakowski, 91–128. Warsaw, 2009.

LaCapra, Dominick. *History in Transit: Experience, Identity, Critical Theory*. Ithaca–London, 2004.

LaCapra, Dominick. "Trauma, Absence, Loss," *Critical Inquiry* 25, № 4. (Summer, 1999): 696–727.

Landsberg, Alison. *Prosthetic Memory: The Transformation of American Remembrance in the Age of Mass Culture*. New York, 2004.

Lanovyk, Bohdan [et al.]. *Istoriia ukraïns'koï emihratsiï. Navch. posibnyk dlia stud. vyshch. navch. zakladiv osvity*. Kyiv, 1997.

Lanzmann, Claude. "Les Non-lieux de la mémoire." In *Au sujet de Shoah. Le film de Claude Lanzmann*, ed. Michel Deguy, 280–93. Paris, 1990.

Lawriwsky, Michael. "The Great Famine of 1932–33. A Symposium 22 October, 2003, 'Australia and the Holodomor: 50 Years of Remembrance'." Accessed February 1, 2021. http://archive.cym.org/au/archives/Holodomor.pdf.

Lefter, Sergey. "Golod byl sdelan special'no. Chto pomniat o Golodomore te, kto ego perezhil." *RBK Ukraïna*, November 11, 2016. https://daily.rbc.ua/rus/show/golod-sdelan-spetsialno-pomnyat-golodomore-1480148878.html.

Leinwand, Aleksandra. "Z cokołów." *Karta*, № 19 (1996): 62–6.

Lenartowicz, J. Krzysztof. *O psychologii architektury. Próba inwentaryzacji badań, zakres przedmiotowy i wpływ na architekturę*. Cracow, 1992.

Levkova, Oksana. "(U)movy samo-(za)buttia." *Nezalezhnyi kul'turolohichnyi chasopys «Ï»*, № 40 (2005). http://www.ji.lviv.ua/n40texts/levkova.htm.

Lewandowski, Maciej. "Rzecz o pomnikach." *Przeszłość i Pamięć*, № 4 (1998): 4–5.

Lewicka, Maria. "Aurea mediocrita, czyli o tym, czy jakość może przejść w ilość." *Roczniki Psychologiczne* 13, № 1 (2010): 51–60.

Lisowska-Magdziarz, Małgorzata. *Analiza tekstów w dyskursie medialnym*. Cracow, 2006.

Lowenthal, David. *The Past Is a Foreign Country*. Cambridge, 1985.

Lysenko, Snizhana. "Cherkashchanyn Vasyl' Pereval's'kyi stvoryv usesvitn'ovidomyi symvol Holodomoru." Uman Info, November 20, 2012. Accessed July 30, 2020, http://uman.info/ua/news/cherkashchanyn-vasyl-perevalskyy-stvoryv-usesvitnovidomyy-symvol-golodomoru--1540.html.

Madera, Andrzej J. *Ukraina na rozdrożu. Między Rosją a Europą*. Rzeszów, 2000.

Maier, Charles. "A Surfeit of Memory? Reflections on History, Melancholy and Denial." *History and Memory* 5, № 2 (1993): 136–51.

Maier, Charles S. "Hot Memory... Cold Memory. On the Political Half-Life of Fascist and Communist Memory." IWM. Accessed November 26, 2013. http://www.iwm.at/read-listen-watch/transit-online/hot-memory-cold-memory-on-the-political-half--life-of-fascist-and-communist-memory/.

"Making the Holodomor Memorial: Context & Questions." University of Maryland School of Architecture, Planning and Preservation. Accessed February 1, 2021. https://arch.umd.edu/events/making-holodomor-memorial-context-questions.

Manastyrsky, Peter J. "30-year anniversary of Holodomor monument in Winnipeg." *Ukrainian Winnipeh,* January 20, 2015. Accessed July 30, 2019. http://www.ukrainianwinnipeg.ca/30-year-anniversary-of-holodomor-monument-in-winnipeg/.

Mark-Fitzgerald, Emily. *Commemorating the Irish Famine: Memory and the Monument*. Liverpool, 2013.

Marochko, Vasyl'. "Holod na Ukraïni (1931–1933 pp.). Prychyny ta naslidky." *Problemy istoriï Ukraïny. Fakty, sudzhennia, poshuky* 1 (1991): 59–68.

Marochko, Vasyl'. "Holodomor-henotsyd 1932–1933 rokiv v Ukraïni. Politychnyi dyskurs." *Istorychna pam'iat'*, № 30–31 (2014): 53–62.

Maron, Jeremy. "Covering the Holodomor: Memory Eternal. Misinformation and Deception Play a Crucial Role in Mass Atrocities such as the Holodomor." Canadian Museum for Human Rights. Accessed February 1, 2021. https://humanrights.ca/story/covering-the-holodomor-memory-eternal.

Marunchak, Michael. *The Ukrainian Canadians: A History*. Winnipeg–Ottawa, 1982.

Marunchak, Mykhailo, *Natsiia v borot'bi za svoie isnuvannia: 1932 i 1933 roky v Ukraïni i diiaspori*. Winnipeg, 1985.

Masl'onko, Maksym. "Holodomor iak chynnyk zovnishn'oï polityky Ukraïny. Istoriia chy isteriia?" In *Problemy mizhnarodnykh vidnosyn*. Vol. 1, 232–47. Kyiv, 2010. Accessed February 1, 2021. http://dspace.nbuv.gov.ua/handle/123456789/58858.

Megill, Allan. "History, Memory, Identity." *History of the Human Sciences* 11 (1998): 37–62. https://doi.org/10.1177/095269519801100303.

Mehyk, Petro. "Viktor Tsymbal (1901–1968)." *Notatky z mystetstva,* № 10 (1970): 47–52.

"Melnychuk Iurii (1921–63)." In *Entsyklopediia ukraïnoznavstva. Perevydannia v Ukraïni.* Vol. 4, 1516. Lviv, 1994.

"Ministro ucraniano inaugura monumento no Parque Tingui." Fundação Cultural de Curitiba. Accessed July 28, 2020. http://www.fundacaoculturaldecuritiba.com.br/noticias/ministro-ucraniano-inaugura-monumento-no-parque-tingui/.

"Mirosław Nizio projektuje Muzeum Ofiar Wielkiego Głodu w Kijowie." InfoArchitekta. Accessed March 31, 2019. https://www.infoarchitekta.pl/artykuly:4-projekty:17748-miroslaw-nizio-projektuje-muzeum-ofiar-wielkiego-glodu-w-kijowie.html.

Misztal, Barbara A. *Theories of Social Remembering.* Maidenhead, 2003.

"Monumento ao Holodomor é instalado no Memorial Ucraniano em Curitiba." *Ecclesia Brasil,* September 19, 2009, https://ecclesia.org.br/news/?p=2505.

Motyl, Alexander J. *Dilemmas of Independence: Ukraine after Totalitarianism.* New York, 1993.

Mozdyr, Mykola. *Ukraïns'ka narodna memorial'na skul'ptura.* Kyiv, 1996.

Mykytovych, Roman and o. Ivan Shevtsiv. "Pam'iatnyky." In *Entsyklopediia ukraïns'koï diiaspory v 7 tomakh,* ed. Vasyl' Markus'. Vol. 4: *Avstraliia, Aziia, Afryka,* 147–8. Kyiv, 1995.

Mytsyk, Iurii. "Z dosvidu zboru svidchen' pro holodomor 1933 r." In *Holod – henotsyd 1933 roku v Ukraïni. Istoryko-politolohichnyi analiz sotsial'no-demohrafichnykh ta moral'no-psykholohichnykh naslidkiv. Materialy Mizhnarodnoï naukovo-teoretychnoï konferentsiï na vidznachennia 65-richchia trahediï ukraïns'koho narodu, Kyïv, 28 lystopada 1998 r.,* eds. Stanislav Kul'chyts'kyi [et al.], 390–407. Kyiv–New York, 2000.

Nader, Luiza. "Afektywne pamiętanie. Moim przyjaciołom Żydom Władysława Strzemińskiego." *Zagłada Żydów. Studia i materiały,* № 8 (2012): 188–213.

Narizhnyi, Symon. *Ukraïns'ka emihratsiia. Kul'turna pratsia ukraïns'koï emihratsiï 1919–1939. Materialy, zibrani S. Narizhnym do chastyny druhoï,* eds. Oleksandr Fedoruk [et al.], compilation Larysa Iakovleva [et al.]. Kyiv, 1999.

"National Holodomor Memorial 'Field of Wheat'." The Kurylas Studio. Accessed February 1, 2021. https://thekurylasstudio.com/memorials/holodomor-memorial-field-of-wheat/.

"New Exhibition at The Ukrainian Museum. Yaroslava Surmach Mills: Retrospective," March 7–September 23, 2018. The Ukrainian Museum. Accessed February 1, 2021. http://www.ukrainianmuseum.org/ex_180307_yaroslava.html.

Nieroba, Elżbieta. "Rola warstwy afektywnej w doświadczeniu muzealnym, narracja o Zagładzie we współczesnym muzeum historycznym."

Zeszyty naukowe Wyższej Szkoły Oficerskiej Wojsk Lądowych im. gen. T. Kościuszki, № 3 (2012): 171–85.

Niewiedział-Bédu, Agnieszka. "Sprawiedliwi wśród Narodów Świata w Polsce 1989–2003. Gry znaczeń w konstrukcji miejsca pamięci." In *Historia, pamięć, tożsamość. Postaci upamiętniane przez współczesnych mieszkańców różnych części Europy*, eds. Maria Kujawska and Bogumił Jewsiewicki, 139–48. Poznań, 2006.

Nijakowski, Lech. *Domeny symboliczne*. Warsaw, 2006.

Nijakowski, Lech. *Polska polityka pamięci. Esej socjologiczny*. Warsaw, 2008.

Nora, Pierre. "Between Memory and History: Les Lieux de Mémoire." *Representations*, № 26, Special Issue: Memory and Counter-Memory (Spring, 1989): 7–24.

Nora, Pierre. "Czas pamięci," transl. Wiktor Dłuski. *Res Publica Nowa*, № 7 (2001): 37–43.

Nora, Pierre, dir. *Les lieux de mémoire*. 7 vols. Paris, 1984–1993.

Nora, Pierre, ed. *Realms of Memory: Rethinking the French Past*. 3 vols. New York, 1996–1998.

Nora, Pierre. "W poszukiwaniu europejskich miejsc pamięci." *Borussia. Kultura, Historia, Literatura*, № 41 (2007): 12–16.

Odnoperchany 1927–1977. Al'bom. Kyiv, 1977.

Odynoka, Linina, Liudmyla Prykhod'ko, and Rostyslav Romanovs'kyi, compilation. *Holodomory v Ukraïni 1921–1923, 1932–1933, 1946–1947. Materialy do bibliohrafiï dokumental'nykh publikatsii*. Kyiv, 2005.

Ohiienko, Vitalii. "Memorial'na polityka vshanuvannia pam'iati zhertv Holodomoru 1932–1933 rr. v Ukraïni." *Hileia. Naukovyi visnyk* 61 (2012): 72–7.

Ohiienko, Vitalii. "Vizual'na kul'tura pam'iatnykiv zhertvam holodomoru v Ukraïni." *Hileia. Naukovyi visnyk* 65 (2012): 114–9.

Olszański, Tadeusz A. *Miejsce UPA w Wielkiej Wojnie Ojczyźnianej. Dylematy polityki historycznej Ukrainy*. Warsaw, 2013.

Onats'kyi, Ievhen, ed. *Mala entsyklopediia Ukraïny*. 16 vols. Buenos Aires, 1957–67.

Ostow, Robin. "Remusealizing Jewish History in Warsaw. The Privatization and Externalization of Nation Building." In *(Re)Visualising National History. Museums and National Identities in Europe in the New Millennium*, ed. Robin Ostow, 157–80. Toronto–Buffalo–London, 2008.

Pam'iati zhertv Holodomoru 1932–1933 rokiv v Ukraïni / To the Memory of the Victims of Holodomor of 1932–1933 in Ukraine. Text H. Furmanchuk, photo O. Mazur, transl. E. Suslin, ed. Ihor Yukhnovskyi [et al.]. Ternopil, 2009.

"Pam'iatnyk berestets'kii bytvi khotily pokryty zolotom." Accessed 30 July 2020. https://gorohiv.rayon.in.ua/news/18525-pamiatnik-v-berestechku-hotili-pokriti-zolotom.

Panchuk, M., and S. Dibrov. "20-Z0-e. Dokumenty, fakty, svidetel'stva." *Kommunist Ukrainy*, № 4 (1990): 70–84.

Panofsky, Erwin. "Iconography and Iconology: An Introduction to the Study of Renaissance Art." *Meaning in the Visual Arts* (1970): 51–81.

Pavlovs'kyi, Vadym. *Vasyl' Hryhorovych Krychevs'kyi: Zhyttia i tvorchist'*. New York, 1974.

Pawluczuk, Włodzimierz. *Ukraina. Polityka i mistyka*. Cracow, 1998.

"Peter Wyhinny Ph.D." *Chicago Tribune*. August 6, 2009. Accessed February 1, 2021. https://www.legacy.com/obituaries/chicagotribune/obituary.aspx?n=peter-wyhinny&pid=131004416.

Po co nam historia?. Introd. Tadeusz Łepkowski, transl. Maria Mróz. Warsaw, 1985.

Pomian, Krzysztof. "Miejsca pamięci w Europie Środkowo-Wschodniej. Doświadczenia przeszłości. Przesłanie na przyszłość." *Przegląd Polityczny*, № 89 (2008): 4–11.

Popovych, Volodymyr, and Roman Senkus. "Kowal Roman-Ivan." *Encyclopedia of Modern Ukraine*. Updated 2013. http://esu.com.ua/search_articles.php?id=9165.

Procyk, Oksana, Leonid Heretz, and James E. Mace. *Famine in the Soviet Ukraine, 1932–33: A Memorial Exhibition, Widener Library, Harvard University*. Cambridge, MA, 1986.

Pyrih, Ruslan, compilation. *Holod 1932–1933 rokiv na Ukraïni. Ochyma istorykiv, movoiu dokumentiv*. Kyiv, 1990.

Rewers, Ewa. "Interferencja pamięci. Ku transkulturowości." In *Pamięć i zapominanie w Europie przełomu wieków*, ed. Zbigniew Drozdowicz: 77–86. Poznań, 2001.

Rewers, Ewa. *Post polis. Wstęp do filozofii ponowoczesnego miasta*. Cracow, 2005.

Riabchuk, Mykola. "Holodomor: The Politics of Memory and Political Infighting in Contemporary Ukraine." In *The Holodomor of 1932–33. Papers from the 75th-Anniversary Conference on the Ukrainian Famine-Genocide, University of Toronto, November 1, 2007*, special issue of: *The Harriman Review* 16, № 2 (November, 2008): 3–9. https://holodomor.ca/wp-content/uploads/2020/04/Harriman-Review-Holodomor-75th-Nov-2008.pdf.

Riabchuk, Mykola. "Kul'tura pam'iati ta polityka zabuttia." *Krytyka*, № 1–2 (2006). http://krytyka.kiev.ua/articles/s.7_1-2_2006.html.

Riabchuk, Mykola. "Mizh hromadians'kym suspil'stvom i novym etatyzmom (Stanovlennia demokratiï i (chy) rozbudova derzhavy)." *Ukraïna. Kul'turna spadshchyna, natsional'na svidomist', derzhavnist'*, № 2 (1995): 201–20.

Riabchuk, Mykola. *Vid Malorosiï do Ukraïny: Paradoksy zapizniloho natsiietvorennia*. Kyiv, 2000.

Ritchie, Nicole Anne. "Queering Museums: Questions of Space, Affect, and the (Non)Normative." MA thesis. University of Toronto, 2015. http://hdl.handle.net/1807/70598.

Rogers, Peter. "Understanding Regionalism and the Politics of Identity in Ukraine's Eastern Borderlands." *Nationalities Papers* 34, № 2 (2006): 157–74. https://doi.org/10.1080/00905990600617730.

Rotoff, Basil, Roman Yereniuk, and Stella Hryniuk, *Monuments to Faith. Ukrainian Churches in Manitoba*. Winnipeg, 1990.

Rozumnyi, Iaroslav. "Ukraïns'kyi mytets' zhyv i tvoryv u Kanadi (Pam'iati Romana-Ivana Kovalia)." *Mystets'ki obriï* 7 (2004) [2005]: 408–10.

Rudling, Per A. "Long-Distance Nationalism: Ukrainian Monuments and Historical Memory in Multicultural Canada." In *Public Memory in the Context of Transnational Migration and Displacement*, ed. Sabine Marschall, 95–126. Cham, 2020. https://doi.org/10.1007/978-3-030-41329-3_4.

Rudling, Per A. "Memories of 'Holodomor' and National Socialism in Ukrainian political culture." In *Rekonstruktion des Nationalmythos? Frankreich, Deutschland und die Ukraine im Vergleich*, ed. Yves Bizeul, 227–58. Göttingen, 2013.

Rudling, Per A. "Multiculturalism, Memory, and Ritualization: Ukrainian Nationalist Monuments in Edmonton, Alberta." *Nationalities Papers* 39 (2011): 733–68. https://doi.org/10.1080/00905992.2011.599375.

Saichuk, Andrii, Iryna Diachenko, and Serhii Ieromenko, "Memorial zhertvam Holodomoru. Tsina pytannia." *Podrobnosti*, November 16, 2008. Accessed July 30, 2020. http://podrobnosti.ua/566586-memoral-zhertvam-golodomoru-tsna-pitannja.html.

Samuel, Raphael. *Theatres of Memory*. London, 1994.

Santner, Eric. "History Beyond the Pleasure Principle: Some Thoughts about the Representation of Trauma." In *Probing the Limits of Representation: Nazism and the "Final Solution,"* ed. Saul Friedländer, 143–54. Cambridge, 1992.

Šapoval, Jurij. "Lügen und Schweigen. Die unterdrückte Erinnerung an den Holodomor." *Osteuropa* 54, № 12 (2004): 131–45.

"Saskatchewan Remembers Holodomor with a Special Service at the Legislature." *Saskatchewan*, November 20, 2017. https://www.saskatchewan.ca/government/news-and-media/2017/november/20/holodomor.

Satzewich, Vic. *The Ukrainian Diaspora*. Routledge, 2002. https://doi.org/10.4324/9780203217498.

Schama, Simon. *Landscape and Memory*. New York, 1995.

Semenko, Iurii, compilation. *Holod 1933 roku v Ukraïni. Svidchennia pro vynyshchuvannia Moskvoiu ukraïns'koho selianstva*. Munich, 1963.

Sendyka, Roma. "Pryzma – zrozumieć nie-miejsce pamięci (non-lieux de mémoire)." *Teksty Drugie*, № 1–2 (2013): 323–44.

Serbyn, Roman, and Bohdan Krawchenko, eds. *Famine in Ukraine: 1932–1933*. Edmonton, 1986.

Ševčenko, Liz. "Sites of Conscience: Reimagining Reparations," *Change Over Time* 1, № 1 (2011): 6–33. https://doi.org/10.1353/cot.2011.0002.

Shapravs'kyi, Serhii. "Traktuvannia osnovnykh elementiv pravoslavnykh kladovyshch z pozytsii khrystyians'koï symvoliky." *Naukovi zapysky [Natsional'noho universytetu Ostroz'ka Akademiia]. Seriia "Istorychne relihiieznavstvo"* 5 (2011): 220–30.

Sharfman, Glenn. "The Quest for Justice: The Reaction of the Ukrainian-American Community to the John Demjanjuk Trials." *Journal of Genocide Research* 2, № 1 (2000): 65–87. https://doi.org/10.1080/146235200112418.

Shevchuk, Oleksandr. *Natsional'no-kul'turni initsiatyvy ukraïns'koï diaspory (kinets' 50-kh – pochatok 90-kh rr. XX st.)*. Kyiv, 1997.

Shevelov, George Yurii. "The Year 1860 in Shevchenko's Work." In *Shevchenko and the Critics,* ed. George S. N. Luckyj, 324–54. London, 1980.

Shkandrii, Myroslav. "Mystetstvo Romana Kovalia." *Zakhidnokanads'kyi zbirnyk,* № 5 (2008): 415–36.

Skoryk, Larysa. "Znaity symvol." *Obrazotvorche mystetstvo,* № 3 (1990): 7–10.

"Skul'ptor Diachenko kazhe, scho ioho pam'iatnyk zhertvam Holodomoru vartyi uvahy" *Ukrinform,* 7 June, 2016. https://www.ukrinform.ua/rubric-culture/2030647-skulptor-dacenko-kaze-so-jogo-pamatnik-zertvam-golodomoru-vartij-uvagi.html.

Slyvka, Iurii. "Ukraïna v Druhii svitovii viini. Natsional'no-politychnyi ta mizhnarodno-pravovyi aspekty." *Ukraïna. Kul'turna spadshchyna, natsional'na svidomist', derzhavnist',* № 3–4 (1997): 3–31.

"Some Aspects in the Life of the Ukrainian Orthodox Church of the USA." Ukrainian Orthodox Church of the USA. Accessed March 23, 2019. https://www.uocofusa.org/history.html.

Stakhors'ka, Liudmyla. "Holodomor ochyma suchasnykiv." In *Holodomor 1932–1933 rokiv iak velychezna trahediia ukraïns'koho narodu. Materialy Vseukraïns'koï naukovoï konferentsiï. Kyïv, 15 lystopada 2002 r.,* 209–12. Kyiv, 2003.

Subtelny, Orest. *Ukraine: A history*. Toronto, 1988.

Subtelnyi, Orest. *Ukraïna. Istoriia*. Lybid, 1991.

Subtelnyi, Orest. "Valentyna Kuryliv: Metodyka vykladannia istoriï." *Pedahohichna dumka,* № 3 (2003).

Swyripa, Frances. *Storied Landscapes: Ethno-Religious Identity and the Canadian Prairies,* Winnipeg, 2010.

Sysyn, Frank E. "The Third Rebirth of the Ukrainian Autocephalous Church and the Religious Situation in Ukraine, 1989–1991." In Serhii Plokhy and Frank E. Sysyn, *Religion and Nation in Modern Ukraine,* 88–119. Edmonton–Toronto, 2003.

Sysyn, Frank E. "The Ukrainian Famine of 1932–3: The Role of the Ukrainian Diaspora in Research and Public Discussion." In *Studies in Comparative Genocide,* eds. Levon Chorbajian, George Shirinian, 1821–215. London, 1999.

Sysyn, Frank E. "The Ukrainian Orthodox Church: Memory and Memorialization of the Holodomor." Accessed July 30, 2020. https://holodomor.ca/wp-content/uploads/2016/05/boundbrook.pdf.

Sysyn, Frank. "Thirty Years of Research on the Holodomor: A Balance Sheet." *East/West: Journal of Ukrainian Studies* 2, № 1 (2015): 4–16. https://doi.org/10.21226/T26P4M.

Szacka, Barbara. "Historia i pamięć zbiorowa." *Kultura i Społeczeństwo*, № 4 (2003): 3–15.

Szacka, Barbara. "Pamięć społeczna a identyfikacja narodowa." In *Trudne sąsiedztwa. Z socjologii konfliktów narodowościowych*, ed. Aleksandra Jasińska-Kania, 37–46. Warsaw, 2001.

Szacka, Barbara. "Pamięć zbiorowa i wojna." *Przegląd Socjologiczny*, № 2 (2000): 11–28.

Szacka, Barbara. "Transformacja społeczna a świadomość historyczna." In *Ofiary czy współwinni. Nazizm i sowietyzm w świadomości historycznej*, 43–64. Warsaw, 1997.

Szacka, Barbara. *Wprowadzenie do socjologii*. Warsaw, 2003.

Szacki, Jerzy. "O kanonie kultury europejskiej uwagi sceptyczne." *Znak* 470, № 7 (1994): 18–9.

Szeląg, Marcin. "Edukacja głupcze! Zadania muzeum na początku XXI wieku." In *Muzeum XXI wieku. Teoria i Praxis*, eds. Elżbieta Kowalska and Elżbieta Urbaniak, 175–81. Gniezno, 2010.

Szolginia, Witold. *Architektura*. Warsaw, 1992.

Szpociński, Andrzej. "Miejsca pamięci (lieux de mémoire)." *Teksty Drugie*, № 4 (2008): 11–20.

Taithe, Bertrand. "Monuments aux morts? Reading Nora's Realms of Memory and Samuel's Theatres of Memory." *History of the Human Sciences* 12, № 2 (1999): 123–39. https://doi.org/10.1177/09526959922120289.

Traba, Robert, and Hahn, Hans Henning. Eds., *Polsko-niemieckie miejsca pamięci*, vol. 1–4 (Warsaw, 2012–2013).

Trembits'kyi, Anatolii, ed. *Muzei pam'iati zhertv Holodomoru na Khmel'nychchyni 1932–1933 rokiv (do 5-richchia vid dnia stvorennia)*. Khmelnytskyi, 2013.

Troebst, Stefan. *Postkommunistische Erinnerungskulturen im östlichen Europa. Bestandsaufnahme, Kategorisierung, Periodisierung / Postkomunistyczne kultury pamięci w Europie Wschodniej. Stan, kategoryzacja, periodyzacja*. Wrocław, 2005.

Trubina, Elena. "Mesta pamiati, monumenty i 'novaia demokratiia'." *Topos*, № 3 (2000). http://journals.ehu.lt/index.php/topos/article/view/485.

Tuan, Yi-Fu. *Space and Place: The Perspective of Experience*. Minneapolis, MN–London, 2001.

"Tvorcha maisternia Sydoruka ta Krylova." Accessed July 27, 2020. https://www.tms.kiev.ua/?section=monuments&lang=ua.

"Two More Holodomor Memorials Unveiled," Association of Ukrainians in Great Britain. November 25, 2018. https://www.augb.co.uk/news-page.php?id=1902.

Tys, Iurii. "Viktor Tsymbal." *Vyzvol'nyi Shliakh,* № 1 (111) (1957): 104–10.

"UCRDC Interviews Child of Holodomor Survivors." Ukrainian Canadian Congress. November 14, 2015. https://www.ucc.ca/2015/11/14/ucc-enewsletter-november-2015/.

"Ukraïns'ka delehatsiia, ocholiuvana Stepanom Kubivym, u bel'hiis'komu Henku vshanuvala pam'iat zhertv Holodomoru." *Vseukraïns'ka nezalezhna suspil'no-hromads'ka hazeta "Kozats'kyi krai,"* September 24, 2018. http://cossackland.org.ua/2018/09/24/ukrajinska-delehatsiya-ocholyu vana-stepanom-kubivym-u-belhijskomu-henku-vshanuvala-pam-yat-zhertv-holodomoru/.

"Ukraïntsi v Priashevi takozh vshanuvaly pam'iat' zhertv Holodomoru v Ukraïni (FOTO)," *Zakarpattia online.* Accessed April 3, 2019. https://zakarpattya.net.ua/Special/187571-Ukraintsi-v-Priashevi-takozh-vsha nuvaly-pam%E2%80%99iat-zhertv-Holodomoru-v-Ukraini-FOTO.

Ushyns'kyi, Oleksandr. "Pro vshanuvannia pam'iati zhertv holodomoru 1932–1933 rokiv v selakh kyïvshchyny. Pershi pam'iatnyky zhertvam henotsydu." *Problemy istoriï Ukraïny. Fakty, sudzhennia, poshuky* 18: *Holod 1932–1933 rokiv – henotsyd ukraïns'koho narodu* (2008): 410–3.

Vasylyk, Mykhailo. *Ukraïntsi Argentyny: istoriia ta suchasnist'.* L'viv, 2009.

Veselova, Oleksandra. "Memorial'ni znaky i pam'iatnyky zhertvam holodu-henotsydu 1932–1933 rr. v Ukraïni." *Kraieznavstvo,* № 1–2 (2009): 169–79.

Veselova, Oleksandra. "Pam'iatni znaky i pam'iatnyky zhertvam Holodu-henotsydu 1932–1933 rr. v Ukraïni." *Problemy istoriï Ukraïny. Fakty, sudzhennia, poshuky* 13 (2005): 434–41.

Veselova, Oleksandra. "Svidchennia ochevydtsiv holodu-henotsydu 1932–1933 rr. v Ukraïni iak dzherelo doslidzhennia ioho prychyn ta naslidkiv." *Problemy istoriï Ukraïny. Fakty, sudzhennia, poshuky* 19 (2010): 82–98.

Veselova, Oleksandra. "Uvichnennia pam'iati zhertv holodomoru-henotsydu 1932–1933 rokiv v Ukraïni." *Ukraïns'kyi istorychnyi zhurnal,* № 2 (2004): 50–67.

Veselova, Oleksandra. "Uvikopomnennia zahyblykh vid holodnoho moru." In *Holod – henotsyd 1933 roku v Ukraïni. Istoryko-politolohichnyi analiz sotsial'no-demohrafichnykh ta moral'no-psykholohichnykh naslidkiv. Materialy Mizhnarodnoï naukovo-teoretychnoï konferentsiï na vidznachennia 65-richchia trahediï ukraïns'koho narodu, Kyïv, 28 lystopada 1998 r.*, eds. Stanislav Kul'chyts'kyi [et al.], 218–42. Kyiv–New York 2000.

Veselova, Oleksandra. "Viddanist' Ukraïni. Trudy i dni Mariiana Kotsia." *Problemy istoriï Ukraïny. Fakty, sudzhennia, poshuky* 20 (2011): 325–34.

Veselova, Oleksandra. *Z istoriï stvorennia i diial'nosti Asotsiatsiï doslidnykiv holodomoru v Ukraïni (ADHU) 1933: monohrafiia.* Kyiv, 2007.

Viedienieiev, Dmytro, and Dmytro Budkov. *Zaruchnytsia hlobal'noho protystoiannia. Trahediia Velykoho Holodu 1932–1933 rr. v Ukraïni v konteksti „kholodnoï viiny" 1945–1991 rokiv*. Kyiv, 2013.

"Vseukrainskii otkrytyi konkurs na luchshii proekt Memorial'nogo kompleksa pamiati zhertv golodomorov v Ukraine." *Format Market*. Accessed April 3, 2019. http://archunion.format-maket.com.ua/golodomor-06-001.shtml.

Wilczyński, Włodzimierz. *Leksykon kultury ukraińskiej*. Cracow, 2004.

Wilson, Andrew. *The Ukrainians: Unexpected Nation*. New Haven–London, 2015.

Wodak, Ruth, and Norman Fairclough. "Critical Discourse Analysis." In *Discourse as Social Interaction*, ed. Teun A. van Dijk, 258–84. London, 1997.

Wolff-Powęska, Anna. "Zwycięzcy i zwyciężeni. II wojna światowa w pamięci zbiorowej narodów." *Przegląd Zachodni*, № 2 (2005): 3–40. https://iz.poznan.pl/plik,pobierz,1039,9fdc38aa0517576b9575cd2920e2ac27/pdf/naka_panfu2013.pdf.

Wolfrum, Edgar. *Geschichte als Waffe. Vom Kaiserreich bis zur Wiedervereinigung*. Göttingen, 2001.

Yates, Frances A. *The Art of Memory*. London, 1966.

Young, James E. *The Texture of Memory: Holocaust Memorials and Meaning*. London–New Haven, 1993.

Yurchuk, Yuliya. *Reordering of Meaningful Worlds: Memory of the Organization of Ukrainian Nationalists and the Ukrainian Insurgent Army in Post-Soviet Ukraine*. Stockholm, 2014.

Zabuzhko, Oksana. "Filosofiia i problema kul'turnoï prytomnosti natsiï." *Ukraïna. Kul'turna spadshchyna, natsional'na svidomist', derzhavnist'*, № 2, (1995): 18–32.

Zastavnyi, Fedir. *Ukraïns'ka diaspora. Rozselennia ukraïntsiv u zarubizhnykh kraïnakh*. Lviv, 1991.

"Zberehty istorychnu pam'iat'." Mizhrehional'na Akademiia upravlinnia personalom. Accessed April 3, 2019. http://maup.com.ua/ua/monuments.html.

Zernii, Iuliia. "Derzhavna polityka pam'iati v Ukraïni. Stanovlennia ta suchasnyi stan." *Stratehichni priorytety*, № 3 (2008): 41–51.

Zhluktenko, Iurii O. *Ukraïns'ka mova na linhvistychnii karti Kanady*. Kyiv, 1990.

Zhurzhenko, Tatiana. "'Capital of Despair': Holodomor Memory and Political Conflicts in Kharkiv after the Orange Revolution." *East European Politics & Societies* 25 (2011): 597–639. https://doi.org/10.1177/0888325410387646.

Zhurzhenko, Tatiana. "Commemorating the Famine as Genocide: The Contested Meanings of Holodomor Memorials in Ukraine." In *Memorials in Times of Transition*, eds. Susanne Buckley-Zistel and Stefanie Schäfer, 221–41. Cambridge, 2014.

Zhurzhenko, Tetiana. "Vshanovuiuchy holod iak henotsyd: superechlyvi znachennia memorialiv zhertvam Holodomoru." *Ukraïna Moderna*, November 28, 2015. https://uamoderna.com/md/zhurzhenko-holodomor-memorials.

Zięblińska-Witek, Anna. "Estetyki reprezentacji śmierci w ekspozycjach historycznych." In *Obóz-muzeum. Trauma we współczesnym wystawiennictwie*, eds. Małgorzata Fabiszak and Marcin Owsiński, 31–48. Cracow, 2013.

Ziębińska-Witek, Anna "Totalitaryzm w nowych muzeach historycznych." In *Historia Polski od-nowa. Nowe narracje historii i muzealne reprezentacje przeszłości*, eds. Robert Kostro, Kazimierz Wóycicki, and Michał Wysocki, 26–44. Warsaw, 2014.

Video:

"Holodomor Monument Unveiling." Produced by *Echoes of Ukraine TV*. February 4, 2015. YouTube video, 23:20. https://www.youtube.com/watch?v=t2N24tf28u8&feature=youtu.be.

"Ianukovych ne vvazhaie Holodomor henotsydom." Produced by Oleksii Obukhov. November 26, 2010, YouTube video, 0:32. https://www.youtube.com/watch?v=YlIcu8zwmK0.

Kurylas, Larysa. "Making the Holodomor Memorial: Context and Questions." Kibel Gallery Lecture Spring 2020, February 21, 2020, YouTube video, 1:18:45, https://www.youtube.com/watch?v=kaoZTuRLOUE&feature=emb_title.

"Reportazh pro pershyi memorial zhertvam Holodomoru." *5 Kanal*. November 22, 2008. https://www.5.ua/suspilstvo/reportazh-pro-pershyi-memorial-zhertvam-holodomoru video-36326.html.

Internet:

https://5.ua
https://arch.umd.edu
http://archunion.format-maket.com.ua
http://arttouryeg.ca
http://canada.mfa.gov.ua
http://cossackland.org.ua
http://digitalcollections.library.cmu.edu
http://drc.usask.ca
https://ebooks.adelaide.edu.au
http://encyclopediaofukraine.com
http://esu.com.ua
https://www.facebook.com/AUGB.SUB

http://fresnostate.edu
http://fundacaoculturaldecuritiba.com.br
http://g.ekspert.infor.pl
https://gorohiv.rayon.in.ua
https://www.govinfo.gov
https://hagan-chamberlain.com
https://holodomor.ca
http://holodomor-monuments.org
https://holodomormuseum.org.ua
https://infoarchitekta.pl
http://iwm.at
http://ji.lviv.ua
http://khpg.org
http://kreschatic.kiev.ua
https://humanrights.ca/exhibition/galleries
https://legacy.com/obituaries
http://magazines.russ.ru
https://map.memorialholodomor.org.ua
http://maup.com.ua
http://memory.gov.ua
http://nadbuhom.pl
https://newpathway.ca
https://paperblog.fr
http://prawo.sejm.gov.pl
http://ratinggroup.ua
http://sharethestory.ca
https://sites.google.com/site/lohocoust/
http://static.rada.gov.ua
https://thekurylasstudio.com
https://tms.kiev.ua
https://ucc.ca
https://www.ucraniano.com.br
http://ukraine3000.org.ua
https://ukrainian.voanews.com
http://www.ukrainiangenocide.org
http://ukrainianmuseum.org
http://ukrainianpeople.us
http://ukrainianwinnipeg.ca
https://www.ukrhec.org
https://ukrinform.ua
http://uman.info
http://umoloda.kiev.ua
https://uocofusa.org

http://the-village.com.ua
http://www.winnipegsun.com
https://wnp.pl
https://youtube.com
https://zakarpattya.net.ua
https://zakon.rada.gov.ua
http://zblizenia.pl

List of Illustrations

73. The Holodomor monument in Snizhkiv, Kharkiv Oblast, Ukraine (1990). Source: "Holodomor Monuments. Kharkivs'ka oblast'." Ukrainian Canadian Research and Documentation Centre. Accessed February 1, 2021. https://www.holodomor-monuments.org/m/kharkiw.html.
74. Viktor Cymbal's painting *The Year 1933*. Source: "Hirki farby Holodomoru: U Kyievi rozpovidaiut' pro khudozhnyka-emihranta Viktora Tsymbala." *Ukraïna moloda* № 076 (August 18, 2020). https://umoloda.kyiv.ua/number/3626/164/149136/.
75. The Holodomor monument in Frontivka, Vinnytsia Oblast, Ukraine. Source: Photography by Mykhailo Potupchyk.
76. The Holodomor monument in Yakymivka, Vinnytsia Oblast, Ukraine. Source: Photography by Mykhailo Potupchyk.
77. The Holodomor monument in Cherkaska Lozova, Kharkiv Oblast, Ukraine (2008). Source: Photography by Igor Turzh, Wikipedia.org.
78. A model of Bohdan A. Shulakewych's monument design (1983). Source: The private archive of Bohdan Ihor Shulakewych.
79. A model of Igor and Liudmyla Grechanyk's monument design (2009). Source: *The Ukrainian Weekly*, № 49 (December 5, 2010): 14.
80. Monument in Berezanka, Mykolaiv Oblast, Ukraine (2007). Source: "Holodomor Monuments. Mykolaïvs'ka oblast'." Ukrainian Canadian Research and Documentation Centre. Accessed February 1, 2021. http://www.holodomor-monuments.org/m/mykolaiv.html.
81. The Holodomor monument in Skomoroshky, Vinnytsia Oblast, Ukraine. Source: Photography by Mykhailo Potupchyk.
82. The Holodomor monument in Obodivka, Vinnytsia Oblast, Ukraine. Source: Photography by Mykhailo Potupchyk.
83. The Holodomor monument in Lublin, Poland (2015). Source: Photography by Wojciech Świątek.
84. The Holodomor monument in Khmelnytskyi, Ukraine (1998). Source: Photography by author.
85. The Holodomor monument in Zhytomyr, Ukraine (2006). Source: Photography by author.
86. Figures of angels in front of the Holodomor memorial in Kyiv, Ukraine. Source: Photography by author.
87. The Holodomor monument in Mykolaiv, Ukraine (1993/2008). Source: wikipedia.org, GNU, FDL.
88. The Holodomor monument in Konotop, Sumy Oblast, Ukraine (2008). Source: "Holodomor Monuments. Sums'ka oblast'." Ukrainian Canadian Research and Documentation Centre. Accessed February 1, 2021. http://www.holodomor-monuments.org/m/sumy.html.
89. The Holodomor monument in Nizhyn, Chernihiv Oblast, Ukraine (2007). Source: "Holodomor Monuments. Chernihivs'ka oblast'."

Ukrainian Canadian Research and Documentation Centre. Accessed February 1, 2021. http://www.holodomor-monuments.org/m/chernigiv.html.

90. The Holodomor monument in Oakville, Ontario, Canada. Source: Photography by author.
91. The Holodomor monument in Windsor, Ontario, Canada. Source: Wikipedia.org, CC BY-SA 3.0
92. The Holodomor monument in Smile, Sumy Oblast, Ukraine. Source: Photography by A.P., Wikipedia.org, GNU FDL.
93. The Holodomor monument in Vyshhorod, Kyiv Oblast, Ukraine. Source: Photography by Yulia Krylova, Wikipedia.org, CC BY-SA 3.0.
94. The Holodomor monument in Litky, Kyiv Oblast, Ukraine (2008). Source: Photography by Olexa Yur, wikipedia.org CC BY-SA.
95. The Holodomor monument in Munich, Germany (2008). Source: Photography by Andrij Nesmasznyj, Wikipedia.org, GFDL.
96. The Holodomor monument in Rochdale, England (2009). Source: Photography by Gerald England, https://www.geograph.org.uk/photo/5340169, CC BY-SA 2.0.
97. The Holodomor monument in North Battleford, Saskatchewan, Canada (2008/2014). Source: John Cairns. "Holodomor Monument Unveiled." *Battlefords News-Optimist*, December 5, 2014. https://www.newsoptimist.ca/news/local-news/holodomor-monument-unveiled-1.1652446.
98. The Holodomor monument in Mala Vovcha, Kharkiv Oblast, Ukraine (2008). Source: "Holodomor Monuments. Kharkivs'ka oblast'." Ukrainian Canadian Research and Documentation Centre. Accessed February 1, 2021. http://www.holodomor-monuments.org/m/kharkiw.html.
99. The Holodomor monument in Clifton, NJ, US (2010). Source: *The Ukrainian Weekly*, № 47 (November 21, 2010): 17.
100. The Holodomor monument in Edinburgh, Scotland (2017). Source: "Inauguration of the Monument to Victims of the Holodomor." Consulate of Ukraine in Edinburgh, 28 November 2017. http://edinburgh.old.mfa.gov.ua/en/news/photos/2238-vidkrittya-ta-osvyachennya-pershogo-v-shotlandiji-pamjatnogo-znaku-zhertvam-golodomoru-19321933-rokiv-v-ukrajini.
101. The Holodomor monument in Leicester, England (2018). Source: "Two More Holodomor Memorials Unveiled," Association of Ukrainians in Great Britain. November 25, 2018. https://www.augb.co.uk/news-page.php?id=1902.
102. Commemorative plaque at Buenos Aires Metropolitan Cathedral, Argentina. Source: Photography by Rainbow Unicorn, Wikipedia.org, CC BY-SA 4.0.
103. The Holodomor monument in Encarnación, Paraguay, is the meeting place of the Ukrainian community on important national holidays.

Source: "Brazil and Paraguay Join International Action to Commemorate Holodomor Victims." *Ukrinform*, October 1, 2018. https://www.ukrinform.net/rubric-society/2549357-brazil-and-paraguay-join-international-action-to-commemorate-holodomor-victims.html.
104. The Holodomor monument in Curitiba, Brazil. Source: "Monumento ao Holodomor é instalado no Memorial Ucraniano em Curitiba." *Ecclesia Brasil*, September 19, 2009, https://ecclesia.org.br/news/?p=2505.
105. The Holodomor monument at St. Demetrius Ukrainian Catholic Church in Toronto, Canada (2011). Source: Photography by author.
106. The Holodomor monument in Khoruzhivka, Sumy Oblast, Ukraine (2007). Source: "Khoruzhivka, Nedryhailivs'kyi raion, Sumy oblast'." Holodomor Museum. https://map.memorialholodomor.org.ua/map/769/.
107. The exhibit at the Canadian Museum for Human Rights in Winnipeg, Canada (2014). Source: Photography by author.
108. The Holodomor monument on the grounds of the Manitoba Legislature in Winnipeg, Canada (2014). Source: Photography by author.
109. The Holodomor monument in Regina, Saskatchewan, Canada (2015). Source: "Saskatchewan Remembers Holodomor with a Special Service at the Legislature." *Saskatchewan*, November 20, 2017. https://www.saskatchewan.ca/government/news-and-media/2017/november/20/holodomor.
110. The Holodomor monument in Toronto, Ontario, Canada (2018). Source: Olha Kyrylenko, "U Toronto vstanovyly memorial zhertvam Holodomoru." *Hromadske*, October 22, 2018. https://hromadske.ua/posts/u-toronto-vstanovili-memorial-zhertvam-golodomoru.
111. Early variant of the monument in Toronto, Canada (2018). Source: The private archive of Oksana Rewa.
112. One of Petro Drozdovsky's conceptions for the Toronto monument (2018). Source: The private archive of Oksana Rewa.

Index